JEWISH SPACE in
CONTEMPORARY POLAND

JEWISH SPACE
IN CONTEMPORARY
POLAND

EDITED BY
Erica Lehrer
and Michael Meng

Indiana University Press

Bloomington and Indianapolis

This book is a publication of

Indiana University Press
Office of Scholarly Publishing
Herman B Wells Library 350
1320 East 10th Street
Bloomington, Indiana 47405 USA

iupress.indiana.edu

Telephone   800-842-6796
Fax   812-855-7931

Manufactured in the United States of America

Cataloging information is available from the Library of Congress.
ISBN 978-0-253-01500-6 (cloth)
ISBN 978-0-253-01503-7 (paperback)
ISBN 978-0-253-01506-8 (ebook)

1 2 3 4 5 20 19 18 17 16 15

Contents

Acknowledgments

THE EDITORS WISH to thank the Jack, Joseph, and Morton Mandel Center for Advanced Holocaust Studies of the United States Holocaust Memorial Museum in Washington, D.C., for its generous sponsorship of the summer workshop "The Politics of Jewish Spaces in Contemporary Poland" in July 2010, out of which this volume grew. We are also grateful to Janet Rabinowitch, former director of Indiana University Press, for her sustaining support for the idea of the book. At IUP, we also wish to thank Raina Polivka and Darja Malcolm-Clarke for seeing the book to press. Kamila Dąbrowska and Dobrochna Kałwa offered constructive comments on the penultimate version of the manuscript at the 2013 "Recovering Forgotten History" workshop in Kraków. The editors also gratefully acknowledge a grant from Concordia University, Montreal, which was integral to the realization of this project. Finally, we thank our copy editor Margaret Hogan; proofreader Douglas Vipond; student assistants Kimberly Moore, Mary Caple, Stephen Milder, and Paul Brown; and of course all the contributors to the volume itself.

JEWISH SPACE IN
CONTEMPORARY POLAND

Introduction

Erica Lehrer and Michael Meng

AMONG OUTSIDE OBSERVERS of Polish-Jewish relations, two divergent images of Poland coexist, each with its own set of powerful emotions. The first is more familiar to North American readers: Poland as an historically blighted land of pogroms, antisemitism, Jewish exclusion, persecution, and murder, and today a place of historical denial by Poles and lingering fear and hostility for Jews, set against a backdrop of silent Jewish ruins, debased and left to crumble. But another image of Poland is emerging among a new generation of close observers. This Poland opposes antisemitism, is embroiled in a process of earnest introspection regarding the involvement of Poles in the historical persecution of Jews, and, most saliently for the present volume, is dedicated to reenvisioning spaces of and for Jewishness, past and present, in the Polish landscape—physical, social, and discursive.

Claude Lanzmann's epic 1983 film *Shoah* seared the image of Poland as a landscape of Jewish death and denial into a generation of viewers, with images of Polish peasant eyewitnesses expressing unreconstructed antisemitic myths and nervously snickering as they talked about the murder of their former Jewish neighbors and the confiscation of those Jews' property. The film suggests that any habitable physical and social "Jewish space" in Poland was permanently obliterated along with the country's Jewish population.[1] But a pair of new films—Yael Bartana's *And Europe Will Be Stunned* and Władysław Pasikowski's *Pokłosie* (*Aftermath*)—powerfully evoke spaces of not only past and present but also future Jewishness, in ways that suggest the advent of a new historical moment. While not nearly as widely viewed—and employing a fictional approach as opposed to using the documentary genre—these films reflect significant present-day social realities: both the inchoate yearnings of and the actual grassroots efforts by non-Jewish Poles and Jews in and beyond Poland to reclaim and expand Poland's Jewish spaces.

Pasikowski's 2012 Polish-made film *Pokłosie* is an allegorical treatment of sociologist-historian Jan Gross's powerful book *Neighbors,* which laid bare the "public secret" that a community of Poles in 1941 had driven their Jewish neighbors into a barn and burned it down.[2] The filmic treatment follows the present-day moral awakening of a young Polish villager who feels an inexplicable pull to collect and reassemble the fragments of his local Jewish cemetery. In his scavenger hunt for the missing tombstones—an endeavor replicated in many Jewish cemeteries across Poland in the last fifteen years—he both uncovers the terrifying truth of what happened to the village's Jews during World War II and incurs the wrath of his fellow townsfolk for his audacity in restoring both the Jewish story and the cemetery's physical space.

Israeli-Dutch artist Yael Bartana's *And Europe Will Be Stunned* is a trilogy of short films developed in collaboration with progressive Polish intellectuals and shot in Warsaw from 2007 to 2011. They chronicle the "fictional" Jewish Renaissance Movement in Poland (JRMiP), a vibrant, youth-based political campaign that has called on 3.3 million Jews to return to Poland. The first film, *Mary Koszmary* (*Nightmares*, 2007), features the movement's leader, performed by young Polish leftist-activist Sławomir Sierakowski, pleading for Jews to return to Poland. He longs for Jews and wants them back, unsettling the archetypal antisemitic Pole as construed by *Shoah* while underlining the ambivalent role of nostalgia in even such "progressive" Polish approaches to Jewishness. Bartana's project dares to envision—however fantastically—Poland as a center of future Jewish life, building on a deep reservoir of largely repressed yearnings for the "vanished world" of the shtetl that exist on both the Polish and Jewish sides of the equation. Indeed, provocatively underscoring the generative intersections of vision and reality, Bartana broke the filmic frame to build a temporary kibbutz training camp in Muranów, the site of the Warsaw ghetto, and the JRMiP itself has a website and manifesto, and held its first congress in Berlin in May 2012.[3]

A range of such new visions of Jewish Poland, both pragmatic and utopian, appear throughout this volume. Shadowed by the earlier image offered by *Shoah*, they provide emotion-laden narratives and counternarratives that offer alternatives and responses to its bleak perspective. *Jewish Space in Contemporary Poland* showcases research by an interdisciplinary group of scholars, illuminating lesser-known engagements with the Polish-Jewish past over the last twenty years. In this period, non-Jewish Poles and Jews (both Polish and foreign) have made Poland home to profound debate and reflection on the loss of its once large—and today minuscule—Jewish minority, representing perhaps the cutting edge of Holocaust memory work in Europe more generally.

This explosion of the past into the present is visible in a variety of media: print, film, photography, theater, music, and even food. But it has been expressed perhaps most strikingly in the built environment and the cultural meanings such physical heritage enables. Across the country, dilapidated synagogues and cemeteries are being restored, Jewish streets recreated, and Jewish museums built. Because Poland was the geographic epicenter of the Holocaust, few other European countries have attracted as much global interest or experienced such intense reflection on the Jewish genocide. But Poland's new conjurings of Jewishness should not be read as simple gestures of reparation for past wrongs, nor as mere mercenary projects of development or instrumental national self-fashioning. Rather, a

"Jewish" presence in both urban and rural landscapes has reemerged in tension and synergy with other remembered minorities, and in complex negotiations with at times divergent local, regional, national, and international groups and interests. These involve primarily Poles and Jews, Americans and Israelis, but also Germans and, to a lesser extent, Roma, Ukrainians, Vietnamese, and even sexual minorities. New global actors have become increasingly interested in "sites of pluralism," even as some spaces—such as Auschwitz and communal properties embroiled in restitution claims—remain contested, fractured grounds. This volume unearths the multiple factors, paradoxes, and possibilities represented by specific sites and memory initiatives.

We take *space* as a common analytical category, considering how the physical, social, and discursive interact to produce with emerging expressions of memory in post-Communist Poland. In the past several years, scholars in anthropology, history, cultural geography, museum and heritage studies, and architectural history have shown increased interest in vernacular spaces and the popular, everyday uses and experiences of monumental sites—including the ways that more ephemeral cultural products like texts, political debates, or new media may impact such physical spaces. Recent studies focus on the building of museums, the revitalization of former Jewish quarters, the return of confiscated property, and "Holocaust tourism." Well-known writers such as Omer Bartov, Svetlana Boym, Ruth Ellen Gruber, Marianne Hirsch, and Michel Laguerre have brought wider attention to Jewish sites and districts in contemporary Europe, and major new Jewish cultural tourism initiatives are currently being launched.[4] Barbara Mann, Julia Brauch et al., and Jurgita Šiaučiūnaitė-Verbickienė and Larisa Lempertienė have offered recent volumes that thematize and theorize Jewish space as an underappreciated analytical tool for plumbing the Jewish cultural and historical experience in its fuller dimensions.[5] Popular interest in the physicality, materiality, and geography of Jewish culture and memory is far from abating.

Despite this new attention to Jewish spaces, there is still a dearth of theoretically sophisticated treatments of the local meanings and lived experiences surrounding Poland's (or larger Europe's) Jewish sites. The "new Jewish Studies" is working to break out of predetermined, normative views of Jewishness to explore how history and identity inform each other, raise questions about difference and solidarity, and recognize that Jewish culture is shaped in a field of interactions with other cultures. Historian Diana Pinto in this volume has theorized about the potential of "the Jewish space" in Europe for new Jewish and European cultural self-conceptions, Jonathan Webber has raised key questions regarding the boundaries and significance of Jewish culture in Europe, Michael Rothberg has envisioned a new paradigm of "multidirectional memory" that considers unacknowledged multicultural and multitemporal interactions which have shaped Holocaust memory, and Barbara Kirshenblatt-Gimblett and Jonathan Karp have called for analyzing Jewishness "as contingent and contextual rather than defini-tive and presumptive."[6]

These important theoretical interventions must be brought more fully into conversation with emerging empirical research. If theoretical advances offer new optics that refocus how we might conceive of Jewish culture and memory, di-rect observation in archival and field research can reveal the cross-fertilizations among projects, interethnic collaborations, and blurred or shared subjectivities emerging around Jewish sites, and how such spaces are negotiated, understood, and sustained by the variously defined Jews and non-Jews who share this field of interest. Indeed, what is most fascinating about the "revival" of Poland's Jewish spaces is the dialogic nature of these developments and the shifting meanings and boundaries of "Jewishness" emanating from them. There is still much work to be done, both in the scholarly and popular realms, to move beyond a vision of Eu-rope as home only to a "vanishing diaspora" and to consider new or overlooked forms of Jewish vitality in Europe.[7]

Finally, this volume aims to intervene in contemporary discussions of plu-ralism, multiethnicity, and cosmopolitanism, contributing a unique perspective from a largely ethnically homogeneous country. Ethnic minorities comprise about 1.8 percent of the Polish population and most are "European," from nearby coun-tries such as Ukraine. Still, like most countries in the world, Poland is confronting questions of cultural, ethnic, religious, and sexual difference, and some Poles have begun to imagine new forms of identity beyond the traditional "Polish-Catholic." Interest in the Jewish past in all its diversity has become a primary tool in plural-ist redefinitions of Polishness.

This volume attempts to understand the construction of pluralism through new uses of Jewish space. Our authors differ in their assessments of such pur-suits. Some see interest in Jewish spaces as a form of democratic renewal for both Poles and Jews; others view it as an attempt at reparation for or redemption from past wrongs; still others suggest that a largely imagined multiculturalism inhibits confronting contemporary injustice—dead Jews, in short, are easier to embrace than gay Poles or a growing immigrant population. Finally, we include voices that remind us of the significance of ongoing conflict over spaces such as Auschwitz and issues such as Jewish property restitution.[8] Our goal, then, is to shed light on the role of the material world in the complex, unfolding encounter with the Jewish past in contemporary Poland, in spaces that conjure up ambivalent, often conflicting memories and emotions. Below we outline in more depth the book's key contributions to the study of space, memory, and pluralism before conclud-ing with a gesture to the multiple layers of time that interact in Jewish spaces to-day, in recognition of the broader historical context that frames the contempo-rary moment.

Space, Heritage, Memory, Nostalgia

Pierre Nora's notion of *lieux de mémoire*—which he described as the external-ized, symbolic, often physical scaffolding for our sense of continuity as collective selves that emerged in modern societies—was introduced to Anglophone aca-demics in 1989, and helped to ignite a trend in which such spatial manifestations of memory have been subject to intense scrutiny.[9] The notion provided a lens through which to assess the reclaiming and recurating of memorial landscapes taking place in emerging postsocialist societies, which for decades a single party state had attempted to control and regulate. The way ideologies were inscribed in the built environment—and were being suddenly reinscribed in a flurry of early 1990s street renaming and monument toppling—became a core component of the new interest in "memory studies" in the academy.

But while drawing attention to space, Nora's depiction of these *lieux* as histori-cal crutches cut off from the more "authentic" social fabric of day-to-day memory that ostensibly bound premodern communities led many scholars to read land-scapes like texts, attending mainly to their discursive aspects. Similarly, the ways that nation-states shaped memory in space to their preferred political ends meant that scholars often granted priority to state actors, rather than to understanding "heritage" more intricately as a node in complex networks of memorial agents, both within and beyond the state.

This volume takes a wide-ranging empirical look at how memory intersects with space in ways that are culturally, socially, politically, and economically con-structed. Our authors shed light on multiple local, national, and transnational vec-tors of meaning, and the dynamic processes by which these are formed and inter-act. Drawing on ethnographic, historical, literary, and sociological approaches, we pay close attention to the multiple ways that Jewish religious sites, museums, urban districts, provincial ruins, and places of Holocaust tragedy are made use of and experienced by a broad range of actors, including local residents, planners, tourists, and Jewish leaders, in Poland and abroad.

A focus on space has multiple benefits: methodologically, spaces turn memory into a thing one can visit, creating touchstones and social catchments that make visible the very process of memory as it is being "collected"—to use James Young's notion.[10] Attention to physical spaces reveals the local manifestations of large, of-ten distant political, legal, and economic shifts, concretizing interpretive gener-alities and thinking through broad analytical categories on the scale of human experience.

Thinking with space also draws attention to the bodies that inhabit and tra-verse it, and the mnemonic force it exerts on them—just as bodies shape, in turn, the spaces around them. Much scholarship on memory privileges cognitive, discursive, or narrative processes over (or as separate from) more fully physical, embodied ways of experiencing the past. Especially given the sudden social ruptures that have scarred and often displaced massive populations in the last century, and the ways that landscapes have been both shattered and renovated in the process, it is crucially important to attend to the ways that "places possess a marked capacity for triggering acts of self-reflection, inspiring thoughts about who one presently is, or memories of who one used to be, or musings on who one might become."[11] Places can draw people into evocative conversations about the presence and influence of otherwise silent pasts. A ground-level view reveals "heritage" to be not simply a set of objects that people possess. While Stanisław Tyszka in this volume highlights the brute realities of disputes over the control of Poland's Jewish properties, the scope and meanings of "heritage" are not defined only by possession of real estate. Rather, heritage emerges from behaviors, practices, and strategies that people *do*.[12] Our authors highlight such social aspects of heritage, how it is influenced and negotiated by the presence and power of a variety of actors—both local and external—that collaborate and conflict.

It is perhaps banal, but it bears repeating that the memory of the "same" events changes depending on where (and when) it manifests and who is doing the remembering. Our volume thus looks at Jewish memory in Polish spaces from a variety of transnational perspectives, all of which have bearing on these simultaneously local and national spaces, and our authors themselves embody a variety of insider and outsider subject positions. Such openness to nontraditional sites and agents of Jewish memory is consistent with shifts in the discipline of Jewish Studies, yet implementing such a perspective in the emotionally freighted landscape of post-Holocaust Poland is particularly tricky, and goes against the grain of much recent writing touching on this area.

A popular perspective holds that European non-Jewish interest in Jews has produced a "virtual" Jewish world devoid of "real" Jews. Tourism and preservation have created kitschy Jewish Disneylands embellished with klezmer music, kosher-style food, and clichéd souvenirs, incorporating alien cultural materials and marketing them as "Jewish."[13] Yet this argument presupposes the existence of "real" Jewishness in a definable, stable, authentic form—a position not only untenable in contemporary humanities scholarship but one that erases local perspectives by reducing Jewish Europe to American or Israeli Jewish concerns.

Thus we are particularly sensitive to the frames of reference that pertain as Holocaust memory is enshrined in new national contexts. If the Holocaust has been put forth as a cornerstone of a newly integrating Europe's shared heritage, Germany has for obvious reasons drawn disproportionate attention. We shift our gaze eastwards toward the perspectives of those for whom the Holocaust is an entirely new frame of reference, and one that may sit uneasily alongside more familiar national narratives of martyrology. In Poland, where over 2 million gentile

Poles were murdered alongside about 3 million Polish-Jewish citizens, followed by forty years of Communist repression—not to mention the longstanding tensions in Polish-Jewish relations in the years leading up to the war—the "Jewish experience" is embedded in frames of understanding that give the work of remembering them today different vectors of meaning.[14] We thus offer a window onto the unevenness of the Europeanization of Holocaust memory, and particularly some unique aspects of its Eastern variant.

But narrating Jewish experience from a Polish perspective is not defined by loss or lack or a need for "catching up" to the West with its established modes of Holocaust memory.[15] Poland is working through and contributing to this memory anew, shining a particular light on the excruciatingly intimate relations of victims, perpetrators, and witnesses that was the reality in these "Bloodlands" of face-to-face and neighborly, as well as industrialized, killing.[16] Poland's grappling with Jewish memory, we argue, is thus particularly painful and trenchant, as well as potentially illuminating and transformative, opening a range of new questions just when Western countries risk self-congratulatory memorial complacency or guilt fatigue.[17]

Of particular interest are the ways that memory projects have implications for identity categories. We suggest how transnational dialogues are bringing "Jewish" memory to bear on debates about Polishness, forcing deep introspection and public discussion about the meaning of "nation" and "citizen" as well as "Pole" and "Jew." These conversations open provocative new questions about cultural ownership and authenticity. The chapters in this volume address questions that common presumptions around clean, stable identity categories obscure: Who has the rights and resources to propagate their perspectives regarding what is "really" Jewish and what is not? How are ethnic groups and cultures formed and sustained, and how are they reestablished in the wake of decimation? What kinds of heritage preservation perpetuate hegemonic/dominant cultural and political agendas, and what modes of tourism pursue memorial counterprojects—or vice-versa? Poland presents an excellent case for considering the role "outsiders" and foreign places may play in the maintenance or reconstruction of "in-group" culture and memory, with important implications for understanding diaspora identity-building practices as well as intercultural relations, reconciliation, and enduring intergroup incommensurabilities.

Finally, while nostalgia is implicitly implicated in many of the chapters in this volume—and is explicitly thematized by Magdalena Waligórska—we are careful in our deployment of this term in relation to the memorial activities our authors analyze because of the simplistic, saccharine, sanitized images it often conjures. Nostalgia is often dismissed as a politically suspect form of memory. But nostalgia, we argue, has a multitude of unexamined textures and layers, which scholars are just now beginning to excavate.[18] A broken, unfulfilled longing for the past, nostalgia may provoke mourning, melancholia, anxiety, and forgetting. Yet it also can motivate curiosity, critique, and action.[19] A similar caution applies to our treatment of "kitsch." Both terms, when expressly theorized, may help to differentiate various qualities of or relationships to memory or aesthetic experience.[20] But they also risk a tacit privileging of culturally specific or class-based regimes of taste, overlooking other ways of relating to the difficult past.[21] At worst, they are labels that serve to judge and dismiss, rather than analyze and illuminate.

Instead of labeling, this volume attempts to describe and open for consideration how and to what effects and ends memory is framed and deployed, and how various discursive, social, and physical spaces enable and constrain what work memories and representations can do for those who experience or evoke them. We seek to recuperate culturally saturated spaces, and their common framing as "heritage," in their full potentialities, not simply as inauthentic and suspicious props but as meeting grounds for interpersonal encounters, for the enactment of morality, for the development of empathy, and for the resignification of identity in more expansive, as well as narrower, terms.

Constructing Pluralism?

Along with uncovering the multiple meanings and actors that inhabit Poland's Jewish spaces, our volume also attempts to expand memory studies by considering the interrelationship between remembrance and pluralism. Julia Brauch et al. suggest that "the public debates on the (re-)localization of Jewish space are perceived as the litmus test for a critical historical consciousness and inclusive identity of European societies."[22] We thus open the question of what the recent surge of Polish interest in physically marking the Jewish past entails for visions of the nation (and policies of the nation-state). Do longings for the prewar past engender more pluralist and cosmopolitan redefinitions of Polishness? Our authors differ in their assessments. Some see memory as a form of cosmopolitan renewal for both Poles and Jews; others view it as an attempt at redemption from past wrongs; still others suggest that celebration of past multiculturalism inhibits confronting pressing contemporary prejudices against other ethnic minorities.

The scholarly study of Holocaust memory—postwar Germany presenting the richest case—has generally focused on the question of *whether* Europeans have remembered the Nazi genocide of European Jews. The concern has been to trace and analyze the patterns of forgetting and recollection, with a now familiar narrative of general repression and silence (1945 to mid-1960s), gradual commemoration (late 1960s to late 1980s), and general, if still contested, acknowledgment of the Holocaust as a major civilizational break in modern European and Western history (1990s to the present).[23] Remembrance itself is the telos here: scholars observe the highly contorted, yet nevertheless still progressively unfolding, processes through which Poles, Germans, French, and so on—who are usually defined ethnically and hermetically as non-Jewish and nonimmigrant—gradually reflect on the Holocaust and the loss of Europe's Jewish population. The moment when the past surfaces as something to contest, discuss, and recognize tends to shape the scholarly agenda.

This volume takes a different approach to the study of memory by turning to the question of *how*, and more centrally, *why*: Why are people in Poland remembering the Holocaust and the history of Polish Jews? What is at stake in a backward gaze? Why do we invest energy in remembering past events that do not seem immediately connected to our everyday lives? Human societies remember the past for multiple reasons, and they often give meaning to the past, even if unwittingly.[24]

Many Poles may remember the past out of simple curiosity or spurred by an historian's fascination with salvaging a forgotten page in the national chronicle.[25] Economic motives are often to some degree at play as brokering of the Jewish past is tangled up with regional development schemes and the still-emergent Polish tourist industry (see chapters by Winson Chu, Erica Lehrer, and Monika Murzyn-Kupisz in this volume). And Jewish memory projects may also be bound up in Poland's emerging impulses at national image management, responding to more than a decade of historical revelations regarding Polish complicity in wartime and postwar crimes against Jews with sanguine representations of Polish-Jewish coexistence. But this book also suggests that in contemporary Poland, deeper searches for meaning are often attached to engagements with the Jewish past. Some Poles involved in Jewish "memory work" invest this activity with a sense of larger purpose. The meanings are polyvalent, but a number of our authors—Konstanty Gebert, Erica Lehrer, Michael Meng, Diana Pinto, and Magdalena Waligórska—touch on one in particular, either directly or tacitly: the possibilities and ambiguities of a liberal democratic philosophy of history centered on the idea of memory as a future-oriented project of enlightenment, that is, a self-critical memory of the nation-state that will help to build more tolerant, pluralist democratic societies.

In this vision, the past is taken as a guide that can instruct and orient Poles in the present and future. This philosophy of history may not be explicitly articulated by actors involved in local memory projects (nor even by some authors in this volume). But one could argue that it is a foundational assumption, a hopeful belief that underlies much memory work in contemporary Poland and beyond. Otherwise, why bother remembering painful events of human suffering that happened decades ago? Certainly there are other philosophical threads at play in the Polish-Jewish case: for example, ethical obligations to ensure harrowing events not be forgotten, or theological commands to absolve sin through reconciliation, the pursuit of emotional catharsis through historical truth-telling, or even superstitious, magical thinking about the qualities of "post-Jewish" sites and objects.[26] Yet we are convinced in today's Poland that memory is frequently being invoked for civic pedagogical ends, to produce the "enlightened knowledge" necessary for present and future national subjects, particularly to refute ethnocultural nationalism or other ideological forms of exclusion.

The idea of memory as a form of enlightened knowledge was theorized most thoroughly by Theodor Adorno and Jürgen Habermas in the context of postwar West Germany.[27] In 1959, Adorno argued that a vigorous "working through" (*aufarbeiten*) of the past could serve the pedagogical function of strengthening German democracy and liberalization.[28] Habermas developed this idea further over the 1980s and 1990s. He claimed that a self-critical memory culture could play a central role in forming a postnational, cosmopolitan identity, or what he called "constitutional patriotism." Memory could provide the motivational and ethical substance of such cosmopolitanism: we can learn from history and build a better society by remembering the disasters of ethnocultural nationalism. While Habermas's arguments usually refer to the German context, his concept of constitutional patriotism applies to—and he has suggested it is emerging in—other liberal democratic nation-states.[29]

Poland, with its unique history and demographics, has been faced since 1989 once again with the question of who Poles are as a nation in a new global order. Remembering the Jewish past and the rupture of the Holocaust are tools for imagining a more plural Poland—and for some, an open, cosmopolitan Polish identity. These cultural reformers imbue memory with pedagogical and political meaning: Józef, the accidental village archeologist-historian in *Pokłosie* or the role played by political activist Sławomir Sierakowski in *Mary Koszmary* represent those for whom memory is linked to profound moral reckoning or more inclusive imaginations of Poland. These figures perform encounters with past and present pluralism, in often awkward but deeply felt attempts to reclaim those Jewish others amid the detritus of whose material heritage they, like many Poles, live.

A skeptic might wonder how representative these characters are; no doubt many Poles interested in the Jewish past and the Holocaust have other motivations for their memory work, not to mention those who have little interest in Poland's Jewish memory and/or embrace an ethnocultural definition of the nation that seeks to protect the ethnic Polish national interest from such potentially self-critical reflections on the past. Or one might question, as Winson Chu does, the extent of critical consciousness—or even pluralistic aims—in recent memory projects in cities such as Łódź, where efforts to embrace German-Polish or Polish-Jewish memory often exclude each other. In his account, a serious, self-critical attempt to think about the complexities of the past seems almost entirely absent in the local political culture of the city.

Still others might critique the notion of "memory as enlightenment" on its own terms. As the authors in this volume show, three primary tensions can be identified within it:

1. For the benefit of what envisioned collective is a given memory project pursued? Cultural-historical or ethnic essentialism can underpin and thus limit self-critical memory projects. If aimed at enlightening a preconceived ethnonational body, memory can exclude citizens or other residents of the nation. Even if Polish Jews are incorporated into the Polish national vision, other "others," such as immigrants or Roma, may be cast as external to the collective that memory is being employed to reform and educate, or, at minimum, such groups' different histories and subjectivities may be denied.[30]

2. Memory of the Jewish past can rest on the essentialization of Jews, associating Jewishness with pluralistic democratic values like liberalism, humanism, cosmopolitanism, or individualism (or alternatively with other ideals such as piety, scholarliness, community cohesion, family values, or even financial acumen).[31]

3. While memories of the Polish Jewish past can flow in multiple directions, they may also remain focused on a narrow set of political issues, such as combatting antisemitism, to the exclusion of critiquing other forms of prejudice, bias, and racism directed against homosexuals, immigrants, and Muslims, among others.[32]

Finally, it is worth considering that the veritable explosion of Jewish memory projects in Poland exist *alongside* the ongoing presence of antisemitism and the persistence of competitive narratives of victimization, as many of our authors discuss in their individual contributions. Antisemitic graffiti and vandalism of Jewish cemeteries and stereotypes of Jews as cash-cows with whom restoration projects can curry favor or greedy schemers vis-à-vis the legal restitution of expropriated prewar property, are important parts of the present-day Polish landscape, existing alongside celebratory Jewish cultural projects. Indeed, while some memory work treats these problems directly, other projects have been accused of being political fig leaves to cover them up.[33]

* * *

The chapters that follow deal primarily with Poland since the collapse of Communism. But the issues of Jewish sites, spaces, and memories are hardly new. While the recent surge and intensity of memory work is distinctive, it is a widespread myth that a blanket of silence fell on Communist Poland until it was finally lifted by liberal democracy in 1989. The notion is underpinned by a linear, teleological conceptualization of Holocaust memory as a process of greater recognition and contestation as time moves forward from the putatively mute decades of the 1950s to the noisier ones of the 1960s onward. Jewish and non-Jewish Poles have thought about, talked about, reflected on, created, and animated Jewish sites since the end of World War II in the most varied of ways, as the contributions by Michael Meng and Slawomir Kapralski illuminate. The physical remnants of prewar Jewish life—or the lack of these—have triggered memories of a suddenly absent population of neighbors in the everyday lives of Poles for nearly four decades. Many of these memories were communicated among small groups of people; the kind of nationwide discussions of the Jewish past taking place in the Polish public sphere today did not, for the most part, occur under Communism. The regime generally delimited public discussions about the Holocaust, although the party-state could never close off all spaces of public discourse, and even created restricted room for some public debate about Polish-Jewish relations in the 1980s.[34] Thus, as readers encounter the stories and arguments that follow, we invite them to keep in the back of their minds the crucial point that the contemporary period rests on a complex, multilayered past.

Notes

1. Stuart Liebman, ed., *Claude Lanzmann's Shoah: Key Essays* (Oxford: Oxford University Press, 2007).

2. Jan Gross, *Neighbors: The Destruction of the Jewish Community in Jedwabne, Poland* (Princeton, NJ: Princeton University Press, 2001); Antony Polonsky and Joanna B. Michlic, *The Neighbors Respond: The Controversy over the Jedwabne Massacre in Poland* (Princeton, NJ: Princeton University Press, 2004).

3. Erica Lehrer and Magdalena Waligórska, "Cur(at)ing History: New Genre Art Interventions and the Polish-Jewish Past," *East European Politics and Society* 27, no. 3 (August 2013): 510–544.

4. Svetlana Boym, *The Future of Nostalgia* (New York: Basic Books, 2002); Ruth Ellen Gruber, *Upon the Doorposts of Thy House: Jewish Life in East-Central Europe, Yesterday and Today* (New York: Wiley, 1994), and *Virtually Jewish: Reinventing Jewish Culture in Europe* (Berkeley: University of California Press, 2002); Marianne Hirsch and Leo Spitzer, *Ghosts of Home: The Afterlife of Czernowitz in Jewish Memory* (Berkeley: University of California Press, 2010); Michel Laguerre, *Global Neighborhoods: Jewish Quarters in Paris, London, and Berlin* (Albany: State University of New York Press, 2008); Omer Bartov, *Erased: Vanishing Traces of Jewish Galicia in Present-Day Ukraine* (Princeton, NJ: Princeton University Press, 2007); Jackie Feldman, *Above the Death Pits, Beneath the Flag: Youth Voyages to Poland and the Performance of Israeli National Identity* (New York: Berghahn Books, 2008); Monika Murzyn, *Kazimierz środkowoeuropejskie doświadczenie rewitalizacji* (Kraków: Międzynarodowe Centrum Kultury, 2006).

5. Julia Brauch, Anna Lipphardt, and Alexandra Nocke, eds., *Jewish Topographies* (Burlington VT: Ashgate, 2008); Jurgita Šiaučiūnaitė-Verbickienė and Larisa Lempertienė, *Jewish Space in Central and Eastern Europe: Day-to-Day History* (Newcastle: Cambridge Scholars' Publishing, 2007); Barbara Mann, *Space and Place in Jewish Studies* (Piscataway, NJ: Rutgers University Press, 2012). Brauch et al. have pointed to the lack of attention to space in Jewish studies as stemming from a bias toward attending to diasporic wandering over territorial attachment, and focus on religion as an organizing principle transcending or standing in for worldly places. They emphasize the need to focus on how Jewish space is *produced*.

6. Jonathan Webber, ed., *Jewish Identities in the New Europe* (London: Littman Library of Jewish Civilization, 1994); Michael Rothberg, *Multidirectional Memory: Remembering the Holocaust in the Age of Decolonization* (Stanford, CA: Stanford University Press, 2009); Barbara Kirshenblatt-Gimblett and Jonathan Karp, eds., *The Art of Being Jewish in Modern Times* (Philadelphia: University of Pennsylvania Press, 2008).

7. Bernard Wasserstein, *Vanishing Diaspora: The Jews in Europe since 1945* (Cambridge, MA: Harvard University Press, 1996).

8. The issue of the legality of Jewish ritual slaughter, or *shehitah*, emerged as a major controversy after the assembling of this volume, but as a barometer, it suggests the volatility and lack of unidirectionality in Poland's changing climate around Jewish issues.

9. The reintroduction of important work by Maurice Halbwachs on collective memory was also a catalyst in this trend. Halbwachs, *On Collective Memory,* trans. Lewis A. Coser (Chicago: University of Chicago Press, 1992).

10. James Edward Young, *The Texture of Memory: Holocaust Memorials and Meaning* (New Haven, CT: Yale University Press, 1993).

11. Keith Basso, *Wisdom Sits in Places: Landscape and Language among the Western Apache* (Albuquerque: University of New Mexico Press, 1996).

12. Lisa Breglia, *Monumental Ambivalence: The Politics of Heritage* (Austin: University of Texas Press, 2006).

13. For analyses of how some of these formations also form spaces of a serious involvement with the Jewish past in Poland, see Erica T. Lehrer, *Jewish Poland Revisited: Heritage Tourism in Unquiet Places* (Bloomington: Indiana University Press, 2013), and Magdalena Waligórska, *Klezmer's Afterlife* (Oxford: Oxford University Press, 2013), which compares Poland and Germany.

14. For historical background on the war time experience that shapes current memories of the "Jewish experience," see Timothy Snyder, *Bloodlands: Europe between Hitler and Stalin* (New York: Basic Books, 2010).

15. Indeed, as several scholars are illustrating, German Holocaust memory is itself undergoing challenges and change, as demographic changes force new questions regarding the "lessons of the past" for grapplings with minorities, cultural difference, and "tolerance." See Andreas Huyssen, "Diaspora and Nation: Migration into Other Pasts," *New German Critique* 88 (Winter 2003): 147–164; A. Dirk Moses, "Stigma and Sacrifice in the Federal Republic of Germany," *History and Memory* 19, no. 2 (2007): 140–142; Michael Meng, "Silences about Sarrazin's Racism in Contemporary Germany," *Journal of Modern History* (forthcoming 2015); Damani J. Partridge, "Holocaust Mahnmal (Memorial): Monumental Memory amidst Contemporary Race," *Comparative Studies in Society and History* 52, no. 4 (2010): 820–850; Michael Rothberg and Yasemin Yildiz, "Memory Citizenship: Migrant Archives of Holocaust Remembrance in Contemporary Germany," *Parallax* 17, no. 4 (2011): 32–48.

16. Snyder, *Bloodlands;* Gross, *Neighbors;* Jan Gross, *Fear: Anti-Semitism in Poland after Auschwitz* (New York: Random House, 2006); Jan Gross and Irena Grudzinska-Gross, *Golden Harvest: Events at the Periphery of the Holocaust* (New York: Oxford University Press, 2012).

17. Brauch et al., *Jewish Topographies,* note that scholarly trends in Central and Eastern European countries have been an important engine for greater attention to space in Jewish Studies (p. 6); the volume by Jurgita Šiaučiūnaitė-Verbickienė et al. is an example of this trend.

18. Svetlana Boym, *The Future of Nostalgia* (New York: Basic Books, 2001); Simon Bunke, *Heimweh: Studien zur Kultur- und Literaturgeschichte einer tödlichen Krankheit* (Freiburg: Rombach, 2009); Peter Fritzsche, *Stranded in the Present: Modern Time and the Melancholy of History* (Cambridge, MA: Harvard University Press, 2004).

19. Sharon Macdonald gives a useful overview of anthropologists and other scholars of Europe who have attempted to tease apart and recuperate some of nostalgia's more critical layers and facets. Macdonald, *Memorylands: Heritage and Identity in Europe Today* (London: Routledge, 2013), 92–108.

20. E.g., see Saul Friedländer, *Reflections of Nazism: An Essay on Kitsch and Death* (New York: Harper and Row, 1984).

21. E.g., see Pierre Bourdieu, *Distinction: A Social Critique of the Judgment of Taste*, trans. Richard Nice (Cambridge, MA: Harvard University Press, 1984).

22. Brauch et al., *Jewish Topographies*,15.

23. Exceptions that analyze the narratives and meanings of memory include A. Dirk Moses, *German Intellectuals and the Nazi Past* (New York: Cambridge University Press, 2007), and Geneviève Zubrzycki, *The Crosses of Auschwitz: Nationalism and Religion in Post-Communist Poland* (Chicago: University of Chicago, 2006).

24. Karl Löwith, *Meaning in History* (Chicago: University of Chicago Press, 1949); Jacob Taubes, *Abendländische Eschatologie* (Bern: A. Francke, 1947).

25. Eva Hoffman's consideration of the motivations of local historian Zbyszek Romaniuk of the small city of Brańsk captures the nuances of the Polish climate for such work. Eva Hoffman, *Shtetl* (New York: Public Affairs, 2007), 24–26.

26. On the superstitious, magical qualities of Jewish spaces, see Magdalena Waligórska, "The Jewish-Style Whodunit in Contemporary Poland and Germany," *East European Jewish Affairs* 43, no. 2 (2013): 143–161, and Erica Lehrer, ed., *Na szczęście to Żyd/Lucky Jews* (Kraków: Ha!art, 2014). The past decade has seen a surge of historical work on the Holocaust by Polish scholars. For example, see Barbara Engelking, "*Szanowny panie Gistapo": Donosy do władz niemieckich w Warszawie i okolicach w latach 1940–1941* (Warsaw: IFiS PAN, 2003); Barbara Engelking, Jacek Leociak, and Dariusz Libionka, eds., *Prowincja Noc: Życie i zagłada Żydów w dystrykcie warszawskim* (Warsaw: IFiS PAN, 2007); Barbara Engelking, *Jest taki piękny słoneczny dzień... Losy Żydów szukających ratunku na wsi polskiej 1942–1945* (Warsaw: Centrum Badań nad Zagładą Żydów, 2011); Jan Grabowski, "*Ja tego Żyda znam!" Szantażowanie Żydów w Warszawie, 1939–1943* (Warsaw: Instytut Filozofii i Socjologii Polskiej Akademii Nauk, 2004); Jan Grabowski, *Judenjagd: Polowanie na Żydów 1942–1945: Studium dziejów pewnego powiatu* (Warsaw: Centrum Badań nad Zagładą Żydów, 2011); Gross, *Neighbors;* Alina Skibińska and Jakub Petelewicz, "The Participation of Poles in Crimes against Jews in the Świętokrzyskie Region," *Yad Vashem Studies* no. 2 (2007): 5–48; Andrzej Żbikowski, ed., *Polacy i Żydzi pod okupacją niemiecką 1939–1945: Studia i Materiały* (Warsaw: Instytut Pamięci Narodowej, 2006); Andrzej Żbikowski, *U genezy Jedwabnego: Żydzi na Kresach Północno-Wschodnich II Rzeczypospolitej* (Warsaw: Żydowski Instytut Historyczny, 2006); and *Zarys krajobrazu: Wieś polska wobec zagłady Żydów 1942–1945* (Warsaw: Centrum Badań nad Zagładą Żydów, 2011). For English summations of this outpouring of research from the *Centrum Badań nad Zagładą Żydów,* see the essays in *East European Politics and Societies* 25, no. 3 (2011): 391–580.

27. The idea of enlightened knowledge comes from Michael Geyer, "The Politics of Memory in Contemporary Germany," in *Radical Evil*, ed. Joan Copjec (New York: Verso, 1996), 170.

28. Theodor Adorno, "What Does Coming to Terms with the Past Mean," trans. Timothy Bahti and Geoffrey Hartman, in *Bitburg in Moral and Political Perspective*, ed. Geoffrey Hartman (Bloomington: Indiana University Press, 1986), 114–129.

29. Jürgen Habermas developed these positions in a number of political writings, including most significantly the following: "Historical Consciousness and Post-Traditional Identity: The Federal Republic's Orientation to the West," in Jürgen Habermas, *The New Conservatism: Cultural Criticism and the Historians' Debate*, ed. and trans. Shierry Weber Nicholsen (Cam-

bridge, MA: MIT Press, 1990), 249–267; "On the Public Use of History," in Habermas, *New Conservatism*, 229–240; "The Finger of Blame: The Germans and Their Memorial," in Jürgen Habermas, *Time of Transitions*, ed. and trans. Ciaran Cronin and Max Pensky (Malden, MA: Polity, 2006), 38–50.

30. On the dilemmas of holism and Holocaust memory, the literature is richest for the German case. See note 15, above.

31. Dan Michman, "A 'Third Partner' of World Jewry? The Role of the Memory of the Shoah in the Search for a New Present-Day European Jewish Identity," in *Contemporary Responses to the Holocaust*, ed. Konrad Kwiet and Jürgen Matthäus (Westport, CT: Praeger, 2004), 123–135.

32. On the multidirectional or cosmopolitan potentials of memory, see Rothberg, *Multidirectional Memory*, and Max Pensky, "Cosmopolitan Memory," in *Routledge Handbook of Cosmopolitan Studies*, ed. Gerard Delanty (New York: Routledge, 2012), 254–266.

33. Magdalena Waligórska, "Der Fiedler als Feigenblatt: Die Politisierung des Klezmer in Polen," *Osteuropa*, nos. 8–10 (2008): 395–408.

34. Iwona Irwin-Zarecka, *Neutralizing Memory: The Jew in Contemporary Poland* (New Brunswick, NJ: Transaction, 1989); Michael Meng, *Shattered Spaces: Encountering Jewish Ruins in Postwar Germany and Poland* (Cambridge, MA: Harvard University Press, 2011); Michael Steinlauf, *Bondage to the Dead: Poland and the Memory of Holocaust* (Syracuse, NY: Syracuse University Press, 1997).

1   "Oświęcim"/"Auschwitz"

Archeology of a Mnemonic Battleground

Geneviève Zubrzycki

I͏ғ "ʜᴜᴍᴀɴɪᴛʏ's ʟᴀʀɢᴇsᴛ cemetery" is known in the world by its German designation—Auschwitz—in Poland it is primarily referred to as "Oświęcim," the Polish name of the small town 50 miles from Kraków where the Nazis set up the world's most notorious concentration and extermination camp.[1] The different names for the same site are related to its respective meanings for the different parties involved. Whereas "Auschwitz" is, for Jews and the world, the symbol of the Holocaust and of universal evil, "Oświęcim" is for many Poles the symbol of Polish martyrdom.[2] It is also the symbolic terrain where Poles articulate their relationship to various others: Germans, who created the camp; Russians, who liberated it; and especially Jews, with whom Poles compete for the ownership of the former camp as a symbol of their own martyrdom. Finally, Auschwitz is the site of the dramatization and enactment of nationalist discourses that have shaped—and divided—Polish public life in the 1980s and 1990s.

"Oświęcim"/"Auschwitz" are multivocal symbols that simultaneously condense and polarize disparate significations. Auschwitz is also what Pierre Nora calls a *lieu-carrefour,* a privileged site where questions of identity are crystallized and fiercely contested by different social groups.[3] Oświęcim, the town, and within it Auschwitz, the former camp, constitute the physical battleground where memory wars have been waged between Jews and non-Jewish Poles, and continue to provide fertile terrain for rearticulating Polish-Jewish relations in the present by addressing the past.

In this chapter, I analyze "Oświęcim"/"Auschwitz" as core symbols, and discuss their respective relation to Auschwitz and Oświęcim.[4] More specifically, I dissect the various layers of meaning "Oświęcim" carries in Poland and discuss the role of the Auschwitz-Birkenau State Museum in the symbol's ideological configuration and reconfiguration. After decades of socializing Poles into a specific reading of history, changes in the narrative of the museum (and other state institutions) have been seen by many Poles as a sudden "Judaization" of Auschwitz, resulting in a "de-Polonization" of "Oświęcim" and its (Polish) memory. Unpacking the meanings attributed to the site itself, and interpreting the changes taking place in the discursive field about the symbol, are keys to understanding a series of controversies surrounding the former camp as well as some of the challenges the museum faces in the twenty-first century.

Auschwitz's Geographic and Historical Contours

Before undertaking our excavation of symbols, let's take a bird's-eye tour of the physical site. What is commonly referred to as Auschwitz is actually a large complex of camps and subcamps, including concentration, extermination, and forced-labor camps covering some 15 square miles (see map 1.1). Auschwitz (or Auschwitz I) was the mother camp, established in 1940 outside Oświęcim mostly for Polish political prisoners; Birkenau (or Auschwitz II) was the largest camp, established almost two miles away from Auschwitz I in 1942 in the small village of Brzezinka, with the main purpose of exterminating European Jewry; and Monowitz (or Auschwitz III, which is not part of the museum) was established in Monowice to provide forced labor to nearby factories such as the large I. G. Farben works.[5] The geography of these camps in relation to the small villages and towns in which they were established during the war is important, since it comes up frequently in debates between Poles and Jews. According to many Poles, controversies arise from avoidable misunderstandings, which they see as the result of a lack of knowledge of the spatial organization of what is, in the rest of the world, often called indiscriminately "Auschwitz."

Several factors have made Auschwitz the site around which collective memories of the Holocaust for Jews and of World War II for Poles have coalesced. Unlike Treblinka, Bełżec, and Sobibór, which were dismantled by the Nazis in 1943 after most Jews of Poland had been killed in the so-called Aktion Reinhard, Auschwitz-Birkenau was still operating shortly before the Soviets liberated the camp on January 27, 1945. Because of the rapid advance of the Red Army in the last months of the war, Nazis abandoned the camp leaving ample evidence of their crimes.[6] Moreover, the Red Army actually liberated prisoners at Auschwitz, whereas at most other camps, they stumbled over ruins with little or no traces of survivors.[7] These factors had important repercussions for memory-making: first, Auschwitz's relatively large number of survivors lived to tell their stories in Poland and throughout the world (although these stories were different depending on the identities of those doing the telling); second, the camp's surviving structures provided solid evidence of Nazi crimes as well as an infrastructure that could host the museum; and last, the number of survivors liberated by the Red Army, the evidence left behind, and the enormity of the crime provided an "ideal" prompt through which the Communist state could construct a shrine to socialism's victory over fascism, and a warning against the excesses of capitalism.

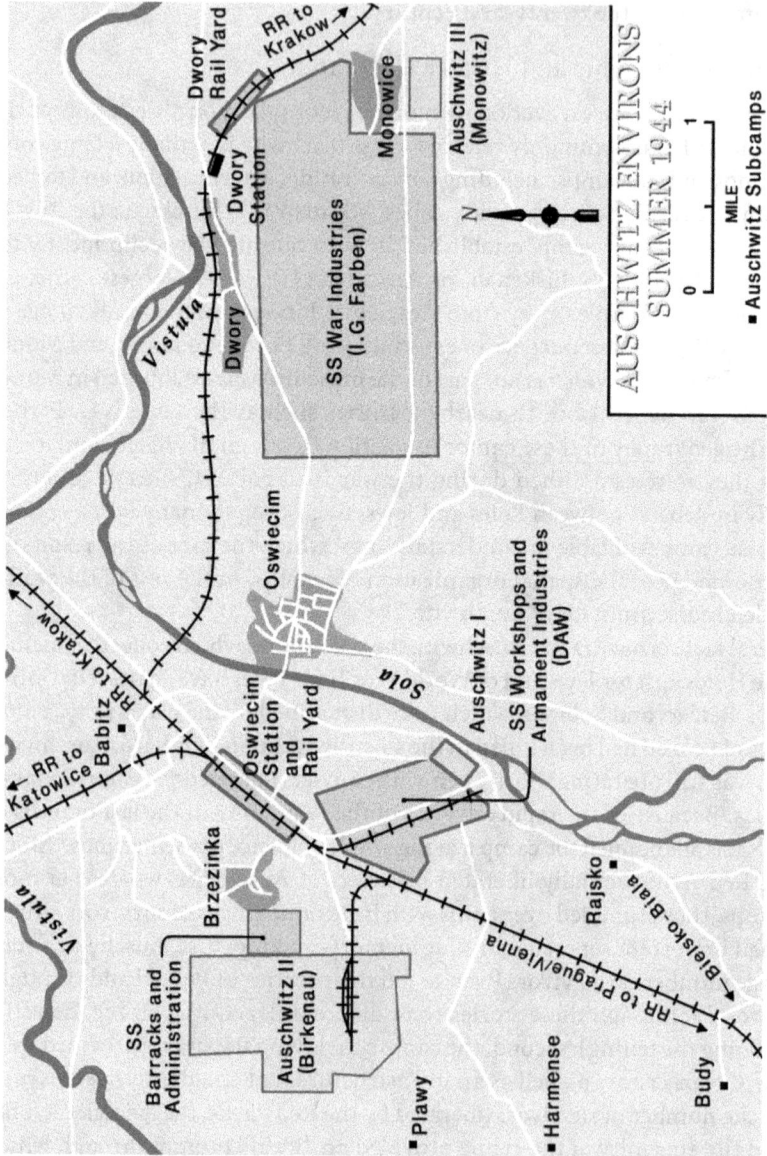

Map 1.1. Map of Auschwitz I, Auschwitz II (Birkenau), and Auschwitz III. Used with permission of the United States Holocaust Memorial Museum, Washington, DC.

"Oświęcim" as Core Polish Symbol

While "Auschwitz" is a complex symbol in its own right, my primary focus in this chapter is on the lesser-known Polish associations with, and constructions of, "Oświęcim." "Oświęcim's" first layer of meaning is related to the camp's history during World War II. Already during the war, the name "Oświęcim" signified Polish suffering under German occupation. Auschwitz was initially created for Polish political prisoners: intellectual and professional elites, members of the resistance, priests, and nuns were the main groups imprisoned there until the Final Solution was implemented in 1942, after which the camp was given the additional and henceforth main function of death camp for the European Jewry, through the creation of Auschwitz II–Birkenau.[8]

While in Polish consciousness the camps in Treblinka, Bełżec, Chełmno, and Sobibór were and are synonymous with the extermination of Jews (because this is primarily where Polish Jews from the liquidated ghettos of Warsaw, Kraków, Łódź, and Lublin were killed), "Oświęcim" became and remained the symbol of Poles' martyrdom during World War II, representing the attempt by Nazis to physically and culturally annihilate the Polish nation—an interpretation that fit neatly into Polish scripts of denationalization by their Western neighbor.

After the war, the Communist state built onto this already common understanding of the camp by creating the State Museum Oświęcim-Brzezinka in 1947 on the basis of a law "on the remembrance of the martyrdom of the Polish Nation and other Nations." As the name of that law suggests, Poles, although not the camp's sole victims, were its main martyrs. The museum was indeed squarely Polish from its inception, but the national narrative was told in the socialist mode and according to socialist parameters, providing a *second* layer of meaning for "Oświęcim" that in many ways reinforced the first, historico-martyrological one. In that narrative, "Victims of Fascism" from Poland and twenty-seven other nation-states were exploited and exterminated at the camp, later liberated by the victorious and just Red Army. According to a Polish publication about the camp, for example, in "Auschwitz there were prisoners of various nationalities, creeds and professions. They included Americans, Austrians, Belgians, Britons, Bulgarians, Chinese, Croats, Czechs, Dutchmen, Egyptians, Frenchmen, Germans, Greeks, Gypsies, Hungarians, Italians, Jews, Letts, Lithuanians, Norwegians, Persians, Poles, Romanians, Russians (and other citizens of the Soviet Union), Slovaks, Spaniards, Swiss, Turks and Yugoslavs."[9] Stated in this fashion, Jews constituted only *one* among *many* groups enslaved and murdered at the camp. That most of the citizens listed above were Jewish was concealed. Note also that the listing is made alphabetically; in the original Polish version, Jews (*Żydzi*) were last on the list, subtly distorting reality one step further. Other examples of this bias can be found in several editions of the official guidebook to the museum, in circulation until the early 1990s. In one section of the guide, a short paragraph informed the reader-visitor of the Nazis' use of Auschwitz for the total extermination of Jews but did so under the subheading "The Nations' Room" (*Sala narodów*). Other groups' fates (such as those of Soviet prisoners of war or Romas) were described using the same term, "extermination," but were brought to the reader's attention with clear subheadings: "The Extermination of Soviet Prisoners of War" and "The Extermination of Gypsies."[10] Jews got no such subheading.

Another instance of the ideological manipulation of the historical record concerns the total number of Auschwitz victims, which was established in the postwar years at a monumental four million. We now know that the actual number of victims was closer to 1.1–1.5 million. This historical distortion, according to scholar James Young, was arrived at "by a combination of the camp commandant's self-aggrandizing exaggerations, Polish perceptions of their great losses, and the Soviet occupiers' desire to create Socialist martyrs."[11] Beyond the thorny issue of historical truth, this inflated number, and the conflation of Jewish and non-Jewish Poles into the category of "Polish citizens" or sometimes simply "Poles," created the long-lasting impression in Poland that Poles had suffered the most deaths and were the greatest victims of World War II. While the use of a "neutral," civic language of citizens was meant to avoid the reproduction of the racial categories defined by the Nuremberg laws,[12] the diminution of Auschwitz's Jewish face was also, if not primarily, a strategic ideological manipulation by the socialist party-state intended to create a socialist shrine, replete with victims (the "Victims of Fascism," Poles at the head) and heroes (the liberating Red Army, the resistance movement). The museum has in recent years revised its narrative and is currently planning a significant overhaul of its general exhibit.[13] It has dropped the socialist rhetoric, and, most importantly, it now stresses that Jews constituted 90 percent of the camp's victims. For Poles, however, who for three generations were socialized to the implied "fact" that they had constituted the majority of prisoners and victims of the camp, this revision of history has not been accepted without resistance.

The *third* and perhaps most counterintuitive and controversial layer of meaning of "Oświęcim" for non-Polish audiences is that of its Catholicism. Members of the Catholic Church's clergy and religious orders were among the camp's first victims, and two were later canonized: Father Maksymilian Maria Kolbe gave his life in exchange for that of a fellow (Polish Catholic) prisoner. He died in the so-called Block of Death, where his cell has been transformed into a shrine. Edith Stein, Sister Teresia Benedicta of the Cross, was a German Jew from Breslau (now Wrocław). A student of Edmund Husserl, she converted to Catholicism, joined the Carmelite order, and died in one of Birkenau's gas chambers. Saint Maksymilian Kolbe and Saint Teresia Benedicta of the Cross are both sources of tensions between Catholics and Jews. The canonization of Father Kolbe is controversial because, before the war, he was the editor of *Mały Dziennik,* a daily newspaper with strongly antisemitic content, and also because his martyr death at Auschwitz offers a narrative of the camp's history that goes against that of the Shoah. Edith Stein's sainthood was contested (by Jews) because of her Jewishness. While she died in the camp as a Jew, in accordance with Nazi racial laws, Catholics understand her death as a religious sacrifice and revere her as a Catholic martyr.

The Catholic identity of the camp was grafted onto the previous layers of meaning of "Oświęcim" in the 1980s with Pope John Paul II's mass at Birkenau in 1979 and the canonization of those two martyrs. As Jonathan Huener shows in his study of commemorations at Auschwitz in Communist Poland, the mass at Birkenau, celebrated by the Pontiff during his first official visit to his homeland, was a turning point in the postwar history of Auschwitz.[14] The papal pilgrimage "to Poland's 'Golgotha' represented the triumph of Polish vernacular notions of Auschwitz and its role in postwar Polish culture."[15] While that mass affirmed and legitimated the Polish idiom of "Oświęcim," it also extended it by proclaiming the universal lessons of "Auschwitz." This move from the national to the universal, however, was cast in a Christian framework that ultimately opened the way for a national-*Catholic* reframing of the site and symbol, which in turn set the stage for some of the most significant controversies surrounding the former camp in the 1980s and 1990s.

The Carmelite Convent Controversy and Its Legacy

The canonization of Edith Stein and Maksymilian Kolbe provided the initial impetus for the establishment of a convent in the immediate vicinity of Auschwitz. The convent was consecrated in 1984 in a building that, while being outside the Auschwitz-Birkenau Museum, is very much part of the history of the camp and overlooks the site (see figure 1.1).[16] During the war, that building (*Theatergebaübe* or Old Theater) was a storehouse for Zyklon B, a chemical used in Germany before and during the war as a disinfecting and pest-control agent—and, beginning in 1941, to asphyxiate camp prisoners. If the presence of a convent at that very site was for many Poles (and even to some Polish Jews) "natural" because of the number of the camp's Catholic victims, it was objectionable for most (non-Polish) Jews.[17] In Polish imagination, however, the camp's grounds were ultimately fused into a coherent and potent whole, conjoining the highly emotional memory of wartime "Oświęcim," the ideological-socialist narrative given to it in the People's Republic of Poland, with the religious significance of Catholic shrines.

After protests from Jewish groups (mostly from outside Poland) objecting to the presence of the nuns at the site, in 1987 an agreement was reached and ratified in Geneva between representatives of the Polish Catholic Church and European Jewish leaders.[18] The accord stipulated that the convent would be moved from the vicinity of Auschwitz by 1989. For various reasons, the nuns failed to move by that

Figure 1.1. Building that housed the Carmelite convent from 1984 to 1993, seen from inside the museum grounds. Photograph by Geneviève Zubrzycki, May 2004

date, and tensions escalated as a group of Jews from New York, under the leadership of Rabbi Avraham Weiss, occupied the grounds of the convent in July of that year and were forcibly ousted from its premises.[19] Protests and resistance followed in Poland, including many declarations by the head of the Catholic Church in Poland, Cardinal Józef Glemp—often unabashedly antisemitic in content and tone.[20]

The second act of this social drama actually began quietly, almost a year before these incidents, when in the fall of 1988, an 26-foot-high cross appeared on the grounds of the convent, the so-called gravel pit. Brought there by a local priest and group of former (Polish Catholic) Auschwitz prisoners, the cross had been part of the altar used during the papal mass at Birkenau in 1979, hence the cross's popular naming as the "papal cross." The cross had been dismantled and stored in a local church's basement for a decade until one night it appeared in the convent's yard. It was erected there without witnesses and without any public or known ritual or ceremony. Although we cannot say with certainty that social actors did not act out of religious motivations, we can safely assume that the gesture was also, if not primarily, a form of protest against the planned relocation of the Carmelite nuns and a tactic to further sacralize the site in order to halt that plan. The Carmelite nuns finally relocated in 1993, when John Paul II personally intervened in the conflict by asking them to leave. The papal cross, however, re-mained on the site, since it had not yet been erected there when the Geneva agree-ment was negotiated and ratified.[21] It would provide a concrete link between the first and third acts of an ongoing social drama about the memory of Auschwitz and the contested place of religious symbols at the site—the War of the Crosses—waged five years later.

With the conflict over the Carmelite convent and its escalation in the early 1990s, "Oświęcim" acquired a *fourth* layer of meaning, as it had come to stand as a symbol of Polish autonomy and sovereignty over what Poles regarded as a key site of their martyrdom. The national significance of the symbol was heightened by what many Poles have understood to be attempts at "de-Polonizing" and "de-Christianizing" the site and the memory of Polish suffering, and as a threat to the Polish state's newly regained sovereignty in 1989. Moreover, fights about the Carmelite convent's location and relocation coincided with society-wide debates about Polish national identity and its relationship to Catholicism, the place of the Catholic Church in the new polity, and a slow but significant process of revision of Auschwitz's history. The fall of Communism and the Carmelite convent con-troversy thus opened up a space and underlined the need for a serious histori-cal reexamination and a significant renarrativization of the site and its history. These processes have all coincided to reinforce nationalist sentiments regarding the camp, its history, and its future, and to interpret narrative revisions of World War II and of Auschwitz as the "de-Polonization" of "Oświęcim" and its prob-lematic "Judaization."

De-Polonizing "Oświęcim" and Judaizing "Auschwitz"

The term "de-Polonization" is generally used to refer to Jewish protests against Christian forms of commemoration and to an entire set of restrictions applied to the former camp and its immediate (and not so immediate) surroundings. Those who use these notions also insist that the museum, which holds the legitimate monopoly of knowledge about the former concentration camp, has gone too far in its revision of history. As noted earlier, the museum's main exhibit has so far remained basically the same since it was initially designed in 1955, but the mu-seum has revised its narrative in its publications, information panels, and guided tours. Most of these revisions concern corrected numbers and the identity of vic-tims. The total number of victims was reestimated, after the opening of Soviet ar-chives in the early 1990s, to be 1.1–1.5 million, 90 percent of whom were Jews from all over Europe. It is now established that approximately 375,000 Jewish Poles and 150,000 non-Jewish Poles were deported to the camp.[22] Of those prisoners, it is es-timated that 80 percent of Jews and 50 percent of non-Jews were killed. The nu-merical revision thus accomplished two things: it rectified the total number of victims away from the inflated 4 million (most of whom, as we have seen earlier, were implied to have been ethnic Poles), and it established the identity of the victims (most of whom, it is now clearly stated, were Jewish). The number of Polish deaths, now estimated at 70,000–75,000, therefore appeared shockingly low for Poles who were socialized into a narrative of millions.

In addition to the revision of the number of victims and their identities, the museum also revised its narrative of World War II. Although Auschwitz I remains the focus of guided tours and hosts the great majority of exhibits (because of its infrastructure), the museum and its guides now place more emphasis than before on Birkenau (Auschwitz II), where most of the killing was conducted and where most victims were Jewish (as opposed to Auschwitz I, where most were gentile Poles).[23] Guides were retrained to emphasize the Jewish identity of the majority of Auschwitz-Birkenau's victims and the uniqueness of the Holocaust, and various explanatory inscriptions were added throughout the museum to underscore the role of the camp in carrying out the Final Solution.[24]

Another significant element in the so-called de-Polonization of the site concerns tourism and visitors at the museum. Before 1989, most visitors to the museum were from the Eastern Bloc (see table 1.1), with Poles constituting the overwhelming majority (see table 1.2). Auschwitz was an important socialist pilgrimage site, and Eastern Bloc visitors conjoined that visit with other tourist activities. With the fall of Communism, the flow of tourists has been dramatically altered. Most foreign visitors are now from "the West"—the United States, Israel, and Western and Northern Europe, as the data in table 1.1 shows.

The East/West inversion, though gradually occurring in the 1990s, is striking: for example, thirty-five times fewer Bulgarians have visited the museum on average per year since the fall of Communism; five times fewer Czechs and Slovaks have come to Auschwitz than Czechoslovaks, and half as many Hungarians. There were, however, three times more French visitors, five times more Americans, eleven times more citizens from Great Britain, and twenty times more Israeli visitors after the fall of communism than there had been, on average, for every year during the 1959–1990 period.

This dramatic shift can be explained by the fact that the fall of Communism decreased the desirability of travel to Poland for citizens of former Eastern Bloc countries, while it increased it for Westerners. Most of these tourists no longer need visas to enter the country, a formerly complicated procedure involving receiving formal "invitations" and other such regulations. In addition, the tourism infrastructure is much more developed now than it was before 1989, with several flights a day to Warsaw and Kraków from all over Europe and North America, and comfortable hotels and restaurants for all tastes (a few now offering kosher meals) yet still relatively affordable to Western wallets compared with other destinations.

Most new "Western" visitors come to Auschwitz to learn and teach about the Holocaust, not to hear about martyrs of the resistance to fascism or the So-

Table 1.1. Foreign visitors to the museum, by country (selection), 1959–2003

Citizens	1959–1990	(avg./year)	1991–2003	(avg./year)
Eastern Europe				
USSR	937,436	(30,240)	—	—
Russia	—	—	8,236	(634)
Ukraine	—	—	15,378	(1,183)
Belarus	—	—	2,007	(154)
Hungary	196,509	(6,339)	44,826	(3,448)
Bulgaria	117,963	(3,805)	1,375	(106)
Czechoslovakia	830,063	(26,776)	—	—
Czech Republic	—	—	40,627	(3,125)
Slovakia	—	—	29,997	(2,307)
East Germany	214,705	(6,926)	—	—
Western Europe/United States/Israel				
West Germany	249,911	(8,062)	—	—
Germany	—	—	471,902	(36,300)
France	197,595	(6,374)	243,335	(18,718)
Netherlands	44,046	(1,421)	116,983	(8,999)
Great Britain	52,254	(1,686)	242,118	(18,624)
Denmark	50,032	(1,614)	129,046	(9,927)
Norway	13,136	(424)	121,918	(9,378)
Sweden	33,472	(1,080)	96,011	(7,385)
Israel	23,496	(758)	198,438	(15,264)
United States	225,089	(7,261)	471,195	(36,246)

Source: From unpublished data, Auschwitz-Birkenau Museum, Visitors' Service Section.
Note: "—" indicates a country that did not exist in those given years.

viet heroes who liberated them. Many are even surprised to hear that the camp was initially established for Poles. Jews in particular now constitute an important segment of visitors. Most come in organized groups, their presence often made visible by the identical white and blue jackets individual group members wear. They come to Auschwitz on pilgrimages and educational tours, the most important being the much-publicized March of the Living.

Since 1988, on Yom HaShoah (Holocaust Remembrance Day), Jews from all over the world—mostly youth from the United States and Canada—gather at Auschwitz I and march the 1.8 miles to Birkenau (Auschwitz II). The two-week-long educational tour ends in Israel in time to observe Yom HaZikaron, Israel Memorial Day, and Yom Ha'Atzmaut, Israel Independence Day. In its promotional

Table 1.2. Visitors to the Auschwitz-Birkenau Museum, 1946–2003

	Total no. visitors	Polish citizens	Foreigners	% Polish visitors
1946–1950	923,045	881,533	41,512	95.5
1951–1955	1,075,218	1,037,525	37,693	96.5
1956–1960	1,132,132	1,010,195	121,937	89.2
1961–1965	2,022,207	1,659,552	362,655	82.1
1966–1970	2,839,092	2,273,027	566,065	80.1
1971–1975	3,556,594	2,789,596	766,998	78.4
1976–1980	3,373,462	2,429,350	944,112	72.0
1981–1985	2,468,748	2,134,548	334,200	86.5
1986–1990	2,935,200	1,882,050	1,053,150	64.1
1991–1995	2,407,800	1,310,983	1,096,817	54.4
1996–2000	2,448,032	1,415,100	1,032,932	57.8
2001–2003	1,322,455	513,053	809,402	38.8*

Source: From unpublished data, Auschwitz-Birkenau State Museum, Visitors' Service Section.
Note: * The decline in visits in the 2001–2003 period is due to two main factors, aside from the fact that the data includes only three years instead of the five used above: the number of foreign visitors was reduced following the terrorist attacks of September 11, 2001, and domestic visitors declined due to education reform in Poland, which impacted the number of Polish school children visiting the museum.

website and preparatory documents, the organizers sponsoring the journey follow the narrative script of Exodus: from Poland to Israel, Egypt to the Promised Land, darkness to light, bondage to freedom.[25]

For the march's participants, the ritual is not only the commemoration of the death of six million Jews but also a powerful corrective to a Polish narrative that had downplayed the role of Auschwitz in carrying out the Nazi Final Solution. For Poles—and especially for locals—it marks the takeover of Auschwitz (the camp) and Oświęcim (the town), reflected in the physical appropriation of the site and town by bodies proudly displaying their Jewish identity with Israeli flags, banners, and windbreakers (some with yellow stars on their sleeves), a white and blue human sea occupying the very space where more than one million Jews were sent to their deaths.

The War of the Crosses

It is in the context of the museum's own narrative revision, the poignant and sometimes tense encounter with the Jewish significations of "Auschwitz," and, more broadly, in the context of the post-Communist reexamination of Polish national identity's relationship to Catholicism,[26] that in the summer of 1998, self-defined "Poles-Catholics" erected hundreds of crosses just outside Auschwitz in the yard of the former Carmelite convent.[27] The War of the Crosses was spurred by rumors a few months earlier to the effect that the papal cross would be removed from the grounds of the former convent at the request of Jewish organizations. A series of commentaries by political figures immediately followed and were thrust into the public arena. One hundred thirty deputies and a group of senators from rightwing parties signed a petition to the government advocating the continued presence of the cross at that site, and Lech Wałęsa spoke out against the removal of the cross in an open letter to Bishop Tadeusz Rakoczy, under whose episcopal authority the town of Oświęcim falls. By mid-March, popular mobilization was under way: Some parishes celebrated special masses for "the respect and protection of the papal cross" alongside vigils for the defense of all crosses in Poland. At the annual March of the Living in April that year, banners and posters with slogans such as "Defend the Cross" and "Keep Jesus at Auschwitz" (in English) were displayed on the gravel-pit fence. By the spring, the issue had become an affair involving, at the domestic level, government officials, the opposition, the Catholic Church, and various civic organizations.

In June, Kazimierz Świtoń, an ex-Solidarity activist, initiated a hunger strike by the papal cross that lasted forty-two days, demanding from the Catholic Church's hierarchy a firm commitment that the cross would remain. After failing to secure such a commitment, Świtoń appealed to his fellow Poles to plant 152 crosses, both to commemorate the (documented) deaths of 152 ethnic Poles executed at that specific site by Nazis in 1941, and to "protect and defend the papal cross." This appeal proved successful: In the summer and fall of 1998, the gravel pit in Oświęcim was transformed into the epicenter of the War of the Crosses, as individuals, civic organizations, and religious groups from every corner of Poland (and from as far away as Canada, the United States, and Australia) answered Świtoń's call to create a "valley of crosses," encouraged by the popular and controversial radio station Radio Maryja. By the time the Polish Army finally removed them in May 1999, 322 crosses stood at the gravel pit.

During that summer, the site became the stage for prayer vigils, masses, demonstrations, and general nationalist agitation. It was the destination of choice for pilgrims, journalists, and tourists in search of a sacred cause, a good story, or a free show. At the national level, the fourteen-month "war" was marked by a series of debates and legal battles, numerous declarations from public officials, and accusations and counteraccusations that embroiled the government in conflict with the opposition, Polish public intellectuals, Polish-Jewish activists, groups from the far right, the Catholic Church, and a schismatic brotherhood claiming to represent "true Catholicism in defense of the Nation." At first, the government stood on the sidelines, invoking the principle of separation of church and state as defined in the Concordat of 1997 in arguing that the papal cross was the property of the Catholic Church, which was responsible for the use of its religious symbols.[28] The church countered that the crosses stood on government property and that the Catholic Church had no monopoly over the symbol of the cross, which belonged to the entire Christian community of believers. Over time, however, as a growing number of crosses appeared at the gravel pit, the crisis became more acute for both the government and the church. For the church, it was rendered more acute by the disobedience of Catholics to the episcopate's request, in late August, to stop planting crosses, and by the persistent involvement of the Society of St. Pius X, a schismatic group. For the government, the situation was exacerbated by demands from Israel and pressure from representatives of the U.S. Congress to remove all crosses from the proximity of Auschwitz at precisely the time when Poland was negotiating the terms of its NATO membership.

In the end, the Polish government and the Catholic Church made concerted attempts to find a solution and regain control of the gravel pit. After many legal battles and the passage of a law regarding "the protection of the grounds of former Nazi camps" on May 7, 1999, a 325-foot-zone was established around Auschwitz, giving the government the legal means to evict Kazimierz Świtoń from the gravel pit, where he had been encamped in a trailer for nearly a year, while the church arranged for the crosses to be relocated to a nearby sanctuary. The papal cross, however, remained. There was thus no resolution of the initial conflict concerning the presence of that specific cross. For this reason, the cross planting action could be qualified as "successful" and is regarded as such by Świtoń himself.[29] By escalating the conflict and radicalizing the demands—from the retention of one cross to the retention of hundreds—the Defenders of the Cross(es) successfully changed the terms for what a compromise would entail. In fact, by the end of the affair, removal of the papal cross was not even considered an option and was not open to negotiations; the removal of Świtoń and the three hundred–odd crosses was the principal objective of most of those involved. If at the outset the papal cross's presence at the gravel pit was not inevitable and different authorities considered the possibility of its removal and relocation, by the drama's conclusion, its presence at that site had been naturalized and made a permanent monument in the landscape of Auschwitz's perimeter.[30]

Even though the War of the Crosses was initiated by marginal characters, the event did mobilize support, and the issues it raised were not marginal but rather became a lightning rod for mainstream commentary and discussion of Polishness, its traditional association with Catholicism, antisemitism, and the state of Catholicism in post-Communist Poland. It brought to light with unusual clarity the challenges of building a plural society in a post-Communist society as it revealed the insidiousness of narratives propagated by the Communist regime and the pervasiveness of ethno-Catholic myths of the nation.[31] Closer to Auschwitz and Oświęcim, it underlined the importance of educating Poles about this history of Auschwitz, but it also highlighted the problematic legacy of that history for the living.

Dissociating Oświęcim and Auschwitz

On May 7, 1999, as part of a law that created a buffer zone around former Nazi camps, which effectively gave the government the legal means to remove Świtoń from the gravel pit and relocate the three hundred–some crosses, the museum changed its official name. From the Oświęcim-Brzezinka State Museum, it was renamed the Auschwitz-Birkenau State Museum in Oświęcim.[32] The rationale behind this modification, according to members of the museum administration, was twofold: first, the appellation should reflect the historical record and thus adopt both camps' original German-language designation. Reestablishing the "Germanness" of the camp would, secondly, dissociate the towns of Oświęcim and Brzezinka, in which the camps were established and where the museum now lies, from the former camps themselves. In addition to this official name change, guides were formally instructed to refer to the camps in their original, German-language designations.[33] The change was made in a conscious effort toward "setting the record straight" and shaping world opinion: by incorporating the German-language place-names into the museum name, the curators wanted to counteract the tendency, especially in the United States, to use the misnomer of "Polish camps" when referring to Nazi camps in today's Poland. Again, this is more than a "mere matter of semantics" as the expression "Polish camps" suggests Poles' central role in the Holocaust, precisely when, for Poles, the fact that "the death camps were located on Polish soil suggests . . . not their national complicity, but their ultimate violation."[34] The implication of Polish camps is thus doubly offensive to them: not only does it diminish the suffering resulting from having served as the primary site of the war, but it accuses them of something that was conducted by their occupiers and tormentors.[35]

The museum's administration is also keen on distinguishing Auschwitz, the former camp and current museum, from Oświęcim, the town in which it is located, which has much deeper roots than the Second World War and a life beyond that tragic history. As a museum employee emphasized to me in an interview, "After the war, a substantial town grew here; almost fifty thousand people, and these people don't live in Auschwitz, but in Oświęcim. We should not associate them with this place; they have their own life, this is their world, their workplaces, their stores, their industries, their recreational sites; this is where their children go to school. We have to separate, radically separate. The camp is Auschwitz-Birkenau, the town is Oświęcim."[36]

Auschwitz, as historical monument, memorial site, and prime symbol of the Holocaust, presents a series of challenges for the town of Oświęcim. Its inhabitants must endure a legacy left to them by the Nazis. The Auschwitz-Birkenau State Museum, far from being a source of revenue for the town, is perhaps better described as a liability. Although it does employ the local population, various proscriptions severely curtail the development of business in the proximity of the former camp. This was not problematic under Communism, when there was little private industry and commerce, and when Oświęcim was a relatively well-off town, with two large industries employing most of the population. With the fall of Communism and concurrent restructuring, however, unemployment has risen significantly, and the need for the development of alternative sources of employment is deeply felt. Large numbers have left Oświęcim in search of employment, most of them youth who see no future in their hometown and have moved to larger cities or emigrated. Restrictions regarding what kinds of businesses can be conducted and where in relation to the former camp are thus seen as a serious impediment for economic development, especially since the former camp is at the heart of the industrial district.

There is a clear tension between Warsaw and Oświęcim over local affairs, a tension palpable between the museum, under the jurisdiction of the Ministry of Culture, and the town.[37] The residents of Oświęcim live in what for many in the world is the symbol of the Holocaust, and see their daily activities restricted not so much by the legacy of history but the weight given to that history. As a town councilman told me with a deep sigh, "Everything here is under a microscope. The world is constantly watching us."[38] The need to distinguish the town from Auschwitz has been ardently felt in the last two decades, beginning after locals were engulfed in loud international controversies like those of the Carmelite convent, the War of the Crosses, and other scandals—often misrepresented in the foreign press—like the planned opening of a supermarket and the existence of a discotheque "in Auschwitz."[39]

Many of these recent "scandals" result from the common use of the name Auschwitz to designate the town of Oświęcim, and from the indiscriminate use of the name Auschwitz to refer to the complex of camps and subcamps throughout the region. But they also result from a different notion of "Auschwitz," the symbol and its spatial location. Poles clearly demarcate the physical site of the Auschwitz-Birkenau Museum from their respective surroundings, Oświęcim and Brzezinka, whereas for many Jews, the containment of "Auschwitz," the symbolic site of the Shoah, within the physical space occupied by the former camp grounds and current museum, is inappropriate. Since the entire area is filled with Jewish ashes, "Auschwitz" extends well beyond the walls of Auschwitz I or the fences of Auschwitz II–Birkenau; it spreads its sacredness in every corner of Oświęcim and its surroundings, which Poles in turn understand as an unfair imposition.[40]

Moreover, while the Auschwitz-Birkenau Museum attracts visitors, Oświęcim enjoys very little of what significant tourist sites and pilgrimage centers usually bring with them. Virtually no cottage industry is worth developing (or allowed to develop) around the museum. Aside from books, DVDs, maps, and grim postcards, there are no "appropriate" souvenirs to sell at Auschwitz. And even if the town or some entrepreneur decided to build a hotel and restaurants for tourists-pilgrims, few would elect to spend the night in the shadow of a death camp.[41] Instead, visitors typically rush back to Kraków, where they can wash away what often turns out to be a difficult visit, and spend money in the royal city's numerous cafés, pubs, and restaurants. Kraków hotels and tourist agencies have rapidly realized the extent of Auschwitz's potential for them, and therefore have developed that market, offering—and loudly advertising—packages that include visits at Auschwitz ("You will meet one of the former prisoners") and "Schindler's list" tours with "optional lunch" in the old Jewish (and currently hip bohemian) neighborhood of Kazimierz, amid the usual itinerary of the Wawel royal castle, Wieliczka salt mines, and evenings of folk dances (see figure 1.2).[42]

If it is so important now for Poles to distinguish Oświęcim, the Polish town, from Auschwitz, the Nazi camp, why was the name "Oświęcim-Brzezinka" used in the museum's official documents until 1999? One reason, as noted at the beginning of this chapter, is that Poles from the beginning of the camp's existence referred to it by its Polish name. The original Polish designations Oświęcim and Brzezinka were also used in the museum's initial name as an attempt to combat the Germanization of a multitude of Polish sites that had occurred during the war, a practice that emphasized German domination and Polish subordination. Using the original Polish names, therefore, underlined the sovereignty of the socialist nation-state after the war. This "return" to Polish place-names was effected at the same time as the names of German cities annexed to Poland following its borders' shift to the west were Polonized. In view of the expressed need to distinguish the town from the former camp, the museum's name change seems reasonable enough, and yet it is still quite infrequent to hear Poles refer to the site as Auschwitz. There is, to be sure, the force of habit behind this insistence on referring to the site by its Polish name, especially in older cohorts of Poles.[43] But there is also strong *ideological* resistance to shifting from one term to the other in certain right-wing milieus. This linguistic change is seen as the recognition and acceptance of the symbol's semantic shift: from Polish martyrdom to Jewish Holocaust and universal evil. These milieus, therefore, insist on calling the camp and the museum by its Polish designation.[44] This reaction is especially surprising coming from the very groups that incessantly insist on the victimization of Poles by Germans, yet it attests to the continued potency and value of "Oświęcim" as a symbol.

Auschwitz in the Twenty-First Century: Bearing the Weight (but Sharing the Cost?) of History

In 2009, the number of visitors to the Auschwitz-Birkenau Museum reached a record 1.3 million. While an astonishing proportion of them were from Western and Northern Europe, the Americas, Israel, and even Asia, Poles have so far remained the largest group, although their number are in sharp decline since the

Figure 1.2. Advertisement of Auschwitz tour. Photograph by Geneviève Zubrzycki, May 2004

fall of Communism (see table 1.2). As many as half of adult Poles, according to national surveys conducted since 1995, have visited the museum at least once in their lifetimes.[45] Many of the Polish visitors are schoolchildren from the eighth grade and above, visiting the museum as part of their Polish history classes.[46] Since 1960, over six million Polish youth have visited the museum.[47] It is clearly a crucial socializing institution on the history of World War II and the Holocaust, and it takes its educational mission very seriously. Its current pedagogical section has put in place special programs for the continuing education of teachers in order for them to better prepare pupils and students for their visits at Auschwitz-Birkenau, and to sensitize them to the Holocaust.[48]

Unlike its educational section, which has been overhauled and significantly expanded, the conservational mission of the museum has fallen short in several regards. The museum faces incredible challenges—the preservation of an amazingly wide variety and types of artifacts over an enormous territory, requiring an unusually diverse set of expert skills and technologies, within a modest budget. While Auschwitz-Birkenau has been recognized as a UNESCO site of world heritage since 1979, until very recently the Polish state was the sole institution responsible for the funding of the museum's activities. That funding has clearly been inadequate. The main exhibit needs a significant reconceptualization, and the infrastructures both at Auschwitz I and II (Birkenau) urgently need maintenance and repair. With budgetary uncertainty, however, it was difficult to start planning. Due to financial constraints and pressing conservation needs, in 2008, the Auschwitz-Birkenau Foundation was established to finance a permanent, long-term plan to preserve the authentic remains of the Nazi concentration and extermination camp. The foundation, under the leadership of the museum's new director, Dr. Piotr Cywiński, has been immensely successful: Less than two years after its creation, pledges amounted to 80 million euros—two-thirds of the required 120 million euros estimated for the new conservation plan. Sixty million euros have been donated from Germany and other EU members, and the United States announced in June 2010 that it would contribute $15 million.

Fund-raising received a boost from a tragic incident in the winter of 2009. On December 18 of that year, the world was stunned to hear that Polish thieves had managed over several hours during a cold snowy night to steal the infamous *Arbeit macht Frei* metal inscription over the entrance gate to Auschwitz I.[49] The historic metal inscription was recovered in less than forty-eight hours, cut into three pieces, but the museum's deficient security system and the broader financial challenges this lapse represented were suddenly in clear view for all to see. With newly raised funds now available, a new main exhibit is being planned and the great majority of the national exhibits, hosted in different blocks of Auschwitz I by countries who were under Nazi occupation, have been completely redesigned—including, most recently, a Jewish exhibit.

Conclusion: "Oświęcim"/"Auschwitz," the Evolution of Two Symbols

To conclude this chapter on Auschwitz and the symbolism of "Oświęcim," it is important to offer some survey data on Poles' changing understanding of "Oświęcim" as it relates to the site and its history. Four surveys taken over the last fifteen years are especially useful to describe the extent of the Polishness of "Oświęcim" on the one hand, and to indicate significant transformations in that perception on the other. These can be attributed to a multitude of commemorative events, the museum's own revised narrative, and the wave of Western visitors that now place Poles in contact with the Jewishness of "Auschwitz" that Jews and the world espouse (see table 1.3). The first survey, conducted in 1995 on the eve of the commemorative celebrations of the fiftieth anniversary of the liberation of Auschwitz, reveals, in accordance with socialist propaganda, that "Oświęcim" was, above all else, for almost three-quarters of adult Poles, the place of martyrdom "of the Polish Nation" or "of several nationalities" (47 percent and 26 percent, respectively). Only 8 percent of Poles associated the site, above all else, with the Holocaust.

The same questions were asked again five, ten, and fifteen years after the first survey. Most striking in these data is the increased consciousness of Auschwitz as the site of the Holocaust: the proportion of those who identified the site with the extermination of Jews was more than five times greater in 2010 than in 1995 (from 8 to 47 percent). The significant boost in the association of the former camp with Jews from 1995 and 2000 could be a result of the War of the Crosses and the intense campaign in the news media on this history of the former camp.

While the surveys from years 2000 and 2005 seem to suggest a trend toward understanding the former camp as the symbolic site of universal evil, of genocide regardless of national/ethnic identity or citizenship—almost three times more respondents identified the site as such in 2000 (13 percent) than in 1995 (5 percent)—that is definitely not the case anymore, with only 3 percent of respondents identifying "Oświęcim" as a site of genocide irrespective of nationality.[50] Finally, the socialist narrative of "Oświęcim" as the site of martyrdom of the Polish nation and other nations has steadily decreased from 26 percent to an insignificant 2 percent in 2010.

What is most striking, looking at the numbers over that fifteen-year period, is the steady growth of the association of Auschwitz with the extermination of Jews on the one hand, and the relative robustness of the association of the site and its history with the martyrdom of the Polish nation on the other. The broader associations are disappearing, leaving Jews and Poles as the primary victims of the camp. Only a tiny fraction of respondents, however—and a shrinking one—understand "Oświęcim" as the symbol of martyrdom for *both* Poles *and* Jews, as if the sharing of the symbol was not imaginable. Note, however, that the Polishness of the former camp was most often selected by people over forty years of age

Table 1.3. Poles' connotations with "Oświęcim"

Question: "With what, above all else, do you associate the word 'Oświęcim'? What is 'Oświęcim' for you?"

	1995 (CBOS) %	2000 (OBOP) %	2005 (CBOS) %	2010 (OBOP) %
Martyrdom of the Polish nation	47	36	37	39
Extermination of Jews	8	32	17	47
Martyrdom of both Poles and Jews	9	5	7	2
Martyrdom of several nationalities	26	10	16	2
Exterm./martyr. of Poles, Jews, other nationalities	a	a	6	a
Genocide irrespective of nationality	5	13	7	3
Other responses	3	2	8	1
Don't know anything about Oświęcim	1	0	0	1
Difficult to say	1	2	2	5

Sources: Centrum Badania Opinii Społecznej (CBOS), *Oświęcim w zbiorowej pamięci Polaków,* 1995; Ośrodek Badania Opinii Publicznej (OBOP), *Oświęcim: Przeszłość a teraźniejszość w opiniach Polaków,* 2000; CBOS, *Po obchodach 60-tej rocznicy wyzwolenia Auschwitz-Birkenau--Obóz w Oświęcimiu w świadomości Polaków,* 2005; OBOP, *Auschwitz w świadomości społecznej Polaków,* 2010.*

Notes:
[a] Response option not given in that survey.
* The first CBOS survey was conducted on January 13–16, 1995, on the basis of a representative random sample of adults living in Poland (N = 1,011). OBOP conducted two surveys, one on January 15–17, 2000 (N = 1,008), and the other on January 28–30, 2000 (N = 1,111), i.e., before and after the commemorative events of the fifty-fifth anniversary of Auschwitz's liberation. The same questions were administered in both surveys to measure the impact of the event on the population's knowledge and perceptions of Auschwitz. The results cited here are those of the *second*, postcommemorative survey. This OBOP survey was designed by and conducted for Dr. Marek Kucia, Department of Sociology, Jagiellonian University, Kraków. The 2005 CBOS survey was conducted from January 28–February 1 of that year (N = 1,333), after the sixtieth anniversary of Auschwitz's liberation. The questions for all three surveys were identical. I am grateful to CBOS and OBOP for making the 1995, 2000, and 2010 surveys available to me at no charge. For analyses and discussions of these (and other) surveys, see Antoni Sułek, "Wokół Oświęcimia: Spór o krzyże na tle wyobrażeń Polaków o sobie i Żydach," *Więź,* no. 481 (November 1998): 61–70, and especially Marek Kucia, "KL Auschwitz in the Social Consciousness of Poles, A.D. 2000," in *Remembering for the Future,* ed. Elisabeth Maxwell (Houndmills, Eng.: Palgrave, 2001), 632–651.

and least often by teenagers, who in turn most frequently indicated the Jewishness of the site.[51] In other words, those socialized in the People's Republic were least likely to associate Auschwitz with the Holocaust.

Other questions were intended to measure not the associations with, but actual historical knowledge about, Auschwitz. In the 2000 and 2010 OBOP (Ośrodek Badania Opinii Publicznej) surveys cited above, between 60 and 67 percent of respondents correctly identified Jews as the group with the largest number of victims. This suggests that most Poles *know* that Jews constitute the majority of the former camp's victims. That knowledge, however, does not seem to alter radically the meaning of "Oświęcim" as a symbol, which suggests the dissociation, in respondents' imaginations, of the symbol "Oświęcim" from Auschwitz the historical site and event. "Oświęcim" belongs to the symbolic sphere of Polish collective memory.

Nevertheless, surveys show that, despite its popularity, the Polish meaning of "Oświęcim" is in slow decline. This could be attributed to the growing knowledge and awareness of Auschwitz's Jewishness. Since it seems difficult to "share" the symbol (only between 2 and 9 percent of respondents between 1995 and 2010 associated "Oświęcim" with the martyrdom of both Poles and Jews), "Oświęcim" has forfeited some of its sanctity for Poles. A second factor for this decline may be the introduction of a "new" and rival symbol in public and official memory, which prior to the fall of Communism was taboo: "Katyń," a series of executions of approximately twenty thousand Polish officers and members of the intelligentsia by Soviet forces in forests near Kozielsk, Starobielsk, and Ostashkow. Unlike "Oświęcim," which was appropriated by the state and given a strong nationalist and socialist emphasis, Katyń was an important symbol in the *underground* and commemorated outside the state—not surprisingly, given that the Soviets were the perpetrator. With the end of Communism and the official recognition of the crime by the USSR in 1990, Katyń was brought into the foreground of Polish discussions of the war, leaving the private and underground spheres of memory to enter its public and official one, and now competing with "Oświęcim" for the status of the nation's holy site of martyrdom.[52]

This multifaceted analysis of the symbols of "Oświęcim"/"Auschwitz" as they relate to Oświęcim and Auschwitz shows that the disputed memory of Auschwitz is partly the result of different experiences of World War II and of historical representations of what took place at the former camps, and the creation of separate symbolic universes around it: "Oświęcim" for Poles, "Auschwitz" for Jews. The symbols' integration into longstanding ethnonational and ethnoreligious narratives of suffering—that of Christ of nations for Poles and of the chosen people for Jews—makes the respective symbols even more potent. Although Poles know that Jews constitute the largest group of Auschwitz's victims, they have appropriated the memory of Auschwitz and woven it into a grand narrative of Polish martyrdom. The prominence of "Oświęcim" in the Polish national narrative and collective memory serves to justify nationalist Poles' claims to the "ownership" of Auschwitz.

Notes

This chapter adapts and updates some of the materials presented in Geneviève Zubrzycki, *The Crosses of Auschwitz: Nationalism and Religion in Post-Communist Poland* (Chicago: University of Chicago Press, 2006). It is based on extensive archival research, ethnographic observations, and interviews conducted during thirty-eight months of fieldwork between 1990 and 2012. I have conducted six months of fieldwork at the Auschwitz-Birkenau Museum in Oświęcim in the winter and spring of 2001, and have followed up on that research with trips in the summers of 2004 and 2010. Additional materials for this chapter include informal conversations and a personal interview with the director of the Auschwitz-Birkenau Memorial and Museum, Dr. Piotr Cywiński (conducted in Ann Arbor on October 25, 2010), as well as materials presented in his public lecture "Auschwitz in the 21st Century" (International Institute, University of Michigan, Ann Arbor, MI, October 25, 2010). A video of the lecture is available at the University of Michigan Center for Russian, East European, and Eurasian Studies, "Auschwitz in the 21st Century," http://www.umich.edu/~iinet/media3/crees/10-11/cywinski_20101025/.

1. Pronounced Osh-VYEN-chim.

2. The symbolic representations of the site should not be conflated with the site itself. I therefore use quotation marks to emphasize the construction and porousness of "Oświęcim" and "Auschwitz" as meaningful symbols. The names without the quotation marks refer to physical sites: Auschwitz is the former camp and current museum/memorial, while Oświęcim is the town where Auschwitz is located. When quoting someone, I keep the term used in the original language. On the various meanings of "Oświęcim" and/or "Auschwitz," see Iwona Irwin-Zarecka, *Neutralizing Memory: The Jew in Contemporary Poland* (New Brunswick, NJ: Transaction Publishers, 1989); Emanuel Tanay, "Auschwitz and Oświęcim: One Location, Two Symbols," in *Memory Offended: The Auschwitz Convent Controversy*, ed. Carol Rittner and John K. Roth (New York: Praeger, 1991), 99–112; Jonathan Webber, "The Future of Auschwitz: Some Personal Reflections," Frank Green Lectures, no. 1 (Oxford: Oxford Centre for Postgraduate Hebrew Studies, 1992); Zvi Gitelman, "Soviet Reactions to the Holocaust, 1945–1991," in *The Holocaust in the Soviet Union: Studies and Sources on the Destruction of the Jews in the Nazi-Occupied Territories of the USSR, 1941–1945*, ed. Lucjan Dobroszycki and Jeffrey S. Gurock (Armonk, NY: M. E. Sharpe, 1993), 3–27; Tomasz Goban-Klas, "Pamięć podzielona, pamięć urażona: Oświęcim i Auschwitz w polskiej i żydowskiej pamięci zbiorowej," in *Europa po Auschwitz*, ed. Zdzisław Mach (Kraków: Universitas, 1995), 71–91; Michael C. Steinlauf, *Bondage to the Dead: Poland and the Memory of the Holocaust* (Syracuse, NY: Syracuse University Press, 1997), 122–144; Antoni Sułek, "Wokół Oświęcimia: Spór o krzyże na tle wyobrażeń Polaków o sobie i Żydach," *Więź*, no. 481 (November 1998): 61–70; Hans Citroen and Barbara Starzyńska, *Auschwitz-Oświęcim* (Rotterdam: Post Editions, 2011); Peter Novick, *The Holocaust in American Life* (New York: Mariner Books, 2000); Tim Cole, *Selling the Holocaust: From Auschwitz to Schindler, How History Is Bought, Packaged and Sold* (New York: Routledge, 2000); Marek Kucia, "KL Auschwitz in the Social Consciousness of Poles, A.D. 2000," in *Remembering for the Future*, ed. Elisabeth Maxwell (Houndmills, Eng.: Palgrave, 2001), 632–651; Marek Kucia,

38 | Geneviève Zubrzycki

Auschwitz jako fakt społeczny: Historia, współczesność i świadomość społeczna KL Auschwitz w Polsce (Kraków: Universitas, 2005); and Zubrzycki, *The Crosses of Auschwitz*. For a study of Holocaust memorial sites in Communist and post-Communist Poland, see chapters 5, 6, and 7 in James E. Young, *The Texture of Memory: Holocaust Memorials and Meaning* (New Haven, CT: Yale University Press, 1993). The most extensive analysis of the politics of commemoration at Auschwitz in Communist Poland can be found in Jonathan Huener, *Auschwitz, Poland, and the Politics of Commemoration, 1945–1979* (Athens: Ohio University Press, 2003).

3. Pierre Nora, *Les lieux de mémoire*, vol. 1, *La République, La Nation* (Paris: Gallimard [Quarto], 1997), 15. Of course Auschwitz is not the only such *lieu-carrefour* in Poland. Westerplatte, the site of the first clash between Germans and Polish forces during the invasion of Poland in September 1939, is another important *lieu de mémoire*. So is Katyń, a series of executions of approximately twenty thousand Polish officers and members of the intelligentsia by the Soviet NKVD in forests near Kozielsk, Starobielsk, and Ostashkow. I discuss the impact in this chapter's conclusion. See also Zubrzycki, *The Crosses of Auschwitz*, 106.

4. In recent years, mnemonic entrepreneurs have attempted to revive a *third* term, Oshpitzin, which, as the website http://oshpitzin.pl explains, is "the name that the Jews of Oświęcim called their town." Created by the Auschwitz Jewish Center—a prayer, study, and research center in Oświęcim, which in Polish is called Centrum Żydowskie w Oświęcimiu, i.e., the Jewish Center in Oświęcim (the town, not Auschwitz the former camp and current museum), the website educates visitors on the Jewish life of Oświęcim prior to the Holocaust. This is part of a growing trend to remember Jews not only as prisoners and dehumanized victims but also as living individuals and communities. The 2001 Birkenau exhibit in the former sauna/disinfecting area in Birkenau, for example, displays family photographs, wedding portraits, and other significant life course events to specifically rehumanize and reindividualize those mass-murdered. As this mnemonic enterprise is relatively recent, it has not become a key category in debates about the physical sites, their symbolic universes, and contested meanings. I thus focus in this chapter on "Oświęcim"/"Auschwitz."

5. For detailed descriptions of the Auschwitz system, see Robert van Pelt and Debórah Dwork, *Auschwitz 1270 to the Present* (New Haven, CT: Yale University Press, 1996).

6. Webber, "The Future of Auschwitz," 3.

7. The Red Army liberated approximately 7,000 prisoners at Auschwitz, who remained in the camp after the Nazis had forced approximately 60,000 others to march west as the Soviets approached. With those who had been released from the camp and those transferred from the Auschwitz system to other camps, the total number of Auschwitz survivors is much larger, in the tens of thousands. Raul Hilberg, *The Destruction of the European Jews*, 3rd ed., 3 vols. (New Haven, CT: Yale University Press, 2003), 3:1046–1048. By contrast, it is thought that less than ten people survived Bełżec, where approximately 500,000 perished, the great majority of whom were Jewish. Between 800,000 and 850,000 Jews were killed at Treblinka, with fewer than 100 surviving to see liberation.

8. Other prisoners in this early period of the camp's history included Soviet prisoners of war, Germans opposed to the Nazis, homosexuals, and Jehovah's Witnesses, as well as assimilated Polish Jews who were targeted as members of the Polish intelligentsia. Ethnic Poles, however, constituted the main group of prisoners during the early period. The memory of the camp is thus a very personal one for many Poles: every tenth adult Pole currently living in Poland has or had loved ones who were prisoners at Auschwitz, and more than one in twenty (6%) actually lost a family member or someone close in the camp. Centrum Badania Opinii Społecznej (CBOS), *Oświęcim w zbiorowej pamięci Polaków*, 1995; Ośrodek Badania Opinii Publicznej (OBOP), *Auschwitz w świadomości społecznej Polaków*, 2010. About a fifth of respondents (22%) declare that members of their families or people close to them were prisoners in

other Nazi concentration camps. CBOS, *Po obchodach 60-tej rocznicy wyzwolenia Auschwitz-Birkenau—Obóz w Oświęcimiu w świadomości Polaków*, 2005.

9. Tadeusz Iwaszko, "The Prisoners," in *Auschwitz: Nazi Extermination Camp* (Warsaw: Interpress Publishers, 1985), 63.

10. Kazimierz Smoleń, *Oświęcim 1940–1945* (Oświęcim: Państwowe Muzeum w Oświęcimiu, 1960), 15–16. The guide to the museum was authored by Kazimierz Smoleń, former prisoner and director of the museum from 1955–1990. It was revised and reedited several times until the narrative revision of the museum in the early 1990s, when it was pulled out of circulation.

11. Young, *The Texture of Memory*, 141. See also Stanisław Krajewski, *Żydzi, Judaizm, Polska* (Warsaw: Vocatio, 1997), 240.

12. Huener, *Auschwitz, Poland, and the Politics of Commemoration.*

13. The first project for the new main exhibition was presented at a session of the International Auschwitz Council in 2007. Now that there are sufficient funds, it will be implemented in successive phases in the next few years. Dr. Piotr Cywiński (director, Auschwitz-Birkenau Memorial and Museum), personal communication, October 27, 2010.

14. Huener, *Auschwitz, Poland, and the Politics of Commemoration*, 185–225.

15. Ibid., 186–187.

16. The spatial status of the convent and its grounds, the so-called gravel pit, is complex: it is outside the fenced area of the former camp and current museum, separated from it by cement block walls and barbwire fences, and bordered by a guard tower. Many Poles have thus argued over the years that this area is *outside* the former camp, using the wall and barbwire fences as the dividing line between Auschwitz the camp and Oświęcim the town, between the sacred and the profane. This spatial interpretation, however, is contradicted by a historical one: prisoners used to work at the gravel pit, and the so-called Old Theater, which housed the Carmelite convent from 1984 to 1993, was used to store Zyklon B during the war. The argument that the building and the gravel pit are outside Auschwitz is also contradicted by the spatial claims of the museum in a quasi-legal document: although the museum did not have formal jurisdiction over the gravel pit until 2004, the museum included it in maps when seeking formal recognition by the UNESCO and inclusion on the World's Heritage list in 1979. The (former) convent and its grounds have therefore been at the center of a border dispute between Poles and Jews about where Auschwitz begins and ends. In the battle over the location of some critical line in space, to borrow Eviatar Zerubavel's apt metaphor, Poles reject the all-encompassing symbolic field of "Auschwitz" and rely on physical demarcations to contain the site. For Jews, "Auschwitz" stands outside any physical construction and exists within its own universe. For some, it is not even part of Poland, hence the proposals made during the War of the Crosses for the extranational territoriality of the site. Eviatar Zerubavel, *The Fine Line: Making Distinctions in Everyday Life* (Chicago: University of Chicago Press, 1993).

17. For an account of Polish Jews' and non-Polish Jews' different reactions to the Carmelite convent, see Krajewski, *Żydzi, Judaizm, Polska*, 228–231.

18. The Polish delegation was composed of Cardinal Franciszek Macharski, archbishop of Kraków; Father Stanisław Musiał, secretary of the Polish Church's Commission for Dialogue with Judaism; and Jerzy Turowicz, editor-in-chief of *Tygodnik Powszechny*. They were joined by three Western European cardinals: Gottfried Danneels of Belgium; Albert Decourtray, archbishop of Lyons and chairman of the French Bishops' Conference; and Archbishop of Paris Jean-Marie Lustinger. The Jewish delegation was headed by Théo Klein, president of the Council of Jewish Organizations in France. He was accompanied by his Belgian and Italian counterparts, Markus Pardes and Tullia Zevi, as well as by French Chief Rabbi René-Samuel Sirat and Professor Ady Steg. Marek Głownia and Stefan Wilkanowicz, eds., *Auschwitz: Konflikty i Dialog* (Kraków: Znak, 1998), 176–177.

19. The deadline by which the nuns were supposed to relocate was, by all accounts, unrealizable. Two years to find a new site that would be acceptable to all parties, to obtain city permits and government clearance, and to secure materials and insure the proper construction was unrealistic in Communist Poland. There was also clear resistance and ill will on the part of the sisters, whose vows were made to that specific convent at that specific site, and who refused to leave. Finally, the affair was further complicated by the fact that, as a monastic order, the Carmelites are not under the jurisdiction of the diocesan bishop but the head of the Carmelite order in Rome. Although Polish, the nuns therefore refused to submit to an agreement ratified by representatives of the Polish Catholic Church.

20. For greater details and a deeper analysis of the Carmelite convent controversy, see Zubrzycki, "Introduction," in *The Crosses of Auschwitz*, 1–33.

21. Stanisław Musiał emphasized this point during one of our conversations (April 9, 2001).

22. Franciszek Piper, *Ilu ludzi zginęło w KL Auschwitz: Liczba ofiar w świetle źródeł i badań 1945–1990* (Oświęcim: Wydawnictwo Państwowego Muzeum w Oświęcimiu, 1992).

23. Despite these improvements, Auschwitz I undeniably remains the locus of the museum. During my fieldwork there in the winter and spring of 2001, Birkenau was typically presented as an "option" rather than as an integral part of the visit. After a three-hour-long, difficult visit to Auschwitz I, the guide typically gave visitors a "break" and then asked them whether or not they wished to continue on to Birkenau. Most declined. The standard visit now includes both Auschwitz and Birkenau, and the admission price includes transport between both camps (this was not the case in the low season a few years ago, when visitors had to walk or hire a cab for themselves and their guide to visit Birkenau).

24. From an assortment of unpublished seminar syllabi for the continuing education of the Auschwitz-Birkenau Museum guides, and from an unpublished document prepared by Mirosław Obstarczyk in 1999 that gives specific instructions to guides on how to conduct visits. I am grateful to Mr. Obstarczyk for making this document available to me.

25. Zubrzycki, *The Crosses of Auschwitz*. The March of the Living is not the only event that starts in Poland and ends in Israel. Jack Kugelmass points out that the symbolism of most organized visits of Jews to Poland is the same: the tours are structured around the themes of destruction and redemption, and almost all of them conclude their travel in Eastern Europe with a longer tour of Israel. Kugelmass, "The Rites of the Tribe: The Meaning of Poland for American Jewish Tourists," *YIVO Annual of Jewish Social Science* 21 (1993): 409. According to him, what is unique about Jewish tourism in Poland is its "antiquarian," rather than "ethnographic," nature: Jewish "tourists" are interested in the dead rather than the living, and the experiences they remember tend to be "those that enhance an already negative opinion. Indeed, they are the experiences they expect to have in Poland, and because they confirm deeply held convictions, they are almost a desired part of the trip" (411). Visiting Poland has now become what Kugelmass calls a "secular ritual" that confirms the identity of the participants as Jews (419). For several other similar examples, see Kugelmass, "The Rites of the Tribe." For vivid descriptions and pointed analyses of the march and Jewish tourism in Poland more broadly, see Erica Lehrer, *Jewish Poland Revisited: Heritage Tourism in Unquiet Places* (Bloomington: University of Indiana Press, 2013). For a discussion of the Zionist narrative in the event, see Novick, *The Holocaust in American Life*, 16. For an excellent analysis on the Israeli memory of the Shoah and the historical and symbolic creation of Yom HaShoah, Yom HaZikaron, and Yom Ha'Atzmaut, see Saul Friedlander and Adam B. Seligman, "The Israeli Memory of the Shoah: On Symbols, Rituals, and Ideological Polarization," in *NowHere: Space, Time, and Modernity*, ed. Roger Friedland and Deirdre Boden (Berkeley: University of California Press, 1994), 356–

371. The opening of the Museum of the History of Polish Jews in April 2013, which focuses on the one thousand years of history of Jews on Polish lands, offers an important counterpoint to the narrative focused on the destruction of Jewish life and culture.

26. I analyze the construction of the link between Polishness and Catholicism in the nineteenth and twentieth centuries in chapter 1 of *The Crosses of Auschwitz,* and devote much of that book to an analysis of its (contested) reconfiguration in the 1990s and early 2000s.

27. At the time, that area was not part of the museum. The Old Theater building and the gravel pit were transferred to the museum in 2004, as the future site of the International Center for Education about Auschwitz and the Holocaust.

28. The Catholic Church is of course differentiated within. See chapter 5 in *The Crosses of Auschwitz* for a detailed analysis of the various opinions and factions within the Polish Catholic Church about the cross(es) at Auschwitz, as well as of the evolution of those opinions during the summer of 1998 until the episcopate took an official position on August 26 of that year.

29. Kazimierz Świtoń, interview with the author, April 25, 2001, and May 23, 2001.

30. Keeping the papal cross at the gravel pit was far from considered a satisfactory conclusion by most abroad and many in Poland—such as Jewish activists and leaders, and liberal Catholics. But it was seen as the only viable option to put an end to the crisis. Interviews with Stanisław Musiał, May 10, 2001; Stefan Wilkanowicz, April 23, 2001; Stanisław Krajewski, May 24, 2004; and Konstanty Gebert, May 25, 2004. For the then chief rabbi of Poland, Pinchas Menachem Joskowicz, the "compromise" was unacceptable, and he personally asked Pope John Paul II to "also remove this last cross from the camp" (*Gazeta Wyborcza,* June 12–13, 1999) during the Pontiff's visit to the Polish parliament on June 11, 1999.

31. For an analysis of ethno-Catholic mythology in Poland and various forms through which it is adapted for political gain and critiqued, see Geneviève Zubrzycki, "History and the National Sensorium: Making Sense of Polish Mythology," *Qualitative Sociology* 34 (2011): 21–57.

32. The renaming was part of a new law regarding "the protection of the grounds of former Nazi camps" enacted by the Polish Sejm on May 7, 1999, which also established a 325-foot protective zone around Auschwitz. On the history of the nomenclature of the grounds of the former Nazi camp, see Jarmen, "Change to the Auschwitz Entry on the UNESCO World Heritage List," Auschwitz-Birkenau Memorial and Museum, http://en.auschwitz.org.pl/m/index.php?option=com_content&task=view&id=470&Itemid=8.

33. The visit synopsis distributed to the guides in 1999 also stressed that they must explain to visitors (especially to Polish ones, who tend to use the Polish names) why this semantic distinction is important: "The goal is to avoid the identification of the town, with its 800-year old history and as part of Polish culture and tradition . . . , with the camp created on its territory by the SS." Ironically, the title of this document used the very terms it instructed its guides not to use. Miroslaw Obstarczyk, "Synopsis of Tours on the Terrain and Permanent Exhibit of the State Museum *Oświęcim-Brzezinka,*" unpublished training guide, 1999, 3.

34. Young, *The Texture of Memory,* 123.

35. There are periodic initiatives by the Polish state and other organizations to counteract that tendency. In 2005, the daily *Rzeczpospolita* initiated a campaign against the term "Polish camps," which was supported by David Peleg, Israeli ambassador in Poland. *Rzeczpospolita* collected several thousand signatures, and Ambassador Peleg insisted in an open letter published in the daily that Jews and Israelis would never accept the concept of "Polish concentration camps." *Rzeczpospolita,* February 3, 2005. The Polish Ministry of Foreign Affairs keeps careful track of all references to "Polish camps" in the international media on a special page of its website, where it posts letters condemning the use of the formulation and includes links to the *Rzeczpospolita* action "Against Polish Camps." See Ministerstwo Spraw Zagranicznych,

"Przeciw 'polskim obozom,'" http://www.msz.gov.pl/Przeciw,polskim,obozom,948.html. Most recently, the New York–based Kościuszko Foundation launched a similar campaign. The preamble of its petition reads,

> WHEREAS the media uses the historically erroneous terms "Polish concentration camp" and "Polish death camp" to describe Auschwitz and other Nazi extermination camps built by the Germans during World War II, which confuses impressionable and undereducated readers, leading them to believe that the Holocaust was executed by Poland, rather than Nazi Germany; WHEREAS these phrases are Holocaust revisionism that desecrate the memories of six million Jews from 27 countries who were murdered by Nazi Germany; WHEREAS Poland was the first country invaded by Germany, and the only country whose citizens suffered the death penalty for rescuing Jews, yet never surrendered during six years of German occupation, even though one-sixth of its population was killed in the war, approximately half of which was Christian; WHEREAS educated journalists must know these facts and not cross the libel threshold of malice by using phrases such as "Polish concentration camps." BE IT THEREFORE RESOLVED that the undersigned request that The New York Times, The Washington Post, the Associated Press, and TIME magazine include entries in their stylebooks requiring news stories to be historically accurate, using the official name of all "German concentration camps in Nazi-occupied Poland," as UNESCO did in 2007 when it named the camp in Auschwitz, "The Auschwitz-Birkenau German Nazi Concentration and Extermination Camp (1940–1945)."

As of December 13, 2010, the petition was signed by 154,107 individuals, including officials, politicians, scholars, activist, survivors, and citizens from Poland, the United States, Canada, and Israel. The Kościuszko Foundation, "Petition on German Concentration Camps," http://www.thekf.org/events/news/petition/. Despite these significant efforts, on May 29, 2012, President Barack Obama referred to "Polish death camps" during the ceremony bestowing a Presidential Medal of Freedom on Jan Karski (Yad Vashem, "The Righteous among the Nations," http://www1.yadvashem.org/yv/en/righteous/stories/karski.asp), a hero of the Polish resistance during World War II. New York Times, "Topics" World War II, http://topics.nytimes.com/top/reference/timestopics/subjects/w/world_war_ii_/index.html?inline=nyt-classifier. While the White House qualified the expression as a "misstatement," Polish Prime Minister Donald Tusk commented on Obama's "ignorance, lack of knowledge, bad intentions." Mark Landler, "Polish Premier Denounces Obama for Referring to a 'Polish Death Camp'," New York Times, May 30, 2012, http://www.nytimes.com/2012/05/31/world/europe/poland-bristles-as-obama-says-polish-death-camps.html.

36. Andrzej Kacorzyk, interview with the author, March 30, 2001.

37. On this tension and its impact on local politics, see the investigative report by Michał Olszewski in the Kraków supplement to Gazeta Wyborcza, May 21, 2004.

38. Jacek Urbiński, interview with the author, April 4, 2001.

39. The opening of the supermarket was planned in a lot across the street from the museum's parking lot. Commercial buildings already existed in that area, and the supermarket was to be opened in a building that was to be renovated and expanded. The discotheque was opened in August 2000 a few miles from the former camp, close to the International Youth Meeting Center in Oświęcim. It was housed in what was during the war a tannery using forced labor. After 1942, the basement of the building was used to search victims' suitcases and shoes for valuables. Victims' hair was also sorted in that building. http://en.auschwitz.org.pl/m/index

.php?option=com_content&task=view&id=139&Itemid=8. For short analyses of several scandals associated with Auschwitz from the perspective of a Polish Jew, see Krajewski, *Żydzi, Judaizm, Polska*, 228–236. I come back to the implications such a conflation between Oświęcim the town and Auschwitz the camp entails for the inhabitants of the small town in a later section.

40. See note 17.

41. There are of course exceptions to this tendency, which concern mostly pilgrims and educational groups. There are now three important centers in Oświęcim that cater to these groups by offering various workshops and promoting Polish-Jewish-German dialogue: The International Youth Meeting Center in Oświęcim (http://www.mdsm.pl), the Centre for Dialogue and Prayer in Auschwitz (http://www.centrum-dialogu.oswiecim.pl), and the Auschwitz Jewish Center (http://208.184.21.217/welcome.asp?page=1). Despite the names of the last two, the centers are all located away from the museum, in the town of Oświęcim. These institutions play an important part in the movement to revise the history of Auschwitz away from its socialist and nationalist narrative by emphasizing the Holocaust and offering venues to discuss its religious and ethical implications. They are also important in fostering dialogue among the main groups involved—Jews, Poles, and Germans—by giving youth from these different nations the opportunity to meet, discuss, and sometimes work together on communal projects. Finally, the Auschwitz Jewish Center offers a space for individual Jewish visitors to connect and learn more about Oświęcim. It also provides important educational resources about the history and culture of Polish Jews before World War II to the local population and other Polish visitors. In an attempt to change its image, Oświęcim adopted a new "motto"—"city of peace"—and now hosts, since 2010, an annual "Life Festival"—a three-day rock festival that attempts to rebuild the town's identity beyond (yet via) its associations with Auschwitz and Birkenau. The narrative presented to would-be visitors (Poles and foreigners) is one where life triumphs over death, peace over war. The Park of the Nations' Reconciliation, planned on the right bank of the Soła River across from the Auschwitz-Birkenau Museum, has a similar goal. The space is meant to become a contemplative one for locals and visitors. Artist Jarosław Kozakiewicz, who won the 2005 competition, designed "The Bridge of Souls" (*Most Duchów*) that will link both shores of the Soła, where victims' ashes were sometimes discharged during the war. The bridge is a twisted structure that evokes a DNA chain or moebius band that symbolizes the passage from life to death but also the reconciliation between opposite parties through their unification. In the words of the artist, the Bridge of Souls "allows a safe crossing between the present and a traumatic history, and between life and death. The passage through the bridge thereby becomes a symbol of transformation" (http://www.kozakiewicz.art.pl/wpis.php?id=35). For photographs and a description of the project in English, see http://polinst.hu/en/node/4478.

42. This market is primarily aimed at non-Jewish individual tourists and groups, as the vast majority of Jews who visit Poland do so within the framework of tour groups organized in their home countries and do not require the services described above. Kugelmass, "The Rites of the Tribe." On the cultural production of Kazimierz in Kraków, see Lehrer, *Jewish Poland Revisited*. In 2009, an art installation by artist Mirosław Bałka was built in Kraków's Podgórze neighborhood, which was the site of the Jewish ghetto during the war. Entitled AUSCHWITZ-WIELICZKA, the installation is a poignant critique of the commodification of the Holocaust and the problematic melding of two sites—the Auschwitz-Birkenau Museum and the Wieliczka salt mines—into a single touristic experience, an "eight-hour monument." The sculpture is made of concrete in the shape of a square tunnel, with holes with the name of the installation on its ceiling. With sunlight, "AUSCHWITZWIELICZKA" is projected on the ground. For photographs, see Kraków Travel, "AUSCHWITZWIELICZKA," http://www.cracow.travel/guide-to-krakow/let-s-visit/podgorze/action,get,id,7978,t,AUSCHWITZWIELICZKA.html.

43. Only 9 percent of Poles use the German term, according to the results of an extensive survey conducted by Marek Kucia, a sociologist at Jagiellonian University in Kraków, while the name "Oświęcim" was used in reference to Auschwitz in almost all of the spontaneous answers given by respondents. Kucia, *Auschwitz jako fakt społeczny*, 103–104.

44. Kazimierz Świtoń, interview with the author, April 25, 2001, and May 23, 2001. Members of the Oświęcim Covenant in the Defense of the Papal Cross at the Gravel Pit, in discussions with the author, March 7, 2001, and April 4, 2001.

45. CBOS, *Oświęcim w zbiorowej pamięci Polaków* (N = 1,011); OBOP, *Oświęcim: Przeszłość a teraźniejszość w opiniach Polaków*, 2000 (N = 1,111); CBOS, *Po obchodach 6otej rocznicy wyzwolenia Auschwitz-Birkenau* (N = 1,133); OBOP, 2010 (N = 1,001). While almost all respondents who declared having visited the Auschwitz-Birkenau State Museum indicated that they had visited Auschwitz I, only two-thirds had also visited Birkenau. A third of Polish visitors, therefore, skip the Birkenau visit. OBOP, *Auschwitz w świadomości społecznej Polaków*, 2010.

46. Visits to the Auschwitz-Birkenau Museum are not part of the official school curriculum, but they have traditionally been included on the "day-trip" circuit, especially in southern Poland. (They were mandatory for pupils of southern Poland under Communism. Krystyna Oleksy, vice director of the museum and director of the Pedagogical Section, Auschwitz-Birkenau State Museum, interview with the author, March 19, 2001, and Andrzej Kacorzyk, Pedagogical Department and coordinator of the postgraduate program for teachers, "Totalitarianism-Fascism-Holocaust," Auschwitz-Birkenau State Museum, interview with the author, March 30, 2001). Students from farther regions also often go to the museum when they visit Kraków and Zakopane, a small resort town in the Tatra mountains. Guides reported to me that the pedagogical benefit for these latter groups was not all that clear since they visit the museum on their way to more "attractive" destinations. Unlike groups that come specifically to the museum as part of their history or Polish classes, these school/tourist groups are not prepared intellectually or "culturally" to visit the site.

47. As cited by Auschwitz-Birkenau director, Dr. Piotr Cywiński, in his public lecture "Auschwitz in the 21st Century," International Institute, University of Michigan, Ann Arbor, October 25, 2010. A video of the lecture is available at the University of Michigan Center for Russian, East European, and Eurasian Studies, "Auschwitz in the 21st Century," http://www.umich.edu/~iinet/media3/crees/10-11/cywinski_20101025/.

48. There are several such programs. Some are directed toward teachers of history, Polish, and religion and ethics, while others are organized jointly with Yad Vashem and consist of courses in Poland and Israel on Judaism, the history and culture of Polish Jews, and the Holocaust. See Andrzej Kacorzyk and Alicja Białecka, "Jesteście po to by dać świadectwo: Program edukacji nauczycieli w Muzeum i Miejscu Pamięci Auschwitz," proposal submitted to the Ministry of Culture, 1999. Aside from the pedagogical initiatives of the Auschwitz-Birkenau Museum, the first Polish high school textbooks about the Holocaust were published in the early 2000s accompanied with teacher's programs, lesson plans, descriptions of specific issues that the Holocaust raises, topics for group discussion, and exercises. See, for example, Robert Szuchta and Piotr Trojański, *Holokaust: Zrozumieć dlaczego* (Warsaw: Dom Wydaw "Mowią Wieki," 2003). See also Jolanta Ambrosewicz-Jacobs and Leszek Hońdo, eds., *Dlaczego należy uczyć o Holokauście?* (Kraków: Uniwersytet Jagielloński, Katedra Judaistyki, 2003), or its English translation, *Why Should We Teach about the Holocaust?* (Kraków: Judaica Foundation, 2004). For a study of ethnic prejudices and antisemitism in Poland and educational pilot programs, see Jolanta Ambrosewicz-Jacobs, *Me, Us, Them: Ethnic Prejudices among Youth and Alternative Methods of Education: The Case of Poland* (Kraków: Universitas, 2003).

49. See, for example, Haroon Siddique, "Arbeit macht frei sign stolen from Auschwitz," *Guardian* (Manchester), December 18, 2009, http://www.guardian.co.uk/world/2009/dec/18

/sign-stolen-auschwitz-death-camp; Judy Dempsey, "Sign over Auschwitz Gate Is Stolen," *New York Times,* December 18, 2009, http://www.nytimes.com/2009/12/19/world/europe/19poland .html; "L'inscription 'Arbeit macht frei' volée à Auschwitz," *Le Monde,* December 18, 2009, http:// www.lemonde.fr/europe/article/2009/12/18/l-inscription-arbeit-macht-frei-volee-a-auschwitz _1282441_3214.html; and "Police: Auschwitz 'Arbeit Macht Frei' Sign Stolen," *The Jerusalem Post,* December 18, 2009, http://www.jpost.com/Headlines/Article.aspx?id=163547.

50. The 2005 survey has "other responses" that could be added to the view that "Oświęcim" is the symbol of genocide regardless of nationality: for example, 2% of respondents declared that they saw it as a place of torture, cruelty, and death without reference to the victims' origins, and another 6% identified "Oświęcim" with the martyrdom and genocide of Poles, Jews, and other nationalities.

51. Kucia, "KL Auschwitz in the Social Consciousness of Poles," 13.

52. See also Zubrzycki, "History and the National Sensorium."

2 Restitution of Communal Property and the Preservation of Jewish Heritage in Poland

Stanisław Tyszka

THE NEXUS BETWEEN property restitution and collective memory is crucial for understanding how countries in Central and Eastern Europe have been attempting to come to terms with their Communist pasts. In each country, public debates about post-Communist property restitution have been linked to prevailing discourses about historical injustices. They have also been dependent on the different ways that dominant political elites understand the democratic state's responsibility for past wrongdoing. In terms of restitution legislation, however, Poland stands out as the only country that has not yet adopted a general law on compensation for individuals who lost property during or after World War II.[1] Since 1989, such legislation has been blocked by former Communists and Poland's liberal and leftist intellectual elite. Restitution has had a profound, though rarely acknowledged, impact on the ongoing debate about Polish-Jewish relations and on the current renaissance of Jewish life in Poland.

Opposition to restitution has dominated public debate in Poland since the fall of Communism. Nevertheless, during the 1990s, the country did adopt legislation that provided for the restitution of property held before the war by the Catholic Church and other major religious organizations, including Jewish communities. When the law on Jewish communal property restitution was passed in 1997, some observers suggested that the restitution of Jewish communal property would become a striking example of how restitution could positively affect collective remembrance. The return and restoration of Jewish communal property, it was thought, would reshape Poland's architectural and cultural landscape in a way that would contribute to the rediscovery of the country's past religious and cultural diversity. Eleonora Bergman, director of the Jewish Historical Institute in Warsaw, who catalogued Poland's remaining synagogues at the beginning of the 1990s, wrote, "When our catalogue of remaining synagogues finally appeared in print, I gave the first copy to the head of the Jewish Community Union, saying, 'All this can be yours.' I was thinking about the community he headed obviously. I wanted the community to adopt all those synagogues and monitor their use and upkeep. This became possible through a regulation that came into force in 1997. Things turned out differently, however."[2] As Bergman suggests, restitution had a very limited impact on the preservation of Poland's Jewish material heritage. This chapter seeks to explain why through an exploration of the legal and institutional ramifications of communal property restitution. The first part of the chapter addresses the origins, provisions, and effects of the 1997 law. It also reflects on how and why legislators understood the problem of preserving Jewish heritage. In this context, it briefly outlines the reception of Jewish restitution claims in Polish public discourse. The second part of the chapter considers several cases of Jewish heritage sites—mostly former synagogues—in order to discuss how restitution has shaped the preservation of Jewish heritage. Finally, the chapter offers some general observations about the relationship between restitution and the preservation of heritage by addressing such questions as: What types of actors contribute to the preservation of heritage sites? How are the meanings and purposes of particular sites negotiated by these actors? Who is deemed responsible for maintaining Jewish historical landmarks, and how is this responsibility justified?

Restitution Legislation

During the 1990s, the Sejm, Poland's parliament, adopted a series of twelve laws to sort out the legal status of the country's major religious organizations. Each of these laws contained provisions regulating the property ownership of churches and religious communities. In order to resolve the issue of present-day ownership of church property that had been nationalized by the Communist regime, these laws established separate commissions comprised of representatives of the government and members of the affected communities to process restitution claims. The law that regulated the restitution of Catholic Church property was passed on May 17, 1989, before the first semidemocratic elections took place in Poland the following month.[3] The adoption of this law was the result of an initiative by the last Communist government, which hoped to buy the church's support, or at least assure its neutrality, during the coming political transition. After the fall of the Communist regime, the law was amended in favor of the church.[4] In the law's updated form, it also became a model for further legislation adopted to regulate the legal status and restitution rights of other religious organizations. On February 20, 1997, the Sejm passed the Law on the Relationship between the State and the Union of Jewish Religious Communities.[5] Interestingly, this was the first law in the history of Polish statehood to regulate comprehensively the status of Jewish communities. In order to process property claims submitted by Jewish communities, the law established the Regulatory Commission for Jewish Religious Communities within the Ministry of the Interior and Administration.

While the legal status of Jewish religious communities and the restitution of Jewish communal property were regulated similarly to that of other churches and religious communities, the situation of Jewish communities differed greatly from other major religious organizations in postwar Poland. There was, for one thing, a lack of legal and cultural continuity between the current Jewish communities and their prewar predecessors. Poland's small Jewish community is currently represented by the Union of Jewish Religious Communities (UJRC), the 1993 replacement for the Religious Union of the Mosaic Faith, which had been established in 1949. Although the UJRC has consistently presented itself as the legal successor to prewar Jewish communities, the Communist authorities never formally recognized the postwar Jewish communities as such. In fact, the handful of Jewish communities that were reestablished in postwar Communist Poland never gained ownership of properties belonging to Jewish religious communities before the war. Instead, the communities were granted only the right to use some of these properties, while the State Treasury retained ownership of the prewar communities' vast holdings.[6] This issue is related to the larger problem of reestablishing continuity of the identities of organizations/corporate bodies in cases where continuity was broken due to legal changes imposed by the Communist regime. In addition to these complicated, technical legal matters, the dramatic change in size of Poland's Jewish community is important to consider. Prior to the war, Poland's Jewish community numbered more than 3 million members. Many of them lived in the eastern territories that Poland lost to the Soviet Union. As a result of the Holocaust and several waves of postwar emigration from Communist Poland, Poland's Jewish community only had about 1,700 official members when the restitution law was passed in 1997. It is, therefore, not only for legal and technical reasons that the 1997 law should be viewed as providing for a *transfer* of properties to new owners (a radically reduced Jewish community with little continuity with the prewar community) as opposed to the *restitution* of properties to their prewar owners.

The factors described above explain, at least in part, why this law was adopted only in 1997, as part of the last package of laws dealing with the status of religious organizations. Some political commentators in Poland emphasized the role of American lobbying in pushing for the adoption of the law, linking it to negotiations around Poland's NATO accession. Statements made by representatives of the World Jewish Restitution Organization (WJRO) seem to justify such conclusions.[7] The organization's vice chairman, Naphtali Lavie, said for example, "We will use all the means accessible to prevent the Czech Republic, Poland and Romania from joining NATO until these countries return all the property to their local Jewish communities."[8] The American government sent its ambassador to the European Union, Stuart Eizenstat, to Poland as a special envoy for property claims in Central and Eastern Europe. He was instructed to raise the issue of restitution of Jewish communal property with the Polish government. Despite these efforts, Poland's accession to NATO was never made conditional on the passage of a property restitution law. Furthermore, while it seems likely that Eizenstat had some influence on the law's passage, it is difficult to trace his negotiations with Polish officials based on the available documentary evidence.[9]

The government submitted the bill on Jewish communities to the Sejm in 1996 with little fanfare. There was also almost no discussion about it in the Polish media. The Sejm, which was dominated by former Communists at the time, passed the bill without much controversy. The new law regulated the status of Jewish religious communities in a comprehensive manner. It rendered the UJRC, formed by the local Jewish communities in the cities of Warsaw, Kraków, Gdańsk, Wrocław, Łódź, Szczecin, Katowice, Bielsko-Biała, and Legnica, the only officially recognized organization representing religious Jews. The law governed many aspects of Jewish life in Poland, including membership in Jewish organizations, the performance of religious and educational activities in public spaces, military service requirements for Jews, and religious holidays. During parliamentary negotiations, one significant provision affecting property issues was added to the government's original bill. This provision (article 22) stipulates that individual Jewish communities, as well as the umbrella UJRC, have the right to purchase, own, and dispose of real and movable property. It also grants representatives of both levels of Jewish communal organization the right to manage freely their properties, and, significantly, it states that the communities may exercise these rights on their own or with the aid of a foundation created especially for that purpose involving foreign organizations composed of Jews originating from Poland and the WJRO. This provision was intended as a compromise stemming from discussions about who should be entitled to take over the property of the prewar Jewish communties— the communities currently living in Poland or the representatives of Polish Jews living abroad.

The law stipulates that a restitution process, called a "regulatory procedure," can be initiated with the regulatory commission at the request of either the UJRC or an individual Jewish community. Separate regulations were adopted for Jewish communal real estate in territories that were part of Poland before the war and for property located in territories that were previously part of Germany. In territories that were Polish before the war and currently part of Poland, Jewish communities are allowed to reclaim certain categories of real estate that were owned by Jewish communities on September 1, 1939, the day of Germany's invasion. But this property can only be reclaimed if it meets one of two conditions. First, the property can be reclaimed if Jewish cemeteries or synagogues were located on it as of September 1, 1939. Second, property can be reclaimed if, as of the date that the 1997 legislation went into effect, the site still contained buildings that had previously served as headquarters for Jewish communities or as places of religious worship, or had been used for charitable, protective, or educational purposes associated with the Jewish faith. In other words, undeveloped real estate could be reclaimed only in the case of demolished synagogues and cemeteries, while other Jewish properties could be reclaimed only if the original Jewish communal buildings still exist. The requirement regarding the original purpose of the buildings is particularly important. In fact, the legislature narrowed the range of properties that could be returned to the Jewish community by eliminating a provision from the original bill that would have allowed for the restitution of buildings that had served sociocultural purposes. This change stemmed from the decision that restitution provisions should regard only property that served religious purposes, broadly understood. In practice, therefore, the 1997 law pertains mostly to former cemeteries, synagogues, prayer houses, community headquarters, schools, ritual baths, preburial facilities, orphanages, old age homes, some hospitals, and undeveloped real estate where synagogues once stood.

In Poland's present-day western and northern territories, which belonged to Germany before the war, the restitution process is different. In these areas, the law applies to the property of Jewish communities that were, as of Hitler's seizure of power on January 30, 1933, operating according to the Prussian Law of July 23, 1847, on the status of the Jews. Restitution may also be sought for property that belonged to other Jewish legal entities or for property that had an undetermined legal status. In these formerly German territories, the restitution procedure can be initiated if one of three conditions is met. The first condition is that the property in question have been the location of a Jewish cemetery or synagogue as of January 30, 1933. The second condition allows restitution proceedings to be initiated in cases where, as of the day that the 1997 law came into effect, buildings that previously served as headquarters of Jewish communities were located on the property in question in towns that still have active Jewish communities. Finally, restitution proceedings can be initiated in order to restore religious worship, charitable, protective, or educational activities associated with the Jewish faith. The scope of restitution is, therefore, more limited here than in the territories of prewar Poland, because only cemeteries, synagogues, and former community headquarters are subject to mandatory restitution.[10] In other cases, Jewish communities could only regain property if they were able to prove that it was needed to conduct religious, charitable, or educational activities in the present day.

The claims submitted by Jewish communities are processed by the regulatory commission, which consists of three government appointees and three UJRC representatives. With the exception of cases pertaining to cemeteries, the regulatory commission has three options to resolve cases about properties located on prewar Polish territory. First, the commission may transfer ownership of the property in question to the Jewish community. Second, in cases where it would be difficult to transfer the property, the commission may choose to award replacement property. Finally, in cases where it would be impossible to either restore the property or offer a suitable replacement, the commission may award financial compensation. With regard to cemeteries and all property in formerly German territories, the regulatory commission's only option for restitution is to transfer the ownership of the property in question to the Jewish community. In these cases, the commission cannot grant replacement property or financial compensation.

What is the *ratio legis* of the law—the purpose of its provisions on communal property restitution? There are a number of possible answers. The transfer of property to Jewish religious communities might be justified, for example, by the fact that such communities require the material resources in order to function. Alternatively, restitution might be considered a means of achieving justice by returning illegally seized property to its proper owners, or at least compensating them for their losses. Property transfers could also be justified as a means of safeguarding the Jewish material heritage in Poland by finding new owners who would care for the sites. While a detailed interpretation of restitution provisions is beyond the scope and purpose of this chapter, it seems worthwhile to consider briefly how the question of heritage preservation appears in the law. Article 17 of the law authorizes Jewish communities to create religious organizations in order to "safeguard the heritage of Jewish culture and tradition." While this is a strong statement about the importance of heritage, it is still clearly subordinated to religious considerations. Article 21, in turn, stipulates that "State, municipal and religious institutions shall cooperate, in a way defined in separate regulations, in order to protect, preserve, document and make accessible the monuments of architecture and art, museums, archives, and religious pieces of art and culture owned by Jewish communities." Here, the law advocates that the restituted properties be preserved and protected. At the same time, as mentioned above, the law gives the UJRC a free hand to manage restituted property as it sees fit, or even to dispose of such property if it wishes to do so. In fact, any restrictions on the exercise of property rights introduced here would be unconstitutional. Article 21 refers, therefore, to the "separate regulations." This is a reference to the general laws on heritage conservation, and these laws have had a considerable influence on the restitution of Jewish communal property.[11]

According to the 1997 law, only individual Polish-Jewish communities and the UJRC are entitled to file restitution claims. Nevertheless, the provision introduced in the Sejm opened the way for foreign organizations to participate in restitution. The involvement of the WJRO, which represents these organizations, formerly depended on the goodwill of local Polish-Jewish leaders. Its role became the subject of long, difficult, and contentious negotiations in which Stuart Eizenstat once again played an important role.[12] Finally, in June 2000, the WJRO and the UJRC signed an agreement to establish the Foundation for the Preservation of Jewish Heritage (FPJH) as a partnership between the two organizations.[13] The

FPJH was registered in Poland in 2002. By creating this foundation, representatives of local communities agreed to allow the WJRO to benefit from the return of communal property in Poland. This was done mainly for political reasons (such as the need for good relations with foreign Jewish organizations and to promote the image of the Polish government internationally) but also as a result of the financial and managerial assistance that the WJRO could provide. The agreement divided Polish territory for the purposes of restitution and heritage preservation. Properties in twenty-two of Poland's forty-nine districts (according to pre-1999 administrative division) are claimed and managed directly by the local communities or the UJRC. The FPJH owns and manages returned properties in the remaining twenty-seven districts. These districts are more distant from the cities where active Jewish communities exist, and constitute about 60 percent of Poland's territory. Real estate within the districts managed by the foundation is transferred to it only after it is formally returned to the UJRC.

Under the 1997 law, the filing deadline for restitution applications was May 11, 2002. A total of 5,504 applications were filed. About two-thirds of them dealt with properties in the districts managed by the foundation, and the rest applied to cases in the UJRC's area. For the sake of comparison, 3,063 applications were filed with the Property Commission for the Catholic Church, 1,200 with the Regulatory Commission for the Evangelical Church of the Augsburg Confession, 472 with the Regulatory Commission for the Polish Orthodox Church, and 168 applications with the Interchurch Regulatory Commission, which covers all remaining churches. The Jewish community, therefore, filed a relatively large number of applications, especially in comparison to the small size of its population. It should also be mentioned, however, that these applications included about a thousand claims for the restitution of Jewish cemeteries. Such claims are either resolved as a result of agreements among local Jewish communities, the government, and municipalities—so long as such agreements are accepted by the regulatory commission—or else they are settled by a decision of the commission. The return of cemeteries has been the least problematic, as their upkeep by the government was expensive, and thus a cost of which they were happy to be relieved.

According to the most recently available statistics, 6,535 hearings had been held as of December 2013. Complete or partial resolutions were reached in 2,398 cases. Some 616 cases were resolved by agreement, 458 were favorably resolved by decisions approving the application in whole or in part, 874 cases were discontinued, 394 were dismissed, 68 had no decision reached, and 44 were suspended.[14] Therefore, 1,074 claims resulted in the return of property, monetary compensation, or an allocation of replacement properties. In those cases resolved by monetary compensation, as opposed to restitution in kind, the agreements with municipalities called for 27,999,035 złotys to be paid to Jewish religious communities. Compensation decisions for property that could not be returned provided for another 55,227,191 złotys paid by the government (altogether, compensation in both types of cases amounts to approximately $27 million).[15]

The representatives of the UJRC and FPJH have complained about the slow pace of the commission's proceedings and problems substantiating claims. Representatives of municipalities, on the other hand, often argue that many applications were based on insufficient material evidence. Problems locating documents that prove prewar ownership of particular assets are obviously caused by the destruction of many archives during the war.

The Social Reception of Restitution Claims

The fact that the commission acts as a sort of court of arbitration, and that it encourages representatives of interested municipalities to participate in the regulations process, means that it works quite slowly. More importantly, however, this inclusive approach has allowed the commission to conduct its work without any major disputes over particular claims, which might capture the interest of the broader public. Indeed, cases tend to be covered in regional, as opposed to national, newspapers, because the reclaimed buildings and properties often served as town libraries, schools, hospitals, or parks, and thus hold significance for local governments and communities.

A survey of articles appearing in the local press since 2002 is revealing. Beyond factual information describing which objects were claimed, the state of negotiations between the municipalities and the Jewish religious communities, and the proceedings and decisions of the regulatory commission, the cases were usually discussed from the perspective of local communities' economic and social interests. The transfer of property to Jewish communities was rarely depicted as the return of property to its rightful owners. This suggests that Polish readers would not see the transactions as underpinned by obvious continuity or the service of justice. Some articles described controversies within local communities caused by the claims. This was particularly common in cases where apartment buildings with tenants were the object of restitution claims. As examples of the variety of responses, consider the following titles from regional newspapers: "They Had to Return a Park to the Jewish Religious Community"; "A Plot with Tenants at Sądowa Street to Be Returned to Jewish Community"; "Will Jewish Community Throw Them out of Their Apartments?"; "Disputed Ownership Title"; "Will the Jews Come and Take the Property?"; and "Will the Jews Take a Large Part of Pabianice?"[16] While some titles are purely descriptive, others suggest a slightly negative, or even antisemitic, attitude toward the claims or claimants.

National newspapers rarely reported on these local property disputes. One set of cases, however, did reach the national media: an apartment building in Łomża and several buildings in Jedwabne, all of which were claimed by the Warsaw Jewish Religious Community. These cases were the subject of a newspaper report entitled "Jews Return for What Is Theirs," which was published as a cover story in the Polish edition of *Newsweek* in March 2004.[17] Among other topics, the report discussed the fears of local community members, including the tenants of the apartment house in question. Some of these fears were expressed in an antisemitic manner. Members of the local community were quoted as saying, for example, "It is going to be like before the war—your streets, our houses [*Wasze ulice, nasze kamienice*]." Some Poles attributed this saying to Jews before the war to suggest the latter's anti-Polish sentiments. Another source of controversy was the magazine's cover, which showed a set of corroded keys allegedly found during the exhumation of Jedwabne Jews. The article caused much public indignation. A few well-known leftist intellectuals signed a protest against the publication entitled "Restitution of Hatred." They accused the article's authors of antisemitism and asked the prosecutor to investigate this case of an "antisemitic poster," as they branded the cover of the magazine.[18]

In the national media, the problems caused by restitution in Łomża and Jedwabne were reduced to the problem of antisemitism, which was attributed either to the journalists or local people. Antisemitism was sometimes a factor in these debates. Yet the restitution claims also directly conflicted with the immediate material interests of local governments and communities. Similar reactions emerged when claims of the Catholic Church conflicted with local interests. Yet this practical aspect of the issue was completely absent in the discussion prompted by the *Newsweek* article. This was in part due to the inappropriate and sensationalist manner in which the issue of restitution was raised in that publication. By resorting to accusing their rightwing political opponents of antisemitism, however, leftist intellectuals also ignored the practical aspect of the debate. Their response reflected a more general unwillingness to discuss the complexity of Jewish property claims since 1989, a situation that has had wide-ranging effects.

Public sentiment about the restitution of Jewish communal property should also be viewed in the context of the broader debate on the restitution of property to individual owners. In this debate, the problem of Jewish property claims has been consistently dismissed or avoided. The Polish leftists and liberal intellectuals who have dominated the public debate on restitution since the beginning of the 1990s have consistently opposed the idea of restoring nationalized property to individual former owners. The editor-in-chief of the popular liberal daily *Gazeta Wyborcza*, Adam Michnik, for example, attacked a class action lawsuit against Poland filed in New York in 1999 by a group of Polish Jews or their heirs who had become American citizens. Michnik called the suit "anti-Polish" and described the very action of filing it as an abuse of history. "There are people," he wrote, "who decided to use the tragedy of the Holocaust as an opportunity to play for big money."[19] Attacking the same lawsuit, former anti-Communist dissidents Jacek Kuroń and Karol Modzelewski wrote, "In the claims by the group of American Jews . . . we see neither sanctity nor tragedy of the Holocaust, only material interest."[20]

These figures subordinated the issue of restitution of Jewish property to their attitudes about the restitution of nationalized property more broadly. Michnik, Kuroń, Modzelewski, and other political commentators of *Gazeta Wyborcza* fervently opposed the draft of a general restitution law passed by the Parliament in 2001. They supported President Aleksander Kwaśniewski's veto, which prevented the bill from becoming law.[21] The reasons for their reluctance toward restitution in general were manifold. First, they tended to juxtapose the arguments of historical justice with those of present-day social justice. Second, because many former owners supported rightwing political parties, leftists feared that the return of property to individual owners might change the political landscape in Poland in ways unpalatable to the leftist elite. Finally, since 1989, many representatives of this elite have advocated the necessity of so-called nomenklatura privatization (*uwłaszczenie nomenklatury*) as part of the political compromise with former Communists. The earlier "propertization" (or material embourgeoisement/ enfranchisement) of the Communist nomenklatura (the stratum of powerful leaders and administrators during the Communist period) has rendered restitution of property to former owners problematic.[22]

Yet, at the same time that they fought against Jewish property restitution, these intellectuals were strong promoters of the so-called Polish-Jewish dialogue and Poland's need to deal with the "dark chapters" of its history. These seemingly contradictory stances lead to the conclusion that Polish intellectual elites radically separated symbolic and material interests in their politics of memory with regard to Polish-Jewish relations. This approach was also applied, to some extent, to policies regarding the preservation of Jewish material heritage.

The Question of Jewish Heritage Preservation

As one of the two beneficiaries of communal property restitution, Jewish religious communities began to reclaim properties a few years before the FPJH was established in 2002. At the beginning of the 1990s, Eleonora Bergman and Jan Jagielski compiled an inventory of Poland's remaining synagogues.[23] Their list included synagogues that represented a wide variety of periods and styles, and that varied greatly in terms of architectural and historical value. While a handful were still used as synagogues, many others had been transformed into museums, cultural centers, libraries, state archives, courts, apartment houses, fire department headquarters, shops, and even pubs. Many were ruined or abandoned, and have continued to deteriorate.[24] Not all of these buildings could be reclaimed through the restitution procedures. While some of them had already been private prayer houses before the war, others had since passed into private hands by the time of the law's passage in 1997. In the latter cases, the regulatory commission could only grant Jewish religious communities replacement properties or financial compensation.

Under the 1997 law, Jewish religious communities were also granted full ownership of properties that they already possessed. They began to reclaim other properties as early as 1998. When the law was adopted, the UJRC was made up of the Jewish religious communities in nine cities, each of which had an active synagogue.[25] These communities were named in the appendix to the law. Since the adoption of the law, the Jewish religious communities in Gdańsk and Wrocław were dissolved as official bodies by the UJRC due to conflicts about restituted property. In accordance with the 1997 law, their holdings were taken over by the UJRC. The centralization of Poland's Jewish religious communities into one umbrella organization is, historically speaking, a novel phenomenon. The prewar religious communities were diverse and autonomous organizations. The UJRC—currently headed by the chief rabbi of Poland, Michael Schudrich, and the president of the union, Piotr Kadlcik—has consistently opposed the emergence of independent Jewish communities in Poland. Communities that are members of the UJRC are responsible for reclaiming properties in their neighboring regions. In a few towns, including Poznań, Wrocław, Lublin, Wałbrzych, and Żary, local branches were established. The situation of former synagogues in places where there is no local Jewish community remains problematic.

The case of the synagogue in Płock shows how the function of Jewish heritage sites in towns without a local Jewish religious community is negotiated by various actors representing different symbolic and material interests. The Small Synagogue in Płock, which is located at 7 Kwiatka Street, is the last freestanding synagogue in the Płock region and one of the few remaining synagogues in the whole Mazowsze province. The two-story building was constructed around 1810 in the classicist style. The building served not only as a prayer house but also as a school, the headquarters of Płock's Jewish community, and, for a time, the rabbi's house. During World War II, the synagogue's interior was completely destroyed. Before the war, around seven thousand Jews lived in Płock. In February 1945, when the first meeting of Płock Jews after the war took place, just twenty-two survivors gathered to establish the local Jewish Committee. In 1949, the Płock Jewish Committee transferred use of the Small Synagogue building to the Gerszon Dua-Bogen Tailor/Knitting/Hosiery Association. This company occupied the building until the beginning of the 1990s. In 1960, the State Treasury was registered as the owner of the former synagogue, having acquired the title by automatic prescription under the law. In 1962, the building was entered into the registry of national monuments as an example of nineteenth-century sacred architecture.[26] After the collapse of Communism in 1989, ownership of the building was formally transferred to the city of Płock. The building was abandoned by the successor of the

Gerszon Dua-Bogen Company in 1992. Until 1997, the local government let it fall into total ruin.

The 1997 law allowed the Jewish religious communities to acquire owner-ship of the synagogue. In May 1998, however, the UJRC and the Łódź Jewish Re-ligious Community reached a settlement with the Płock municipality, whereby the Jewish Religious Community relinquished all rights to the property in return for 224,000 Polish złotys (approximately $64,000).[27] The agreement, which was accepted by the regulatory commission, stipulated that the municipality of Płock could freely dispose of the building so long as it did not turn it into a church, bath, tannery, or public toilet. In addition, no "indecent activities" were to be car-ried out in the building. In particular, the building was not to be used for adult entertainment or as a dance hall. These conditions were set in rabbinic responsa authored by Rabbis Chaskel O. Besser and Amiel Wohl from New York. The re-sponsa were attached to the agreement. The agreement also stipulated that there were no religious symbols on the property that needed to be removed under Jew-ish religious law. It singled out the remaining wooden framework of the aron ha-kodesh (Torah ark), and noted that it was not to be considered a religious symbol. That wooden framework was the only artifact of the synagogue's original interior that had survived decades of war, misuse, and neglect.[28]

Almost immediately, the Płock city council listed the synagogue building as available for purchase. In 2001, the council reversed its decision to sell the build-ing, slating it to become a public art gallery instead. There were plans to create an exhibit commemorating the Jews of Płock in one of the gallery's rooms. But financial and organizational problems prevented the proposed project from be-ing executed. In January 2004, the city council decided to auction the building off, but because it was listed in the register of historic monuments, any potential buyer of the former synagogue would have to have its plans for the building ap-proved by the provincial heritage conservation officer. Prospective buyers would also be required to observe the conditions set in the agreement accepted by the regulatory commission.

Quite unexpectedly, the decision to sell the synagogue sparked strong pro-tests in Poland and abroad. Opposition came from representatives of the Israeli and American branches of the Płock Landsmanschaft,[29] members of the Jewish community in Poland, and a historian of Płock Jews. The criticisms voiced by Konstanty Gebert, a journalist and prominent representative of the UJRC, are particularly significant. Gebert argued that the municipality should turn the syna-gogue into a museum of Płock Jews—a project beyond the means of the UJRC's own finances—rather than sell it. According to Gebert, the UJRC could not af-ford the costly repairs required to restore most of Poland's remaining synagogues. In places where there was no active Jewish community and the local synagogue building was in poor condition, he argued, rather than try to regain the synagogue, the union should instead settle for financial compensation. At the same time, Gebert laid the responsibility for taking care of dilapidated synagogues on the Polish communities:

> A Jewish museum? Some people might bristle at the idea. "And why should we organize a Jewish museum there, if the Jews themselves gave the synagogue back?"
>
> The answer is simple. The Jews gave the synagogue back because they cannot afford to renovate it, and there would be nobody to pray in it. There are no Jewish citizens of Płock left. But that makes the duty lying upon the citizens of Płock to remember their fellow-townspeople even stronger. . . . If the town is not just a collection of random buildings with random people living in them, if local identity is more than just a regional vignette on a brochure advertising the beauty of the town and its surroundings, identical to everywhere else, if we do not want the past to be shaped and cut in an arbitrary way, then memory becomes a fundamental issue. The Jews of Płock are a part of that memory.[30]

Gebert thus tied the preservation of Polish Jews' material legacy to the moral duty to remember the victims of the Holocaust, as well as to a particular (re-)configuration of local identity in which a community's former Jews should be seen as an integral part of its fabric, and not as outsiders whose material heritage is someone else's responsibility. He argued that the responsibility for commemorating the Jews of Płock rested entirely upon the local community, and that the Jewish religious communities did not share this burden. It would seem, therefore, that he understood the issue of property restitution to be separate from the moral obligation to commemorate those who perished in the Holocaust. This understanding is consistent with the general separation of symbolic and material interests in Poland's public discourse on Jewish property restitution. Such an approach is, of course, legitimate in legal terms, as the Jewish communities have the right to dispose of their property however they see fit.

The case of the Płock synagogue suggests questions that are relevant for the problem of Jewish material heritage preservation more generally: What is the relationship between synagogues' former religious purposes and the preservation of Jewish heritage for historic and cultural reasons? Who should be responsible for the heritage and on what grounds? In the Płock case, the beneficiaries of restitution assumed that this heritage site could be disposed of because it was not being used for religious purposes. But there was also a conflict between the formal, legal aspects of ownership, under which the municipality was free to dispose of its assets, and political limitations on the exercise of property rights revealed by the protests against the community's proposed sale of the synagogue building. It seems significant that the building in question was a municipal property, as it was apparently regarded as a sort of collective property by protesters. The fates of dozens of other former synagogue buildings held by private owners have not stirred similar outcries.

Some members of Poland's Jewish community have criticized the UJRC's treatment of Jewish heritage sites. They take issue with the fact that the organization often chooses to accept financial compensation for heritage sites instead of seeking property restitution. They also complain that the UJRC often chooses to sell heritage sites once they have been restituted.[31] For the most part, these controversies have failed either to arouse the interest of the national media or to affect Polish public opinion more generally.[32] Among the more active Jewish critics of the UJRC's policy is Bolesław Szenicer, who served as the longtime director of the Jewish cemetery in Warsaw at Okopowa Street. The UJRC dismissed Szenicer from that position, allegedly due to his criticism of the union's policy of selling reclaimed Jewish heritage properties.[33] After being dismissed, Szenicer set up the Jewish Old Testament Community in Poland, which opposes the UJRC. Szenicer also began publishing a low-budget monthly magazine, *Głos Gminy Starozakonnych* (The Voice of the Old Testament Community), which he used to discuss the demolition of Jewish heritage properties. Among the buildings sold by the communities and subsequently demolished, he listed the Butcher's Synagogue in Siedlce, the Reindorf Synagogue and Mikvah in Otwock, and mikvahs (ritual baths) in Krzeszowice and Mińsk Mazowiecki.[34] Representatives of the UJRC responded to these accusations by arguing that the buildings in question were usually ruined, that there were no Jews who could use them for religious purposes, and that preference was given to the material needs of the Jewish community (including the welfare system, educational activities, and rabbis' salaries). In order to finance these needs, the UJRC explained, they had to sell some buildings.[35] The validity of these arguments cannot be verified because the finances of the UJRC are not publicly disclosed nor subject to audit. But it is reasonable to question such arguments considering how small the Jewish community is in relation to the millions of złotys the UJRC receives each year from selling or renting reclaimed properties.[36] Nevertheless, criticism such as Szenicer's has had little effect on the UJRC, which remains reluctant to use its funds to preserve Jewish heritage sites.

The fate of former synagogues has been debated in a few other cities as well. The most well-known case is probably that of the New Synagogue in Poznań, which the Germans transformed into a swimming pool for Wehrmacht soldiers in 1940. The New Synagogue continued to be used as a swimming pool throughout the era of the Polish People's Republic and even after 1989. Finally, under the 1997 law, the ownership of the building was transferred to the UJRC. In 2006, Marcin Libicki, an art historian and rightwing member of the European Parliament, proposed that the synagogue be purchased from the Jewish Religious Community and demolished. He suggested that the community ought to build a new synagogue in a different location. Libicki attempted to justify his controversial proposal by arguing that the erection of the synagogue by German Jews at the beginning of the twentieth century was part of the *Kulturkampf* aimed against Catholicism and Poles. Since the small Jewish community in Poznań uses a prayer house located on Stawna Street, plans to turn the New Synagogue into a cultural center or hotel were made. According to local Jewish leaders, however, these plans could not be realized due to a lack of funds. Because these plans for the building cannot be carried out, the Jewish community continues to lease it to the swimming pool operator. Representatives of the UJRC argued that the immediate closure of the pool was not advisable, because draining the water might threaten the building's structure.[37]

In some cases, the Jewish religious communities have undertaken commemorative initiatives around Jewish heritage sites. One example is the previously mentioned synagogue in Otwock, which was returned to the Warsaw Jewish Religious Community in 1999. The community sold the synagogue to a development company the next year. In the middle of 2003, the synagogue was demolished and a large building with apartments and shops was built in its place. In 2009, a commemorative stone was unveiled in front of the new building. Its inscription reads, "Here, on 6 Górna Street, there was a building containing a synagogue and a mikvah. In 1939, circa 11,000 Jews lived in the city. To the memory of Jewish inhabitants of Otwock." The stone was placed cooperatively by the Jewish Religious Community in Warsaw and the development company.

A similar approach was taken in the case of a building that once housed a Jewish hospital at 15 Leszno Street in Warsaw. Until 1941, that building housed a facility for Jewish children and old people. The Warsaw Jewish Religious Community took control of the building under the provisions of the 1997 law, and in 2009, the community decided to demolish it. Interestingly, this decision was accompanied by a public relations campaign in which the representatives of the community sent local newspapers a press release entitled "Jewish Religious Community Will Save the Former Hospital on Leszno Street from Oblivion." The authors of this statement informed the press that they wanted to document the history of the building. They appealed to readers to provide them with testimonies or photographs. They also explained that, although they would have liked to keep the hospital, it was in such bad condition that it was necessary to demolish it. The destruction of this historic building was criticized by experts in Jewish Studies including Jacek Leociak, author of numerous publications on the Warsaw Ghetto.[38]

Indeed, the UJRC can point to very few success stories as regards the preservation of material heritage. Beyond the few synagogues it has saved for religious use, its only notable success was the opening of a new synagogue in the building that once housed the famous Chachmei Lublin Yeshiva. This building, located in the city of Lublin, was returned to the Jewish community under the 1997 law.

The community renovated it and transformed the former yeshiva into a synagogue, a mikvah, and the Lublin Jewish Religious Community headquarters, all of which opened with much fanfare in February 2007. Further plans call for the rest of the building to be made into a hotel. It is worth noting that the American government had already paid a compensation claim related to this building in 1964.[39] The Theological Seminary Yeshivath Chachmey in Southfield, Michigan, received the compensation as the Lublin school's successor. The money given to the Michigan seminary was taken from a $40 million fund that the U.S. government had received from the Polish People's Republic as part of a 1960 agreement that provided compensation for property of American citizens nationalized by the Communist regime.[40] Such transactions show another facet of the complex workings of restitution, namely the occasional oversight (due to anything from administrative chaos to corruption) of previously paid compensation.

The previously discussed controversy surrounding the Płock synagogue speaks to another important issue related to the preservation of Jewish heritage in Poland, namely the involvement of nongovernmental organizations. As a result of the debate prompted by the town of Płock's decision to sell the synagogue, a group of private people—local entrepreneurs and community activists, including a "Righteous among the Nations" honoree and a Catholic priest—formed the Płock Synagogue Association. This group proposed that a museum of Jews from Mazovia and an education center for young people be located in the heritage site. Acting without the support of any large institution, the association managed to interest the governments of Płock and Mazowieckie provinces in their idea. Accordingly, in 2006, the municipality loaned the association the building free of charge. In 2010, the town of Płock sold the building to the association for 1 percent of its real value. In the meantime, the association managed to secure financing for restoration work and the creation of the museum. The synagogue's reconstruction is predicted to cost 9 million złotys, of which the association has collected 1.3 million. The rest of this sum will come from European Union funds (specifically from the Regional Operational Program of the Mazowieckie Province).

Nongovernmental organizations have played an important role in the preservation of other Jewish landmarks as well. In the small northeastern town of Sejny, for example, the Borderland Foundation (Fundacja Pogranicze) renovated and now rents the White Synagogue. This synagogue was initially reclaimed by the UJRC through the restitution process.[41] In Olsztyn, the Borussia Foundation is renovating a preburial house that was constructed in 1913 based on designs made by the famous architect Erich Mendelsohn. The foundation intends to establish a center for intercultural dialogue there.[42]

Foreign organizations, too, have made a significant contribution to the preservation of Jewish heritage sites in Poland. In 1998, the Chevra Lomdei Mishnayot Synagogue in Oświęcim was the first Jewish communal property to be returned to a Jewish religious community in Poland. The Bielsko-Biała Jewish Religious Community, which received the synagogue, donated it to the Auschwitz Jewish Center Foundation, which was established in 1995 in New York. The building was completely restored to its prewar condition as described in survivors' testimonies and recollections. It reopened in September 2000. In Kraków, the Center for Jewish Culture "Judaica Foundation" was established in 1993 in a former prayer house built in the 1880s by the B'nei Emuna Prayer and Benevolent Society. Renovations to the building were made possible by financial aid from the U.S. Congress. Yet, under the 1997 law, the Jewish Religious Community in Kraków filed a claim for financial compensation for this building with the regulatory commission. The claim was approved.[43] In Leżajsk, a synagogue was opened in 1998 in the building of a former mikvah. This synagogue, which serves mostly Hasidic Jews who come to visit the tomb of Rabbi Elimelech Weissblum, was a project of the Hasidim Leżajsk Poland Foundation. The legendary Rabbi Menachem Mendel's synagogue in Rymanów was bought from the FPJH by the Congregation Menachem Zion Yotzei Russia of Brooklyn, New York. The congregation's leader is Rabbi Avraham Reich, who is a direct descendent of Rabbi Mendel. In 2005, the congregation reconstructed the building, which was almost entirely ruined.

The second major beneficiary of restitution is the Foundation for the Preservation of Jewish Heritage. In contrast to the UJRC, the foundation is not a religious organization. It operates in those areas of Poland that are located far from existing Jewish communities. Since 2004, it has been headed by Monika Krawczyk, an attorney from Warsaw. As the foundation's chief executive officer, Krawczyk is responsible to a council composed of representatives from the UJRC and the WJRO. The foundation's aims are threefold. First, it protects properties that bear particular religious or historical significance. Second, acting as the plenipotentiary of the UJRC, it reclaims properties that belonged to Jewish religious communities before World War II. Third, it manages returned properties.[44] The foundation's policy with regard to the preservation of Jewish material heritage is outlined in its annual reports. The 2009 report listed six main areas in which the foundation is active: cemeteries, memory, revitalization, education, Jewish Studies, and antisemitism.[45] The order in which these areas are listed in the report reflects their importance for the foundation.[46]

Taking care of Jewish cemeteries is the foundation's top priority due to the religious significance accorded to cemeteries in Judaism.[47] The foundation organizes the tidying up of cemeteries and builds fences around them. It should be noted, however, that the foundation is by no means the only institution taking care of Poland's Jewish cemeteries. A number of foreign organizations, including the Nissenbaum Foundation and the Poland Jewish Cemeteries Restoration Project, have been involved in this activity since the 1980s.[48] Also, as of March 2010, the FPJH had no special budget for cemetery restoration.[49] Under the category "Memory," the annual reports list the participation of FPJH representatives in numerous commemorative ceremonies, including the unveiling of monuments and plaques. These markers are funded either by the FPJH or private Jewish donors. "Revitalization" includes the reconstruction of important Jewish landmarks. Most of this work has been undertaken within the "Hassidic Route" project that the foundation has carried out since 2005. The project's aim is to develop a tourist route linking together towns containing important Jewish monuments in southeastern Poland and possibly also western Ukraine. The foundation's major educational program is called "To Bring Memory Back." The program's goal is to encourage students to search for the remains of Poland's multicultural history, and to take care of Jewish cemeteries. Students participating in the program reconstruct the history of their towns and explore Jewish traditions and culture. In 2009 alone, the program involved about 4,800 students at 175 schools all over Poland. The program has been sponsored by the Polish government and by private foundations. In the field of Jewish Studies, the foundation's major activity is the Polin website, which it has been developing since 2006.[50] This website, which is available in both Polish and English, presents information about the history and development of Jewish communities throughout Poland. It also contains information about the Holocaust and Jewish material heritage sites. In 2009, the project was supported by the Polish Ministry of the Interior and Administration and the San Francisco–based Taube Foundation for Jewish Life and Culture. Finally, the foundation's activities in the field of antisemitism include reporting on incidents of antisemitic speech (such as leaflets, public speeches, and graffiti) or acts of vandalism directed against Jewish heritage sites.

The area of activity most relevant for the purpose of this chapter—that is, the exploration of relationships between property restitution and the preservation of heritage—is the foundation's revitalization projects. The FPJH's policy in this respect is formulated as follows: "In order to preserve [Jewish landmarks] for future generations, it is necessary to adapt them to the contemporary realities and the needs of local communities. Our strategy is based on the belief that authentic and sustainable revitalization proceeds only in cooperation with local partners. Such approach fits well within the priorities of the regional policy of the European Union."[51] Two important features of the foundation's policy are described within this statement. First, the foundation limits its activities to those places where it can find local partners.[52] This means that the FPJH sees itself more as a coordinator than an initiator of renovation projects. In practice, the foundation's local partners are municipalities or nongovernmental organizations. Second, the statement's reference to the EU reveals that the foundation is looking for external funds to pay for its revitalization projects.

As of February 2013, the foundation had conducted only one revitalization project. It renovated the Renaissance Synagogue in Zamość and turned that building into a house of prayer, an information center for the FPJH's Hassidic Route project, and the Museum of the History of the Jews of Zamość. The newly renovated synagogue was opened in April 2011. In 2008, the project received a grant from Iceland, Liechtenstein, and Norway through the European Economic Area Financial Mechanism and the Norwegian Financial Mechanism, which covered 85 percent of the renovation costs. The remaining 15 percent was financed by other donors and the FPJH itself. The foundation's representatives indicated that this was a "pilot project." They have also publicized further renovation projects planned for the synagogues in Kraśnik and Przysucha. The FPJH is currently seeking funding for restoration works in Kraśnik, where it is working in cooperation with the municipal council to open a cultural center in the town's former synagogue. At the same time, the foundation advertises having taken up "numerous educational activities in Kraśnik, aiming to involve the inhabitants in taking care of their town's multicultural heritage."[53]

These revitalization efforts have been developed within the framework of the Hassidic Route project that was launched by the foundation in 2005. In 2011, the route included twenty-three towns in Poland's Lublin and Subcarpathian provinces. The foundation has published a series of brochures devoted to the history of these towns' Jewish communities. The foundation has also been effective in securing outside financing for the project. In 2005 and 2006, the project was supported by the PHARE (Poland and Hungary Assistance for Reconstructing of Their Economies) 2003 European Union Interreg IIIA program for infrastructural projects preparation, an initiative that aims to stimulate cooperation among regions in the European Union. In 2007, the Ministry of Labor and Social Policy supported the project within the framework of its Citizen Initiative Fund program. In 2008, 2009, and 2010, the project was supported by the Taube Foundation for Jewish Life and Culture.

It is difficult to estimate the extent to which the few revitalization projects coordinated by the foundation are financed by funds it has received through the restitution process (including funds received as financial compensation for properties that could not be restituted and income from the rent or sale of reclaimed properties). The representatives of the foundation say that their annual financial reports are audited under the provisions of Polish law. Yet these reports have not been made available to the public, which has led to speculation about the foundation's finances.

Despite this lack of transparency, it is clear that financial matters influence the foundation's approach to synagogue restoration projects. In fact, its representatives have complained about the requirements imposed on them by conservation officers, who can order the repair of heritage sites and impose fines if repairs are not completed. Similarly to the UJRC, therefore, the foundation usually prefers financial compensation to the return of synagogues. It is even willing to relinquish properties awarded to it through a restitution claim rather than complete costly renovations. For example, the FPJH decided to donate an early nineteenth-century synagogue in Bydgoszcz-Fordon to a local nongovernmental organization because no buyer could be found and conservators demanded that the building be repaired immediately.[54] The new owner, the Yakiza Foundation, plans to use the synagogue building as a center of culture and gallery of alternative art. In the case of the early baroque Great Synagogue in Tykocin, which was built in 1642 and is one of the oldest synagogues in Poland, the foundation settled for financial compensation. This settlement meant that the synagogue remained under the control of the Office of the Marshal of Podlaskie Voivodship. The decision was made despite the fact that the Great Synagogue was thoroughly restored in the late 1970s and now hosts the Museum of Jewish Culture. In the case of the ruined 1927 synagogue in the small village of Wielkie Oczy, the FPJH simply dropped its claim to the property during the regulatory commission proceedings because of the large costs of restoration they would have had to bear.[55]

The former synagogues that are best preserved are probably those occupied by government-financed museums. This category includes, for example, the Old Synagogue in Kraków, the Great Synagogue in Łęczna, the New Synagogue in Leszno, and the synagogues of Włodawa. Such synagogues are typically owned by municipalities. In the case of Leszno's New Synagogue, for example, the Jewish Religious Community received compensation from the Regional Council of Wielkopolska, which continues to own the building. Recently, however, the Jewish museum in Łańcut's synagogue was taken over by the FPJH. The situation of the complex of seven synagogues in Kraków's Kazimierz district, which are a popular tourist attraction, is unique. All seven synagogues have now been renovated and are owned by the local Jewish Religious Community. The renovations were financed primarily by the Social Committee for the Restoration of Kraków's Monuments. The committee's budget is set by Kraków's president's office.[56]

Conclusion

The popularity of events and initiatives related to Jewish culture, food, and history, and the fact that Jewish culture has recently become very fashionable in certain middle-class urban circles, has had only a limited effect on the preservation of Jewish material heritage in Poland. There is a clear contrast between the popularity of Jewish culture as a new trend in urban cultural consumption patterns and the number of dilapidated former synagogues and Jewish cemeteries languishing in small towns.

The so-called renaissance of Jewish life in Poland is, for the most part, a renaissance without Jews.[57] The absence of Jews in Jewish heritage preservation efforts—while in part attributable to the minuscule number of Jews in today's Poland—is also at least partially due to the lack of legislation concerning the restitution of property to individual owners of expropriated homes, stores, or factories. It is possible to speculate that if more heirs of individual owners had been allowed to regain their properties, at least some of them would come back to Poland and contribute to the preservation efforts. In terms of justice, an interesting paradox exists with regard to the restitution of formerly Jewish property in post-Communist Poland. Many Jewish heirs to dispossessed citizens of the Second Republic of Poland (1918–1939) were not allowed to reclaim their properties after 1989, even though their moral title to this property seemed clear. At the same time, the property of prewar Jewish religious communities has been transferred to organizations whose moral entitlement to that property is less apparent.

When considering the impact of restitution on the preservation of Jewish heritage, it is important to ask the question, "who benefits?" In fact, this question must be asked in two ways: Who benefits from restitution? And who benefits from the restoration of Jewish heritage sites? The Jewish religious communities use restitution first and foremost as a source of income to cover their daily expenses. While they have preserved synagogues used for religious purposes, they are not particularly interested in the preservation of Jewish material heritage in general. The WJRO through the FPJH has, in turn, pursued a rather vague policy with regard to Jewish material heritage, even though it has declared the preservation of Jewish material heritage to be its main objective. It is readily apparent that the foundation focuses more on commemorative initiatives (placing plaques or organizing memorial events) than on revitalization projects that physically restore or rebuild. The foundation's policy is also based on the assumption that heritage sites in small towns will serve not Jews but the local, ethnically Polish community, since Jews are no longer present among the local inhabitants. The foundation tends, therefore, to rely on cooperation with local institutions and on public funds in order to carry out revitalization projects.

The main actors responsible for financing the preservation of Jewish material heritage are still the government and municipalities. Restitution of communal property has not considerably changed this situation. In some cases, prolonged regulatory commission procedures have even delayed publicly sponsored renovation projects.[58] In recent years, nongovernmental organizations have also become important initiators of renovation projects. They, too, depend on public funds for their projects. Funds from the European Union, however, appear to be a significant new means of financing initiatives in this area. Nongovernmental organizations continue to propose cultural projects that comply with the fashionable policy of promoting "multiculturalism." Because of the lack of other significant ethnic and religious minorities in contemporary Poland, this trend often finds expression in projects related to the rediscovery and commemoration of the heritage of Polish Jews.

Notes

1. For a discussion of restitution in Central and Eastern Europe see, for example, Csongor Kuti, *Post-Communist Restitution and the Rule of Law* (Budapest: Central European University Press, 2009); Andrzej K. Koźminski, "Resitution of Private Property: Re-privatization in Central and Eastern Europe," *Communist and Post-Communist Studies* 30, no. 1 (1997): 95–106; and Mariana Karadjova, "Property Restitution in Eastern Europe: Domestic and International Human Rights Law Responses," *Review of Central and East European Law* 29, no. 3 (2004): 325–363.

2. Eleonora Bergman, "Introduction," in *Niewinne oko nie istnieje,* ed. Wojciech Wilczyk (Łódź: Atlas Sztuki, 2009), 1.

3. Ustawa z dnia 17 maja 1989 r. o stosunku Państwa do Kościoła Katolickiego w Rzeczypospolitej Polskiej, *Polish Official Gazette,* 1989, no. 29, item 154.

4. According to the new provisions, the church was additionally entitled to reclaim property nationalized in Warsaw. Another new provision stipulated that the church entities could be granted real estate in the northern and eastern territories, which was understood as compensation for property left in the former Polish eastern territories seized by the Soviet Union. See ibid., 1991, no. 107, item 459.

5. Ibid., 1997, no. 41, item 251.

6. Lucjan Dobroszycki, "The Jewish Community in Poland, 1944–1947: A Discussion on Post-War Restitution," in *She'erit hapletah: Rehabilitation and Political Struggle,* ed. Yisrael Gutman and Avital Saf (Jerusalem: Yad Vashem, 1990), 1–16.

7. The World Jewish Restitution Organization was formed in 1992 to pursue the recovery of Jewish property in Central and Eastern Europe. It is composed of the following organizations: Agudath Israel World Organization, American Gathering/Federation of Jewish Holocaust Survivors, American Jewish Joint Distribution Committee, B'nai B'rith International, Center of Organizations of Holocaust Survivors in Israel, Conference on Jewish Material Claims against Germany, European Jewish Congress/European Council of Jewish Communities, World Jewish Congress, and World Zionist Organization.

8. Marilyn Henry, "Fifty Years of Holocaust Compensation," *American Jewish Yearbook* 102 (2002): 58.

9. Stuart Eizenstat, *Imperfect Justice: Looted Assets, Slave Labor, and the Unfinished Business of World War II* (New York: Public Affairs, 2003).

10. In practice, the regulation on community headquarters affected only four cities: Gdańsk, Wrocław, Legnica, and Szczecin.

11. See the Act of 15 February 1962 on the Protection of Cultural Heritage, *Polish Official Gazette,* 1962, no. 10, item 49, and the Act of 23 July 2003 on the Protection and Care of Historic Buildings, ibid, 2003, no. 162, item 1568.

12. Eizenstat, *Imperfect Justice,* 42.

13. For a discussion of the contentious negotiations leading to the establishment of the FPJH, as well as the nature of the conflict between international and Polish-Jewish organizations, see Itamar Levin, *Walls Around: The Plunder of Warsaw Jewry during World War II and Its Aftermath* (London: Praeger, 2004).

14. The case is dismissed when the application does not fulfill the requirements set in the 1997 law. The proceedings can be discontinued for various reasons, for example, when the application is withdrawn by the communties' representatives. Such a decision cannot be appealed. A suspended case can be reopened if new evidence is submitted.

15. Anna Szustakiewicz, Działalność Komisji Regulacyjnej do Spraw Gmin Wyznaniowych Żydowskich, Stan na dzień 31 grudnia 2013 r., http://propertyrestitution.pl/download/files/restytucja_mienia/uaktualnienia/komisja_ds_gmin_wyznaniowych_zydowskich.pdf.

16. Aleksander Król, "Musieli oddać park Wyznaniowej Gminie Żydowskiej," *Polska Dziennik Zachodni,* July 17, 2008, 1; Marek Holak, "Działka z lokatorami przy Sądowej ma być oddana Gminie Żydowskiej," *Pałuki i Ziemia Mogileńska,* October 21, 2008, 1; Waldemar Bocheński, "Gmina żydowska wyrzuci ich z mieszkań?" *Tygodnik Nowy Ziemia Pilska,* no. 51/2005, 1; Magdalena Hodak, "Sporny tytuł własności," *Dziennik Łódzki,* no. 283/2005, 13; Danuta Miechowicz, "Przyjdą Żydzi i zabiorą?" *Tygodnik Zamojski,* no. 110/2004, 1; Renata Kamińska, "Czy Żydzi odbiorą kawał Pabianic," *Zycie Pabianic,* November 15, 2004, http://www.zyciepabianic .pl/wydarzenia/miasto/nasze-sprawy/czy-ydzi-odbiora-kawal-pabianic.html.

17. Karol Olecki, "Żydzi wracają po swoje," *Newsweek,* March 28, 2004, 1.

18. "Restytucja nienawiści," *Gazeta Wyborcza,* April 6, 2004, 1.

19. Adam Michnik, "Kłamstwo w cieniu Shoah," *Gazeta Wyborcza,* August 3, 1999, 1.

20. Jacek Kuroń and Karol Modzelewski, "Cena reprywatyzacji," *Gazeta Wyborcza,* January 27, 2001, 1.

21. For a broad discussion of Polish public debates on property restitution, see Stanisław Tyszka, "Property Restitution and Collective Memories in the Czech Republic and Poland after 1989" (Ph.D. diss., European University Institute, Florence, January 2011).

22. For example, in June 1989, Adam Michnik told the Serbian magazine *NIN:* "If the people of the nomenklatura enter joint-stock companies and become their co-owners, they will have interest in defending these companies, and the system of joint-stock companies destroys the Stalinist order." June 25, 1989, 51, quoted in Antoni Dudek, *Ślady PeeReLu: Ludzie, wydarzenia, mechanizmy* (Kraków: Arcana, 2001), 161. See also Jerzy Szperkowicz, "Uwłaszczać i nie żałować" (To Enfranchise and Not to Regret), *Gazeta Wyborcza,* September 25, 1989, 1.

23. Eleonora Bergman and Jan Jagielski, *Zachowane synagogi i domy modlitwy w Polsce: Katalog* (Warsaw: Jewish Historical Institute, 1996). See also Samuel Gruber and Phyllis Myers, *Survey of Historic Jewish Monuments in Poland: A Report to the United States Commission for the Preservation of America's Heritage Abroad* (Jewish Heritage Council World Monuments Fund, November 1995).

24. See the album of photographs of former synagogues in Wilczyk, ed., *Niewinne oko nie istnieje.*

25. Six prewar synagogues are still in use by Jewish religious communities. They are the Nożyk Synagogue in Warsaw, the Remuh Synagogue and the Tempel Synagogue in Kraków, the New Synagogue in Gdańsk-Wrzeszcz, the White Stork Synagogue in Wrocław, and the Reicher Synagogue in Łódź. The other Jewish religious communities use smaller houses of prayer established after the war. These are located on 3rd of May Street in Bielsko-Biała, on Julian Ursyn Niemcewicz Street in Szczecin, on 3rd of May Street in Katowice, and on Chojnowska Street in Legnica.

26. *Polish Register of Monuments,* entry no. 513 from March 28, 1962, National Heritage Board of Poland, Warsaw.

27. Regulatory Commission for Jewish Religious Communities, file reference number: W.KŻ-I-32/98, Ministry of the Interior of Poland, Warsaw.

28. Presently, the Płock synagogue's aron ha-kodesh is held at the Mazowsze Museum.

29. A society of immigrants from the same town or region.

30. Konstanty Gebert, "Co dalej z synagogą?" *Gazeta Wyborcza,* January 20, 2004, 1.

31. Another example is the New Synagogue in Ostrów Wielkopolski, which was originally opened in 1860. The New Synagogue is the only preserved metropolitan synagogue in Poland that was built in Moorish Revival style. In 2006, the municipality of Ostrów Wielkopolski paid the UJRC 225,000 złotys to drop its claim to the synagogue. The synagogue was supposed to become a "Center of the Three Cultures" (Polish, Jewish and German), named for the poet Wojciech Bąk, the philosopher Israel Meir Freimann, and the writer Edzard Schaper.

32. For an exception, see Piotr Pytlakowski, "Dajcie nam zgodnego rabina" (Give Us an Accommodating Rabbi), *Polityka* 42 (October 2002), http://archiwum.polityka.pl/art/dajcie -nam-zgodnego-rabina,376120.html. An English translation of Pytlakowski's article is available at http://starozakonni.w.interia.pl/Polityka%20Oct%202002%20%5BEnglish%5D.doc.

33. See ibid. and Bolesław Szenicer, interview with the author, February 11, 2008. Szenicer claims that the UJRC was dominated by "new Jews," a group of young and ambitious former participants of the educational camps organized by the Lauder Foundation from 1989 onward. These camps were for people who wanted to study Jewish traditions, learn about their roots, or simply convert to Judaism. According to Szenicer, these "new Jews" did not necessarily care about the preservation of Jewish heritage.

34. Szenicer, interview with the author. See also Bolesław Szenicer, "Gmina Wyznaniowa Starozakonnych," http://starozakonni.w.interia.pl/index.html.

35. Andrzej Zozula, UJRC, interview with the author (Warsaw, March 12, 2008).

36. Since 1989, the Jewish communities have represented, at most, a few thousand people. The estimate of income is conservative if compared to the sums received in compensation (see footnote 14) and considering the market value of real property owned by the UJRC in the expensive districts of central Warsaw.

37. Piotr Kadlcik, interview with the author, December 28, 2010; Monika Krawczyk, interview with the author, February 15, 2008.

38. Tomasz Urzykowski, "Ocalmy budynek szpitala przy Lesznie 15" (Let's Save the Building of the Hospital on Leszno Street), *Gazeta Wyborcza*, May 5, 2009, 1.

39. Jakub Wyszyński, "Jesziwa do zwrotu?" *Biuletyn Gminy Wyznaniowej Żydowskiej w Warszawie* 44, no. 6 (December 2007–January 2008): 1.

40. United States of America–Polish People's Republic, "Agreement, with Annex, Regarding Claims of Nationals of the United States. Washington, July 16, 1960," *The American Journal of International Law* 55, no. 2 (April 1961): 540–544.

41. See the Borderland Foundation's website at http://pogranicze.sejny.pl/.

42. See the Borussia Foundation's website at http://www.borussia.pl/.

43. For a discussion of the conflict about the prayer house in the Jewish community of Kraków, see Magdalena Kursa, "Atrakcyjny Kazimierz," *Gazeta Wyborcza*, January 6, 2009, 1.

44. Foundation for the Preservation of Jewish Heritage in Poland, *2009 Annual Report*, http://fodz.pl/download/fodz_annual_2009_www.pdf.

45. Ibid.

46. Based on interviews with the foundation's leaders and analysis of their work.

47. Krawczyk, interview with the author.

48. For more information, see the Nissenbaum Foundation's website at http://www .nissenbaum.pl/ and the Poland Jewish Cemeteries Restoration Project website at http://www .pjcrp.org/.

49. Stewart Ain, "Wanna Buy a Historic Shul in Poland?" *The Jewish Week*, March 2, 2011, http://www.thejewishweek.com/news/international/wanna_buy_historic_shul_poland.

50. The Polin website is located at http://www.polin.org.pl.

51. Foundation for the Preservation of Jewish Heritage in Poland, *2009 Annual Report*, 12.

52. This search for local partners has, in some cases, created public controversy. For example, someone wrote in spray paint on the wall of the nineteenth-century synagogue in Klimontów: "Do you want to rent this building? Call 0224366000," and "Have an idea for what could be in this building? Call 0224366000." The telephone number is for FPJH's Warsaw office.

53. Foundation for the Preservation of Jewish Heritage in Poland, *2009 Annual Report*, 19.

54. *Polish Register of Monuments*, entry no. A/261/1 from May 25, 1991; Krawczyk, interview with the author.

55. The synagogue is listed in the *Polish Register of Monuments,* entry no. A-353 from May 8, 2009.

56. The Social Committee for the Restoration of Cracow's Monuments website is located at http://www.skozk.pl/.

57. Richard Bernstein, "Letter from Europe: Watching Over Poland's Ghosts, in a Spirit of Renewal," *New York Times,* July 27, 2005, http://www.nytimes.com/2005/07/27/international/europe/27letter.html?pagewanted=all&_r=0.

58. One such project is the synagogue in Leszno, which is to be renovated by the municipality.

3 Muranów as a Ruin
Layered Memories in Postwar Warsaw

Michael Meng

Goods, clothes, synagogues, apartments—things—were, for the most part, all that was left of Jewish life in Poland after the Holocaust;[1] traces, fragments, remnants, ruins, the detritus of genocide, littered streets and homes:

> In the abandoned flats
> scattered bundles,
> suits and comforters,
> and plates and stools,
> fires are still dwindling,
> idle spoons lie about,
> thrown out in a hurry
> family photographs.[2]

Such fragments remained for decades after the war. Some seventy years after Władysław Szlengel wrote his poetry about abandoned Jewish objects, photographer Wojciech Wilczyk traveled across Poland to document the condition of its remaining prewar synagogues; he found many in ruins and others functioning as storage houses, movie theaters, and stores. Along with his photos, Wilczyk recorded the sights, sounds, and emotions that he experienced while encountering these spaces. About the synagogue in Działoszyce, he wrote:

> Large ruins with no roof, with traces of its onetime splendor. Apparently, this was one of the most beautiful classicist synagogues in pre-war Poland. I go inside; I find the smell so prevalent in abandoned places. Empty alcohol bottles and beer cans lying about everywhere in the nettles and undergrowth, of course. . . . I see that a man I noticed in a nearby parking lot has followed me into the middle of the ruins. . . . He says he always checks in here when he's passing by Działoszyce, that he can't bear to look at the devastation. If only he got all six numbers in the lottery (he often plays) he'd put all the loot—or a substantial part of it, anyway—toward renovating this place. It's marked by tragedy—he says—people were killed here during the war. And the fire at the end of the '60s, in his opinion, was a clear case of arson.[3]

Jewish ruins are the focus of this chapter, which reads ruins as spatial embodiments of time—chronotopes—that humans invest with various meanings
and narratives.[4] Ruins are containers of multiple temporalities: layers of time flow
through and interact in their crumbling stones.[5] Yet, ruins are also quite particular containers of time insofar as they mark ravage and catastrophe, whether
the cause of ruination is natural or historic, whether the process of decay is slow
or rapid: a vacated factory building degenerating over decades; a city rendered
into ash in days of aerial bombs; a landscape turned into rubble within seconds of
the earth's trembling plates. Ruins seduce, attract, and frighten people who gaze
on them. Their sublime destruction and their layered accretion of time tell histories about life and death. The ruin is, as Max Pensky writes, "a cipher or mark
whose very enigmatic character qualifies it both for occult significance and as a
sign of the constant threat of an insignificant social world threatened at all moments with the omnipresence of guaranteed oblivion."[6] Ruins are especially unstable and ambivalent reincarnations of the past into the present and future.

This chapter gazes upon one ruin: Warsaw's most concentrated area of interwar Jewish life—the neighborhood of Muranów—which comprised the bulk of
the wartime ghetto and which the German occupiers turned into a massive ruin
after the uprising of 1943.[7] Broadly moving from 1945 to the present and drawing on a medley of architectural, artistic, and written sources, I build a collage of
various and juxtaposing meanings invested in Muranów. I take three snapshots
of mostly non-Jewish Polish encounters with the area as a pile of ruins immediately after the war; as a socialist-realist housing complex in the early 1950s; and
as a space of remembrance and introspection in the contemporary period. This
composite image, hardly total, seeks to collect a few fragments from Muranów's
postwar history and reveal some of the ways in which Poles have dealt with this
space. After reconstructing these three images, I stay with the contemporary period to consider some of this volume's central questions: How do Jewish spaces
such as Muranów relate to Poland's future? What kind of pluralism can Poles
build from their multiethnic past?

Ruins

In 1945, 11,229 of Warsaw's 25,498 buildings were demolished, and approximately
25 percent of the city's streets were destroyed.[8] The total cost of damages amounted
to an estimated 21.9 billion złoty, which today would be about $54.6 billion.[9] As
W. E. B. Du Bois observed after his visit to Warsaw in 1949: "Some streets had been
so obliterated that only by using photographs of the past could they tell where the
street was."[10] Warsaw's former prewar Jewish district was the most severely destroyed part of the city. A Jewish survivor who returned to Warsaw just after the
war recalled, "Over a wide area, there was nothing but powdered rubble—ruins,

ruins, ruins. . . . My entire life had been part of the lively rushing stream that had poured through these streets and alleys. I had known every corner, every house, every cobblestone. Where was it all?"[11] The debris indeed seemed to reach sky-ward, transforming Warsaw into the urban archetype of modernity in Walter Benjamin's understanding of history as a cycle of ruination. Although Benjamin was not alive to gaze at Warsaw's ruins, the kind of questions he might have asked while looking across the city's wreckage are among the ones I would like to ex-plore in this chapter: Does the past endow present and future generations with an injunction to remember? If so, what political, social, and cultural meanings are to be invested in memory? How is such extreme destruction and violence to be or-dered and narrated into some semblance of human significance?

One can find many answers to these questions in early postwar Warsaw, but here I present briefly three attempts to make sense of the city's carnage, begin-ning with the reflections of Jacob Pat, a journalist born in Białystok who trav-eled to Poland from the United States in 1946. Pat wrote about his experiences in *Ashes and Fire,* a travelogue that first appeared in Yiddish in 1946 and then in English translation in 1947. Walking through Warsaw, a city he had lived in for nearly twenty years, he barely could distinguish its streets amid all the fragments that made up the postwar urban landscape. The wreckage made him lament Jew-ish suffering and death:

> For the fourth time today I visited the former Warsaw Ghetto. This time I came to bid a last farewell. I remember that first day in Warsaw when I dared not en-ter upon this sea of carnage that stretched out before me; I turned back. When I returned I found myself climbing and scuttling up and down hill over these monstrous ruins. I came once more, and spent long hours searching for traces of the years I had spent among the streets of this city. But all these once familiar streets were heaped into one everlasting funeral pyre. And now I come to say good-bye, to seal the picture of Israel's grave forever in my heart.[12]

Rather than aestheticizing ruins, as some postwar observers of urban rubble were apt to do, Pat invests them with emotive power as ciphers of Jewish perse-cution. He situates the ghetto ruins within a lachrymose history of Jewish afflic-tion, and he embraces traditional Jewish injunctions to remember past suffering and commemorate the dead.[13] He takes up the archetypal and affective task of memory and mourning: "'Great like the sea is thy breach; who can bring healing to thee?' The ancient, everlasting words of Jeremiah's *Lamentations* ring in my ears. Once again the sea of Jewish suffering runs high. The waves roar, they rise and fall, carrying me with them." Moreover, Pat produces some of his most emo-tive prose, complete with somatic motifs, when he writes about ruins. Shattered stones make him tremble, shiver, numb, shake, and cry. The sights and sounds of these spaces incite intense memories and bodily reactions. As Pat writes, "And my father's house has left nothing behind—no balcony, no door, no threshold. Only a small, snow-covered pile of rubble, swept by a cold wind. . . . I stood there in the hollow silence of my father's house, facing its nothingness. I cried."[14]

If Warsaw's ruins made Pat lament and compelled him to remember, they terrified Bronisław Wojciech Linke, a painter who created horrifying images of Warsaw's destruction just after the war. Linke's ruinology involves no aestheticization of violence, no reverie on the sublimity of decay, no melancholia about what has been lost. Rather, his watercolors—painted mostly in 1946–1949 and collected in a 1959 portfolio titled *Stones Screaming* (*Kamienie krzyczą*)—cast ruins as "ugly, unkind, sinister, and horrid."[15] Conjoining architectural and somatic destruction, Linke created images of skeletons, ghosts, rubble, twisted beams, fire, and burnt brick: a ruined building emerges from the rubble as a revenant; a ghost plays a fiddle to possibly mangled street lamps; dead bodies float upward over a desolate apartment building. In *Mystery* (1947), three human-shaped ruins play fiddles over a crane pulling an infant out from the womb of a partially buried woman whose hands are folded in prayer. On the painting's right side, a newspaper clipping torn out vaguely in the shape of a human contains newspaper headlines about "ruins" and "Warsaw's population rises again." The fiddlers wear crowns of barbed wire that seem to imitate Christ's crown of thorns.

With these contorted images of life, fecundity, and resurrection, is Linke gesturing at Warsaw's redemption, reprising mythic narratives of Poland as the Christ among the Nations whose sacrificial suffering will save the world? Such a redemptive vision circulated widely after the war.[16] But Linke's ruins may be challenging this meme. His ruins horridly pull viewers back to the past, insisting that the future must be rooted in remembering and mourning human barbarism; present and future generations must recall the past because otherwise, as Benjamin warned, it will disappear irretrievably. Indeed, Linke's watercolor *El Mole Rachmim*,[17] Lord of Many Mercies, depicts a Jew clothed in a torn prayer shawl as a ruin of the Warsaw Ghetto. Painted in 1956, the work took up the Jewish injunction to remember at a time when forgetting in the public sphere was dominant: the erection of socialist-realist apartments were burying the ruins of the Warsaw Ghetto. More boldly, Linke connects Jewish and Polish suffering together into one meditation on Nazi violence. *El Mole Rachmim* dramatizes the specificity of Jewish persecution but also sublimates it into the whole of urban wreckage. In so doing, it transmits a multidirectional memory of ruination, violence, and mass death in *Warszawa/Varshe*.[18]

Because Jewish and Polish memories of the Nazi occupation have collided often and intensely over the past seventy years, a skeptic might question here how "representative" such a multidirectional memory is. The archive of multidirectional memory in early postwar Poland may indeed be small, but it may be

Figure 3.1. Bronisław Wojciech Linke's *El Mole Rachmim,* 1956. Courtesy of Muzeum Narodowe w Warszawie

more extensive than we think, at least in Warsaw. Another, if quite differently expressed, iteration of multidirectional memory comes from the Polish capital in the form of Bohdan Lachert's attempt to memorialize the ghetto space in his design for the rebuilding of Muranów. An avant-garde, modernist architect during the interwar period, Lachert set out to transform Muranów into a new housing complex of square, functional, and unadorned apartment buildings erected among ample green space. He was, though, aware that his new project would be sitting on top of the former ghetto. Partly for practical reasons and partly for symbolic effect, he decided to build his apartments on top of the ruins and to use the ghetto rubble mixed with concrete for their foundations. Lachert left the fronts of the buildings unstuccoed and used a rusty red brick to capture the somberness of the ghetto space. As he put it, "The history of the great victory of the nation paid for through a sea of human blood, poured out for the sake of social progress and national liberation, will be commemorated in the Muranów project."[19] While his buildings might initially appear to be strictly modernist in their design and aesthetic, they went beyond mere function to express the Nazi past. Lachert's project infused the modernist future with the past.

This temporal pastiche of past and future was meant to stimulate remembrance. Lachert envisioned his project as complementing the Warsaw Ghetto Monument, which was erected in 1948 slightly north of his housing complex. Natan Rapoport's monument heroically commemorated the Warsaw Ghetto Uprising, depicting on its western side proletarian-looking figures brandishing arms as they almost jump out from the granite in which they are carved. The eastern side shows twelve Jews, their heads slouched, reluctantly moving to their fate.[20] Lachert, who wrote an expert commentary on the monument, praised Rapoport's design and stressed that the "grim atmosphere of this great mausoleum, erected among a cemetery of ruins, soaked with the blood of the Jewish nation," must remain as "new life comes into existence."[21]

Lachert's project attempted to bring Polish and Jewish suffering together into a single progressive, socialist memory. One suffering did not have to diminish the other, and one memory did not have to belong to one ethnic group; they could flow in distinct, yet complementary directions to recall the past and construct a better future under socialism. In his orientation toward the future, Lachert's encounter with the ghetto ruins was distinct from Pat's lamentation on loss and Linke's mediation on barbarism. His vision for building a new Muranów on top of and from the ghetto ruins architecturally articulated the dialectic of destruction and regeneration: ruination would engender new life. And yet, even as Lachert's project looked to the socialist future to transcend Warsaw's prewar capitalist past, it remained deeply cognizant and expressive of Muranów's wartime past as a space of mass persecution and murder.

Socialist Realism

By 1949–1950, the modernist principles that shaped Lachert's project and much of Warsaw's reconstruction up to that point were rejected for the new architectural style—socialist realism—spreading across the Soviet bloc with the beginning of Stalinism. Originating in early 1930s Moscow, socialist-realist architecture documented the historic triumph of Communism over capitalism by showcasing the historic movement from the dark, dirty, cramped, and chaotic capitalist city to the light, clean, spacious, and orderly socialist city.[22] Critiquing the austere and functional designs of modernism, socialist-realist architecture emphasized ornamentalism, form, and meaning. It stressed the building of beautiful and decorative facades by typically turning to classical architecture to construct aesthetically pleasing and politically meaningful buildings.[23] In the late 1940s and early 1950s, socialist realism was imported to Eastern Europe. Warsaw saw the completion of its most celebrated socialist-realist architectural project in 1955—the Joseph Stalin Palace of Culture and Science. Built in grandiose neoclassical style and towering almost 800 feet high, the building, Stalin's gift to Poland, dominated Warsaw's skyline, as it does to this day.

In the wake of this architectural shift, Lachert's plans were criticized for their modernist expression and alleged gloomy representation of the ghetto space. In 1952, a four-page assessment of his project appeared in the journal *Architektura*. The author, Jerzy Wierzbicki, provided formulaic rejections of Lachert's design at the peak of Stalinism. Just as critics in the Soviet press during the 1930s had derided modernist buildings as boxlike barracks, so too now did Wierzbicki claim that Lachert's apartments resembled faceless "blocks." He also disapproved of Lachert's architectural representation of the ghetto space through the construction of dark brick facades: "The buildings in the original design are overwhelmed by monotony, are sad, grey. . . . A rubble hollow brick fills the walls, a concrete frame goes around the window and marks the molding of the building." He concluded bluntly, "Muranów does not attain a fully positive expression."[24] The fallout proved decisive. Lachert's buildings were stuccoed and small designs were painted on their white surfaces. Muranów was now to be a cheerful, bright, and colorful place for the working class.[25] The stuccoing painted over literally and figuratively Lachert's attempt to represent a space "soaked with the blood of the Jewish nation."[26]

This transformation of Muranów into a socialist-realist housing complex was invested with significant political meaning in early postwar Warsaw. Muranów's rebuilding metonymically represented the emergence of a new socialist Warsaw, a moment in the city's history marked by the Communist victory over the bourgeois capitalist past and by Poland's revitalization from the destruction of Nazism.[27] This temporal narrative was reprised through two motifs in the press. First, Communism was transporting Poles from darkness to light, from capitalist hardship to socialist prosperity. In 1951, for example, the *Polska Kronika Filmowa* (Polish Newsreel, *PKF*) depicted a working-class family moving into Muranów. With the sun beaming through the windows of their new apartment, the newsreel showed the family with wide smiles as the narrator informed, "50,000 working people will live in Muranów."[28] A new society of material comfort was coming into existence on the rubble of the *ancien régime*. Second, the trope of "a new life emerging on the ruins" circulated repetitiously in press articles and newsreels about Muranów.[29] As one newspaper article put it: "Muranów today is no longer a deathly silence of lifelessness. Today life is bursting forth there."[30] Similarly, a *PKF* newsreel documented workers and ordinary Varsovians collecting building materials from the rubble. "In September, tens of thousands of Varsovians turned up to clear the rubble of the area of Muranów," the narrator explained. "Selected and cleaned bricks serve for building the foundations and interior walls of the new housing estate—Muranów C."[31]

This dual framing of Muranów as a space of rebirth and Communist triumph displaced the area's wartime history. This layer of time was not repressed from consciousness all together; some articles touched on the Nazi ghettoization and murder of the Jews. But such references were immediately marginalized by images of life and prosperity. The wartime past was forgotten through what Freud called negation: the violence of the ghetto appeared only for its significance to be refused.[32] Muranów's stuccoed apartments propelled Warsaw into the socialist future, displacing the death and destruction that lay underneath its foundations. The pastiche of socialist realism, with its magnanimous appropriation of classical designs, replaced the pastiche of Lachert's mnemonic modernism.

Remembrance and Introspection

Forty-five years after construction workers erected the last apartment buildings in Muranów in 1967, the amnesia of socialist realism still limns the area. On their way to work, school, the store, or the park, most Varsovians probably think little of the past that lies around and below them; everyday life demands forgetting, and memory beyond the needs of everyday life demands effort. Although Muranów's postwar socialist past is omnipresent, its prewar and wartime pasts can only be encountered through pictures, diaries, memoirs, newspaper clippings, stories, and testimonies because, with only a few fragmentary exceptions, nothing spatially remains of these pasts.[33] And yet, memories of Muranów have exploded over the past decade in art, film, literature, prose, photography, architecture, cyberspace, and even in everyday life.[34] The area's multiple temporalities—the prewar history of Jewish life, the wartime history of ghettoization and genocide, and the postwar history of building an amnesiac socialist future—have provoked attention from Poles as never before.[35]

These involuntary memories of Warsaw's Jewish past are often stimulated quite suddenly and unexpectedly. When journalist and writer Beata Chomątowska rented by chance an apartment on Elektoralna Street to be near her work, she at first did not realize where she was living until she went on a walk through Muranów. Crossing Nowolipie, Nowolipki, and Stawki streets, the past suddenly appeared to her. "I knew these streets from numerous prewar and wartime photos," she explained.[36] She decided to document Muranów's pasts, as well as the postwar erasure of them, in a project titled "Stacja Muranów," which appeared first as a website in 2010 before being published as a book two years later.[37]

The book unearths Muranów's prewar, wartime, postwar, and contemporary layers of time through a mélange of voices, perspectives, and images. Loosely organized into eleven thematically overlapping chapters, it forms a montage of fragments, interruptions, discontinuities, and repetitions. The book's temporal narrative is more cyclical and layered than linear. While Chomątowska does not invoke Benjamin, her temporal structure comes close to his conception of multiple pasts flowing into the present, and her historical methodology replicates his interest in building a montage of temporal fragments that have largely been forgotten or discarded.[38] In each chapter, she returns to the rupture of the Holocaust, the disavowal of that rupture in the early postwar years, and the continued efforts of Varsovians to make sense of living on the ghetto ruins. This repetition seems to suggest the constant reincarnation of the past in each successive moment of time. Even as the district has changed over the past seventy years, its layered pasts continue to permeate the present and future.

This nonlinear temporal structure underpins Chomątowska's multilayered historical narrative, which she reconstructs through newspaper clippings, photos, memoirs, diary entries, architectural plans, and oral interviews. Refusing to order these pieces into a distinct narrative pattern, she weaves together juxtaposing stories about the district over the twentieth century: Jewish life before the war; Jewish death during the war; Lachert's attempt to commemorate the Holocaust; the negation of the wartime past by socialist realism; efforts to encounter the district's multiple histories after the collapse of Communism. These layers of time interact and counteract throughout the book. The first chapter opens with a black-and-white photograph of three women and a young boy standing on a backstreet of prewar Muranów, with a streak of sunlight shining on their smiling faces. Four pages later, a color photo of Bank Square taken in 1979 shows a sun-glistening skyscraper being built on the space where Warsaw's Great Synagogue once stood. This montage uncovers the complex interactions of multiple temporalities in one urban space. It reveals Muranów as a ruin—a space of layered times that coheres

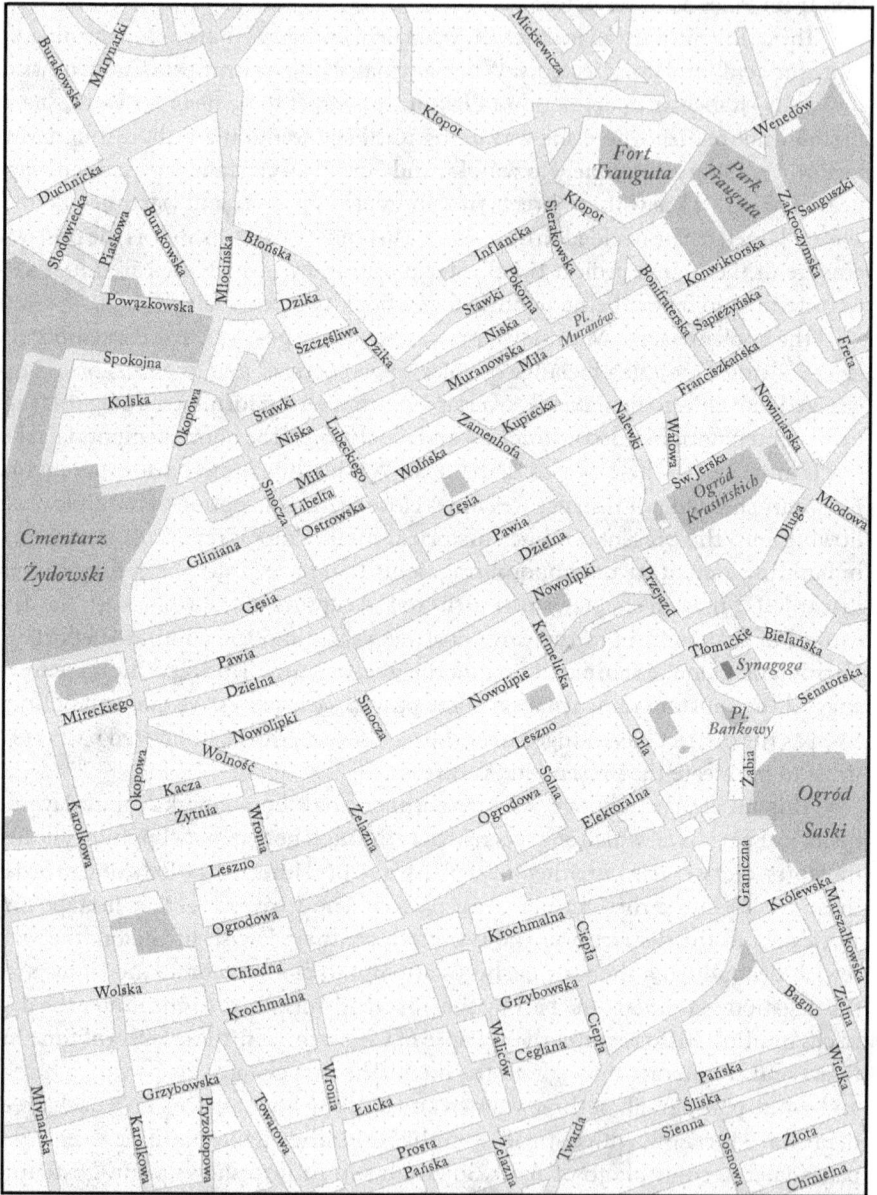

Map 3.1. Map of prewar Muranów. Map based on *Plan m.st. Warszawy*, 1934, Science Library of the Ivan Franko National University of Lviv.

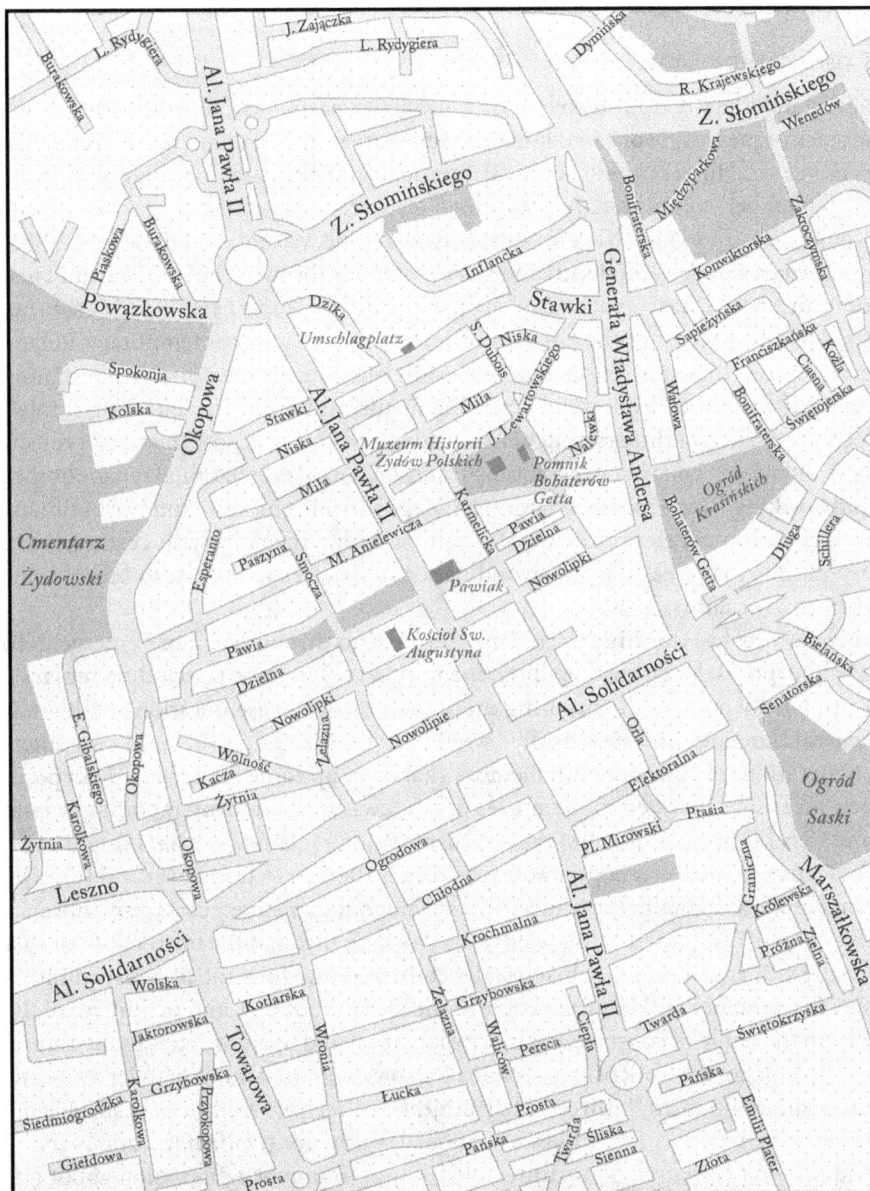

Map 3.2. Map of contemporary Muranów. Map based on *Warszawa: Plan miasta*, 2011, Marco Polo.

around not some climatic or eschatological endpoint but rather around the district's tumultuous and varied histories.

Cosmopolitanisms

Chomątowska's textual recovery of Muranów's pasts—as one among many examples of memory work in contemporary Warsaw (and Poland more broadly)—raises several broader philosophical questions at the core of this volume: Why do we remember events that are not immediately related to our everyday lives? Why would we want to look back on such a catastrophic, violent, and dark past? What are the advantages and disadvantages of memory for life? The antiquarian curiosity to know what happened in the past seems too superficial in this case, not least because many of the carriers of Jewish memory in contemporary Poland and in post-Holocaust Europe more broadly often invest memory with profound political and social aspirations. Coming historically from the left, artists, intellectuals, writers, scholars, and activists involved in Holocaust memory projects have often been engaged in critiquing traditional modes of national remembrance and thinking. These memory actors challenge patriotic, mythic, and hermetic narratives and memories of the nation-state, imbuing memory with cosmopolitan aspirations that seek to look beyond national histories or at least to break down their mythic auras.[39]

But why has this urge to critique nationalism through memory emerged? To what purposes does a cosmopolitan memory serve? In these concluding remarks, I can hardly hope to do anything more than broach these questions with a few general thoughts, and specifically I would like to do so by gesturing at two different iterations of cosmopolitan memory that open up some of the varied purposes and meanings invested in memories of the Jewish past in contemporary Poland and Central Europe. The first type of cosmopolitan memory—what I might call a "reflective, critical cosmopolitanism"—recalls the past to transform and improve democratic societies in the future. This cosmopolitan memory casts remembrance as a form of "enlightened knowledge."[40] Working through the horrors of the past ideally will engender more historically conscious and tolerant citizens: an introspective memory will cleanse people of the ideas, emotions, and prejudices of the past in the name of constructing more egalitarian and open societies in the future.

In Poland, the work of artist Joanna Rajkowska is an example of reflective, critical cosmopolitanism.[41] Three of her projects—*Greetings from Jerusalem Avenue* (*Pozdrowienia z Alej Jerozolimskich*, 2002), *Oxygenator* (*Dotleniacz*, 2006–2007), and *Minaret* (*Minaret*, 2009, unrealized)—aim to provoke discussion about tolerance and identity in Poland. The first project featured a palm tree erected at the intersection of Jerusalem Avenue and New World Street to mark the absence of Warsaw's prewar Jewish community; the second involved a pond on a green space around Grzybowski Square to stimulate reflection about the area's multiple functions as a space of Warsaw's prewar Jewish life, of the failed Communist future, and of the capitalist present; and the final project attempted to transform a paper mill smokestack in Poznań into a minaret to ask "where we—Poles—are in the process of opening ourselves up to strangers, others, foreigners."[42]

As Rajkowska explained in an interview with artist Artur Żmijewski, she hopes to advance cosmopolitanism through her artistic projects. "I am disgusted by the idea of the nation-state," she remarked. "I dream of a non-national or a supranational state." If her vision might be viewed as utopian, Rajkowska also attempts to unsettle in everyday life some of the dominant ways in which Poles think about themselves and their pasts. As she further remarked, "When the opportunity arose to build a sign of the presence of Muslims [in Poznań], it became clear that we need to discuss the comfortable and nostalgic image of Poles—the victim, and at the same time, the defender of all values."[43]

This activist, introspective cosmopolitanism differs from the second type of cosmopolitan remembrance of the Jewish past in Poland and Europe: "redemptive cosmopolitanism," which symbolically reincorporates Jewishness into the present as a marker of achieved tolerance and multiethnicity in the new Europe. After Nazism and Communism, Europe has seemingly arrived as a tolerant, democratic, and liberal continent. It has learned from its horrific past and repented its sins. This self-celebratory narrative of democratic redemption sets up Nazism as the cataclysmic failure of Western liberal democracy and codes European Jewish culture as a unique carrier of tolerance, liberalism, cosmopolitanism, and humanism.[44] The years 1945 and 1989 emerge as cathartic moments of progressive culmination toward the telos of liberal democracy, and the celebration of Jewishness redeems Europe from its violent past through the act of recovering a cultural heritage transvalued as a cultural code for the positive values of European civilization.[45]

Redemptive and reflective cosmopolitanism should not be seen as distinctly opposite; rather, they may circulate, if in tension with each other, in the same memory project. Let us take for example the speech by Sławomir Sierakowski, delivered in *Nightmares* (*Mary Koszmary*, 2007), the first film of Yael Bartana's trilogy about Polish and Israeli memories and identities. The setting, the film announces, is Warsaw's "Olympic stadium." Built in 1955 by the Communist state, the stadium stands as an archetypal ruin, with vegetation covering its weathered stones. Sierakowski, a well-known leftist-activist, proclaims in Polish:

> Jews. Fellow countrymen. People. Peeeeople. You think the old woman who still sleeps under Rifke's quilt doesn't want to see you? Has forgotten about you? You're wrong. She dreams about you every night. Dreams and trembles with fear. Since the night you were gone and her mother reached for your quilt, she has had nightmares. Bad dreams. Only you can chase them away. Let the three million Jews that Poland has missed stand by her bed and finally chase away

the demons. Return to Poland, to your/our country! . . . This is a call, not to the dead but to the living. We want three million Jews to return to Poland, we want you to live with us again. We need you![46]

Sierakowski goes on to critique antisemitism and ethnocultural nationalism before returning to his argument that Poland needs Jews to redeem its sins. As he speaks, a group of young devotees—clad in Communist-style scout uniforms—write on the field the following phrase: "3,300,000 Jews can change the life of 40,000,000 Poles." Shortly afterward, Bartana cuts to an aerial shot of stone pillars in what remains of the stadium's bleachers; the camera stays on this image for about seven seconds. With the screen darkened and somewhat blurred, the pillars look like tombstones. The film creates juxtaposing images of ruination and rebirth.

The speech, which Sierakowski cowrote with writer and leftist-activist Kinga Dunin, is replete with historic references, images, and idioms: the wartime seizure of Jewish goods, objects, and property; the murder of Jews during the Holocaust; the postwar emigration of Jews from Poland; the psychoanalytic command to work through nightmares; and nationalistic narratives of suffering. The speech and the film's propagandistic style also play with redemptive narratives. The return of Jews to Poland promises to heal the tensions between Jews and Poles, who, when they see each other, will finally allow the "armor" to fall. Redemption from past sins will seemingly follow this cathartic moment of reconciliation. "Without you," Sierakowski says, "we will remain locked away in the past; with you, a future will open up for us." What will this future entail? Sierakowski envisions a cosmopolitan moment of togetherness and shared humanity. Poles and Jews will lose their particular affiliations and identifications as "chosen peoples" and become "Europeans." Cosmopolitanism will save Poland, Europe, and the world from "a new outbreak of nationalisms," and liberate the world from the violent ethnonationalism of the twentieth century.[47]

How might we read this speech? On the one hand, we might see it as playful: it overtly mocks the utopianism of nationalism, fascism, Communism, and cosmopolitanism. Sierakowski performs as a clownish disciple whose histrionics subvert the faith and whose exaggerated parody of messianic Polish nationalism staves off any notion of salvation, any prospect of hope. On the other hand, Sierakowski and Bartana appear serious about their cosmopolitan commitments and about provoking discussions about the past to address political questions about exclusion, discrimination, and persecution in the present-future.[48] Perhaps their project embraces a kind of Socratic irony that seeks to stimulate dialogue about the progressive power of memory to advance more cosmopolitan societies.[49] As the leader of Poland's leftist political milieu Political Critique, Sierakowski wants Poles to engage in a discussion about the *idea* of three million Jews returning to the country. He looks back on the past to critique the mythologies of Polish nationalism in the hope of opening up more civic, democratic, postnational attachments in Poland. He subverts the faith in emancipatory memory only to reinforce it. In short, his memory politics might be exposing some of the tensions in building pluralistic societies through memory: cosmopolitan memory may be reflective but it may also be redemptive; it may stimulate political critique and it may provoke self-satisfaction; it may strengthen democracies and it may celebrate the apotheosis of democracy.[50] While recollections of the Holocaust and the prewar Polish Jewish past seem likely to continue into the near future, the precise role that introspective remembrance may be able to play in building more pluralist societies remains at the moment unspecified.

Notes

1. I wish to emphasize "for the most part" here because—despite the massive human void left after the Holocaust—Jewish social, cultural, religious, and political life also continued in Poland after 1945. See Natalia Aleksiun, *Dokąd dalej? Ruch syjonistyczny w Polsce 1944–1950* (Warsaw: Trio, 2002); Grzegorz Berendt, ed., *Społeczność żydowska w PRL przed kampanią antysemicką lat 1967–1968 i po niej* (Warsaw: Instytut Pamięci Narodowej, 2009); Grzegorz Berendt, *Życie żydowskie w Polsce w latach 1950–1956: Z dziejów Towarzystwa Społeczno-Kulturalnego Żydów w Polsce* (Gdańsk: Wydawnictwo Uniwersytetu Gdańskiego, 2006); August Grabski, Maciej Pisarski, and Albert Stankowski, *Studia z dziejów i kultury Żydów w Polsce po 1945 roku* (Warsaw: Trio, 1997); Audrey Kichelewski, "A Community under Pressure: Jews in Poland, 1957–1967," *Polin* 21 (2008): 159–186; Joanna Nalewajko-Kulikov, *Obywatel Jidyszlandu: Rzecz o żydowskich komunistach w Polsce* (Warsaw: Instytut Historii Polskiej Akademii Nauk, 2009); Jaff Schatz, *The Generation: The Rise and Fall of the Jewish Communists in Poland* (Berkeley: University of California Press, 1991); Marci Shore, *Caviar and Ashes: A Warsaw Generation's Life and Death in Marxism, 1918–1968* (New Haven, CT: Yale University Press, 2006); Bożena Szaynok, *Ludność żydowska na Dolnym Śląsku 1945–1950* (Wrocław: Wydawnictwo Uniwersytetu Wrocławskiego, 2000); and Feliks Tych and Monika Adamczyk-Grabowska, *Następstwa zagłady Żydów: Polska 1944–2010* (Lublin: Wydawnictwo Uniwersytetu Marii Curie–Skłodowskiej, and Warsaw: Żydowski Instytut Historyczny im. Emanuela Ringelbluma, 2011).

2. Władysław Szlengel, "Things," quoted in Bożena Shallcross, *The Holocaust Object in Polish and Polish-Jewish Culture* (Bloomington: Indiana University Press, 2011), 22.

3. Wojciech Wilczyk, *Niewinne oko nie istnieje/There's No Such Thing as an Innocent Eye* (Łódź: Atlas Sztuki, 2009), 683.

4. M. M. Bakhtin used the word "chronotope" to denote "the intrinsic connectedness of temporal and spatial relationships that are artistically expressed in literature." Bakhtin, "Forms of Time and of the Chronotope in the Novel," in *The Dialogic Imagination: Four Essays*, ed. Michael Holquist, trans. Caryl Emerson and Michael Holquist (Austin: University of Texas Press, 1981), 84.

5. Reinhart Koselleck, *Zeitschichten: Studien zur Historik. Mit einem Beitrag von Hans-Georg Gadamer* (Frankfurt am Main: Suhrkamp Verlag, 2000).

6. Max Pensky, "Three Kinds of Ruin: Heidegger, Benjamin, Sebald," *Poligrafi* 16 (2011): 65–89.

7. In 1938, 90.5 percent of the inhabitants of Muranów were Jewish (Gabriela Zalewska, *Ludność żydowska w Warszawie w okresie międzywojennym* (Warsaw: PWN, 1996), 63). Although Muranów was not a ghetto as defined as a compulsory, segregated, and enclosed area of Jewish residence (such as Frankfurt's *Judengasse* until the early nineteenth century), it was often imagined and discursively marked as a "ghetto." For discussion on Muranów and the spatial history of Jewish life in Warsaw, see Eleonora Bergman, "The 'Northern District' in Warsaw: A City within a City?" in *Reclaiming Memory: Urban Regeneration in the Historic Jewish Quarters of Central European Cities*, ed. Monika Murzyn-Kupisz and Jacek Purchla (Kraków: International Cultural Centre, 2009), 287–299; Barbara Engelking and Jacek Leociak, *The Warsaw Ghetto: A Guide to the Perished City*, trans. Emma Harris (New Haven, CT: Yale University Press, 2009), 1–24; Peter J. Martyn, "The Undefined Town within a Town: A History of Jewish Settlement in the Western Districts of Warsaw," in *The Jews in Warsaw: A History*, ed. Władysław Bartoszewski and Antony Polonsky (Cambridge: Blackwell, 1991), 55–83; Katrin Steffen, "Connotations of Exclusion—'Ostjuden,' 'Ghettos,' and Other Markings," *Simon Dubnow Institute Yearbook* 4 (2005): 459–479; Alina Cała, "The Discourse of 'Ghettoization'—Non-Jews on Jews in 19th- and 20th-Century Poland," *Simon Dubnow Institute Yearbook* 4 (2005): 445–458; and Zalewska, *Ludność*.

8. Krystyna Czarnecka, Grażyna Kurpiewska, and Joanna Szapiro-Nowakowska, "Straty w nieruchomościach," in *Straty Warszawy 1939–1945: Raport* (Warsaw: Urząd Miasta Stołecznego Warszawy, 2005), 373; Tomasz Stanisław Markiewicz, "Powrót do życia—Warszawa leczy rany zadane wojną," in *Straty Warszawy*, 618.

9. The dollar amount was calculated according to its value in 2004. Wojciech Fałkowski, "O mieście, które miało zginąć. Prace nad opisaniem i oszacowaniem strat Warszawy i jej mieszkańców," in *Straty Warszawy*, 12.

10. W. E. B. Du Bois, "The Negro and the Warsaw Ghetto," *Jewish Life*, May 1952, 15.

11. Bernard Goldstein, *The Stars Bear Witness* (New York: Viking, 1949), 286.

12. Jacob Pat, *Ashes and Fire*, trans. Leo Steinberg (New York: International Universities Press, 1947), 12.

13. Yosef Hayim Yerushalmi, *Zakhor: Jewish History and Jewish Memory* (Seattle: University of Washington Press, 1996).

14. Pat, *Ashes and Fire*, 11, 13, 69, 85, 128, 70.

15. Quote from Maria Dąbrowska's foreword in B. W. Linke, *Kamienie krzyczą* (Warsaw: Wydawnictwo Artystyczno-Graficzne RSW Prasa, 1959), 6.

16. See, for example, *Warsaw Accuses: Guidebook to the Exhibition Arranged by the Office of Reconstruction of the Capital Together with the National Museum in Warsaw, Warsaw, May-June 1945* (Warsaw: Czytelnik, 1945), and Stanisław Albrecht, *Warsaw Lives Again!* (Warsaw: Committee on the Exhibition "Warsaw Lives Again," 1946).

17. This is the spelling Linke gives. A direct transliteration of the original Hebrew would be El Male Rachamim; El Moleh Rachamim is a spelling that follows Yiddish pronunciation.

18. Here I am building on Michael Rothberg, *Multidirectional Memory: Remembering the Holocaust in the Age of Decolonization* (Stanford, CA: Stanford University Press, 2009).

19. Bohdan Lachert, "Muranów–dzielnica mieszkaniowa," *Architektura*, no. 5 (1949): 129, 132.

20. On the monument, see James Young, *The Texture of Memory: Holocaust Memorials and Meaning* (New Haven, CT: Yale University Press, 1994), 155–184.

21. Archiwum Żydowskiego Instytutu Historycznego (AŻIH), Centralny Komitet Żydów w Polsce (CKŻP), Wydział Kultury i Propagandy, 308/217, Bohdan Lachert report, April 28, 1948. For additional evidence on Lachert's intentions here, see Lachert, "Muranów–Dzielnica mieszkaniowa" and "Historia powstania osiedli Muranowa Południowego," unpublished manu-

script of which excerpts are published in Piotr Matywiecki, *Kamień graniczny* (Warsaw: Oficyna Wydawnicza Latona, 1994), 491–494.

22. Katerina Clark, *Moscow, The Fourth Rome: Stalinism, Cosmopolitanism, and the Evolution of Soviet Culture, 1931–1941* (Cambridge, MA: Harvard University Press, 2011), 100–101. On building the new Moscow, see Karl Schlögel, *Moscow, 1937*, trans. Rodney Livingstone (Malden, MA: Polity, 2012), 33–53.

23. Clark, *Moscow*, 108–114.

24. Jerzy Wierzbicki, "Dzielnica mieszkaniowa Muranów (Próba krytyki)," *Architektura*, no. 9 (1952): 222–223, 224, 225.

25. "Tynkowanie Muranowa," *Stolica*, May 15–31, 1951, 3.

26. AŻIH, CKŻP, Wydział Kultury i Propagandy, 308/217, Bohdan Lachert report, April 28, 1948.

27. For example, see "Zbudujemy nową Warszawę—stolicę państwa socjalistycznego: Przemówienie przewodniczącego KC PZPR, Prezydenta R.P. Bolesława Bieruta na I warszawskiej konferencji partyjnej," *Stolica*, July 17, 1949, 3–7.

28. "Nowe mieszkania na Muranowie," *Polska Kronika Filmowa*, 1951.

29. Feliks Weber, "Osiedle mieszkaniowe Muranów," *Stolica*, June 11, 1950, 5.

30. "Miliony cegieł, miliony złotych," *Stolica*, September 25, 1949, 2.

31. "Odbudowa Warszawy. Budowa szybkościowca," *Polska Kronika Filmowa*, 1949.

32. As Sigmund Freud wrote, "The content of a repressed idea or thought can get through to consciousness, then, on condition that it is negated. Negation is a way of acknowledging the repressed, indeed it amounts to a lifting of the repressed, although not, of course, an acceptance of what is repressed" ("Negation," 1925). The piece is reprinted in *The Penguin Freud Reader*, ed. Adam Phillips (New York: Penguin, 2006), 96–97. On forgetting through negation, see also Ali Behdad, *A Forgetful Nation: On Immigration and Cultural Identity in the United States* (Durham, NC: Duke University Press, 2005).

33. The tenement houses on Próżna Street are the main exception. See Janusz Sujecki, *Próżna: ocalona ulica żydowskiej Warszawy* (Warsaw: Ortis, 1993); Rafał Chwiszczuk, *Ulica Próżna i Dzielnica Żydowska w Warszawie/Próżna Straße und das jüdische Viertel Warschau* (Warsaw: Austriackie Forum Kultury, 2008).

34. On everyday memories of the area, see Adrian Wójcik, Michał Bilewicz, and Maria Lewicka, "Living on the Ashes: Collective Representations of Polish-Jewish History among People Living in the Former Warsaw Ghetto Area," *Cities* 27, no 4 (2010): 195–203.

35. The recent recovery of Jewish memories of Warsaw rests alongside the persistence of competitive narratives of victimization among non-Jewish Poles and Polish Jews. On the built environment of contemporary Warsaw, see Elżbieta Janicka, *Festung Warschau* (Warsaw: Wydawnictwo Krytyki Politycznej, 2011). More broadly, see Geneviève Zubrzycki, *The Crosses of Auschwitz: Nationalism and Religion in Post-Communist Poland* (Chicago: University of Chicago, 2006).

36. Beata Kęczkowska, "Stacja Muranów—przewodnik po dziejach dzielnicy: Rozmowa z Beatą Chomątowską," *Gazeta Wyborcza*, October 22, 2012, http://warszawa.gazete.pl/warszawa, 1,34861,12712707,Stacj_Muranow_przewodnik_po_dziejach_dzielnicy.html.

37. Beata Chomątowska, *Stacja Muranów* (Wołowiec: Wydawnictwo Czarne, 2012).

38. For a concise discussion of Benjamin's methodology of montage, see Max Pensky, "Method and Time: Benjamin's Dialectical Images," in *The Cambridge Companion to Walter Benjamin*, ed. David S. Ferris (New York: Cambridge University Press, 2004), 177–198.

39. By "cosmopolitan memory," I am attempting to identify a key tension in self-critical memory projects that seek to challenge or look beyond the myths, vocabularies, and conventional identities of the nation-state. Cosmopolitanism, since its earliest origins among the Cyn-

ics and Stoics, has denoted a human attachment to an order, belief, or value beyond one's particular place or standpoint. While cosmopolitanism comes in many forms, they all converge around the basic interest in striving to look beyond one's world without ever being able to transcend it. That last point about the inherent limit of cosmopolitanism is crucial. The cosmopolitan cliché of the rootless nomad who has no grounding in any place and who avoids embracing any perspective is misleading: how can finite beings arrive at a groundless position or ascend to a synoptically indifferent viewpoint? We simply cannot. We always stand somewhere and our vision always remains partial. Thus cosmopolitanism is always rooted; there's always a tension between the cosmos and the polis, between the universal and the particular, between the postnational and the national. The concept of "rooted cosmopolitanism" has been developed most thoroughly by Kwame Anthony Appiah, *Ethics of Identity* (Princeton, NJ: Princeton University Press, 2005), chap. 6.

40. Michael Geyer, "The Politics of Memory in Contemporary Germany," in *Radical Evil,* ed. Joan Copjec (New York: Verso, 1996), 170.

41. For other examples in contemporary Poland, see Erica Lehrer and Magdalena Waligórska, "Cur(at)ing History: New Genre Art Interventions and The Polish-Jewish Past," *East European Politics and Society* 27, no. 3 (2013): 510–544.

42. Joanna Rajkowska, "Minaret," project description published on her official website, www.rajkowska.com.

43. "Sztuka publicznej możliwości: Z Joanną Rajkowską rozmawia Artur Żmijewski," in *Rajkowska: Przewodnik Krytyki Politycznej* (Warsaw: Wydawnictwo Krytyki Politycznej, 2010), 237, 241.

44. The evaluation of European Jewishness as a carrier of some of the most positive values of modern European history is a contemporary take on an older, postemancipation discourse of Jewish contributions to European civilization. See Moshe Rosman, *How Jewish Is Jewish History* (Portland, OR: Littman Library of Jewish Civilization, 2007), 112–130.

45. Of course, the transvaluation of Jewishness as a positive cultural code of cosmopolitanism could not be more different from the antisemitic cultural code of "Jewish cosmopolitanism." See Shulamit Volkov, "Antisemitism as a Cultural Code: Reflections on the History and Historiography of Antisemitism in Imperial Germany," *Leo Baeck Institute Yearbook,* no. 23 (1978): 25–46.

46. This translation from the Polish is taken from *And Europe Will Be Stunned* (London: Artangel, 2012), 120.

47. Ibid., 120, 121.

48. As Bartana put it in New York, "I want a Poland to be a country or a community which is prepared to take three million Jews." Quote from "Conversations with Contemporary Artists: Yael Bartana," Solomon R. Guggenheim Museum, New York, NY, January 24, 2012, http://www.youtube.com/watch?v=qbTjO2QSYRQ.

49. Yael Bartana quoted in Dorota Jarecka, "Śmierć lidera," *Wysokie Obcasy,* April 11, 2011, http://www.wysokieobcasy.pl/wysokie-obcasy/1,53662,9399606,Smierc_lidera.html; "Till Imagination Takes Us Back—A Conversation with Yael Bartana," *Ma'arav,* April 29, 2012, http://www.maarav.org.il/english/2012/04/till-imagination-takes-us-back---a-conversation-with-yael-bartana/.

50. These antinomies are perhaps clearest—to look briefly beyond Poland—in contemporary Germany, which has a surfeit of public memory over decades of discussions about the Holocaust. Holocaust memory in Germany has long been imbued with the political aim of producing a more enlightened, tolerant, and pluralistic society. Since the late 1980s, Germany's mainstream politicians, journalists, writers, and academics have generally embraced a critical memory culture that has compelled many of them to oppose blatant forms of antisemitism,

xenophobia, and prejudice. Germany's far-right political parties, which have posted some of the weakest election numbers in Europe over the past twenty years, have been politically marginalized partly because of Germany's public sensitivity to the past. But while rightwing political parties have been discredited, and expressions of overt antisemitism in the public sphere have generally become taboo, new forms of xenophobia, racism, and prejudice, especially against Muslims and migrants, have spread among segments of German society. Meanwhile, Holocaust memory in Germany has become over the past decade increasingly depoliticized, staid, and ritualistic. As a symbol of Germany's redemption from Nazism, Holocaust memory asserts and displays Germany's successful transformation into a tolerant, liberal democracy. This symbolically redemptive function of memory helps to diffuse recognition of new forms of exclusion in Germany society. At the same time, though, some memory activists in Germany have started to critique this staid memory culture in the hope of renewing the aspiration that memory can build a more open, tolerant, and pluralistic society. For example, in 2008, Aktion Sühnezeichen Friedensdienste hosted a nine-month-long seminar with a group of migrant women from the Berlin district of Neukölln. Astrid Messerschmidt, a specialist in intercultural pedagogy who reflected on the project's significance, critiqued the sense of "pride" that has surfaced in Germany about its "achieved working through of the past." Aktion Sühnezeichen Friedensdienste, *Neuköllner Stadtteilmütter und iher Auseinandersetzung mit der Geschichte des Nationalsozialismus* (Berlin: Aktion Sühnezeichen Friedensdienste, 2010), 26. For analysis and contextualization of this project, see Michael Rothberg and Yasemin Yildiz, "Memory Citizenship: Migrant Archives of Holocaust Remembrance in Contemporary Germany," *Parallax* 17, no. 4 (2011): 32–48. See also Michael Meng, "Silences about Sarrazin's Racism in Contemporary Germany," *Journal of Modern History* (forthcoming 2015).

4 Stettin, Szczecin, and the "Third Space"

Urban Nostalgia in the German/Polish/ Jewish Borderlands

Magdalena Waligórska

A LARGE, EYE-CATCHING PIECE of red graffiti proclaiming "I miss you Jew!" (*Tęsknię za tobą Żydzie!*) appeared in 2010 at Rondo Giedroycia, one of the major traffic circles in Szczecin. Perplexing many passersby, the slogan was not incidental but rather part of a larger project that the Warsaw performer Rafał Betlejewski started on International Holocaust Remembrance Day the same year. "I miss you Jew!" is a controversial art project consisting of the author, joined by a growing number of followers across Poland, painting the programmatic graffiti in various public places. Additionally, the participants can write commemorative entries about particular Jews they miss on the project's website. Betlejewski, whose idea has been both praised as an apt provocation and criticized for being kitsch and offering easy redemption, explains that his aim is to provide a platform for collective longing.[1] The graffiti "I miss you Jew!" which invokes Jews who died in the Holocaust or were forced to emigrate in 1968, appeared in many places related to Jewish life, for example in the vicinity of synagogues or in former Jewish districts.[2] Also in Szczecin, the motto appeared in a space popularly considered "Jewish": the district of Niebuszewo.

Szczecin's nostalgia for its Jews verbalized in Betlejewski's graffiti is part of the broader nostalgia for a multicultural past, which came to the fore in particular when the city was competing for the status of the European Capital of Culture 2016.[3] Niebuszewo has become the locus of this longing, a spatial metaphor that has come to epitomize the broader, multilayered, troubled history of the city. Narrating the Jewish past of Szczecin is, however, a less straightforward task than the "I miss you Jew!" graffiti campaign might suggest. First of all, Jewish historical sites have been wiped out of the topography of Szczecin. Second, Jewish heritage in the city is inextricably intertwined with its German past, as the city (under its former name, Stettin) belonged to Germany before it became in 1945 part of Poland's so-called Recovered Lands. Given that Polish historiography for decades insisted that these new western borderlands were essentially Polish, the German past of the city is difficult to incorporate into the framework of Szczecin's Polish

Figure 4.1. "I miss you Jew!" graffiti in Szczecin, 2010. Photograph by Magdalena Waligórska

history, centered around the myth of a new beginning and the city's "return" to Poland. As Szczecin—along with other Polish municipalities—is rediscovering its Jewish heritage, celebrating Jewish culture in official festivities, and incorporating the "Jewish element" into the city image, this urban nostalgia unfolds not only in the context of material renovation, commemoration, and reenactment, but also engenders a particular discursive space.

The question this chapter addresses is how contemporary prose and performance art spatialize the memory of Jewish and German presence in Stettin/Szczecin and map Jewishness in the urban space. Analyzing urban novels, autobiographical writing, and art projects that address the Jewish past in Stettin/Szczecin, I investigate the particular conditions of urban nostalgia in the "Recovered Lands," where the Jewish legacy is inseparable from the German, and where the rediscovery of Jewish spaces thus entails a process of cultural translation and "overwriting" of contested spaces.

In the twentieth century, Stettin/Szczecin was peripheral both to the pre-1939 Third Reich and the post-1945 Poland. Heavily damaged in the Second World War, the city changed hands several times in the immediate postwar period and retained for a relatively long time a multiethnic population of Germans, Poles,

Ukrainians, and Jews, trying to find new homes in the aftermath of the war.[4] Nor does Szczecin feature prominently on today's map of Jewish heritage in Poland.[5] While the former region of Galicia, as well as the areas of central and eastern Poland, boast of their Jewish past and offer Jewish heritage tourist trails like the "Hassidic Route"[6] or the "Shtetl Route,"[7] Szczecin, together with the rest of the western borderlands, exists only on the margins of the narrative of the Polish-Jewish past.

Stettin/Szczecin, however, has not been irrelevant for the Jewish history of the twentieth century. In 1940, Stettin was the site of the first, experimental deportation of Jews from the territory of the Third Reich. Six years later, Jewish life unexpectedly boomed in the city again, as it became a major transit point for emigrating Holocaust survivors. This two-act Jewish history of Stettin/Szczecin left few material traces, but in its wake, there remains a complex legacy of destruction, amnesia, and myth-making that is paradigmatic for former German territories incorporated into the new borders of post-1945 Poland more generally.

Jews in Stettin (Act One)

The first mention of the Jewish population in western Pomerania dates back to the Middle Ages. The early Jewish settlements in Stettin, however, practically ceased to exist in the seventeenth and eighteenth centuries. In 1683, only one Jew was allowed to reside in the city, an employee of the Berlin rabbi, supervising the trade of kosher wine. And although in 1753 the Prussian authorities came up with a peculiar, unrealized plan to found a Jewish town in Pomerania, Jews actually resettled in the region only after the 1812 March Edict of the Prussian king Friedrich Wilhelm granted them citizen rights.[8] The beginning of the nineteenth century witnessed a dynamic growth of the new Jewish community in Stettin. A small wooden synagogue was erected in 1834, and in 1875, the community, counting already over two thousand members, celebrated the opening of a new, impressive Moorish-style synagogue.[9] In 1938, the Stettin Jews were a community of nearly three thousand, organized into diverse social and cultural associations and clubs. There was an Association of Jewish Front Soldiers, a rowing club, and a tennis club.[10] On the night of November 9, 1938, not only the synagogue but also the two sport club buildings were set on fire. On the next day, most male Jews of Stettin were deported to Sachsenhausen. Although they soon returned, the dramatic events were only a prelude to the definitive deportations to come.[11] Jewish Stettin came to an end on February 13, 1940, when 1,124 Jews, together with their non-Jewish spouses and children, were deported to the district of Lublin in the General Government.[12] Most of them were murdered in the concentration camps Bełżec, Treblinka, and Auschwitz. The burnt-out synagogue was fully demolished in 1940 and never rebuilt.

Jews in Szczecin (Act Two)

Jews did reappear in Szczecin, however, as soon as the war was over. They were Polish Jews, "repatriated" primarily from the USSR, where they had survived the war. In June 1946, there were 30,951 of them registered in Szczecin, but they did not intend to stay for long. In December 1946, half of them had already left the city; six months later, less than seven thousand Jews remained in Szczecin.[13] The authorities, especially after the Kielce pogrom in 1946, where local inhabitants attacked Holocaust survivors, killing over forty of them, located many newcomers in the district of Niebuszewo, where it was thought that a large Jewish community would be better protected against anti-Jewish violence.[14] Jews lived in Niebuszewo together with Germans who had not yet left the city. The district had several prayer houses, one of only two yeshivas in the country at that time, two Jewish nursery schools, and five kindergartens. In 1946, a Jewish primary school opened. Niebuszewo became a Jewish neighborhood, with Yiddish spoken in the streets. There was a Jewish People's University, a library, and theater and dance groups. There was also a Jewish militia station and a bakery. This extended Jewish infrastructure, however, was temporary. Szczecin, the base for the Bricha agency, which organized legal and illegal emigration of Jews to Western Europe and Israel, was more a Jewish transit point than a final destination.[15]

Although most Jews had left Szczecin by 1958, Niebuszewo, also known as Lejbuszewo (from the Jewish male name "Lejb") in local city slang, remained the seat of a small Jewish community. In the late 1950s, Jews from the Soviet Union were still arriving there. A ritual slaughterhouse and kosher canteen existed in the district until the 1960s. Szczecin was also a site of Jewish cultural life.[16] Eliasz Rajzman (1909–1975) and Hadasa Rubin (1912–2003), among the last Yiddish-language poets in postwar Poland, both lived and published in the city. There was even a Jewish band, Następcy Tronów (Heirs to the Throne), which gave concerts and took part in music contests across Poland.[17] The antisemitic campaign of 1968, which resulted in the emigration of a third of local Jews, came as a final, tragic caesura to Jewish life in Szczecin.[18] In 2010, the Jewish community counted approximately sixty members, most of them elderly and in need of support. There is a prayer hall and kosher kitchen that distributes meals. Mikołaj Rozen, the head of the Jewish community in Szczecin, however, was not optimistic about the future, stating in 2007 that the community is "slowly coming to an end."[19]

Reflective Nostalgia

"Szczecin is as hard as the victor's boot / Szczecin is as strong as a sailor's hand" reads the proud verse of the poem "Szczecin" by Leszek Goliński, published in a 1946 volume under the programmatic title *The Oder Murmurs in Polish* (*Odra szumi po polsku*). "We have not come here to long," declares the lyrical subject, "but to rule, to resist and create."[20] Indeed, in the immediate postwar period, the authorities of the new western borderlands found longing undesired, if not outright suspect. Poland received the "Recovered Lands" as a compensation for her eastern borderlands, the Kresy, which, according to the decisions taken by the Big Three (Stalin, Roosevelt, and Churchill) at the Yalta Conference in February 1945, were to be annexed by the Soviet Union. As officials were trying to legitimize Polish claims to these ex-German territories, writers hastily took to penning a Polish mythology of the Recovered Lands, celebrating, if not the intrinsically "Polish" landscape, then the conclusiveness of the hard "victor's boot." The incontestable, fortified border was the key image of this narrative.

After over four decades of intensive attempts to inscribe the city into the mythos of the Recovered Lands, overwriting its German history with a Polishness reeking of fresh paint, Szczecin seems to be wary of such singular metanarratives.[21] Today, the city, aspiring to the title of a "Baltic Neopolis," not only acknowledges its German past as a tourist attraction but also boasts multicultural influences, promoting itself with the slogan "Szczecin—Here the borders blur."[22] The hard-and-fast frontier, it seems, is no match for amorphous longing.

Nostalgia has become an important topos in new artistic projects that question the monolithic image of Szczecin as a Polish city, investigating blank spots, discontinuities, and fragmentation in its history. Urban nostalgia, as Svetlana Boym argues in *The Future of Nostalgia,* can take two directions. Restorative nostalgia, characteristic of nationalist projects in particular, "proposes to rebuild the lost home and patch up the memory gaps." It is a quest for a "truth," which relies on myth-making and aims at a reconstruction of the past. Reflective nostalgia, conversely, "lingers on ruins, the patina of time and history, in the dreams of another place and another time," offering a "meditation on history and passage of time." It does not put forward a vision of an absolute truth, but instead "cherishes shattered fragments of memory."[23]

If the post-1945 myth of the Recovered Lands implied a restorative nostalgia (however strained the idea of the "return home" was), it is reflective nostalgia that seems to underlie Szczecin's current longing for the past. Rediscovering the repressed past of the city, contemporary artists and writers choose rather to linger on ruins, uncovering the fragmented, paradoxical, and distorted chapters of the city's history and awakening the ghosts of its "others." This rediscovery of Szczecin's previous inhabitants and minorities is implicated in both the more general wave of nostalgia for Poland's past multiethnicity, and the more localized attempts to reinterpret the history of the Recovered Lands and acknowledge their German heritages.

Indeed, the rise of interest in the Jewish past took on the dimensions of a true explosion in post-1989 Poland. Literary, historiographic, and artistic projects dealing with the Jewish past have proliferated in an unprecedented way. Festivals of Jewish culture mushroomed across the country, and the revitalization of Jewish sites became an imperative to many local communities. This revival of memory about Jews inspired both canonical art forms, and the cutting-edge productions of unorthodox street art, video, installation, and performance artists. The initiatives of renowned authors like Zbigniew Libera (*LEGO Concentration Camp*, 1996), Artur Żmijewski (*The Game of Tag*, 1999; *Our Songbook*, 2003; *A Pole in the Closet*, 2006), Joanna Rajkowska (*Greetings from Jerusalem Avenue*, 2002), or Wilhelm Sasnal (*Maus*, 2002) have been accompanied by a plethora of other, lesser-known projects, which often pose difficult questions about the past of Polish-Jewish relations or anti-Jewish violence. This memory work has a particular edge in places like Szczecin. The German Stettin, with its post-1945 migrations, must be the departure point for any quest for the Jewish Szczecin, and its rediscovery profoundly affects the emotional topography of the city.

In his *Places on the Margin*, Rob Shields points to the ways in which such social topographies of cities take shape. "Social spatialization," in his definition, embraces "both discursive and non-discursive elements, practices and processes," generating "place-images" or "spatial metaphors" that convey a particular set of associations. This cultural mapping relies both on collective mythologies and actual interventions in the physical space.[24] The discursive space of contemporary literature and urban art, which reassess the past through the lens of reflective nostalgia, has the potential to radically "respatialize" urban realities. And the case of Szczecin is an excellent illustration of how the recent upsurge of memory about Germans and Jews opens new, complex patterns of urban nostalgia, which not only reinterpret the city as a site of cultural pluralism but also expose hybridity and cultural translation as key modes of coexistence in a multiethnic urban context.

Ruins

Artur D. Liskowacki's *Eine kleine* (2000) and Inga Iwasiów's *Bambino* (2008) are two well-received and rewarded Polish novels that attempt a reflective gaze on Szczecin's troubled history. Both *Eine kleine*, which plays during and immediately after the Second World War, and *Bambino*, which embraces the first postwar decades, paint fragmented, disquieting visions of the city's past, creating what Boym called an "emotional topography of memory" where the personal and historic events overlap.[25] Picturing the city as a heterogeneous conglomerate of people, languages, and traditions, Liskowacki and Iwasiów also map the intersections of the Jewish and German spaces in Stettin/Szczecin.

Liskowacki's *Eine kleine* is an homage to a city in transition. Narrating the metamorphosis of Stettin into Szczecin from the perspective of his German protagonists, Liskowacki creates a literary bridge between the city's German and Polish eras, documenting dramatic epilogues but also tracing continuities. Jews appear as marginal figures in the story, as ephemeral, fading personages-in-passing, captured on the brink of the catastrophe and, later, as scarred survivors. Their absence, however, haunts the inhabitants of Stettin; their abandoned spaces prove an organic part of the city's identity.

The Jews in *Eine kleine* belong undoubtedly to the German element. Doctor Liedermann, a physician, is so assimilated that he even wears a traditional Tirolean hat. When the Stettin synagogue is burning on Kristallnacht in 1938, Liedermann is among the crowd of onlookers. He takes this opportunity to loudly announce, "Well, just a piece of Moorish rubbish. . . . It only clashed with the spirit of this city: Teutonic, Gothic, Hanseatic."[26] As his non-Jewish friend, still facing the smoldering remnants of the synagogue, urges him to emigrate, Liedermann answers indignantly, "Why on earth should Germans leave their houses now?" (140). And indeed, the Jewish characters of *Eine kleine* remain in Stettin until the end, holding on to their daily routines, incredulous to the darkening atmosphere around them.

Liskowacki portrays Germans and Jews in prewar Stettin as neighbors. They peek into each other's windows, meet each other in the street, and observe each other. Yet the "disappearance" of Jews happens almost seamlessly, hardly disrupting the order of the urban universe. New tenants almost imperceptibly occupy the emptied Jewish apartments and silently take over Jewish businesses. Not a single sign reminds passersby of the recent deportations. August Kugel, however, a journeyman baker and member of the Nazi Party, takes note of the increasing discrimination that Rosemann, his Jewish neighbor, has to face. It does not escape Kugel that Rosemann has been deported. Looking into the windows of his friend's abandoned apartment, Kugel contemplates his absence:

> In Rosemann's windows on the first floor there were thick yellow sheer curtains and only on one window sill could you see a geranium in a flowerpot. This geranium was still standing there in the spring, when new tenants were moving in; it blossomed red and gray. Seeing it, Kugel felt a stab of pain at the bottom of his stomach, but also some sort of satisfaction. Like when you predict the result of a match. Even if it is a defeat. In S. one needs apartments, so many families have to squeeze in overcrowded flats. (32)

The gaze of Kugel is one of an opportunist, a typical German *Mitläufer* (opportunist), who acts upon personal interest rather than ideological conviction. After the 1944 air raids of Stettin, Kugel gets himself a set of elegant furniture from a bombed-out house. He deserts his unit when Russians march into the city in 1945, and then eagerly adapts to the post-1945 Communist reality in Szczecin. His indifference toward the "disappearance" of Jews is symptomatic here of the popular postwar German claim to ignorance about what happened to Jews ("Wir haben es nicht gewusst"). Picturing Kugel's brief moment of reflection in front of his neighbor's window, Liskowacki captures the very process of repression. Kugel does realize the fate of Rosemann but subdues empathy with an attempt at rationalization: Germans can really use the space vacated by Jews.

But although the Jews of Stettin gradually fade from the image of the city without leaving any noticeable void for Liskowacki's protagonists, Jewish spaces come to take on a symbolic significance as the German Stettin faces its own armageddon. When the city is turned to rubble, the universal destruction brings the fragmented Jewish and German spaces into unison. Heini, an orphaned German boy, is a curious wanderer through the city, collecting abandoned, destroyed objects. In a nearby hospital, he finds a German military Cross of Merit. His uncle, however, throws it away, explaining that the cross is stained with "innocent blood." Later, the boy retrieves the cross from among the nettles at the Jewish cemetery, where he often wanders, admiring the depictions of human hands on the gravestones. Picking up the medal, Heini scrutinizes it with interest: "He had a good look at it, to see if the blood stains were still to be seen. But they were not, it was shining, like new. And since Heini found a piece of a yellow bone right next to it, he thought it would be best to put the bone and the cross on the stone slab. The one that had a seven-branched candlestick carved on it and strange letters, as if worms gnawed out winding corridors in the stone" (187). The Jewish cemetery becomes the resting place for the incompatible, unwanted, even shameful detritus of the German Stettin. A temporary enclave of the recent past, it has to be discarded in order to create Szczecin. Thus, it is at the cemetery that Heini hoards some of the odd broken objects that he has salvaged from the rubble: a barometer, a jar of mustard, a coffee grinder—shards of the lost world. When the last Germans leave Szczecin in the 1950s, Heini asks his departing friend, Hummel, to take a suitcase full of these Stettin remains to Germany. Among the countless bits of bric-a-brac and urban fragments, there is also a piece of a Jewish matzevah (memorial stone) in his suitcase. But the emigrating Hummel, head of the German Cultural Association in Szczecin, abandons the mysterious suitcase in a park, departing without it. When a passerby discovers Heini's collection, this Stettin still-life seems to take on a life of its own:

> There will be a barometer with a broken glass falling out of the suitcase, a coffee grinder, the ribbon of the Iron Cross and a silver spoon with a monogram, and a black half-moon of Schumann's *Mondnacht,* and behind them: a linden tree covered in golden dust, a Cadelle beetle, the Jewish stone hands, a kettle-drum with crossed drumsticks, an iron stove, a handful of salt roasted red in the fire . . . and so much more that it's impossible to walk away with it, to collect what has been scattered and is floating in the air, getting lost in the grass. (224–225)

The Jewish (blessing?) hands in stone make an organic part of this oneiric miniature of Stettin. They become a universal symbol of loss. Heini's suitcase, in fact, accommodates the whole city. It seems to be a metaphor for what Doreen Massey calls "coexisting heterogeneity" and an urban space that is "becoming." It is chaotic, subsuming various trajectories. Liskowacki lingers on ruins, creating a narrative that breaks the monolithic, uniform myth of Szczecin's past. He points to paradoxical overlaps and "contemporaneous plurality."[27] Walter Benjamin, and later Svetlana Boym, described this quality as "porosity."[28] "Porosity is a spatial metaphor for time in the city," wrote Boym, "for the variety of temporal dimensions embedded in physical space."[29] Cities in transition are particularly prone to porosity as they are sites of improvisation. They are incongruous, consisting of layers belonging to different time periods. They contradict the total vision of the city that the authorities or city planners might want to adopt.

Liskowacki's novel documents the process of what Sara Upstone calls "overwriting," which she explains is when a "new reality is layered over the old, which nevertheless continues to exist as a trace."[30] This overwriting first takes place when the Jewish spaces of Stettin are being erased from the cityscape, and Jewish apartments and establishments are taken over. It occurs for the second time when the post-1945 city is changing hands and street names. The urban coordinates come to be expressed in a new language (Polish), but the emotional topography of the protagonists in the "city of S." remains the same. Michał Cichy, in his reading of *Eine kleine,* interprets the novel as a portrayal of the death of Stettin and the birth of Szczecin, two entities that share neither a common history nor even the same space.[31] Liskowacki's city, however, is not sanitized but porous. *Eine kleine* expresses doubt in the possibility of brand-new beginnings, warning that history remains stuck to the sites where it took place and that the dead haunt those who replace them. Stettin is a layer of the palimpsest of Szczecin, one that will never be effaced.

Train Station

Although *Eine kleine* plays in the immediate postwar years, it hardly acknowledges Szczecin as a major node of Jewish emigration. Liskowacki's protagonists see Jews as an anonymous mass, "loitering around the town waiting for the transport" (175). Paradoxically, however, these Jews share the German fate, joining the flow out of the city, often with forged German documents. As Hummel is emigrating from Szczecin, he suddenly recollects a disquieting encounter with a stranger he met several years before at the same railway station:

> Hummel remembers one of the first transports, nine years before, and a short
> man with a few days' black beard who, passing by, with a movement of his head
> pointed to the carriages of the train that just came in and muttered something

in a soft, lame German. Hummel didn't hear it, or rather didn't understand it and was looking at him in silence. This apparently disconcerted the man who, after a moment of hesitation, overcoming as if in this very last minute some old, stale fear, whispered, looking vigilantly at Hummel: "The same train that you were sending us on. And now: you and us, together." He looked straight into Hummel's eyes, testing the effect of his words. And he shrugged his shoulders. As if discarding what he just said. Hummel didn't manage to answer and the blackish one immersed himself in the crowd thickening at the entrance to the station. (222–223)

The meeting with the emigrating Jew prefigures Hummel's own exodus from Szczecin. The Yiddish-speaking Jews, who are headed to Palestine, symbolize the predicament of the city, even though they are alienated figures, external to both Stettin and Szczecin. The Jews travel through the city without leaving a trace, uprooted, unaffiliated, vulnerable. Arriving from the East, like Poles, and departing westward, like Germans, they comprise one part of the general migratory flux in and out of Szczecin, where people carry their "suitcases, bags and bundles, their travel documents, their hatred, their sorrow, their remembering, their entanglement in the past, now shrunk to the dimensions of this station, this train, this carriage" (222).

Although the narrative of *Eine kleine* enfolds in a time frame that embraces both Act One and Act Two of Jewish history in Stettin/Szczecin, Jewish spaces in the text serve merely as inert, symbolic backdrops. Likewise, Jewish protagonists, like the assimilated Doctor Liedermann (the "German Jew") and the nameless Holocaust survivor at the train station (the "Polish Jew," perhaps?), are archetypal characters without any depth. They are heralds of the upheavals to come, a prefiguration of the German fate. The burning synagogue foreshadows the fires that are going to consume the defeated fortress of Stettin. The train station teeming with Yiddish-speaking migrants mirrors the predicament of the German expellees. The key Jewish space of the novel is the cemetery, a monument to Jewish absence that pervades the novel. Like the synagogue and the railway platform, it is given a universal dimension as the spatial metaphor of ultimate symbiosis. It is the place where Jewish bones rest alongside the German Iron Cross of Merit. Death and migration, Liskowacki seems to suggest, unite the persecuted and the persecutors.

The figure of Heini, the collector of urban wreckage, opens up a perspective on yet another kind of space: the space of transit. Heini collects personal belongings from destroyed houses, things that used to signify something in the household's original context but are now exposed to the elements. They have become silent witnesses of wartime destruction and postwar migrations. "Private property," as Joachim Schlör notes, "has, for both the individual memory and the collective memory, a deep emotional significance."[32] Objects of private use like a "silver spoon with a monogram" connote home. Their dispersal in the public space of the bombed street and their vulnerability (only a "half-moon" remains of the broken Schumann record) stand for the dissolution of home, which no longer provides shelter. This transition in the objects' role from significant personal belongings to meaningless, fractured pieces of debris stands either for death or displacement. The objects filling Heini's suitcase, itself a powerful symbol of migration, are an assemblage of things left behind, by both deported Stettin Jews and departing Germans. As such, they "become embodiments of conditions and circumstances—bearers of memories, of hopes," as Schlör puts it. They might "mediate memory" or perform "a bridging function" between the place where they were abandoned and their former owners, but they also symbolize the void, the collapse of the old order.[33] Heini chooses Germany as the ultimate destination of the symbolic Stettin suitcase, but it never reaches this end. Instead, the suitcase is suspended in between, doomed to endless transit. In a way, it reminds the Polish Szczecin of the city's legacy of dispossession and displacement.

Home

Inga Iwasiów, in her *Bambino,* depicts those who remained. Ulrike/Ula, a Stettin-born German, and Stefan, a Jew who settles in Szczecin after the war, both wish to leave the past behind but cannot escape it. Their love affair in postwar Szczecin is staged in the enclosed, almost fortified space of Ula's apartment. The dichotomy between inside and outside is crucial here. For Ula and Stefan, two "others" in Szczecin, the home is a protected space. It is an enclave where they can be themselves, and where they are protected from their neighbors' prying gazes. At the same time, it is also a place inhabited by ghosts. It is here that each of them remembers and relives their traumatic pasts. Ula is haunted by postwar rapes and Stefan by the concentration camp. Ula, who entirely "polonizes" herself, occupies the apartment that belonged to her parents. The apartment itself, therefore, is a direct link to her past and her old identity. She sleeps in her parents' old bedroom, isolated from the outside world by heavy, tightly fitted curtains: "These curtains. In the beginning it seemed to her that everyone sees her. And that everyone wants to know whether she is not thinking about her father and her brothers. What she is thinking about when she mixes German with Polish, entering so quickly, overnight, onto the streets, onto the signboards, into her head."[34] The room behind the heavy curtains, however, is not a protected idyll but a trap. "Close, close the room tightly," thinks Ula, trying to forget the Russian voices and laughter that she still hears in there, "this one room in which, perhaps, there is something, something can be heard" (148). The sealed-off apartment is also the space where Ula draws boundaries between her own unspoken past and Stefan's. Trying to rationalize his silence, she thinks to herself, "Two stories per person could sneak out even from such a well-secured room" (149). Therefore, she asks no questions about Stefan's scars and the number tattooed on his arm. When he finally tells her how his family died, she regrets that he shared it with her. "He was right to spare her," she thinks. "He was right. Nobody is ready to share with anyone. . . . She has her own kinds of death too. She closes the windows for them. So that they don't get out" (205–206).

Both Ula, a cook, and Stefan, a teacher, remain in Szczecin despite massive postwar emigration waves. They decide to inhabit the myth of the Recovered Lands, which promises a new beginning for everyone. The illusion of Szczecin's hospitality, however, ends in 1968. Stefan, urged to leave by the secret police, decides to emigrate. Iwasiów presents this exodus as Stefan's leaving a vacuum not only in Ula's bedroom but in the very texture of the city:

> This train must have a very strong locomotive to tear the people out of here. Even those who wanted to leave, who were looking forward to it. They leave behind addresses, apartments, trails. He [Stefan] should be pulled back by the school building, solid, heavy. He liked teaching there, facing the blackboard, looking out of the window. He liked especially these intermezzos. Her flat, fortified with the barriers of curtains, locks. With touch. The bar, piles of plates, heavy pots. . . . She is imagining buildings, streets, people on park benches. All of these objects from A to infinity attached with an anchor (we are in a port city) to the train. (209)

Although Iwasiów depicts rootedness in this very literal way (people are anchored to places where they lived their lives), her novel rarely deals with the urban exterior. It is the home that is the main point of reference for Ula and the backdrop of her relationship with Stefan. Ula's apartment is the space that accommodates her German books (the only visible marker of her identity) and her emancipated lifestyle (her lovers come to visit her by night). The apartment is also the space where the true stories of Ula and Stefan are narrated. Sara Upstone, in her analysis of the spatial politics of the postcolonial novel, notes that the domestic sphere, often portrayed as an "idealized and apolitical location" is in fact a "site of power contestation."[35] The home, as an alternative to public, institutionalized space, can thus be a subversive niche. This is true in both Liskowacki's *Eine kleine* and Iwasiów's *Bambino*. In both novels, the home represents the subaltern in an urban space that is undergoing a dramatic shift in power relations. Not unlike postcolonial reality, under Communism, the home is the space of resistance in a society that stigmatizes otherness.

Neighbors

In post-1945 Szczecin, Jews and Germans not only found themselves in a similar, precarious position as subalterns, but their marginal positions also opened up the possibility of solidarity between them. This entanglement of Jewish and German fate is reflected not only in literary fiction but also in autobiographical accounts of that time. Jews and Germans often shared their spaces. They were neighbors or fellow inmates in hospitals. Sometimes they were even friends. In her memoirs, Taube Kron writes about an elderly German woman who took care of her child. Kron, in turn, became the wet nurse of a German baby whose mother was unable to breastfeed, and who was ostracized by the Polish women in the maternity ward.[36] Similarly, Anna Frajlich mentions her ersatz grandmother, a German woman who worked for her Jewish family as house-help.[37] The vicinity of Jews and Germans in the immediate postwar years was conditioned not only by their spatial proximity (Niebuszewo was one of the places where Jews and Germans lived side by side) or linguistic affiliation (Jews, many of whom spoke Yiddish or German, could communicate with Germans much better than Poles), but also by the shared stigma of otherness.

The region of western Pomerania after 1945 was a place where anti-German and anti-Jewish violence was a fact. The Warsaw-based Jewish newspaper *Dos Naje Leben* reported several cases of Jews in Szczecin being murdered, robbed, shot at, or beaten up in 1946 and 1947.[38] In the summer of 1946, for example, a crowd of around one hundred people attacked Jews in the streets. Three people were injured before the situation was defused by the local militia.[39] Many Germans in the area also felt unsafe during the immediate postwar period. In 2008, the local Institute of National Remembrance in Szczecin reported that, during the winter of 1945–1946, grave atrocities had been committed against Germans by the local militia in the Polish-governed town of Świnoujście/Swinemünde, 35 miles north of Szczecin.[40] In her memoir, Katarzyna Weintraub also recounts the attempted lynching of a German woman in Szczecin. Upon seeing a group of people stoning her, Weintraub's father pulled the German woman out of the crowd and brought her home. The woman, who remained in Szczecin to look for her missing child, stayed with the Jewish family, who assisted her in her search until she finally found her son in a Polish orphanage.[41] The commonalities of the Jewish and German fates in Szczecin concerned not only life in Szczecin but also emigration. There were Jews who left the city with forged German identity cards, and Germans who joined Jews on the illegal trucks smuggling people across the border.[42] Paradoxically, not only the living Jews and Germans experienced a similar fate but also the dead. In the postwar campaign to "polonize" Szczecin, both German and Jewish cemeteries were destroyed, and the broken fragments of the pre-1945 tombstones were later recycled as building material.

Szczecin in the aftermath of the Second World War was not only a city on Poland's geographic and social periphery—the notorious "Wild West." It was also a marginal location in Homi Bhabha's sense, a liminal, "interstitial" space, a space in between, which has the potential to become a site of negotiation, a "third space." Used originally in reference to the language of political critique, Bhabha's concept of the third space denotes a space of negotiation where binary and antagonistic positions yield to a rearticulation, "which contests the terms and territories of both." It is also the space of the "negotiation of incommensurable differences," which "opens up a space of translation: a space of hybridity." It is, furthermore, a space that is "remaking the boundaries, exposing the limits of any claim to a singular or autonomous sign of difference—be it class, gender or race." The space of "thirdness" is, in other words, a creative site where dissonance, friction, and discontinuity generate conditions for the emergence of something new that is "neither the one nor the other."[43] Such a marginal space, Sara Upstone adds, is also "a site of marvelous realities that is fragmented, multicultural and constituted of both the real and imagined."[44] It might be because of the uncanny, the fantastic, and even the heretical ideas implied in the questioning of boundaries and the emergence of borderline identities that makes literature and performance art such an apposite space for articulating them.

Szczecin is a space of translation in many dimensions. One of these is composed of the very language for denoting certain spaces and objects. The adjectives *poniemiecki* and *pożydowski* ("formerly German" and "formerly Jewish") are unique modifiers that effectively capture Central Europe's post-1945 shifts of borders and ownership. A *poniemiecki* or *pożydowski* house—and it is in this particular collocation that the adjective is most often used—is not a German or Jewish (*niemiecki* or *żydowski*) space, but a *Polish* one. Although an object described as *poniemiecki* or *pożydowski* might have changed hands as result of theft, seizure, or confiscation, the adjective connotes transfer, almost inheritance of a sort. It signifies appropriation but also overwriting, adaptation, and even adoption. In the context of the so-called Recovered Lands, *poniemieckość* (a derivative abstract noun) is the basis of local identities. Formerly German houses were "translated" into Polish, painted over with new Polish-language signs. Ex-German objects became incorporated into Polish households. In Szczecin, they were also incorporated into Jewish households. Katarzyna Weintraub gives a poignant example of this cultural subsumption in her family:

> In this omnipresent formerly German reality [*w poniemieckiej rzeczywistości*] the expression "family heirloom" [*po babci*, literally "inherited from one's grandmother"] was a kind of a metaphor, a mental shortcut referring exclusively to the Rosenthal set of thin ivory porcelain. It was an identical set that grandfather bought for grandmother in 1932, on their trip to Berlin. Irony, or maybe destiny, wanted it that this *poniemiecki* service connected, like a thin thread, the world of our Szczecin house with that on the Vilnius Antokol, the home of the grandparents I never knew.[45]

Szczecin was indeed a space where such a post-1945 German-Jewish cultural translation was possible. The households that emerged there in the postwar years were compounded. The urban space was being translated from *niemiecki* to *poniemiecki*. Weintraub's family lived at that time with a German woman, Frau Keinert, who took part in their Sabbath dinners. Weintraub remembers that the Sabbath challah on their Szczecin table was covered with a napkin that Frau Keinert embroidered with the phrase *Guten Appetit*.[46] The Jewish home in Szczecin thus formed part of the third space, the space where dichotomies gave way to unforeseen and unlooked-for translations.

Niebuszewo

The third space, at the intersection of the Polish, Jewish, and German, attracts artists who not only narrate the complex history of Szczecin but also physically "touch" urban spaces with their work. Many of these art projects take place in Niebuszewo, the district that has been turned into a laboratory for retrieving Szczecin's memory.

On a rainy evening in 2007, a trilingual slogan, "Be yourself—take on a different identity," appeared on one of the buildings in Niebuszewo. Two other slogans— *Die Kultur ist unser Glück* (Culture is our fortune) and *Historia buduje lepszą przyszłość* (History guarantees a better future)—were illuminated nearby. Playing on Nazi and Communist propaganda, as well as the language of commercials, Bartosz Wójcik, a Szczecin-based multimedia artist, tried to raise the question of which history and whose past will come to define the identity of Szczecin. The artist believes that the city, whose past was amputated and whose layers of diverse heritage were excluded from the official post-1945 discourse, could paradoxically only construct its identity by deconstructing the dominating metanarratives and acknowledging the traces of the other in the urban texture.[47]

Wójcik, who is also the head of the local cultural association OFFicyna, has long been engaged in the rediscovery of Szczecin's multicultural past. OFFicyna, founded in Niebuszewo by a group of independent artists in 1998, has been very active in the field of social art. The association organizes workshops, issues a periodical entitled *Niebuszewiak,* curates a museum about Niebuszewo, and stages art projects in cooperation with the district's inhabitants. In 2008, OFFicyna published a map of Niebuszewo featuring not only places associated with the district's various minorities (for example, the German factory, the Jewish school, the place where Roma used to set up camp), but also the sites of urban legends (like the former house of the notorious Butcher of Niebuszewo who was said to have killed children and processed the human flesh into a macabre homemade *bigos*). The map came into being with the help of local people, who brought their personal photos and shared their own stories about the neighborhood. OFFicyna soon started organizing walking tours through the district and, in 2009, published a guidebook to Niebuszewo. The guidebook compiles historical facts and inhabitants' reminiscences, but it also documents street art projects staged by the association.

Figure 4.2. Niebuszewo, 2010. Photograph by Magdalena Waligórska

Spacerkiem po Niebuszewie (*Strolling around Niebuszewo*) generates a new narrative about a part of the city that suffered from a reputation as a dilapidated and dangerous area for decades. Not only does it present the district as architecturally interesting; it also creates the myth of an "urban arcadia," where different minorities lived peacefully side by side in "the atmosphere of a little town of the Polish eastern borderlands (*Kresy*)."[48] The Kresy, the eastern territories that Poland lost after 1945, is an important topos here. First, the image of the Kresy, originally inhabited by Poles, Jews, Ukrainians, Belorussians, and Lithuanians, often serves in Poland as a spatial metaphor for multiethnicity. Second, since Szczecin was the destination of many "repatriated" eastern Poles after 1945, the suggestion is made that the city is an extension of the Kresy, and that the multiethnicity of eastern Poland is somehow reproduced in the new Polish western borderlands. This heterogeneity is, moreover, framed as a value that defines Szczecin's new identity. As the authors of the guidebook put it, Niebuszewo, a paradigmatic melting pot, is "the lens of west Pomeranian identity."[49]

"Moving Houses" (*Przeprowadzka*), a theater project undertaken in 2009 by the Kana Theatrical Center, pointed to how fragmented and polyphonic the voices of this urban arcadia can be. The performance, directed by Weronika Fibich, was an attempt to narrate the Jewish and German history of an urban space *in and through that space*. Using locations such as an old German factory, the Niebuszewo railway station, an antiquities shop with old German furniture, and a tenement house in the formerly Jewish neighborhood, Fibich combined theater, oral history, archival research, and multimedia effects in a performance that was intended to evoke the migratory experience of the district's post-1945 population. In preparation for the project, which took over a year, Fibich carried out a series of interviews with present and former inhabitants of Niebuszewo. Among the Jews and non-Jews whose memories she recorded were those who emigrated from Szczecin after 1968. Thus, the experience of settling into an alien space only to be forced to abandon it once again became the leitmotif of the performance.

"Moving Houses" opens in the former factory building, where video interviews with the inhabitants of Niebuszewo are projected onto rough industrial surfaces. The unusual setting breaks the aura of secure hominess in which the film material was shot. The spectators, who roam freely from one projection to another, receive fragmented, disquieting narratives through their headphones, which prepare them for further exploration of the spaces of migration. Divided into groups and equipped with empty boxes and travel documents (a facsimile of a 1969 "exit-visa" stating that its owner is no longer a Polish citizen), the spectators are loaded onto an old truck and taken to further destinations. Upon their arrival in one of the three locations, they hear more interviews and encounter archival materials about the first Polish settlers in Szczecin and the everyday objects abandoned by the deported Germans.

The experiences of post-1945 Polish settlers, who arrived in a city of rubble that felt like a "living cemetery," are interwoven with the narratives of Jews who left the city in the aftermath of the 1968 antisemitic campaign.[50] In documenting how the Polish city overgrew and superseded the German one, Fibich does not leave out painful moments. The Szczecin of 1945 was not a welcoming place. Chaim Sucholicki, who arrived in Szczecin right after the war from a work camp in Kamchatka, remembers how people would be found dead in the streets at dawn. Bloodstains in the snow reflected nighttime violence, an ever-present hazard among the ruins. Daniel Waksman recalls how his parents, who were looking for an empty apartment to move into, found a German hanged in the attic of one. The urban spaces found by both Jewish and non-Jewish settlers are marked by death, and their domestication takes time.

The Niebuszewo that Fibich's interviewees remember is "home," but it is a home that they had to work strenuously to adopt and it was, therefore, never idyllic. German houses that became Jewish homes, German cemeteries that served as playgrounds for Jewish children, and German cutlery decorated with swastikas— used by children as trinkets—were all subsumed into *poniemieckość*. Such abandoned objects received new meanings and were invested with new emotions. The

Germans themselves are, unfortunately, not among the narrators of *Przepro-wadzka*. They have no voice and exist exclusively through the objects and spaces that once belonged to them. Only the inclusion of German narratives in the project would give a full picture of Szczecin's migrations, but it proved easier for the makers of "Moving Houses" to reach Polish Jews who emigrated after 1968 but who still return to Szczecin for their "'68 Reunions" than the Germans expelled after 1945.[51] Despite this silence, however, Fibich's performance visualizes spaces permeated by German absence. These spaces the post-1945 settlers in Nie-buszewo—whether Jewish or non-Jewish—colonize with their own brittle, impermanent order.

In 1968, the transient nature of the hospitality provided by the new Szczecin became clear. Some of the voices in *Przeprowadzka* speak of hostility and violence against Jews, recalling the traumatic events that made their families leave Poland. Róża Judkewitz cannot forget the cobblestone street that she walked with her brother on the way home from school. There they were attacked by other children who shouted abuse and threw stones at them. The construction workers paving the street did not react at first, but when Róża's brother reached for a stone to throw back at their attackers, the workers caught him and brought him to a militia station. Upon collecting his son from the cell where he had been locked up after the incident, Róża's father decides, "This is enough now. Now we will make the application to leave."[52] Interviewed years later in Hamburg, Róża Judkewitz remembers the fear that accompanied her on her way home that day but also the terracotta lilies of the valley that adorned the entrance to her house in Szczecin. They remain her favorite flowers today.

Fibich seems to be fascinated by the multiple layers of personal history that accrete in a single urban space. Part of her performance takes place in a tenement house that overlooks a picturesque park. The site is a popular spot for family photo sessions. The artist, who found archival photographs of the park, placed half-transparent prints of them on the window panes of the building. Thus, looking out onto the park, spectators also look into the past. The photos become a prism that forces viewers to rethink the physical space before them. Current residents' emotional attachments to a place they know so well are overlaid with the emotions of others who were connected to it previously. "Moving Houses" is, therefore, an exercise in "respatialization." The spectators are not only exposed to other people's emotional topographies of Szczecin; they are also forced to relive some of the disorientation and anxiety experienced by those who had to emigrate. Their documents taken away from them at the beginning of the show, they are transported to unknown destinations and forced to carry cumbersome boxes.

Szczecin's overwriting of Stettin took place not only in the realm of the living but also among the dead. The visual artist Karolina Freino's 2007 project "Walls and Sandpits" (*Murki i Piaskownice*) addressed the obliteration of Stettin's ne-

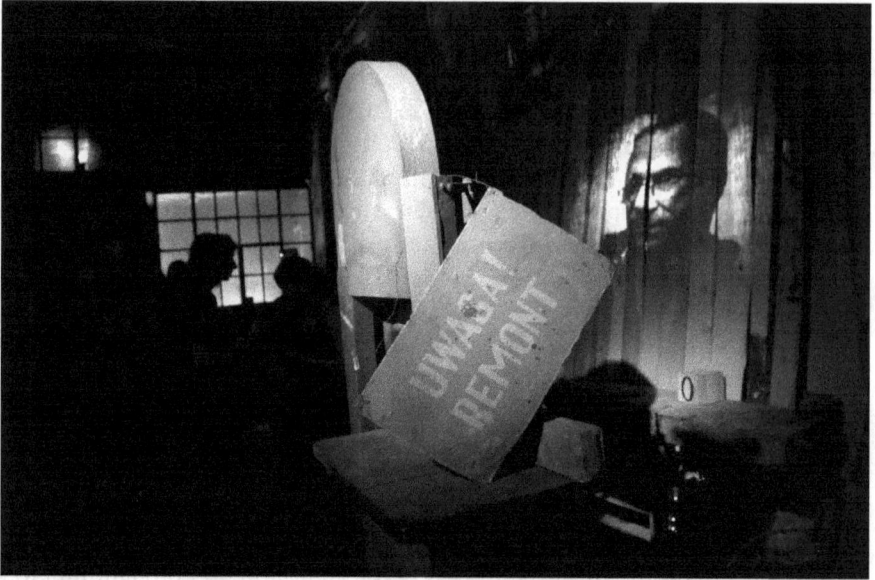

Figure 4.3. *Moving Houses,* 2009, an oral history interview projected on the wall of a former factory in Niebuszewo. Photograph by Ewa Ciechanowska

cropolis. Documenting the desecrated and fragmented German and Jewish tombstones recycled into Szczecin's walls, sandpits, and pavements, Freino mapped the whereabouts of these rejected fragments of the city's past and carried out an act of cultural translation, returning living significance to this funerary debris. Freino photographed forty sites where broken tombstones were used as building material and published a series of diptych death notices in the local newspapers. The notices, which appeared over the course of a month in four local papers, featured photographs of the fragmented tombstones, descriptions of their current locations, and Polish translations of their inscriptions. By deciphering the epitaphs, Freino restored the stones' meaning as texts of mourning and moved them from the realm of pure functionality to the sphere of the sacred. Her death notices, truncated, unfinished, and mutilated, are powerfully expressive. They provoke a discussion about the annihilation of other cultures in Szczecin and, at the same time, perform a symbolic ritual of mourning.

Evoking the universal experience of bereavement, Freino's project probes the limits of empathy across ethnic boundaries. Her death notices are not, however, an attempt to mend the damage. Rather, they delineate a third space. The stones they depict cease to be anonymous walls and pavements, but their original whole-

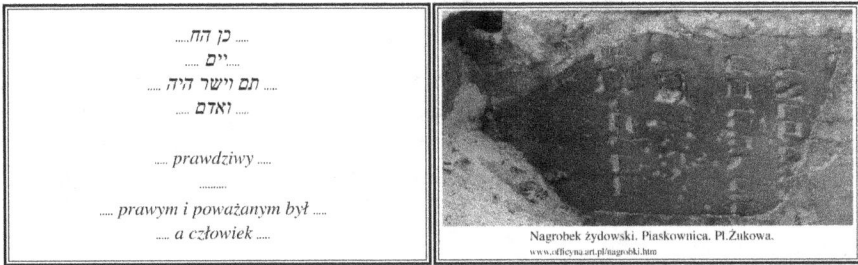

Figure 4.4. An obituary by Karolina Freino, 2007: ". . . a real. . . . /. . . . /. . . . he was a righteous and respected. . . . /. . . . but a man. . . ." A matzevah found in a sandpit in Żukowa Square, Szczecin. Photograph by Karolina Freino

ness is not restored either. In the act of translation, some of their meaning is salvaged, but the broken epitaphs eventually testify to the impossibility of retrieving the original text. They remain unclear, mysterious, dissonant. Although Freino's project tries to remedy oblivion, it does not restore order. It only documents destruction.

"Walls and Sandpits" provoked considerable reaction in the city. The author received many letters in support of her initiative. Others sent her information about where further tombstones could be found. Even the Municipal Conservator responded with an explanation of the desecrated tombstones' legal status. The destroyed necropolis seems, in fact, to be inspiring an outpouring of commemorative projects. In 2006, the municipal authorities opened a lapidarium for German tombstones at the central cemetery in Szczecin. Mikołaj Rozen, head of the local Jewish community, made plans for a similar initiative at the former Jewish cemetery. He wants to relocate Jewish matzevot that were previously recycled or abandoned all across Szczecin. Rozen believes that placing the matzevot in rows suggesting the layout of a Jewish cemetery (even without the actual human remains, which were disinterred in 1982) would not only be a respectful way to accommodate the displaced tombstones, but also a means of reclaiming a historic Jewish space.[53]

The problem of misused Jewish matzevot is not limited to Szczecin. As Łukasz Baksik's 2010 photography exhibition "Matzevot for Everyday Use" (*Macewy codziennego użytku*) poignantly illustrated, Jewish cemeteries were desecrated and their matzevot recycled in localities throughout Poland. Gravestones removed from Jewish cemeteries were not only used to pave streets and build stairs, barns, park pergolas, or septic tanks. They were also converted into querns, grinding wheels, and even Catholic tombstones.[54] To confront the problem, Baksik, together with a "Society for Creative Initiatives ę," launched an educational project entitled "Matzevah Return Manual" (*Instrukcja Powrotu Macewy*). The educational program proposed by the activists develops practical ways of retrieving misused matzevot in local communities. In many cases, this manual of what to do "if you stumble upon a matzevah" is the first attempt to map Jewish spaces in the consciousness of the local inhabitants.[55] Retrieving matzevah fragments, therefore, means also retrieving memory.

Conclusions

This process of regaining memory appears to be well underway in Szczecin. The nostalgia for a different time and place may actually be more acute in the Recovered Lands than it is elsewhere in Poland. The "repatriated" population of Szczecin was discouraged not only from openly expressing nostalgia for their homes abandoned in the Kresy but also from acknowledging the true nature of the post-1945 expulsion of Germans or the antisemitic campaign of 1968. The city seems to contain, therefore, enough potential for longing. Yet, as Yi-Fu Tuan notes in *Space and Place*, migration does not always result in sighing for the past. "When a people deliberately change their environment and feel they are in control of their destiny, they have little cause for nostalgia." It is different, however, when rapid changes take place, and people feel they are "spinning out of control." In moments of uncertainty, "nostalgia for an idyllic past waxes strong," warns Tuan.[56] The year 1989 marked a very important turning point for the memory of others in the so-called Recovered Lands. A possibility for addressing the traumas related to the post-1945 mass migrations to and from Szczecin was opened in tandem with rapid systemic changes that deeply transformed the lives of the people. This moment of upheaval also triggered a revisioning of local identities.

"Preservation is fine for the past that is long past, but yesterday is thought of as something to dump," writes Kevin Lynch.[57] By the 1990s, the interwar years and the immediate postwar period already belonged to a past distant enough to be worthy of revisiting. At the same time, the Communist myth of the Recovered Lands as essentially Slavic and culturally homogeneous lost its appeal. And as this yesterday was discarded, Szczecin found itself in need of an alternative narrative of its past.

The contemporary prose and art projects that aim to rediscover the Jewish and German spaces of Stettin/Szczecin ought to be considered both in the framework of Upstone's post-space, and Bhabha's third space. The new narratives about Stettin/Szczecin that such projects offer open ways to resist the post-1945 myth of spatial order that claimed Szczecin as a purely and timelessly Polish city. Further, as these narratives critically interrogate myths of unity and reveal processes of cultural translation, they transcend even the dichotomy of Stettin versus Szczecin. In so doing, they open up a fascinating third space where the city's German,

Polish, and Jewish elements converge, a process that both acknowledges and creates hybrid and transient realities that escape straightforward categorization.

The historically brief moment of post-1945 ethnic heterogeneity fascinates both artists and cultural organizers. The guidebook to Niebuszewo created by OFFicyna seems to envision the district as a kind of borderland arcadia, a place that serves as Szczecin's symbolic melting pot, accommodating Poles, Jews, Russians, Ukrainians, Roma, and even Germans. Yet this multiethnic enclave has also become an object of critical inquiry. The projects I discuss here present urban spaces not only as hybrids, reflecting the past *coexistence* of cultures, but also the brutal attempts to efface otherness.

The multiethnic Szczecin has undoubtedly become an attraction. With new, guided tours and art events organized throughout the district, Niebuszewo has reemerged on the city map as a neighborhood worthy of attention. But its voices (via Fibich's "Moving Houses") and its walled-in secrets (in Freino's "Walls and Sandpits") reveal truths that clash with saccharine visions of Szczecin as a Polish/German/Jewish melting pot. The respatialization of Germanness and Jewishness in the cityscape, undertaken in contemporary writing and performance art, corresponds to a degree with municipal authorities' attempts to present Szczecin as a city with a multicultural past and "blurred borders." On the other hand, these new narratives compellingly illustrate how postwar emigration waves and the events of 1968 put a definitive end to the city's multicultural past. If these projects express a nostalgia for the multiethnic history of Stettin/Szczecin, they also make clear that it is irretrievable. Viewing the Polish/German/Jewish borderlands through the rearview mirror, these new narratives also demonstrate that, as Svetlana Boym puts it, "The object of nostalgia is further away than it appears."[58]

Notes

I wish to thank the head of the Jewish Socio-Cultural Association in Szczecin, Róża Król; the head of the Jewish Community in Szczecin, Mikołaj Rozen; the head of the Cultural Association OFFicyna, Bartosz Wójcik; and Robert Grabowski from Szcecin's Municipal Press Office, as well as Małgorzata Frymus, Karolina Freino, Weronika Fibich, and Ewa Ciechanowska for their kind help and for granting me access to archival, multimedia, and visual material related to their artistic projects.

1. See Paula Sawicka, "Nie tak łatwo odczarować słowo 'Żyd,' ale próbujmy." *Gazeta Wyborcza Warszawa*, March 25, 2010, 2; Jerzy Bralczyk and Agnieszka Kowalska, "Odczarujmy słowo 'Żyd,'" *Gazeta Wyborcza Warszawa*, March 23, 2010, 2; and Dorota Jarecka, "Kicz to sztuka szczęścia. Prowokacja czy ściema," *Gazeta Wyborcza*, May 29–30, 2010, 21. For more details on the project, see: http://www.tesknie.com/.

2. See Agnieszka Kowalska, "Z tęsknoty za Żydem," *Gazeta Wyborcza Warszawa*, January 19, 2010, 1; "Pokażmy, że tęsknimy," *Gazeta Wyborcza Warszawa*, March 6, 2010, 2; and Wojciech Karpieszuk, "Żydzi—tęsknimy!" *Gazeta Wyborcza Warszawa*, March 29, 2010, 3.

3. "Strategische Prioritäten für die Bewerbung Szczecins um den Titel Kulturhauptstadt Europas 2016" (leaflet).

4. Tadeusz Białecki, "Pierwsze lata polskiego Szczecina 1945–1949," in *Dzieje Szczecina 1945–1990*, ed. Tadeusz Białecki and Zygmunt Silski (Szczecin: Wydawnictwo 13 Muz, 1998), 51–73; Tadeusz Białecki, "Ludność," in ibid., 161–188.

5. Although Szczecin is featured on the Virtual Shtetl website, an interactive documentation project of the Museum of the History of Polish Jews in Warsaw, the regions belonging to the so-called Recovered Lands have the smallest number of entries in comparison to the other regions of Poland; see http://www.sztetl.org.pl/en/city/szczecin/. The Foundation for the Preservation of Jewish Heritage in Poland does not list any revitalization projects in the Szczecin region; see *Annual Report 2013*, http://fodz.pl/download/1fodz_raport_2013_www.pdf.

6. For more information on the Hassidic Route, see the Foundation for the Preservation of Jewish Heritage in Poland, the Hassidic Route, n.d., http://fodz.pl/download/FODZ_ulotka_szlak_en.pdf.

7. See the guidebook by Agnieszka Sabor, *Sztetl: Śladami żydowskich miasteczek* (Kraków: Austeria, 2005).

8. Jacob Peiser, *Die Geschichte der Synagogen-Gemeinde zu Stettin* (1935; Würzburg: Holzner Verlag, 1965), 21; Andreas Brämer, "Der lange Weg von der Duldung zur Emanzipation (1650–1871)," in *Die Geschichte der Juden in Deutschland*, ed. Arno Herzig and Cay Rademacher (Bonn: Ellert and Richter Verlag, 2008), 80–97.

9. See Piotr Fiuk, "Architektura dziewiętnastowiecznej synagogi szczecińskiej," in *Żydzi oraz ich sąsiedzi na Pomorzu Zachodnim w XIX i XX wieku*, ed. Mieczysław Jaroszewicz and Włodzimierz Stępiński (Warsaw: DiG, 2007), 163–173.

10. "Synagoga" and "Żydzi," in *Encyklopedia Szczecina*, ed. Tadeusz Białecki (Szczecin: Uniwersytet Szczeciński, 1999), 441–442, 739–740.

11. Peiser, *Die Geschichte der Synagogen-Gemeinde zu Stettin*, 127–128.

12. Wolfgang Wilhelmus, "Die Lubliner Judenliste: Die erste Deportation deutscher Juden vom 13. Februar 1940 aus dem pommerschen Regierungsbezirk Stettin," in *Die Namensliste der 1940 aus dem Regierungsbezirk Stettin deportierten Juden: Zeitgeschichte Regional*, Heft 3, Januar (Rostock: Geschichtswerkstatt Rostock, 2009), 4–13.

13. "Żydzi," in *Encyklopedia Szczecina*, 739–740.

14. Anna Kafel, "Niebuszewo–dzielnica niechciana," in *Spacerkiem po Niebuszewie* (Szczecin; Wydawnictwo Forma, 2009), 67.

15. Marcin Stefaniak, "Nielegalna emigracja Żydów z Pomorza Zachodniego w latach 1945–1948," in *Żydzi oraz ich sąsiedzi na Pomorzu Zachodnim w XIX i XX wieku*, 365–376; Janusz Mieczkowski, "W poszukiwaniu miejsca–z historii Żydów w Szczecinie," *Pogranicza: Szczeciński Dwumiesięcznik Kulturalny* 4 (2003): 75–88; *Spacerkiem po Niebuszewie*, 82–83.

16. Janusz Mieczkowski, *Między emigracją a asymilacją: Szkice o szczecińskich Żydach w latach 1945–1997* (Szczecin: Towarzystwo Społeczno-Kulturalne Żydów w Polsce, 1998).

17. Małgorzata Frymus, "Następcy Tronów," *Pogranicza: Szczeciński Dwumiesięcznik Kulturalny* 4 (2003): 86–88.

18. See Eryk Krasucki, *Żydowski marzec '68 w Szczecinie* (Szczecin: Towarzystwo Społeczno-Kulturalne Żydów w Polsce, 2008).

19. Mikołaj Rozen, "Żydzi w Szczecinie," a speech given during the seminar "Żydzi na polsko-niemieckim pograniczu–po śladach," Groß Neuendorf, 17 June 2007, available at the website *Transodra Online*, http://www.transodra-online.net/pl/node/1421. See also Róża Król, "Współczesne problemy środowiska Żydów szczecińskich," in *Żydzi szczecińscy: Tradycja i współczesność: materiały z sesji naukowej, 27 czerwca 2003*, ed. Kazimierz Kozłowski and Janusz Mieczkowski (Szczecin: Dokument, 2004), 155–159.

20. Leszek Goliński, "Szczecin," in *Odra szumi po polsku*, ed. Leszek Goliński and Franciszek Fenikowski (Poznań: Wydawnictwo Zachodnie, 1946), 30. In the original, "Szczecin jest twardy jak but zwycięzcy / Szczecin jest mocny jak dłoń żeglarza / Nie przychodzimy tu, aby tęsknić / Lecz by panować, by trwać i stwarzać!"

21. For a discussion of a similar case of a formerly German Polish city of Wrocław, see Gregor Thum, "Wrocław and the Myth of the Multicultural Border City," *European Review* 13, no. 2 (2005): 227–235.

22. "Szczecin: Tu zacierają się granice," *Urząd Miasta Szczecin*, http://www.szczecin.eu /baltic_neopolis/atuty_miasta/szczecin_takze_wyjatkowe_polozenie_geograficzne.html.

23. Svetlana Boym, *The Future of Nostalgia* (New York: Basic Books, 2001), 41, 49, 50.

24. Rob Shields, *Places on the Margin: Alternative Geographies of Modernity* (London: Routledge, 1992), 7, 31, 46.

25. Ibid., 52.

26. Artur Daniel Liskowacki, *Eine kleine* (Szczecin: Wydawnictwo 13 Muz, 2000), 140–141. All English-language translations are by me; hereafter cited in the text.

27. Doreen Massey, *For Space* (London: Sage, 2005), 9, 59.

28. Walter Benjamin, "Naples," in *Reflections* (New York: Schocken Books, 1986). Cited in Boym, *The Future of Nostalgia*, 76–77.

29. Boym, *The Future of Nostalgia*, 76–77.

30. Sara Upstone, *Spatial Politics in the Postcolonial Novel* (Farnham: Ashgate, 2009), 6.

31. Michał Cichy, "Requiem dla Stettina," *Gazeta Wyborcza*, June 16, 2001, 19.

32. Joachim Schlör, "'Take Down Mezuzahs, Remove Name-Plates': The Emigration of Objects from Germany to Palestine," in *Jewish Cultural Studies*, vol. 1, *Jewishness: Expression, Identity, and Representation*, ed. Simon J. Bronner (Oxford: The Littman Library of Jewish Civilization, 2008), 138.

33. Ibid., 142, 147.

34. Inga Iwasiów, *Bambino* (Warsaw: Świat Książki, 2008), 71. All English-language translations are by me; hereafter cited in the text.

35. Upstone, *Spatial Politics in the Postcolonial Novel*, 115, 116.

36. Taube Kron, "Droga do domu," *Pogranicza: Szczeciński Dwumiesięcznik Kulturalny* 4 (2003): 25.

37. Anna Frajlich, "Mój Szczecin?" *Pogranicza: Szczeciński Dwumiesięcznik Kulturalny* 4 (2003): 32.

38. Clippings from *Dos Naje Leben*, nos. 12, 18, 46 from 1946 and no. 27 from 1947, cited in the appendix to Peiser, *Die Geschichte der Synagogen-Gemeinde zu Stettin*, 154–157.

39. Eryk Krasucki, "Antyżydowski tumult w Szczecinie w 1946 r.," *Gazeta Wyborcza Szczecin*, February 1, 2008, 7.

40. Adam Zadworny, "Zabijali Niemców z zemsty," *Gazeta Wyborcza*, 18 January 2008, 4.

41. Katarzyna Weintraub, "Karp pożydowski," *Pogranicza: Szczeciński Dwumiesięcznik Kulturalny* 4 (2003): 36.

42. See Stefaniak, "Nielegalna emigracja Żydów z Pomorza Zachodniego w latach 1945–1948," and Joanna Wójcik, "Lejbuszewo? O niebuszewskim tyglu kultur i religii," in *Spacerkiem po Niebuszewie*, 82.

43. Homi K. Bhabha, *The Location of Culture* (London: Routledge, 1995), 28, 218, 25, 219.

44. Upstone, *Spatial Politics in the Postcolonial Novel*, 14.

45. Weintraub, "Karp pożydowski," 41:
W tej wszechobecnej poniemieckiej rzeczywistości określenie "po babci" było rodzajem przenośni, skrótem myślowym odnoszącym się wyłącznie do serwisu Rosenthala z cienkiej porcelany koloru kości słoniowej. Taki sam serwis dziadek kupił dla babci

w 32 roku podczas wspólnej podróży do Berlina. Ironia czy też może zrządzenie losu sprawiły, ze poniemiecki serwis połączył jak nikłą nicią świat naszego szczecińskiego domu z domem nieznanych mi dziadków na wileńskim Antokolu.

46. Ibid., 43.

47. Bartosz Wójcik, interview with the author, June 10, 2010.

48. Stowarzyszenie OFFicyna, *Spacerkiem po Niebuszewie*, 85: "atmosfera kresowego polskiego miasteczka."

49. Ibid., 16.

50. Chaim Sucholicki, interview with Weronika Fibich, in "Przeprowadzka," Kana Theatre Association, Szczecin, 2009.

51. Reunions of Jewish émigrés from Szczecin, organized by the local Socio-Cultural Association of Jews in Poland, took place in 2003, 2007, and 2010.

52. Róża Judkewitz (Zylberberg), interview with Weronika Fibich, in "Przeprowadzka," Kana Theatre Association, Szczecin, 2009.

53. Mikołaj Rozen, interview with the author, June 8, 2010.

54. Agnieszka Kowalska and Łukasz Baksik, "Macewy codziennego użytku," *Gazeta Wyborcza: Duży Format*, October 28, 2010, 8–10.

55. Society for Creative Initiatives ę, "Instrukcja Powrotu Macewy," http://instrukcjapowrotu.blogspot.com/.

56. Yi-Fu Tuan, *Space and Place: The Perspective of Experience* (London: Edward Arnold, 1977), 195.

57. Kevin Lynch, *What Time Is This Place?* (1972; Cambridge, MA: MIT Press, 1993), 42.

58. Boym, *The Future of Nostalgia*, 354.

5 Rediscovering the Jewish Past in the Polish Provinces

The Socioeconomics of Nostalgia

Monika Murzyn-Kupisz

> For our towns and villages the history of the shtetl is the greatest opportunity
> for a future. Quite simply, this is the past of these places, and without it we will
> not succeed in building an identity for the present.
>
> —Jarosław Zatorski, Mayor of Chmielnik[1]

IN FEBRUARY 2008, the premiere of the play *Żyd* (Jew) was staged at the municipal theatre in Bielsko-Biała. It provoked strong and differing reactions from Poles. While some Poles severely criticized the production or reacted to it with anger and outrage, others praised *Żyd* and lauded Artur Pałyga, its young Polish playwright, for creating a thought-provoking piece. The play is set in an economically depressed, provincial Polish town, a former shtetl. Its characters are a group of local teachers who have gathered to discuss how to welcome a guest to their school. But they are not expecting an ordinary visitor. Instead, the guest is a Holocaust survivor who grew up in town and once attended the school.

In his preparations for the Jew's visit, the school's principal evokes one of the most significant aspects of the evolving relationship between former shtetls and their Jewish history. The principal eagerly participates in the planning, pushing for public ceremonies to honor the visitor. The principal's pleas are calculated, however. They are due in large part to his assumption that the Jew must be rich. Thus, the principal reasons, if the Jewish visitor is sufficiently impressed by the town's welcome, he might be convinced to contribute money to refurbish the rundown school. Yet there is much more to the Polish-Jewish relationship than economics. In Pałyga's play, the teachers' meeting opens the floodgates for an outpouring of Polish attitudes toward Jews. Some of the teachers' comments reveal ignorance, while others invoke painful memories, strong stereotypes, and even prejudices. Conflicting emotions, ranging from guilt, shame, and hatred to nostalgia, admiration, and acknowledgment of the great Jewish contributions to Polish culture, are all voiced at the meeting. Since some of the characters are too young to have firsthand knowledge of Jews, they derive their views mainly from folklore and stereotypes. The older teachers, on the other hand, are able to draw on personal recollections from the 1950s and 1960s.

Both the play's content and the way that Polish audiences have responded to it point to how economic issues have become enmeshed with the multifaceted relationship between Poles and Jews. Perhaps most significantly, the play has shown how questions regarding Poles' attitudes toward Jews prior to, during, and after the Second World War now shape debates about Jewish heritage in Poland.[2] The difficult, unsettled context that *Żyd* brings out into the open is crucial to the ongoing "rediscovery" of Jewish heritage in Poland. My chapter considers what this rediscovery means for towns like the fictional one presented in *Żyd*, that is, former shtetls in the Polish provinces.

First initiated in the 1980s but intensifying after the fall of Communism in 1989, a gradual revival of memory of Jews has been underway across Poland. The growing significance of this process of rediscovery has been evident in several ways, including the rising popular interest in sites connected to the Jewish past, increased media coverage of matters related to Jewish heritage, and the many new scholarly publications on the topic. In addition, many vestiges of Jewish presence, such as synagogues and cemeteries, have been restored, and commemorative plaques and monuments have been created across the country. These efforts to restore memories of Poland's Jewish past have emerged both because of grassroots initiatives and because of externally organized projects. In many cases, restoring a locality's Jewish past has provided the basis for new cultural events and tourist attractions. Due to frequent visits by Jews and non-Jews alike, restored sites of Jewish memory have contributed to the stronger visibility but also commercialization of Jewish heritage throughout Poland.

This chapter takes up the ongoing discussion of the post-Communist rediscovery of Jewish heritage in Poland, and seeks to broaden it in three ways. First, it examines provincial towns. This focus is distinct from other studies, which have tended to look at contested spaces or prominent sites of commemoration in major urban centers. Primarily, the current research has addressed general tendencies, these urban sites' states of physical repair, or problems related to their commercialization.[3] These studies, however, have overlooked less known provincial towns, despite the fact that they have a special pride of place in the landscape of Jewish memory as former shtetls.[4] Indeed, provincial towns warrant particular attention precisely because of their disproportionately large Jewish populations prior to World War II.

Second, my research pays more attention to the dynamic process of interaction between individual actors and physical sites of Jewish heritage. In particular, I look at actors' diverse motivations and attitudes toward the sites with which they are engaged. Although a few scholars have begun to address this interrelation between tangible and intangible heritage in the Polish-Jewish context, much work remains to be done.[5] Further study will help to illuminate the social and cultural underpinnings of the physical changes to the Polish landscape, and address the ways that these changes are understood.

Third—and this is perhaps my key contribution—I insist on the necessity of integrating analysis of Jewish heritage brokering into a broader socioeconomic context. As I see it, this integration means exploring internal and external socioeconomic factors that may either inspire and facilitate the process of Jewish heritage rediscovery or hinder and even prevent it from taking place. As demonstrated by Pałyga's play, Jewish heritage revival cannot be understood without examining the roles of individual agents making choices within the complex socioeconomic contexts in which revival processes take place. Such contexts include, among others, the return to a market economy, local entrepreneurship, the revival of democratic local and regional governance, European integration, and general trends in the tourism market.

The town of Chmielnik, located 20 miles south of Kielce in central Poland, illustrates some of the opportunities and challenges surrounding Jewish heritage in small towns. Like other former prewar shtetls, Chmielnik was an important site of Jewish life. A Jewish community had existed there since the seventeenth century. Before the Second World War, Jews made up approximately three-quarters of the town's population. Jews also held a dominant position in local economic and cultural activities, shaping the town's traditions and its built environment.[6] For all these reasons, Jewish heritage—both its tangible and intangible expressions—constitutes a major part of the town's history, albeit one that after 1945 was unwanted, forgotten, or suppressed in local memory.

In contrast to many other places that have significant but untapped Jewish heritage potential, Chmielnik has witnessed a surge of diverse activities linked to Jewish heritage. Some of these efforts take novel approaches to celebrate the former shtetl's Jewish past. This is particularly interesting given that the Kielce region is commonly associated with Jewish suffering, the Holocaust, antisemitism, and the Kielce pogrom (July 4, 1946).[7] Furthermore, many former shtetls in the region are also widely thought to be in socioeconomic decline and are said to lack cultural vitality.[8] What is central, then, to Chmielnik—a seemingly unlikely site for the celebration of Jewish heritage—is the link between the rediscovery of heritage and local development strategies.

In this chapter, I examine this link and begin by introducing contemporary concepts of heritage, including the notion of "dissonant heritage" and its role as an asset in local development. I then consider the diverse groups of actors involved in heritage development in general and in the rediscovery of Jewish heritage in

Poland in particular before turning to the case of Chmielnik.[9] Finally, I explore the internal and external factors that have driven the rediscovery of Jewish heritage in Chmielnik and made the town so far a "success story" in this regard. My conclusion addresses the significant pitfalls and risks associated with the process of Jewish heritage revival in Poland, focusing particularly on challenges that affect small towns.

The Concept of Heritage: Actors and Stakeholders in the Heritage Market

From a socioeconomic perspective, cultural heritage is understood as a ubiquitous and heterogeneous set of tangible elements and immaterial values. These elements and values are derived from the past, but they are used for contemporary purposes.[10] Current approaches to heritage emphasize the need for an inheritor who welcomes and makes use of such relics. This use may be symbolic, meaning that the relics are used to build identity in the present. Heritage may also be put to commercial use, often in the form of tourist and leisure products.[11] Put another way, it can be said that "the concept of heritage relates to the ways in which contemporary society uses the past as a social, political or economic resource."[12] Thus, only those elements of the past that society deems useful will be preserved, promoted, and given a function independent of their professionally established artistic or historic value.

In examining the role of heritage, one must, therefore, distinguish between artifacts of the past that are accepted by local residents and those that are rejected as "dissonant" heritage. Gregory J. Ashworth and John E. Tunbridge distinguish four types of heritage dissonance.[13] The first is "disinherited heritage" or "heritage without inheritors," which emerges when migration, border shifts, ethnic cleansing, or other tragic events force an ethnic or religious group to depart from its former territory. In such cases, the promotion of homogenous national heritage often obscures or eliminates the legacy of absent ethnic or regional minorities. These groups' rich historical experiences may be ignored or distorted in official public representations of the past. A related second type is "non-conforming heritage," or heritage that, in absence or despite the presence of inheriting populations, is incompatible with dominant norms, ideologies, or the public image of an area.

How local residents perceive the place in which they live plays a key role in the creation of heritage. In presenting their past, people typically wish to accentuate the positive aspects of their town or region. They tend to highlight achievements of which they are proud and to conceal or at least downplay the significance of events that reflect negatively on their community. Elements of the past related to wars and other tragedies—the third type of dissonant heritage, referred to as "distasteful heritage" or "heritage of atrocity"—are rarely preserved and celebrated by inhabitants of regions whose image would be tarnished if such memories were openly recalled. But local inhabitants are not always fully in control of their heritage. In some cases, the identity of a town or region may be dominated by its "difficult" heritage, a state of affairs that may even relegate centuries of peaceful existence and development to the sidelines despite the desires of local people.[14] Even elements of the past that are widely accepted can create problems when they are used as heritage. Complex meanings are often simplified for easier digestion by mass audiences, and political or commercial factors may also influence the portrayal of particular aspects of the past. These influences result in aestheticized and distorted versions of history, which may not be in line with the local population's image of its past or historic records, creating the fourth type of dissonant heritage, the so-called distorted heritage.

Dissonance may also result when the same heritage is used by different actors or when it functions simultaneously on different identity levels—from personal and local to regional, national, and international. Furthermore, the socioeconomic changes that have taken place around the globe in the last decades have only increased the demand for heritage by inspiring a growing nostalgia for the real or (more often) imagined past.[15] Matters are further complicated by the fact that cultural heritage is currently seen as an important asset for local development and a potential competitive advantage in many places. As such, heritage is a resource that impacts the cultural activities or aesthetics of a given site, serving as the basis for the development of local pride, thereby strengthening identity, knowledge, creativity, and cohesion within a local community. Heritage may also help to attract tourists and shape the image of a given locale for potential investors and new residents. In effect, heritage can play a key role in the local economy by directly or indirectly influencing the creation of jobs and new sources of income.[16]

Given its tremendous economic significance, there are a broad range of stakeholders who have great interest in the meaning of and market for heritage. These stakeholders may act as discoverers, producers, or consumers of heritage; sometimes they even fulfill more than one role. Legal owners of the tangible elements of heritage, insiders such as local residents and members of local cultural associations, who often have intimate knowledge of heritage and local tourism entrepreneurs, can both be considered producers and consumers of heritage. Public authorities and organizations also hold significant stakes in heritage. In some cases, these bodies are in fact the owners of heritage. They may also provide financial support or shape policy and legislation related to heritage production.

There are important external actors, as well. Among them are different types of tourists, including those who consume heritage when they visit a given place out of nostalgia, as well as those who consume heritage for leisure, educational, or religious purposes. A second set of important external actors is composed of scholars and academic researchers. Members of this group help to "discover" heritage by providing information to other actors, but they also try to influence decisions about heritage in their own right. Finally, the media takes part in the heritage market by providing information and interpretation. Much like academics, the media may shape heritage by either promoting or downplaying some of its features.[17]

The case of Jewish heritage in contemporary Europe is a textbook example of the diverse spectrum of stakeholders involved in the heritage market. In post-Holocaust, post-Communist Europe, in particular, few aspects of Jewish culture are entirely restricted to the inner circles of Jewish religious or community life. Rather, they are often present in broader civic fora (particularly what Diana Pinto has called "Jewish spaces") and are thus subject to non-Jewish interpretation, participation, and influence.[18] In fact, in the Polish case, the group of stakeholders involved in the rediscovery of Jewish heritage at the local level is often overwhelmingly or even exclusively composed of non-Jewish actors. These include Polish enthusiasts intent on "discovering" this aspect of their locality's heritage, and academics involved in research projects on the Jewish past. Local leaders and elites, such as democratically elected municipal authorities (since 1990), the Catholic clergy, teachers, and employees of cultural institutions, may also influence local attitudes and activities, especially in smaller communities. These actors' motivations run the gamut from the wish to strengthen local identity, to the desire to improve the aesthetics of selected sites, to a sense of nostalgia for the past, to a desire to deal with the difficult past, to an understanding of Jewish heritage as a chance to attract tourists and promote the municipality. The overall interest level of contemporary local communities, including young people, local entrepreneurs, and artists, in becoming involved in heritage rediscovery is also important.

Despite the fact that only a tiny Jewish community remains in present-day Poland, Jewish actors exert influence on the country's Jewish heritage. These Jewish stakeholders include both the official Jewish communities in larger Polish cities, which act as owners and managers of Jewish communal property, and a range of Jewish visitors from, and institutions based, abroad.[19] These various Jewish actors have strikingly different attitudes, needs, and expectations with respect to Poland's Jewish heritage.[20] Associations of Jews hailing from a given Polish town may be interested in preserving prewar memories, for example, but not their physical spaces. After years of ambivalent exile from their birth places, some former Jewish residents or their descendants may decide to (re)visit Poland, searching for their roots, commemorating the Holocaust, participating in cultural events, or even paying visits to individual Polish families.[21] Hassidic Jews often travel as pilgrims focused on religious experiences. Israeli youth often come to Poland on national "civil religious pilgrimages" that takes them to death camps and other sites of extermination, with the aim of strengthening national identity and group belonging.[22] Other Jews are driven by sheer curiosity or encounter Jewish heritage by chance during a vacation.[23] Regardless of Jews' motives for visiting Poland, however, it is clear that in the end, their involvement in matters of Jewish heritage is the result of an individual or collective choice: some visiting Jews wish to cooperate with local actors while others do not.

Finally, public authorities at the regional and national levels play a role in the development and management of Jewish heritage. These actors make decisions about the inclusion of Jewish heritage in broader development strategies and policies, or the availability of EU funding for heritage projects. Now that even non-Jewish tourists, both foreign and domestic, have begun to show interest in visiting Jewish heritage sites, developing these sites has become an important issue for public authorities. The information provided by the media on Jewish heritage projects influences local attitudes and the demand of tourism.

The growing significance of Jewish heritage in Poland's major cities has begun to spill over to the country's smaller towns, as well.[24] Even in these small provincial towns, the same broad range of stakeholders—from local people to Jewish communities, government officials, academics, the media, visitors, and tourists—are involved. Looking at the process by which Jewish heritage is rediscovered and put to use in former shtetls thus offers a window into the process of heritage formation. By turning now to the town of Chmielnik, I offer an in-depth look at one case of Jewish heritage formation in the Polish provinces.

The Changing Fortunes of a Little Town and Its Present-Day Socioeconomic Context

Chmielnik has existed as a settlement since the Middle Ages. It received city rights in the sixteenth century and became an important center of Calvinism and the Polish Brothers pacifist movement (also known as Aryanism) during the Reformation. In the second half of the seventeenth century, however, Catholicism once again became the city's dominant religion, a change that was evident in the erection of a new baroque church. Nevertheless, Chmielnik's Jewish community also emerged during the same century. The Jewish quarter initially developed north of the main square, and by 1638, it had grown to include a synagogue. A Jewish cemetery was also created around this time. When the Aryans were expelled from the city in 1658, Jews took over their homes and shops. Before long, Jews had come to dominate trade and production in Chmielnik.[25] By the late eighteenth century, Jews constituted over half of the local population, and at the turn of the twentieth century, 78 percent of the town's inhabitants were Jews. In this sense, Chmielnik was a typical shtetl.

Jews continued to dominate Chmielnik's townscape during the interwar period. Although many Jews moved to bigger urban centers such as Kielce or simply left Poland, until World War II four out of five craft workshops and stores in the town remained Jewish. For the most part, these small businesses provided services

Figure 5.1. View of the market square in Chmielnik prior to World War II. United States Holocaust Memorial Museum, courtesy of Varda Kleinhandler Cohen

for Catholic peasants living in the surrounding countryside. Jews also dominated local gastronomy, and they were particularly renowned for their goose dishes. Thanks to Jews, therefore, Chmielnik became well known for the production and distribution of goose meat. Jews were also owners and managers of larger enterprises such as the local quarries, a gypsum factory, a printing house, a distillery, and a sawmill.

Much of the town's built environment belonged to Jews. In the interwar years, the Jewish community owned and used a baroque synagogue, four prayer houses, a cheder (elementary school), a mikvah (ritual bath), and three schools. Much of this landscape was constructed during the nineteenth century. In 1820, a new Jewish cemetery was opened on Mrucza Street. Following major fires in 1849 and 1876, the town center was renovated. Wooden houses were replaced by brick and stone buildings, giving the town a more elegant look. Jews were also quite active in the community. In addition to participating in religious congregations and the Polish-Jewish city council, Jews worked in a variety of associations focused on culture, education, sports, and charity for the poor, sick, and disabled. Despite its small size, Chmielnik was thus a dynamic town whose prewar atmosphere, traditions, and outlook were largely determined by its Jewish community.[26]

Figure 5.2. A party of the Jewish Kleinhandler family in Chmielnik, 1936. United States Holocaust Memorial Museum, courtesy of Varda Kleinhandler Cohen

During World War II, the Nazis turned almost the entire town into a ghetto. At its peak in early 1941, the Chmielnik Ghetto housed some thirteen thousand Jews.[27] Many of these Jews were removed in October 1942, and by March 1943, the ghetto had been completely liquidated. Most of the Jewish inhabitants of Chmielnik were murdered at Treblinka or other extermination sites. Only about five hundred Chmielnik Jews survived the war. Very few of these survivors returned to the town, and those who did left Chmielnik for good after the Kielce pogrom.

The war brought many other significant losses to Chmielnik. Over three hundred private buildings were destroyed, and many more were damaged. Public buildings such as the town hall and the post office were also destroyed, as were industrial buildings and facilities, including the city's power station and about seven hundred shops and six hundred craftsmen's workshops. Losing its Jewish residents and suffering such physical destruction left the town without much of a chance to prosper in the new political situation that followed World War II. Its economy declined sharply. Like many other former shtetls, Chmielnik's population declined. By 1950, the town's population had dropped to less than half its prewar figure.[28] Furthermore, even once the town's population began to rebound because of migration from the surrounding countryside, it "became an ethnically homogeneous, typically Polish and Catholic town."[29]

Figure 5.3. Jews who have been expelled from Płock wait on a street to be resettled in the Chmielnik Ghetto, 1941. United States Holocaust Memorial Museum, courtesy of Varda Kleinhandler Cohen

Catholic Poles moved to the town and replaced Chmielnik's once large Jewish population. Despite the vivid memories of older residents, the former shtetl's Jewish past went publicly untold. The synagogue that the Nazis had desecrated was converted into a warehouse and then abandoned. Eventually, the building fell into disrepair despite plans to turn it into a cultural facility. The small building that had once housed a Jewish school was adapted to serve as Chmielnik's new town hall. Almost nothing remained of the Jewish cemetery on Mrucza Street. The Nazis had used shards of the broken matzevot (headstones) to pave roads during the war, and the Poles continued this practice after the war's end. The few surviving Jews who dared to revisit their hometown during the 1980s or early 1990s were reportedly met with hostility or indifference.[30] The main square, which was no longer used as a trading or meeting place, devolved into a poorly maintained, overgrown park adorned with a statue commemorating Red Army soldiers. It seemed that the only memories of Jewish life in Chmielnik were those held by Holocaust survivors or inscribed in the Chmielniker *yizkor* book.[31]

The political and economic transformations that occurred in Poland after the fall of Communism were initially very hard for Chmielnik. Similar to other small settlements that had stagnated during the Communist period, the little

Figure 5.4. The market square in Chmielnik after renovation, 2010. Photograph by Monika Murzyn-Kupisz

town struggled to find new ways to keep itself afloat after 1989. The intensive out-migration that occurred during the 1990s made the town's future even bleaker. Finally, after 2000, this out-migration stopped. Chmielnik has, in fact, staged a remarkable resurgence over the past decade. Between 1999 and 2008, the number of economic entities in the municipality increased from 583 to 727. This wave of entrepreneurial activity was far greater than in other nearby towns. The town has also significantly upgraded its infrastructure, renovating public buildings, adding new athletic and cultural facilities, and expanding access to the water supply and sewage system. Chmielnik now far outstrips other small communities as well as many nearby larger settlements in measures like the percentage of houses connected to the municipal water supply.[32] Although the town has not yet been able to attract a major new industrial investor, Chmielnik seems much more prosperous today than it was ten or twenty years ago. This apparent prosperity is confirmed by the town's high position in many regional development rankings and by the general good impression that it makes on visitors. The local cultural center has been renovated and enlarged. A building combining the functions of a town hall and a library was completed in 2011, allowing the town administration to relocate from the former Jewish school. Newly renovated houses now grace the town square. The once overgrown plaza has been redesigned and adorned with a variety of sculptures, flowerbeds, and a picturesque well.

The new town center's attraction is a Jewish-style restaurant located on the main square. During my visits, the restaurant's staff and local customers happily directed me to Chmielnik's Jewish heritage sites, a significant departure from the negative stereotype of backwater towns in the Kielce region, still confirmed by other former shtetls such as Działoszyce. Overall, in other words, Chmielnik has both prospered economically and grown far more comfortable with its Jewish past over the past ten years.

Jewish Heritage in Contemporary Chmielnik

Today, Chmielnik is often referred to as an example of a town where a striking change of attitude toward Jewish heritage has taken place.[33] In fact, in 2009, the town received the Rev. Stanisław Musiał Award for social initiatives promoting Christian-Jewish and Polish-Jewish dialogue.[34] Over the course of the last decade, Chmielnik's Jewish heritage has been rediscovered in diverse ways and inspired many activities, most of them linked with the locally initiated "Meetings with Jewish Culture" festival. Not only is the town's Jewish past officially acknowledged, but it seems to be increasingly tolerated, accepted, and at times even embraced by the residents of Chmielnik. The town is also now actively promoted to tourists as a former Jewish shtetl.

It is easy today for both Poles and foreigners to learn something about Chmielnik's Jewish past. Professional historians and amateur local history enthusiasts have become increasingly interested in this topic since the late 1980s, a trend that is reflected in the growing number of publications on the history and heritage of Chmielnik. The town is included in both scholarly works and popular literature on history and architecture in the Kielce region. Several monographs on the town, including residents' memoirs, have recently been published. Although such general interest publications do not focus explicitly on the subject, references to Chmielnik's Jewish heritage are present in all of them. Since 1989, Chmielnik has also been featured in writings on Jewish culture in Poland, including works published both domestically and abroad. Most importantly, researchers have begun to take particular interest in the town's Jewish past. Local archivist Piotr Krawczyk has been among the most active in this regard. Krawczyk writes of becoming increasingly convinced that "we cannot tell the history of Chmielnik without Jews."[35] He explains his conviction on the town's official municipal website: "The history of the Jewish community is intimately linked with the town's history . . . as it was the main director and creator of all events and situations in the settlement's centuries long existence. . . . That is why it is very important to become acquainted with the history of past times as well as ponder on how . . . despite different religious denominations, the town's residents jointly built the prosperity and greatness of Chmielnik."[36] Krawczyk has published a number of short texts and articles in the local and regional press based on his research. He also coauthored the first Polish monograph focusing on Chmielnik's Jewish heritage, which was published in Polish in 2006 and English in 2007.[37] Not only does this book present a general picture of Jewish life in prewar Chmielnik and describe the annihilation of Chmielnik's Jews; it also refers to particular people, customs, and events. References to the coexistence of Poles and Jews, the importance of Jews in the town's history, and Jewish heritage sites are also visible in the town's promotional materials and on its official website.

The town was among the first former shtetls to conduct an amateur oral history project. Supervised by their teachers, local secondary school students interviewed the town's oldest residents and recorded their recollections of life in Chmielnik prior to World War II. These testimonies revealed how deeply ingrained the Jewish presence is in the memories of the elderly, even if the recollections that they passed on to Chmielnik's young people were mainly rosy childhood memories influenced by subsequent life experiences and framed in the present-day atmosphere. All of the elderly residents acknowledged that Chmielnik was a Jewish town, and most of them stressed this point.

Such activities aimed at rediscovering the little town's Jewish past are inspired and actively supported by the local authorities. The town's popular mayor, Jarosław Zatorski, has played a significant role in furthering Chmielnik's Jewish heritage rediscovery. According to Zatorski, who has been reelected repeatedly since 1993, Jewish heritage is "our pride but also an obligation to remember."[38] He describes Jewish heritage in Chmielnik as both a touchstone for local identity building and a vehicle for promoting the town to tourists and potential investors.

In 2001, local authorities decided to emphasize the central role Jews played in Chmielnik's history during celebrations of the town's 450th anniversary. This was the first time since World War II that Chmielnik's Jewish past was put on display for the general public. A "Day of Jewish Culture" was added to the anniversary festivities. The streets were decorated and a market fair that recalled the town's prewar atmosphere was held. Even the dilapidated synagogue was opened to visitors. With assistance from their own teachers, a Jewish schoolteacher from Warsaw, and professional actors, local school children put on plays with Jewish themes. Chmielnik's association of retired people took part by preparing dishes according to Jewish recipes that they still remembered. It was after this first celebration that the mayor and his staff came up with the idea of developing a Jewish culture festival intended to both "put Chmielnik on the map" and increase the local community's awareness and appreciation of this part of its past.

Since 2003, the "Meetings with Jewish Culture" festival has taken place annually in Chmielnik and become a major success. Through dance workshops, exhibitions, performances by well-known Polish klezmer artists, and lectures and

Figure 5.5. A local klezmer group performs in the street during the 2012 "Meetings with Jewish Culture." Photograph by Monika Murzyn-Kupisz

meetings with Holocaust survivors, the festival serves as an introduction to Jewish culture as both a local and universal phenomenon. Moreover, the festival actively involves many locals, especially young people. Although some of the festival events are the work of professional artists, a significant portion of the events feature amateur singers and dancers. Theatrical presentations by enthusiastic local school students are one of the event's highlights.[39] Local artists, entrepreneurs, and craftsmen are also involved in the festival.

One of the intentions of the festival organizers is to promote openness toward outsiders and strangers. Face-to-face encounters at the festival facilitate dialogue between Jews who once lived in Chmielnik and the Catholics who live there today. As Chmielnik's mayor remarked, the "Day of Jewish Culture" in 2001 had but one major flaw: "It lacked the possibility of an authentic meeting with a real Jew."[40] Using archivist Piotr Krawczyk's contacts among Jews who had previously lived in Chmielnik, the festival's organizers set out to remedy this situation. As a result of their efforts, a former Chmielnik Jew, Meier Mały, has been invited to the festival every year as its honorary guest. Each year, he recounts his experiences living in Chmielnik, surviving the Holocaust, and settling in Israel, explaining Jewish customs and traditions all the while. Mayor Zatorski stresses that the festival's success owes much to Mały, who has "contributed greatly through his visits, encouraging and mobilizing us!"[41]

Figure 5.6. A music performance on the stage on Chmielnik market square during the 2012 "Meetings with Jewish Culture." Photograph by Monika Murzyn-Kupisz

Figure 5.7. Mayor Jarosław Zatorski and former Jewish resident of Chmielnik Mayer Mały laying flowers at the monument next to the Chmielnik synagogue as part of commemoration activities during the 2012 festival. Photograph by Monika Murzyn-Kupisz

Over time, other Jews have also begun to attend the festival, with more than eighty taking part in 2010. Mostly former residents, some of these visitors brought their families so that their children and grandchildren could see Chmielnik.[42] Many members of the younger generations were surprised by the warm welcome they received from the town's residents and local authorities. Arlene Garfinkel Speiser, whose parents survived the Holocaust, noticed a drastic shift in Chmielnik over the course of just eighteen years. When Speiser first visited the town, the experience was anything but welcoming. "In 1990, Speiser found the Jewish cemetery in ruins, and its broken tombstones paving Chmielnik's sidewalks. Spray-painted swastikas marred the synagogue. She heard people mutter, 'Go home, Jews'." Upon her return in 2008, however, Speiser found restoration work underway in both the cemetery and the synagogue. Mayor Zatorski even "kissed her hand at the ceremonies honoring five Holocaust survivors."[43]

A woman named Joyce Ann, whose father, Irwin Wygodny, grew up on a farm near Chmielnik, said she sees the festival itself as essential to the increased interactions between Poles and Jews. After her visit to the festival, Joyce Ann explained that she felt "that the festival is important to everyone at a lot of levels." She emphasized the significance of the festival as a place where "Polish people can meet Jewish people and know that we are real and not so different from them." She even said that she found "the integration of Jews and Poles during the festival" to be its "most impressive" aspect.[44]

Other Jewish visitors also remarked upon the integration on display at the festival. One former Jewish resident of Chmielnik repeatedly commented that she "must be dreaming" after watching a chorus of girl and boy scouts sing "Shalom Alecheim" in Hebrew and Polish. When she saw the Polish and Israeli flags flying side by side, "her heart beat nearly out of her chest."[45] Even Jewish guests without personal connections to Chmielnik have praised the festival. Miriam Akavia, a well-known Kraków-born Israeli writer who is the president of the Society for Polish-Jewish Friendship in Israel, was moved by the interactions between Jews and Poles she saw in Chmielnik. She said, "I am touched by everything I have seen here. . . . For many years, I have been working for the dialogue and friendship between our nations. We have managed to destroy many stereotypes, but there is a lot left to do. Events such as yours are very helpful in creating the dialogue."[46] The former Israeli ambassador to Poland, Shevach Weiss, also expressed his gratitude to the festival's organizers. "Our hearts are now open," he said, "because your young people are so interested in the past and often they ask their parents about their [former Jewish] neighbors."[47]

Government officials and regional leaders have noted the importance of the Chmielnik event for the local population. During the third festival, for example, Joanna Grzela, the deputy governor of the Kielce region, said, "It is a great honor for me to be here today with you and the guests from Israel. I am proud that . . .

Chmielnik . . . once a year becomes the capital of Jewish culture. . . . But the most important thing is that these young people are learning about Jewish culture, about tolerance and respect towards other nations."[48] Jerzy Daniel, the editor-in-chief of a regional cultural monthly, commented in a similar vein at the second festival:

> Today's meeting is the meeting of residents of Chmielnik, present and past. . . .
> [T]he fact that following a local government initiative mutual contacts take
> place allows young people to get to know who the Jews were: their grand-
> parents' former neighbors . . . get a chance to experience that Jews are not only
> some exotic individuals with beards and peyes coming from old paintings and
> photographs, but normal people with their own customs, tradition and cul-
> ture. It is good that we start speaking about the past without mutual preju-
> dices and complexes.[49]

Yet the young people of Chmielnik are not the only ones who have been affected by the opportunities for interaction provided by the festival. These interactions may reach far beyond this small town, playing a role in changing Poland's image in the eyes of Jews around the world. Following World War II, Poland was seen by Jews as little more than the site of the Holocaust. It was considered a backward, antisemitic country. Concentration camp sites were the main places Jews came to Poland to visit. Festivals like the one in Chmielnik, however, are starting to challenge this image. Due to press coverage, such events have affected not only the children of Holocaust survivors but also Jews with no Polish connections, as well as international public opinion more generally.

The festival has allowed local authorities to show the outside world—and especially the town's former Jewish residents—that present-day inhabitants of Chmielnik wish to commemorate the town's Jewish past, not to negate it. This signal of Polish interest in the Jewish past has inspired Holocaust survivors to offer the town financial assistance, thus making the rediscovery of Chmielnik's Jewish heritage a joint Polish-Jewish effort. The extent of cooperation between Poles and Jews was made evident during the 2005 festival. A monument on the side of the synagogue that emphasized the town's multicultural heritage was unveiled that year. While the funds for this undertaking were sent from Israel by the Kalish family, the project's design and implementation were left up to the local authorities. The monument commemorates the Jewish community and emphasizes the coexistence in Chmielnik of two nations—the Poles and the Jews. These points are expressed both in the monument's form and its poetic inscription.[50]

The rededication of the Jewish cemetery during the 2008 festival was another marker of Polish-Jewish cooperation. The idea to restore the cemetery came from the Cultural Association of Chmielnik. Again, the Kalish family contributed financially, while local authorities and the cultural center organized the de-

Figure 5.8. The "Oak Trees" memorial on the wall of Chmielnik synagogue. Photograph by
Monika Murzyn-Kupisz

Figure 5.9. The entrance to the rededicated Jewish cemetery on Mrucza Street in Chmielnik. Photograph by Monika Murzyn-Kupisz

sign and construction work. This extensive project transformed the cemetery into a memorial site. All the extant fragments of matzevot were assembled to form a monument, and the few remaining tombstones were cleaned and restored to their original places. Finally, a protective wall was built around the cemetery. The cemetery's new entrance gate features inscriptions in Hebrew, Polish, and English.

The synagogue building, while until recently largely in ruins, has been from time to time open to the general public as a site for Jewish cultural events. Particularly during the festival, the space surrounding the synagogue was filled with stalls and presentations. Yet town officials had larger aspirations for the former synagogue; they wanted the building to be lively year round. The success of the festival strengthened the municipality's 2006 application to the Ministry of Culture and National Heritage for financial assistance for basic renovations to the building. As no preservation work had been done since the 1960s, repairing the building's roof and gutters was crucial to prevent further deterioration, and served as the first step in a broader renovation project. Local authorities subsequently made the synagogue's restoration a priority in all local development strategies.[51] In 2008, they successfully applied for European Union regional funds in order to cofinance the project, entitled "Cultural and Education Centre—The Shtetl of the Świętokrzyskie Region," which concluded in 2013. Its total cost amounted to

7.2 million złotys ($2.5 million). Most of this sum—6.6 million złotys—was spent within the framework of the EU cofunded project (4 million provided by the European Regional Development Fund, 1.6 million by the municipality of Chmielnik, and 1 million by the Ministry of Culture and National Heritage of the Republic of Poland). The municipality also provided an additional 0.6 million złotys necessary for project-related expenses outside the EU cofunded project (data obtained directly from the municipality). The project is the most important element of Chmielnik's town center regeneration scheme, a status evident from the fact that one-fifth of the total regeneration budget for the entire municipality was allotted to restoring the synagogue.[52] In October 2009, regional authorities further acknowledged that they considered the project significant when they provided an additional 825,000 złotys to promote it.

Nizio Design International, a Polish firm well known for its innovative work designing museums, thematic expositions, and memorial places including the Museum of the Warsaw Uprising, has prepared an architectural and interior design concept. The multifaceted project includes a museum about the history of the town and its Jewish community, a modern cultural facility for local residents, and a memorial to the Chmielnik Jews who died in the Holocaust. At the same time, the design emphasizes the ambiance of the prewar shtetl. According to the plans developed by Nizio, the aim of the project is "to create a site vibrant with life." The designers foresaw the synagogue simultaneously as "the modern symbol of Chmielnik, . . . a tourist attraction, a cultural center, and a platform for meetings and scientific exchange."[53]

The project both explicitly acknowledges the town's multicultural past and highlights the significance of its Jewish community. The project will also employ an exciting new curatorial approach, one that understands the museum as a place of dialogue between the past and the present, and emphasizes audience engagement.[54] To achieve these varied ends, the synagogue's exterior was restored and renovated without significant changes, but the interior features an unusual cube-shaped architectural element, the so-called House of Light. Located in the former sanctuary, the House of Light is connected with the women's gallery via a flat roof made partially of glass. It serves as a concert and exhibition space.

Other elements of the synagogue were also restored or renovated in interesting ways. The bimah (pulpit), which was destroyed by the Nazis, was recreated based on prewar records, but the new bimah is built of glass, making it seem simultaneously real and unreal. The space between the House of Light and the original sanctuary walls forms the "shtetl streets." They function as exhibition space in which the history of the town and its Jewish community is presented. The exhibit runs from the Chmielnik Jewish community's origins, through the thriving nineteenth and early twentieth centuries, right up to present-day efforts to "reclaim memory." The Jewish heritage of other shtetls in the region, such as Działoszyce or Szydłów, is also mentioned. A library, as well as conference space and concert rooms, were set up in other parts of the building. Finally, the memorial to local Holocaust victims was built 50 feet north of the synagogue. It is composed of another, contrasting cube, the "House of Shadow." Visitors enter the cube through narrow openings, and once inside they face the names of the town's Holocaust victims written on the walls.

The Jewish festival and the extensive efforts to renovate Chmielnik's former Jewish spaces have inspired a variety of other endeavors connected with Jewish culture. Local artists have increasingly incorporated references to Jewish heritage in their art. In 2004, a klezmer band, "The Chmielnikers," emerged from the local cultural center. It was the first such group in the region. A non-Jewish Chmielnik family opened the small restaurant mentioned earlier called "Cymes" (a Polish word meaning "first-rate" borrowed from the sweet carrot and potato dish called "tsimes" in Yiddish) on the main square. The restaurant references Jewish culture in its decor and menu, which emphasizes the town's traditional goose dishes. Cymes is frequented not only by tourists; it has also become a meeting place for local residents. Thus, the restaurant has become a potential meeting place for the town's Christian Polish residents and visiting Jews, making it quite similar to several venues in Kraków's Kazimierz.[55]

The parish priests, and especially the parson, have also taken on an important role in the effort to reconnect Chmielnik with its Jewish heritage. Each year during the Jewish festival, the priests conduct an ecumenical service and prays the Kaddish (Jewish mourner's prayer). But significantly, their involvement extends to other times of the year as well. A special program introduces the main Jewish holidays to Catholic worshippers, presenting Jews as "Elder Brothers in Faith." On Palm Sunday in March 2010, for example, Hebrew psalms accompanied the presentation of ceremonies from a Jewish Passover Seder at the parish church.

The rediscovery of Jewish heritage is crucial to enhancing local pride and promoting Chmielnik as an interesting place to visit. The festival and related activities have been featured on television and radio programs and in newspaper articles in both Poland and abroad. All of this activity and attention has made Chmielnik an inspiration for other small towns in the region and even some towns farther afield. During the second iteration of the Chmielnik festival, the nearby town of Szydłów joined in. Since that time, one day of the festival always takes place there. Działoszyce and Pińczów participated in the third festival, and a Jewish heritage trail among the localities has been prioritized in regional tourism development plans. In short, the remarkable success of Chmielnik's Jewish festival and the town's growing spectrum of related events and activities have allowed the former shtetl to become a model for development in the region.

From Dissonant to Accepted: Making Jewish Heritage "Polish"/"Ours"

Chmielnik's open embrace of its Jewish heritage has had many positive consequences and caused observers to describe the rediscovery process as a success
story. I find that multiple, mutually reinforcing factors have contributed to the
town's special character. Among these is the existence of local enthusiasts who are
dedicated to uncovering the town's Jewish past. Over the past decade, the positive attitudes and dedicated efforts of a cast of strong local leaders (including the
mayor,[56] Catholic priests, employees of the local cultural center, and school teachers) have been essential to overcoming local people's initial predominant indifference and in some cases hostility toward all things Jewish. While the erection
of monuments in general is currently en vogue throughout Poland, Chmielnik's
authorities have tended to emphasize the town's past cultural diversity in the memorial stones, sculptures, busts, and plaques that they have dedicated.[57] Although
the local community does at times criticize the excessive number of new sculptures in the town's public spaces, they are now accustomed to such commemorative activities. The Jewish past has thus become a known, tolerated, and increasingly accepted part of local heritage.

Improving public aesthetics, restoring material heritage, renovating public
spaces, and strengthening local identity through cultural activities are all important elements of the local authorities' policy agenda. Jewish heritage has been
integrated into this broader vision of community development, a priority that is
reflected in the comparatively high and clearly growing share of spending on culture and heritage in the municipal budget. In a town where unemployment remains much higher than the regional average, heritage and culture did not initially
rank high in the local budget, but that has changed. From 1999 to 2008, municipal
spending per inhabitant doubled, but, as shown in figure 5.10, the amount spent
per person on culture and heritage in 2008 exceeded 1999 levels by almost nine
times. In 1999, the municipal government spent, in total, 272,519 złotys on "culture and art." In 2008, in contrast, 2,298,615 złotys ($789,902 based on exchange
rates as of December 30, 2008) was spent on "culture and national heritage." From
a metropolitan or foreign perspective, this may not seem like a lot of money (as it
is not even enough to cover the costs of one medium-size conservation project),
but for a small town in central Poland, it is a very sizeable sum.[58]

"Reclaiming memory" in Chmielnik is emerging as a long-term process in
which diverse activities involve multiple generations and various sections of the
local community. Not only young people but also their parents and grandparents
serve as participants and audiences. Members of these older generations provide
historical testimony and create the local products or artworks that are featured
at cultural events. In fact, Jewish heritage is presented in Chmielnik within the
framework of mainstream, local, Polish, predominantly Catholic memory. That

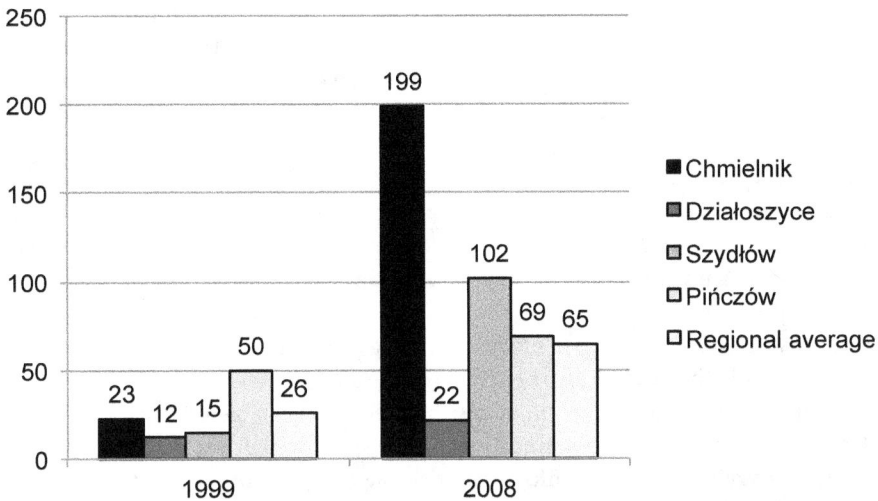

Figure 5.10. Spending per resident on culture and heritage in the municipal budget of selected former shtetls in Świętokrzyskie (Kielce) region in 1999 and 2008 in złotys. Główny Urząd Statystyczny Regional Data Bank

is to say, shared experiences and interactions between (Catholic) Poles and Jews are presented as a completion of the town's historical record rather than a radical revision of it. Indeed, some of the memory "restoration" activities are placed in a Christian context, and thus made to appear more familiar to the local community. Such "Catholization" of Jewish memory may offend the sensibilities of some Jewish observers, but it is also perhaps the most effective—or maybe the *only*—way for local residents to begin dealing with the memory of their prewar Jewish neighbors.

Presenting Jewish traditions to the general public in the parish church is a striking means of bringing Chmielnik's Jewish heritage into its current residents' daily lives. As mentioned above, an ecumenical church service has become an integral part of the annual Jewish festival. A Catholic mass containing the Jewish Kaddish involves both the local population and foreign Jewish guests. Following Christian practice, flowers are also brought to Jewish memorial sites and candles are lit at them. Catholic priests from the region do not simply participate passively in the festival as audience members or figureheads; they serve as active performers. Because priests are highly influential figures in the community, their participation legitimizes, shapes, and thus greatly advances the rediscovery of the town's Jewish past.

Finally, Jewish heritage is taking on lasting importance in Chmielnik because local authorities actively employ it as a new basis for local development in a town without a preexisting tourism sector. As the mayor has put it, "Jewish heritage is our main chance to make the town known and attractive."[59] This is an important contrast to other nearby former shtetls, which are known and promoted as tourist destinations based on their prominent Christian monuments or royal traditions, despite their Jewish histories. Chęciny, for example, boasts the ruins of a royal castle, while Szydłów markets itself as "Polish Carcassonne." Pińczów, which benefits from its position as the county seat, possesses significant Christian monuments and emphasizes the golden years of Protestantism and the brief yet heroic establishment of the Republic of Pińczów at the end of World War II in its image.

In addition to the internal factors driving the rediscovery of Jewish heritage in Chmielnik, the process also benefits from a range of external factors. First, discovering local and regional uniqueness has been fashionable in Poland and other Central European countries since 1989.[60] Uncovering the "exotic" multicultural heritage of religious and ethnic minorities is an important part of this trend. In Poland, this has included not only the discovery of Jewish heritage but also the Greek-Catholic heritage of the Lemkos and the German heritage of the country's western and northern territories.[61] Nevertheless, the fascination with Jewish heritage that has recently developed all across Europe privileges Jewish heritage discovery projects. Political support from the national and regional levels of government furthers this process, while Jewish heritage rediscovery projects in larger Polish urban centers provide another source of positive reinforcement.

Chmielnik also faces difficulties in its efforts to "discover" its Jewish heritage. But in comparison to other former shtetls, the town seems well equipped to handle many of them. The town's status as a regional leader and trendsetter gives it a clear competitive advantage in the commercialization of its Jewish heritage projects, though town leaders are keenly aware that other small localities are hot on their heels in this regard. Seen in this light, town officials' significant investment in their pioneering synagogue project can be interpreted as an attempt to sustain Chmielnik's edge. The availability of European Union funds for heritage projects further motivates the search for sites to "discover" and renovate. These funds enable many projects to be undertaken that local authorities could not otherwise afford. Location and access can also pose difficulties for the redevelopment of former shtetls. Although almost all former shtetls are peripheral backwaters, Chmielnik is in a relatively good position because it is located near an important crossroads of the main intraregional Kraków-Kielce road. Given these many factors and variables, Chmielnik's promising path toward redevelopment cannot be replicated in cookie-cutter fashion by other small towns. This is because the existence of rich heritage sites and the positive attitudes of local leaders are only two of the many conditions that have caused the Chmielnik project to flourish.

Increasing numbers of former Jewish residents and their descendants have begun to search for roots in Poland in the post-Communist era. As I have found in the case of Chmielnik, although their memory of Poland is often dominated by the tragedy of the Shoah, when dialogue is initiated between former Jewish residents and present-day Polish local communities, survivors and their families are often willing to support local Jewish heritage regeneration activities both morally (e.g., legitimating them through attendance at cultural and commemorative events) and financially, either by providing funds for specific memorial activities or, indirectly, through their tourist spending. The support of Jewish foundations and organizations, whether large-scale sources like the World Monuments Fund or more modest, often practical assistance from domestic Jewish institutions, is important. Direct encounters between Jews and non-Jews in the physical space of former shtetls or during joint visits to Poland and Israel in turn lead to the dismantling of some mutual stereotypes and suspicions. For example, according to the Chmielnik mayor, much of the anxiety of Chmielnik's local population with respect to Jews vanished when they saw that Jewish visitors to the town were motivated by nostalgia and identification rather than desires to solely emphasize their Holocaust experiences or reclaim property.[62]

Property ownership is another key factor in efforts to restore material heritage sites. In this regard, too, Chmielnik has been relatively fortunate.[63] The case of the synagogue restoration project is perhaps the most telling. As a result of intensive negotiations between Chmielnik officials and the Katowice Jewish Community, the latter decided to withdraw its claim to the property. Their agreement, which was supported by the Association of Chmielnik Jews in Israel, which is on very good terms with the Chmielnik local authorities, requires the town to restore the former synagogue and convert it into a museum and educational center. In contrast, the rediscovery process taking place in Pińczów, which started much earlier, lost impetus in part because the municipality is not the local synagogue's legal owner and could not, therefore, restore the building.[64] In Działoszyce, neither the current legal owner of the ruined remains of the synagogue located in the center of town—the Katowice Jewish Community—nor the municipal authorities seem to have any idea how to deal with the town's Jewish past.

The Chmielnik "success story" is, thus, the result of many factors, both internal and external. Local interest and town officials' support for rediscovery projects have been crucial, but factors like location, property ownership, and Chmielnik's place within the larger Polish and European heritage restoration projects have contributed greatly to the town's success as well. The contrast between Chmielnik and other former shtetls reveals just how important these factors have been. Indeed, though heritage restoration is a local project in Chmielnik, it must be viewed as part of a larger competitive framework. In addition to the competition for redevelopment funds and tourist spending, support and praise by the media makes diverse audiences aware of the Jewish heritage rediscovery process taking place in particular localities and engenders a sense of pride among local residents.

Challenges and Problems

Chmielnik and select other former shtetls in the Polish provinces have clearly made progress in terms of their relationships to Jewish heritage at the local level, a trend that is evidenced by the recent quantum leap from oblivion to acknowledgment, increasing tolerance, and, in some cases, growing embrace. Nevertheless it is clear that uneasy issues remain.[65] Almost any presentation of Jewish heritage may be worthy of initial praise. Yet local leaders and townspeople participating in the rediscovery of Jewish heritage must eventually take on the more complex, multiperspectival presentation of Jewish heritage. In this regard, major projects such as the innovative restoration concept for the Chmielnik synagogue can become either qualitative milestones in the understanding of a town's Jewish heritage or lost opportunities.

The prewar worlds of Jews and Christians were characterized by "side by side" existence rather than coexistence. Relations between the two communities were both symbiotic and ambivalent.[66] Yet, the memory of the shtetl is being modified in both Jewish and Polish consciousness due to changing social, political, and historical contexts. To many Poles, the shtetl embodies nostalgia for an idealized provincial past—and it also represents a time before the moral breach of the Holocaust.[67] Accordingly, they typically emphasize mutual links between Poles and Jews and peaceful coexistence in a framework of picturesque multiculturalism. Jews, by contrast, may see it as a backward place of deprivation and antisemitism, or conversely a site of ideal *Jewish* communal harmony and intimacy, entirely separate from the Christian population, who is widely perceived to have abandoned them during the Shoah. In both cases, Jews tend to emphasize segregation and the trials of Jewish-gentile relations.[68]

The original plans for the exhibition that is to be housed in the restored synagogue suggest some cognizance of these divergent worldviews, and a desire to engage visitors in understanding them. According to these plans, the exhibit was to use diverse archival materials in order to illustrate the multidimensionality of Jewish life in Chmielnik prior to World War II. A film in which two of the town's prewar inhabitants, a Pole and a Jew, walk through the city and explain the different meanings and memories that particular sites hold for them accompanies the archival materials. Still, the exhibit tends to focus only on the positive theme of coexistence and to exclude more contentious topics. Visitors are thus left to meditate on contentious issues individually, inside the separate space of the Holocaust monument. Such aesthetization of Chmielnik's Jewish past may not advance reconciliation among Poles and Jews, but it may have appeal among non-Jewish tourists, who are searching for pleasure, enjoyment, and "staged" authenticity rather than knowledge about the past.[69]

Excessive commercialization of Jewish heritage is also a threat, though for now it remains a rather distant one in the provinces. Although souvenirs and publications related to Jewish heritage are sold annually during the Jewish festival, there are still no local shops in Chmielnik selling such items year round. As in Poland's larger urban centers, however, it will be hard to avoid superficial presentations of Jewish heritage, which may enforce negative stereotypes despite good intentions. The inclusion of Jewish themes in local art is a good example. Despite their awareness of the diversity of Jewish life in Chmielnik prior to World War II, local artists prefer to depict only orthodox Jews, whom they consider more "picturesque."

This fetishization of orthodox Jews is not the only way in which local artists have resorted to stereotypes in their depictions of Jews. A portrait of Leopold Kozłowski, known as "The Last Klezmer of Galicia," shows the grinning musician holding what appears to be a bag of money. This painting is an excellent example of the intermingling of different frames of reference; it allows us to see how one person's genuine positive motivation can be another's offensive stereotype. To understand such a multivalent artifact in its local context, one must know that the portrait is part of a broader series of paintings intended as a tribute to Polish— and specifically Chmielnik—Jews by the local painter Małgorzata Gładyszewska. In the case of this particular portrait, the artist was personally acquainted with her subject, to whom she was grateful for performing at the festival, for which she designs stage backdrops. Kozlowski has approved the portrait, which was displayed as part of an exposition during the festival one year, and has traveled with Chmielnik students during Jewish-themed performances in other towns.

In other paintings in the series, Gładyszewska has depicted Jews in traditional orthodox attire, but these works are set in particular local spaces, reminding the local audience that Jews used to be real, living parts of the local landscape. Jews' former place in Chmielnik is expressed in the title of the exhibition, "I Can Hear Their Footsteps, I Can See Their Faces." From the local Polish perspective, then, the painting series can be seen as an expression of the powerful nostalgia for the town's lost Jews. As with many other popular references to Jewish heritage in contemporary Poland, the series is open to countervailing interpretations, however. The depictions may seem ghostly, inauthentic, or even disrespectful to some Jews, particularly those from abroad, yet from the local perspective, the paintings can be considered genuine attempts to come to terms with one's own group identity.[70] Artworks like Gładyszewska's paintings may thus be understood and interpreted differently by the local community, sympathetic Jewish visitors connected to the town, and other Jews or Poles.

Within the Jewish community, differences of opinion about the rediscovery of Jewish heritage in Chmielnik are not confined to the realm of art, however. Some Jews are unwilling to even participate in commemorative activities jointly with Poles. There have, as yet, been no orthodox or Hassidic Jews among the five thousand people who visited the dilapidated synagogue every year even prior to the completion of the restoration project. Observant Jews will also be unlikely to attend the festival or visit the renovated synagogue. At minimum, religious Jews would find the juxtaposition of the "House of Light" in the former synagogue and the "House of Shadow" Holocaust memorial on the former cemetery grounds in conflict with the traditional understanding of Jewish burial sites as "houses of life" or "houses of eternity."[71] In addition, some Jewish visitors to former shtetls such as Chmielnik may question the local population's motives in suddenly embracing their town's Jewish heritage. They may see it as an instrumental, mercenary attempt to attract visitors and garner external funds. The fifty thousand visitors projected to arrive in Chmielnik each year in order to see the renovated synagogue will undoubtedly make a sizable contribution to the local economy. In anticipation of them, a local entrepreneur is already building a hotel in the town center. Yet without the financial assistance received through tourism, Jewish heritage sites' improved state of repair will be difficult to maintain. The ten jobs that will be created by the synagogue project will be filled by young, well-educated locals who might otherwise depart for larger urban centers. These workers will become skilled "heritage brokers," forming an important, daily human interface to the museum for Polish and Jewish visitors alike.[72]

Direct contacts between Poles and Jews weaken mutual stereotypes about the past and present. Interest in Poland's Jewish heritage is a catalyst of such encounters. Every year, a group of Chmielnik residents including students, teachers, and persons involved in the organization of the festival travels to Israel. They meet Israeli youth and former Chmielnik residents, and visit Yad Vashem as well as Jewish and Christian historic sites. In exchange, former Jewish residents of Chmielnik, their families, other Israeli youth, and Jewish visitors from the United States visit the small town both during the festival and on other occasions. Given these interactions, Chmielnik has the potential to become a unique social space in which gentiles and Jews interact and meaningfully engage in Jewish culture both as its audience and its creators. In that sense, the Jewish heritage of Chmielnik may create "a malleable, discursive space, in which groups do not simply articulate established positions but actually come into being through their dialogical interactions with other."[73]

Whether or not this will happen depends much on the ability of diverse actors, most of all Chmielnik's present-day Polish community but also the town's present and potential Jewish partners, to continue the process of rediscovery. These actors must see the rediscovery project as an unfinished, long-term challenge to both restore heritage sites and present them to visitors to stimulate tourism, and as an opportunity to pose and openly reconsider difficult issues and questions related to the redefinition of individual and group identity.[74] The aim to "put Chmielnik on the map" through redevelopment and tourism, coupled with an understanding of the town's Jewish heritage as an inseparable part of its local identity, are key to the continuance of this process and to its eventual success. As I have shown

Figure 5.11. Portrait of Leopold Kozłowski, "The Last Klezmer of Galicia," painted by Chmielnik artist Małgorzata Gładyszewska. Photograph by Monika Murzyn-Kupisz

in this chapter, however, this rediscovery is dependent not only on goodwill and public interest in Jewish heritage but also on a variety of other factors. Most significant among these are the socioeconomic dimensions of nostalgia, such as the attitudes and capabilities (e.g., organizational, financial, cultural) of different actors and stakeholders, the economic situation of a particular town, the status of property ownership, and the evolving demand of tourism.

Notes

The views or opinions expressed in this chapter, and the context in which the images are used, do not necessarily reflect the views or policy of, nor imply approval or endorsement by, the United States Holocaust Memorial Museum.

1. Quoted in Agnieszka Sabor, "In Search of Identity," in *Reclaiming Memory: Urban Regeneration in the Historic Jewish Quarters of Central European Cities,* ed. Monika Murzyn-Kupisz and Jacek Purchla (Kraków: International Cultural Centre, 2009), 120.

2. Eva Hoffman, *Shtetl: The Life and Death of a Small Town and the World of Polish Jews* (Boston: Mariner Books, 1998); Joshua D. Zimmerman, ed., *Contested Memories: Poles and Jews during the Holocaust and Its Aftermath* (New Brunswick, NJ: Rutgers University Press, 2003); Dorota Glowacka and Joanna Zylinska, eds., *Imaginary Neighbors: Mediating Polish-Jewish Relations after the Holocaust* (Lincoln: University of Nebraska Press, 2007); Robert Cherry and Annamaria Orla-Bukowska, *Rethinking Poles and Jews: Troubled Past, Brighter Future* (Lanham, MD: Rowman and Littlefield, 2007).

3. Works addressing urban spaces include Ruth E. Gruber, *Virtually Jewish: Reinventing Jewish Culture in Europe* (Berkeley: University of California Press, 2002); Ian Leveson and Sandra Lustig, eds., *Turning the Kaleidoscope: Perspectives on European Jewry* (New York: Berghahn Books, 2006); and Murzyn-Kupisz and Purchla, eds., *Reclaiming Memory*.

4. For one of the few such studies, see Sławomir Kapralski, "Battlefields of Memory: Landscape and Identity in Polish-Jewish Relations," *History and Memory* 2 (2001): 35–58. For specialist guidebooks addressing the topic, see Agnieszka Sabor, *Sztetl: Śladami Żydowskich Miasteczek* (Kraków: Austeria, 2005), and Ruth E. Gruber, *Jewish Heritage Travel: A Guide to Eastern Europe* (Washington, DC: National Geographic, 2007).

5. For attention to such interactions, see Erica Lehrer, "Repopulating Jewish Poland—in Wood," *Polin* 16 (2003): 335–355; Monika Murzyn-Kupisz, "Reclaiming Memory or Mass Consumption? Dilemmas in Rediscovering the Jewish Heritage of Krakow's Kazimierz," in Murzyn-Kupisz and Purchla, eds., *Reclaiming Memory,* 363–396; Erica Lehrer, this volume; Michael Meng, *Shattered Spaces: Encountering Jewish Ruins in Postwar Germany and Poland* (Cambridge, MA: Harvard University Press, 2011); and Jean-Yves Potel, *La fin de l'innocence: La Pologne face à son passé juif* (Paris: Éditions Autrement, 2009).

6. Marek Maciągowski and Piotr Krawczyk, *The Story of Jewish Chmielnik* (Kielce: Chmielnik Municipal Office, 2007); Marek Maciągowski, *Społeczność żydowska w Chmielniku w XIX i XX wieku* (Poznań: Wydawnictwo Poznańskie, 2012).

7. Jan T. Gross, *Fear: Anti-Semitism in Poland after Auschwitz: An Essay in Historical Interpretation* (New York: Random House, 2006); Hoffman, *Shtetl.*

8. Elżbieta Trafiałek, *Starość w miasteczku Chmielnik* (Kielce: Gens, 2002).

9. My research includes analysis of statistical data, scholarly and tourism literature, memoirs, radio programs, municipal strategies, and promotional materials. I also visited Chmielnik and other former shtetls in the region and conducted interviews with local community leaders from 2010 to 2013.

10. Thus heritage consists, *inter alia*, of material evidence such as individual buildings, sites and complexes, artifacts, and archival documents, as well as traditions, customs, rituals, and skills.

11. Peter Howard, *Heritage: Management, Interpretation, Identity* (London: Continuum, 2003); Gregory J. Ashworth, Brian Graham, and John E. Tunbridge, *Pluralising Pasts: Heritage, Identity and Place in Multicultural Societies* (London: Pluto Press, 2007); Ullrich Kockel and Máiréad Nic Craith, eds., *Cultural Heritages as Reflexive Traditions* (New York: Palgrave Macmillan, 2007); Brian Graham and Peter Howard, eds., *The Ashgate Research Companion to Heritage and Identity* (Aldershot: Ashgate, 2008).

12. Brian Graham, Gregory J. Ashworth, and John E. Tunbridge, *A Geography of Heritage: Power, Culture and Economy* (London: Arnold, 2000).

13. Gregory J. Ashworth and John E. Tunbridge, eds., *Dissonant Heritage: The Management of the Past as a Resource in Conflict* (Chichester: Wiley, 1996).

14. See, for example, Sharon Macdonald's discussion of Nuremberg's struggles to manage the ruins of the Nazi rallying grounds in her book *Difficult Heritage: Negotiating the Nazi Past in Nuremberg and Beyond* (New York: Routledge, 2009).

15. David Lowenthal, *The Past Is a Foreign Country* (Cambridge: Cambridge University Press, 1985); Svetlana Boym, *The Future of Nostalgia* (New York: Basic Books, 2001).

16. World Bank, *Cultural Heritage and Development: A Framework for Action in the Middle East and North Africa* (Washington, DC: World Bank, 2001); Xavier Greffe, Sylvie Pflieger, and Antonella Noya, *Culture and Local Development* (Paris: Organisation for Economic Co-operation and Development, 2005); Jim McLoughlin, Jaime Kaminski, and Babak Sodagar, eds., *Heritage Impact 2005: Proceedings of the First International Symposium on the Socio-Economic Impact of Cultural Heritage* (Budapest: EPOCH [Excellence in Processing Open Cultural Heritage, an EU 6th Framework Programme], 2006); Allan Peacock and Ilde Rizzo, *The Heritage Game: Economics, Policy and Practice* (Oxford: Oxford University Press, 2008).

17. Howard, *Heritage*, 2003.

18. Diana Pinto, "The Jewish Space in Europe," in Leveson and Lustig, eds., *Turning the Kaleidoscope*, 179–186; Diana Pinto, "Negotiating Jewish Identity in an Asemitic Age," *Jewish Culture and History* 2–3 (2013): 68–77.

19. Michal Firestone, "The Conservation of Jewish Cultural heritage as a Tool for the Investigation of Identity," in Murzyn-Kupisz and Purchla, eds., *Reclaiming Memory*, 53–62.

20. Jonathan Webber, ed., *Jewish Identities in the New Europe* (London: The Littman Library of Jewish Civilization, 1994).

21. They "feel simultaneously attracted and repelled by their birthplaces." Monika Adamczyk-Garbowska, *Patterns of Return: Survivors' Post-war Journeys to Poland* (Washington, DC: United States Holocaust Memorial Museum, Centre for Advanced Holocaust Studies, 2007), 17.

22. Jackie Feldman, *Above the Death Pits, Beneath the Flag: Youth Voyages to Poland and the Performance of Israeli National Identity* (New York: Berghahn Books, 2008).

23. Noga Collins-Kreiner and Dan Olsen, "Selling Diaspora: Producing and Segmenting the Jewish Diaspora Tourism Market," in *Tourism, Diasporas and Space*, ed. Tim Coles and Dallen Timothy (London: Routledge, 2004), 279–290.

24. Gruber, *Virtually Jewish*, 2002; Leveson and Lustig, eds., *Turning the Kaleidoscope*; 2006; Sabor, "In Search of Identity."

25. Maciągowski and Krawczyk, *The Story of Jewish Chmielnik*, 2007.

26. Michał Marusieński, *Zygzakowate szczęście: Wspomnienia 1911–1949* (Kraków: Secesja, 1991); Adam Penkalla, *Żydowskie Ślady w Województwie Kieleckim i Radomskim* (Radom: Tramp, 1992); Suzan Hagstrom, *Sara's Children and the Destruction of Chmielnik* (Spotsylvania VA: Sergeant Kirkland's Press, 2001); Stanisław Rogala, *Chmielnik—Miasto i Gmina* (Kielce: Gens, 2003); Amelia Sołtysiak, *Chmielnik i Ja* (Kielce: Jedność, 2007); Krzysztof Urbański, *Almanach Gmin Żydowskich Województwa Kieleckiego w Latach 1918–1939* (Kielce: Muzeum Narodowe w Kielcach, 2007); Maciągowski and Krawczyk, *The Story of Jewish Chmielnik;* "Memorial Book of Chmielnik: Yizkor Book of the Annihilated Jewish Community (Poland): Translation of *Pinkas Chmielnik. Yisker bukh noch der Khorev-Gevorener Yidisher Kehile*," ed. Ephraim Shedletski (Tel Aviv: Former Residents of Chmielnik in Israel, 1960).

27. Piotr Krawczyk, "Dzieje Gminy Żydowskiej w Chmielniku," www.chmielnik.com.

28. According to national censuses, in 1921, there were 7,693 residents in Chmielnik. In 1950, there were 3,139, and in 1988 and 2002, there were 4,123 and 4,127, respectively.

29. Trafiałek, *Starość w miasteczku Chmielnik*, 24.

30. Suzan Hagstrom, "Cultivating Her Roots: Holocaust Survivors' Relative Visits Poland with Her Eyes Wide Open," *Jewish News Detroit*, September 25, 2008, A40–41; Suzan Hagstrom,

"Return to Poland: Orlando Survivor Revisits a Traumatic Past and Glimpses a Promise of the Future," *Heritage Florida Jewish News*, July 25, 2008, 3A, 14A.

31. Yizkor books (from the Hebrew "you will remember") are memorial books that rec-ollect and memorialize Jewish communities. Books such as the one referred to here were typi-cally created by societies of survivors from the same town after the Holocaust. Written and compiled by amateur writers, who recall the life in their hometown, they are an important and unique source of primary information on the vanished Jewish communities in Central and Eastern Europe.

32. Poland Central Statistical Office, "GUS: Central Statistical Office Regional Data Bank," www.stat.gov.pl.

33. Suzan Hagstrom, "Greenspun Visits Polish Hometown to See Her Renovated Syna-gogue," *Heritage Florida Jewish News*, http://www.heritagefl.com/story/2013/07/12/features /greenspun-visits-polish-hometown-to-see-her-renovated-synagogue/1032.html.

34. Sabor, *Sztetl*, 2005; Hagstrom, "Return to Poland," 2008; Arkadiusz Stempin, "*Czy należy bać się Strachu?*" *Znak* 6 (2008): 126–132; Katarzyna Weintraub, *Wspomnieć tych co miasto budowali*, Polish Radio in Kielce, broadcast by Radio MultiKulti, Rundfunk Berlin-Brandenburg (RBB) radio broadcast, August 31, 2007. In 2009, Chmielnik youth dance groups that used Jewish themes in their performances were awarded two main prizes at the Carnival of Cultures in Berlin.

35. Maciągowski and Krawczyk, *The Story of Jewish Chmielnik*, 15.

36. Krawczyk, "Dzieje Gminy Żydowskiej w Chmielniku."

37. Maciągowski and Krawczyk, *The Story of Jewish Chmielnik*. The newest, even more in-depth scholarly monograph focused on the history of the Jewish community in Chmielnik in the nineteenth and twentieth centuries was published in 2012. See Maciągowski, *Społeczność żydowska w Chmielniku*.

38. Ibid., 9.

39. Katarzyna Weintraub, pers. comm. with author, July 2, 2010; school teachers from Chmielnik, pers. comm. with author, June 30, 2010.

40. Jarosław Zatorski, pers. comm. with author, September 3, 2010.

41. Ibid.

42. Jarosław Zatorski and staff, pers. comm. with author, September 3, 2010.

43. Hagstrom, "Cultivating Her Roots."

44. Hagstrom, "Cultivating Her Roots."

45. Hagstrom, "Return to Poland."

46. Maciągowski and Krawczyk, *The Story of Jewish Chmielnik*, 252.

47. Ibid., 247.

48. Ibid., 260.

49. Marek Maciągowski and Piotr Krawczyk, *Żydzi w Historii Chmielnika* (Kielce: FPHU, 2006), 247.

50. The main part of the monument consists of two oak trees with intertwining branches symbolizing the two nations living side by side. The inscription (in Hebrew, English, and Pol-ish) reads, "History does not stride along main roads but rather strolls on the side streets of peaceful little towns. In memory of the heritage of the Jewish-Polish community of Chmiel-nik 1565–1942. June 19, 2005. Founded by the Kalish Families in Israel in memory of Chmiel-nik Jews."

51. EPRD, *Strategia Rozwoju Społeczno-Gospodarczego Miasta i Gminy Chmielnik* (Kielce: EPRD, 1999); EPRD, *Studium Uwarunkowań i Kierunków Zagospodarowania Przestrzennego Miasta i Gminy Chmielnik* (Kielce: EPRD, 2002).

52. Akordbud-Consulting Sp. z o.o., *Lokalny Program Rewitalizacji dla Miasta Chmielnik na Lata 2007–2013, Aktualizacja 2009* (Chmielnik: Urząd Miasta i Gminy Chmielnik, 2009). Data on the cost of the project comes directly from the municipality.

53. Nizio Design International, "Projekt Koncepcyjny w Murach Dawnej Synagogi," www .nizio.com.pl.

54. Timothy Ambrose and Crispin Paine, *Museum Basics* (London: Routledge, 2008); Sheila Watson, ed., *Museums and Their Communities* (London: Routledge, 2007).

55. See Erica Lehrer, this volume.

56. The mayor is not affiliated with any political party. In the most recent elections (November 2010), he received an all-time high 61.5% of the vote. He also has the direct backing of almost one third of the city council, politicians who were recruited, like him, from a local political grouping, which means that he may effectively exercise strong leadership.

57. As many as ten different commemorative plaques or sculptures were placed at different sites within the town after 2000. These include two monuments to Chmielnik's Jews.

58. In 2008, the municipal authorities of Chmielnik spent more money on culture and heritage than the authorities of the nearby county seat of Pińczów, even though Pińczów has more than twice as many inhabitants as Chmielnik. Chmielnik also outspends other former shtetls with significant material remains of Jewish heritage and a rich history of Jewish presence. The amount spent on culture and heritage per person in Chmielnik is twice the amount spent in Szydłów, almost three times what is spent in Pińczów, and a striking nine times more than is spent in Działoszyce (see figure 5.10).

59. Jarosław Zatorski, pers. comm. with the author, September 3, 2010.

60. Monika Murzyn, "Heritage Transformation in Central and Eastern Europe," in Graham and Howard, eds., *The Ashgate Research Companion to Heritage and Identity*, 315–346.

61. Alla Sokolova, "Jewish Sights: Exoticization of Places and Objects as a Way of Presenting Local 'Jewish Antiquity' by the Inhabitants of Little Towns," in *Jewish Space in Central and Eastern Europe: Day-to-Day History*, ed. Jurgita Šiaučiūnaitė-Verbickienė and Larisa Lempertienė (Newcastle: Cambridge Scholars Publishing, 2007), 261–280. See also Waligórska, this volume.

62. Jarosław Zatorski, pers. comm. with the author, September 3, 2010.

63. This pertains both to the ownership of the most significant Jewish landmark—the synagogue—and to the ownership of housing. Although the town center's urban layout has remained quite unchanged, two-thirds of the present-day housing in Chmielnik has been built after 1944 and its legal status is to a large extent settled, which surely impacts on attitudes toward Jewish visitors. Author's calculations based on GUS data of the 2002 national census, Poland Central Statistical Office, "Główny Urząd Statystyczny: Central Statistical Office Regional Data Bank," www.stat.gov.pl.

64. Jerzy Znojek, the supervisor of the regional museum in Pińczów, pers. comm. with the author, May 2, 2010.

65. Tolerance is not, of course, synonymous with reconciliation and acceptance. See Wendy Brown, *Regulating Aversion: Tolerance in the Age of Identity and Empire* (Princeton, NJ: Princeton University Press, 2006).

66. Samuel Kassow, "The Shtetl in Interwar Poland," in *The Shtetl: New Evaluations*, ed. Steven Katz (New York: New York University Press, 2007), 123.

67. Eugenia Prokop, "The Image of the Shtetl in Polish Literature," *Polin* 4 (1989): 128–142.

68. Israel Bartal, "Imagined Geography: The Shtetl, Myth and Reality," in Katz, ed., *The Shtetl*, 179–192.

69. See, for example, John Urry, *The Tourist Gaze* (London: Sage, 2002).

70. Lehrer, "Repopulating Jewish Poland"; Erica Lehrer, "Review," *Cultural Analysis,* 4 (2005), www.socrates.berkeley.edu; Steven Saxonberg and Magdalena Waligórska, "Klezmer in Kraków: Kitsch or Catharsis for Poles?" *Ethnomusicology* 3 (2006): 433–451; Ruth E. Gruber, "Beyond Virtually Jewish . . . Balancing the Real, the Surreal and Real Imaginary Places," in Murzyn-Kupisz and Purchla, eds., *Reclaiming Memory,* 63–79.

71. Joachim Jacobs, *Houses of Life: Jewish Cemeteries of Europe* (London: Frances Lincoln, 2008).

72. Lehrer, this volume.

73. Michael Rothberg, *Multidirectional Memory: Remembering the Holocaust in the Age of Decolonization* (Stanford, CA: Stanford University Press, 2009), 5.

74. Already after completing the chapter this dilemma has been clearly voiced in the Polish opinion-forming press. In June 2011, a very critical text on Chmielnik's efforts to rediscover its Jewish past was published in the *Tygodnik Powszechny,* a liberal, Catholic weekly. In the opinion of its author, little more than superficial entertainment accompanied by a lack of deeper, serious reflection over the Polish-Jewish past were visible in Chmielnik, making it a textbook example of the shallowness of recent Polish embracing of the Jewish past focused on the organization of crowd-drawing, festive celebrations rather than serious commemoration. According to the article's author, "Chmielnik resembles Poland in a nutshell: there are questionable heroes, many dead and few living Jews, a joyful but slightly shallow festival." Zuzanna Radzik, "Bohater i Żydzi," *Tygodnik Powszechny,* July 3, 2011, http://tygodnik.onet.pl /kraj/bohater-i-zydzi/w7pyk. This critique was soon strongly rebutted. In a piece published in the same magazine two weeks later, Agnieszka Sabor praised the long-term-oriented, grass-roots efforts with respect to Jewish heritage, making Chmielnik unique in the Polish provinces. As she pointed out, "Little Chmielnik has dared to do something no other town or city in Poland has done so far. . . . The local government, supported by a few enthusiasts, made the Polish-Jewish dialogue its main political objective. This policy is implemented consistently and systematically—taking the risk of losing each, consecutive local elections." Sabor, "Stereotypy są jak chwasty," *Tygodnik Powszechny,* July 17, 2011, http://tygodnik.onet.pl/kraj/stereotypy-sa -jak-chwasty/ovd8p. Chmielnik authorities have also responded, though indirectly, by creating an event accompanying the annual commemoration of the deportation of Jews from Chmielnik to Treblinka concentration camp, which takes place in September. In 2011, the first edition of a "Meeting with the Cinema with Jewish Motifs" film festival was organized in the town, in which watching such films is an occasion for young people to discuss the complex and difficult issues linked with Jewish presence in Poland and Polish-Jewish relations.

6 Amnesia, Nostalgia, and Reconstruction

Shifting Modes of Memory in Poland's Jewish Spaces

Sławomir Kapralski

Memory and Space

Since the 1990s, the Jewish past has begun to reappear in Polish memory as part of a nostalgic vision of colorful "multiculturalism." This view of the past glosses over everyday occurrences of antisemitism, as well as the tragedy of the Holocaust. At the local level, this translates into a predilection for renovating dilapidated synagogue buildings or developing the Jewish section of the local museum over constructing memorials to Jewish Holocaust victims. The renovated synagogues and museums themselves have come to play an essential role in the way that Jewish memory has returned to Poland.

In his 1986 essay "Of Other Spaces," Michel Foucault investigated the importance of such spaces in contemporary society. He argued that we have privileged space over time as the main frame within which we orient ourselves in our everyday lives.[1] Foucault's claim may be exaggerated, but the role played by former cemeteries and dilapidated synagogues in the revival of Jewish memory in Poland is one among many examples that suggest, at minimum, a trend toward the privileging of space over time.[2] In fact, the growing role played by space in late modernity clearly differentiates the present period from classical modernity, when linear time and narrative were emphasized. Similarly, if classical modernity was the age of history, as Foucault asserts, then it could be argued that late modernity is the age of memory. With its loosening of our connections to the spaces in which we are located due to the cross-cutting communication networks in which we participate, late modernity is perhaps metaphoric of the capricious, nonlinear work of remembrance.[3]

It is in such "flows of space and communication" that we form and express our perceptions of the past and our attitudes toward it, and use these to orient and scaffold our senses of collective self.[4] The term "memoryscape" captures this complex relation of intertwined processes. Memoryscape is a memorial landscape—both material and symbolic—through which "collective memory is commonly spatialized."[5] Drawing on Arjun Appadurai's work, I use the suffix "-scape" to imply several characteristics of memory's relation to space: its fluidity, its relativity based on perspective, and its imagined quality.[6] In spite of all its materiality, the tangible landscape of memory is constituted in dialogue with the imaginations of those who refer to it. This inherent ambiguity of the concept allows it to account for the complicated interplay of things and words, which only together form our frames of remembrance.

The spatialization of memory is not only a free play of fluidities, perspectives, and imaginations, however. It is also political, involving practices that manipulate cultural similarities and differences, and sanitizing history by introducing a dominant, privileged way of seeing.[7] A memoryscape can thus be defined as a "site of concentrated cultural practice," the main function of which is to order the meaning of the past. This involves presenting historical and intercultural relationships so that they appear coherent, and organizing difference so that it is not subversive. Memoryscapes contain many memories, some of which are in symbolic conflict—often in parallel to other, real-world conflicts that embroil the communities from which these diverse memories emanate. For this reason, memoryscapes as sites of cultural practice are "constantly engaged in efforts not only to normalize or homogenize but also to hierarchize, encapsulate, exclude, criminalize, hegemonize, or marginalize practices and populations that diverge from the sanctioned ideal."[8] Memoryscapes thus do more than simply express and convey memories. They also erase the memories of those without sufficient resources to participate, or silence uncomfortable memories that haunt those who physically control a given landscape. Yet even sanctioned memories are not simply conferred from the past or "copied" from the memories of a particular group into the memoryscape. Rather, all memories are distorted in ways that legitimize a given group's claim to control a territory, its meaning, and its history.

On the one hand, then, memoryscapes are products of power relations. On the other hand, memoryscapes themselves contribute to the construction of consciousness of the past, with various aspects remembered and forgotten.[9] In this role, memoryscapes become focal points around which we build our collective identities in the present. The process is further circular: once constructed, such identities themselves influence the shape of memoryscapes, by using them for their own symbolic expression. Memoryscapes are thus transformed into meaningful, concrete places through the hierarchic relations of power and the community's cultural constructs.[10]

Thus, memoryscapes have the peculiar characteristic of being, according to Clifford Geertz's terminology, both "models of" and "models for."[11] Memoryscapes are "models of" because they become, over time, representations of the remembered past. Yet, memoryscapes may also be consciously designed to emphasize and amplify those aspects and interpretations of the past desired by those with the power to shape them. In this way, memoryscapes are "models for"—they are instructions or "frames" for our memories in which certain memories are more likely or able to emerge than others.[12] Memoryscapes, then, exercise through their spatial and discursive components a coercive power over the ways that we perceive social relations in a given territory, and act as permanent reminders of who we are.

To the extent that their presence is representative of Poland's Jewish past, sites like synagogues and cemeteries, and discourses associated with them, can be "models of" the past. But these sites are also made into "models for" the past by local officials who reshape them and determine which aspects of them will be emphasized and which will be downplayed or even erased. Using examples from several provincial Polish towns that once had significant Jewish populations, I analyze how local people have interacted with such sites since World War II. I show how Jewish sites, and the broader Polish memoryscape they inhabit, are manipulated by local officials to shape local identities. But as I argue, the sites themselves, in their material realities, also play a role in this process; they are messengers from the past that assert a sovereign agency that must be managed.

Jews in Poland's Memoryscapes

By wiping out a Jewish world that had been a substantial part of Poland's landscape for centuries, the Holocaust radically altered many Polish towns in ways both demographic and material. The postwar exodus of Holocaust survivors further diminished the few traces of Jewish memory remaining in Poland, and the handful of Jews who decided to stay against all odds were too weak to significantly influence Polish society. As a result, James E. Young has argued, Poles "were left alone with their own, now uncontested, memory of events."[13] Young's statement is, however, only partially true because *sites* of Jewish memory remained in Poland even after almost all of the Jews were gone. Despite attempts to seize Jewish property or the use of Jewish spaces for non-Jewish purposes, ruined synagogues and desecrated cemeteries, to point to the most monumental forms, have remained in the landscape. The presence of these material remnants has ensured that Jewish memory remains anchored in Polish memoryscapes in inescapable physical terms. These generally dilapidated traces of the Jewish past still exist because of active resistance from Jewish organizations and the ambiguous attitudes of local and national authorities during the Communist era. The ways these Jewish sites and spaces were treated was contested in heated debates that divided "Jews" and "Communists," "Jews" and "Poles," and also different Jewish institutions.[14] The approaches fall into three general categories: oblivion, erasure, and preservation. They do not follow one another chronologically; we find all of them in any period of contemporary Polish history. The disposition of each site of Jewish memory depends upon the particular configuration of power relations and the constructs of identity that dominate a given time and place. Further, "preservation" of the Jewish past by Poles may itself take very different forms. These range from just and fair representation to manipulative distortion or alleged "restorations" that result in pretentious imitations.

The Holocaust: Erased and Represented

The 1990s were marked by the "revival" of Jewish memory in Poland. Changes in the way that the Holocaust is taught to schoolchildren and the development of special programs addressed to teachers in this field were two of the most significant elements of this revival. In addition, a number of commemorative ceremonies conducted under the auspices of government officials have helped to focus public opinion on previously neglected Jewish aspects of Polish history. At the same time, Polish-Jewish relations have received substantial attention in the mainstream media. This process of change has also involved Auschwitz-Birkenau, where Jewish institutions helped to refurbish the museum there. The new exhibition at Auschwitz emphasizes the camp's role as the symbol of the Holocaust. It also clearly indicates that Auschwitz-Birkenau was first and foremost a site of mass extermination, where men, women, and children were sent to death simply because they were Jewish.

Poles also started to interact more frequently with the increasing numbers of Jewish visitors to Poland during the 1990s, interactions that included meetings between Polish and Israeli high school students. At the same time, Poles have witnessed the revival of Jewish communal life in their country. A growing number of Poles are rediscovering their Jewish roots or deciding to reclaim previously repressed or rejected Jewish identities. This process has been assisted by various Jewish organizations, which have become visible both as protectors of the material remnants of Jewish culture in Poland and as supporters of Jewish religious, cultural, and educational initiatives. Correspondingly, a certain number of Poles, acting out of genuine interest, intellectual curiosity, or economic motives, have engaged in Jewish cultural initiatives. These range from opening a "Jewish" restaurant to setting up a klezmer band to organizing a festival of Jewish culture. All of these initiatives have contributed to the phenomenon described by Ruth Gruber as "virtual Jewishness," that is, a certain form of Jewish culture produced by and addressed to non-Jews.[15]

The intellectual debate about Polish-Jewish relations at the time of the Shoah has continued, and it is now free from the constraints of censorship. This debate peaked following the publication of Jan T. Gross's book *Sąsiedzi* (*Neighbors*) in 2000. During the public discussions about Gross's book, which describes how the

Polish inhabitants of Jedwabne had murdered in 1941 at least 340 of their Jewish neighbors, the "whole of Polish society was convulsed by an extraordinary self-examination."[16] These discussions, which continued (albeit with decreased intensity) after the publication of Gross's *Fear* in 2006 and then again with the publication of *Golden Harvest* in 2011,[17] have divided many sectors of Polish society, including the Roman Catholic Church. Nevertheless, Gross's work, on account of the public discussions it ignited, has greatly contributed to the "return of memory" of Jews and the Holocaust.

In spite of the processes outlined above, Poland's Jewish past in general and the Holocaust in particular have not become part of the country's "living memory." If anything, recent surveys suggest that understanding of the unique qualities of the Jewish past has decreased among Poles over the past decade. In 1992, 46 percent of Poles believed that Jews suffered more than Poles during World War II. In 2002, however, only 38 percent held that opinion. The number of respondents who believed that Poles suffered more than Jews rose from 6 to 10 percent. In fact, 47 percent of those surveyed in 2002 believed that Poles and Jews had suffered equally during World War II, compared to 32 percent of those surveyed in 1992.[18]

It seems, then, that although Poles were exposed to more factual information about, and many more representations of, the Holocaust in the decade from 1992 to 2002, they have failed to integrate it into their cognitive structures. In an earlier article, I explained this surprising development with reference to the discursive features of memory and the local circumstances of Polish debates about Jews.[19] Here I add the spatiality of memory to the equation via the notion of memoryscapes, the context in which memories are produced and reproduced in relation to the physical landscape.

I suggest that it is precisely the lack of material and spatial frames that accounts for the disconnect between the information Poles have received and the way that they think about it. Material and spatial frames are significant because they form a scaffolding that absorbs and reflects the meaning of the past as it is elaborated in national intellectual debates, and help to transform this meaning into vernacular social memories. Without being articulated spatially, representations of the Holocaust, which are largely intellectual and "textual," may serve as "models of" Holocaust representation but fail to be "models for" considering the Holocaust in popular memory. Without spatial frames, representations of the Holocaust may not be effective tools for transmitting to Poles a deep, enduring understanding of what happened to the Jews in the past and what that means for the present.

The representations of the Holocaust in Poland largely lack spatial frames, in particular ones that would be created on purpose by those who control Poland's memoryscapes. One factor influencing this tendency is the fact that in many localities, modest Holocaust memorials were created by Jewish survivors in the first years after the war. These memorials were usually located in Jewish cemeteries, and thus were all but invisible to ordinary Poles. Nevertheless, awareness of these memorials' existence may have caused local authorities to assume that commemoration of the Holocaust was "done," and allowed them to focus on less difficult aspects of their municipalities' cultural histories. The synagogue building in Łańcut is a prime example of this trend. For many years, the former synagogue served as a storage area. When it was finally renovated—with the financial assistance of the Polish government and local businesses—it became the Jewish part of the local museum in 1990.

Over the past decade, Jews have only been represented in Łańcut's memoryscape through the kind of musealized and aestheticized references to the town's former Jewish community in the synagogue-museum. The Holocaust has still not been commemorated publicly, and the existing, rather dilapidated Holocaust memorial, built shortly after World War II in Łańcut's Jewish cemetery, was not included in the town's commemoration strategy, which focused on the landmarks that would be more attractive for tourists. In 2007, in the process of restitution of Jewish communal property, the synagogue building was returned to the Jewish community, represented by the Foundation for the Preservation of Jewish Heritage (FPJH) in Poland (see Tyszka, this volume), and for some time it has been closed to visitors. In 2008, it reopened and remains open for visits May to August (in the remaining months, visits are possible upon prior appointment with the FPJH). One might expect that in the new situation, the museum and local authorities will turn to the memory of the Holocaust as a means of commemorating Łańcut's Jews. No significant activities of this kind, however, have been seen so far.

Such progressive developments can be seen in other locations, even in places where Jewish memory was previously present in local memoryscapes. In Tarnów, for example, a Holocaust memorial built by the local community of survivors is centered around the remaining column of the town's New Synagogue, which was destroyed by the Nazis. The Tarnów memorial, together with the area of the cemetery where it is located, is well maintained and periodically renovated. The work of upkeep is carried out by the local museum and the Society for Protection of Jewish Monuments, a group that was organized by local Poles interested in their town's Jewish past. More recently, a memorial tablet was placed at the corner of Żydowska (Jewish) Street and the main square. This plaque marks the spot where thousands of Tarnów Jews were murdered during the so-called actions of liquidation in 1942. The tablet indicates that memory of the Holocaust is now present in the town's center.

Tarnów's newest commemoration, a tablet funded by an Italian entrepreneur who now lives in Tarnów, is further evidence of the Holocaust's presence in the town's memoryscape. The text on the table, in Polish and English, reads:

The inhabitants of these houses were among the
40,000 tarnowians slaughtered by the german murders
during the horrific years of the bestial aggression.
To these martyrs, unified in the same God, City and Sacrifice,
we submit. Eternal honour to their memory. The fellow-citizens.[20]

The text on the new tablet is an interesting attempt to create a "unified memory" of the Jewish victims of the Holocaust and the Polish victims of World War II. Its reference to 40,000 deaths may refer to the total wartime loss of "Tarnowians" (the Jewish population of Tarnów shortly before the war is estimated at 25,000). The fate of Jewish victims has, therefore, been equated with that of Poles. What is more, by stating that all these victims shared the "same God, City and Sacrifice," the tablet has become a factor in the construction of a joint Jewish-Polish "community of memory" in Tarnów. Because it implicitly challenges the uniqueness of the Holocaust, however, this statement has proven controversial. Nevertheless, the tablet remains an interesting intervention into the memoryscape that is clearly intended to serve as a "model for" a certain experience of the past.[21] Given the long period of time that Jews were excluded from the Polish community of memory, it seems quite likely that the tablet will affect the ways that local people perceive Jews. It is possible, however, that the tablet will simply further Polish society's growing tendency to treat Jewish and Polish suffering during World War II and the Holocaust as identical.

Attempts to represent the memory of the Holocaust in public in the town of Rzeszów do a better job of distinguishing Jewish and Polish experiences. The first commemoration in Rzeszów was a memorial plaque placed on the wall of one of the town's two surviving synagogue buildings. This building now houses an art gallery, the municipal archives, and a small research unit that studies the region's Jewish history. The plaque was jointly funded by Rzeszowian Holocaust survivors abroad and town authorities. The next commemoration in Rzeszów was a memorial slab placed in a park in front of the synagogue buildings. This park was once the town's Jewish cemetery. The text on this tombstone-like slab reads, "This is the site of a sixteenth-century Jewish cemetery that was destroyed during World War II by the Nazi occupiers. In the summer of 1942, Jews were gathered here before they were deported to a death camp." In a single act of commemoration, this text connects the long history of Rzeszów's Jewish community with local Jews' destiny during the Holocaust. In doing so, it reclaims the whole area as both a Jewish memoryscape and a representation of the Holocaust.

Despite these successes, however, significant difficulties face those who seek to represent the Holocaust in Poland's memoryscapes. The nature of these difficulties can be seen in the landscape of Żołynia and the Jewish cemetery in Przeworsk.

Invisible Holocaust

A large sign proudly informs visitors to Żołynia that the town was awarded a military cross for supporting the resistance during World War II. This sign is evidence that memory of the war is carefully preserved by the people of Żołynia, a small town located between Łańcut and Leżajsk. Closer inspection reveals that Żołynia's memory of the war is rather selective, however.

In the corner of the town's main square there is a small monument crowned by an eagle with its wings outstretched—the Polish national emblem. The inscription on this monument explains that it is dedicated "To the memory of the inhabitants of Żołynia, fallen for the Fatherland in the years 1939–1945 and murdered by Hitlerites." The names of twenty-four people executed in 1943 follow. The fact that all the names on this list are those of Poles poses an important question: what happened to the other inhabitants of Żołynia—namely, the Jews? The answer, of course, is that they, too, were "murdered by Hitlerites," in numbers much greater than those Poles executed for supporting or belonging to partisan units active in the surrounding forests. Nevertheless, the "Community of Żołynia," which erected the monument in September 1983, neglected to include the names of Jews on the inscription.

This decision, however consciously or unconsciously made, results in the symbolic exclusion of Jews from the "Community of Żołynia." As it happens, the inhabitants of Żołynia today comprise only Poles. Yet with the implicit projection of this state of affairs onto the past, local people have excluded Jews from the town's collective memory as well. This exclusion is a clear sign of the conflation of the town's mental and physical landscapes. The physical elimination of the Jews, while carried out by the Nazis, facilitated the subsequent symbolic elimination of the memory of the Jews by the Poles. If one reads between the lines, the monument in Żołynia might make its statement this way: "This is Poland, the land of Poles, who have their own, glorious and tragic—but exclusively Polish—history."

The historical dimension of this phenomenon of exclusion is quite significant. Jews were long considered to belong to another, alien world. They were not perceived as full members of the "community." The indifference of many Poles to the Holocaust can be at least partially explained by this fact. Because the murdered Jews were perceived as alien, their history was considered a separate stream of events, albeit one that overlapped at times with Polish history. In the process of homogenization, the history of Poland came to be seen as *Polish* history—that is, the history of ethnic, Catholic Poles. The Żołynia monument is thus a powerful tool for manipulating the memoryscape, a spatial means of historical domination.

The politics of the Żołynia monument are worth recounting. The monument was erected in 1983 when the regulations of martial law, introduced in 1981, were gradually being relaxed. As a sign of that relaxation, leaders of the Communist party and the military tried to play up their devotion to Polish history and tradition. Since no monument could have been built at that time without the consent of local party officials, it is logical to assume that their consent was prompted by the policy of relaxation, which included concessions for local commemorations of Polish tradition. Commemorating Jewish tradition would have muddied the authorities' clear populist nationalist intentions, and created obstacles in the process of restoring legitimacy to a regime that had imposed martial law.

Yet Jewish memory has, in a way, returned to Żołynia after all. Josef Waldman, a Jew whose family once lived in the town, built a new fence around the old cemetery site and offered a cash reward for tombstones that had been removed from the cemetery. Perhaps unsurprisingly, the financial incentive offered by Waldman caused some of the tombstones to turn up rather quickly. They have since been returned to the cemetery. After years of oblivion, then, the cemetery has reemerged as a visible sign of the Jewish presence in Żołynia.

In Przeworsk, a small town east of Łańcut, Jews had developed a rich community life in the town since settling there in the sixteenth century, and on the eve of World War II, they comprised nearly 50 percent of the population. The synagogue building in Przeworsk did not fare as well as Łańcut's synagogue during the war. The Nazis leveled the Przeworsk synagogue and also removed gravestones from the Jewish cemetery, which they used to pave the courtyards of the local sugar refinery. During the Nazi occupation, the cemetery was used as an execution site. Jews who were caught trying to escape transports to the camps were brought there and shot. Having been desecrated and filled with difficult memories, the former cemetery has proven a particularly challenging node in the local memoryscape. Since the war's end, the cemetery terrain has been dealt with variously, seeing phases of oblivion, erasure, and commemoration.

Immediately after the war, the former cemetery was left empty and untouched. The site remained in oblivion until a new section of the road connecting Kraków and Przemyśl was built in Przeworsk. The construction work damaged the southern side of the cemetery. In 1969, a little more of the site was erased. A huge monument commemorating the twenty-fifth anniversary of the town's liberation was erected in that year.[22] The monument, known as *Pomnik Walki i Męczeństwa* (Monument of Fight and Martyrdom), stripped away the cemetery's western edge. In the early 1980s, the municipal council voted to build a bus station on the eastern side of the cemetery, leaving no trace of the original site.

Jan Sasak, a local stonecutter who served on the municipal council at the time, voted against the proposed bus station. When he was outvoted, Sasak suggested that the town at least put up a sign indicating the site's previous use as the town's Jewish cemetery. Unsupported by his colleagues on the council, Sasak decided to take action on his own. He built and installed a modest stone monument with an inscription commemorating the Jews murdered during the war in the northeast corner of the new bus station. A few years later, the stone was moved—without Sasak's knowledge or consent—to the southeast corner of the former cemetery site, next to a taxi stand. The stone's former location had apparently been intended for commercial purposes. Its new location made it much less visible to or accessible by visitors.

The history of the former Jewish cemetery in Przeworsk is exceptional; the sites of Jewish cemeteries in the region, while often left empty and unprotected, are rarely used for construction projects. The story of the Przeworsk cemetery does, however, illuminate a general pattern of removing—whether consciously or not—Jewish memory from the landscape. Building a road and bus station on the former cemetery exemplifies a "functional approach" to sites of Jewish memory. This line of reasoning goes: the Jews are no longer here; their gravestones were already removed by the Nazis; life must go on, and local people need roads and bus stations. This argument was popular among local authorities in the 1950s. Since that time, urban and industrial developments have led to growing conflicts with moral and religious claims to protect the areas of Jewish cemeteries, sites commonly seen as "problems" for the local authorities.[23] While this functional approach can certainly be interpreted as evidence of open or latent antisemitism, one cannot dismiss other relevant factors. The lack of sensitivity in the case of the road construction project must be understood in the context of the early postwar period's lingering practical problems: living amid the ruins of both the devastation of the built environment and the distortion of the moral world imposed by the Nazis. Later, in the 1980s bus station case, an already more advanced process of forgetting was accelerated by an increased focus on the pressing Polish political events connected with social unrest and the rising of the Solidarność (Solidarity) movement.

The 1969 monument can be interpreted somewhat differently. It was a conscious attempt to present the Communist vision of history. It was, furthermore, prepared in a particular way in order to legitimize the Communist authorities. Still, the monument's construction coincided with the government's official antisemitism campaign, and this fact may have influenced the decision about where it ought to be built or, at a minimum, silenced any potential concerns about whether it was appropriate to build such a monument on the site of a former Jewish cemetery.

The monument itself is an example of Communist manipulation of history. It consists of two separate structures. The first is composed of three columns, symbolizing three decades of Communist Poland. This structure is adorned with the Communist version of the Polish national emblem. It features an eagle without a crown (the crown, as the symbol of royalty, had been removed from the emblem by the Communists). Below the national emblem is yet another emblematic eagle: the symbol of the Piast dynasty, the first royal dynasty to rule the Polish lands.

The Piast dynasty's eagle does not have a crown either, since the dynasty was not granted its royal title until after the emblem had been established as its symbol.

The monument is a clear attempt to anchor Communist rule in Polish history by presenting Communist rule as a logical and legitimate stage in the history of the Polish state. Further, the Communists often made positive references to the Piast dynasty's rule, in contradistinction to the multinational Polish-Lithuanian Commonwealth. The politics of this historical favoritism seem clear, based on the Polish state's existence within the Soviet sphere of influence: the Poland of the Piast dynasty was similar in size to Communist Poland, while the Polish-Lithuanian Commonwealth reached far into areas that had since become the western parts of the Soviet Union. But the Piast dynasty could also have been seen favorably in such comparisons for ideological reasons. According to the official Communist interpretation of history, the commonwealth was a belligerent, expansionist state based on serfdom and an egoistic exploitation of its resources by the aristocracy. Moreover, the homogeneity of Poland's population during the Piast dynasty was often presented in favorable opposition to the "negative" multinational character of the commonwealth and the interwar Republic of Poland. Through such comparisons, the Communists suggested that the forced homogenization of Poland after World War II was, in fact, a "return to the roots" of Polish statehood.

The second part of the Przeworsk monument, an upside-down pyramid that vaguely resembles a memorial candle, has the symbol of the Polish Military Cross on its front wall. Its inscription reads, "To the heroes of the revolutionary struggles, loyal sons of the Przeworsk soil, those who fought against the oppression of the prewar rightwing Polish government, against the Nazi occupiers and against the forces of reaction, for national and social liberation, for socialist Poland." The vision of history expressed in this inscription identifies prewar, "capitalist" Poland and postwar anti-Communist groups with the Nazis. National liberation is identified here with the Communist political program, which excluded non-Communist members of the Polish resistance from the officially approved pantheon of "national martyrs." Together with the symbolism of the twin eagle emblems, this inscription makes the Communists' vision for the monument clear. "Socialist" Poland is the telos of Polish history, and those who did not participate in the process of its manifestation do not belong to "Us." They are rather "Them," the enemy. Jews, similarly, found no place in the homogenous Communist vision, as they were blurring its ideological divides. While the logical steps to this conclusion may have been different, Polish Communists and Polish nationalists thus shared a vision of Poland that was ethnically homogeneous, with no place for Jews.

The history represented in the Przeworsk memoryscape has thus been falsified in multiple ways: Jewish memory has been erased by both the destruction of the cemetery and the logic of history embodied by the monument, and ethnic Polish vernacular memory has been denied by the latter. The only attempt to preserve Jewish memory was the initiative of a single individual, Jan Sasak, in an idiosyncratic act of "counter-monumentalization," the modesty and genuineness of which contrast strikingly with the bombastic Communist monument.

Since 1989, the issue of "de-communizing" Poland's public spaces has been raised frequently, with varying emphases. Indeed, the process of destroying the monuments of the *ancien regime*, and replacing Communist street names with new names honoring formerly erased national heroes, is a common phenomenon in post-Communist Eastern and Central Europe more generally. The process intensifies when rightwing nationalists win elections, and slows down when the political pendulum swings to the left. The town of Przeworsk, however, has chosen a unique means of dealing with its Communist monument, leaving it in place but radically altering its form in 2000.

The most striking alteration to the monument was the addition of the crucified figure of Jesus that has been affixed to the columns, which represent three decades of Communist rule. This change was intended to symbolize Communist repression of Poland's Catholic identity. It offered an alternate kind of "closure" to Poland's national history by replacing its Communist telos with a religious one. The addition of Christ's figure to the monument was also intended to symbolize the way that the true essence of Polish nationhood liberated itself from decades of oppression, overcoming the Communists' antireligious stance. Polish victimization was once again transformed into the victory of the oppressed. This victim-to-victor trope is closely linked to the romantic-religious vision of Poland as the "Christ of nations." It is reminiscent of the final scene of the great Polish romantic drama, *The Un-Divine Comedy* by Zygmunt Krasiński (1835). In this scene, the seemingly victorious leader of a "godless" social revolution dies when he is confronted by a vision of Christ. The revolutionary's last words, "Galilee vicisti," or "You won, man of Galilee," attest to the fact that social revolution without God cannot succeed, and that one cannot build a better world without God.[24]

The Catholic concept of redemption is also evident in the monument's transformation. Benedict Anderson's idea of nationalism as a "secular transformation of fatality into continuity, contingency into meaning," suggests the way that Catholic redemption can be applied to Polish identity.[25] Because the cross is the ultimate sign of redemption, adding it to the monument not only reflects the historical victory of the true Polish identity; it also signifies an attempt to redeem the evil caused by that identity's long repression. Nationalist discourse, on the other hand, makes the nation's memoryscapes into sites for the cultural practice of collective immortalization. Thus, the memoryscape helps national identity to survive ruptures by evoking a "future imaginable throughout the past," and by building and celebrating national identity as primordial, unified, and continuous.[26] The modern nationalisms described by Anderson use secularized discourses to this end. More traditional nationalisms, however, in which religion is an important factor of national unity, may employ religious discourse as well.

A new inscription was also added to Przeworsk's monument in 2000. It reads:

"Open the door for Christ"
(John Paul II)
To the victims of the struggle for freedom and human dignity.
In the Millennial Year
to honor
the pontificate of the Polish Pope
John Paul II.
Community of Przeworsk.

This inscription describes the redemption of Polish identity that is embodied by the monument's transformation. First, the values expressed in Polish history have been redefined as freedom and dignity. Second, Polish identity has been linked to Christianity through references to Christ and to the second millennium. Finally, the authority of the pope—perhaps the only Polish person living or dead held in high esteem by all Poles—has been invoked to cement this redemption.

The figure of Christ "crucified by Communism" is, therefore, a sign of a key internal conflict within Polish memory. It is also an attempt to confirm the persistence of the "true essence of Polishness" in spite of ruptures caused by the "evils" of Communism. At the same time, the figure is a sign of nationalist eschatology and theodicy. This last point may be another reason that local authorities have been unwilling to commemorate the town's Jews. The former Jewish cemetery has been turned into a *Polish* memoryscape—a symbolic territory of Polish redemption and reconciliation of different groupings within Polish society. Thus, the inclusion of Jews would only complicate the picture and turn attention to an evil that was even worse than three decades of Communism, and a group that has suffered even more than the Poles. Commemorating Jews would also return attention to the site's original function as a Jewish cemetery. For these reasons, Jews have been excluded from the local memoryscape. Such "differential deprivation of history," in which nondominant groups have no chance to demonstrate the "lasting visibility of their own past," is a key means by which dominant groups gain existential strength.[27]

While the Jewish strand of Polish history has been almost entirely elided from the Polish perspective, the divided site reveals a much more central crack in Polish history: the conflict between the "dark force" of Communism on the one hand and Polishness and Christianity on the other. In this way, Przeworsk's former Jewish cemetery has become a site of striving for ethnic Polish collective immortalization, reinforcing an ethnic Polish "community of history and destiny."

In the process, ethnic Poles achieve a "measure of immortality" by ensuring that individual Polish achievements will "live on and bear fruit in the community"—their *own* community.[28]

Memory, Space, Identity: Toward a Typology

In the final section of this chapter, I would like to offer a theoretical model that may help to organize and structure the variety of attitudes toward Polish-Jewish memoryscapes that have been presented in the previous sections. This model also has an explanatory function. It tries to avoid the static perception and monolithic treatment of "the Poles" that has weakened other discussions of Jewish memory in Poland. The model presented here presupposes that memoryscapes are produced locally, and that localities differ across time and space. While such local populations have been ethnically Polish since the Holocaust, they are nevertheless socially and culturally heterogeneous and have been forced to collectively reinvent themselves. Physical space and materiality itself—with the traces of the past they contain—are active factors in this process. In this model, the concrete forms of Poland's local Jewish memoryscapes are interpreted as a consequence of each community's own shifting identity and its relation to space, rather than a simple materialization of Polish-Jewish relations.

Memory's relationship with space and identity is based on an interesting paradox. According to David Lowenthal, a common vision of the past is a necessary element of collective identity.[29] The answer to the question "Who are we?" must therefore be founded in the image of who a group *was*. At the same time, however, the present identity of a group is precisely what makes that group's past relevant. This is because any "living" past is someone's past, and that past has a meaning in the present. As John R. Gillis succinctly explains it, the essential meaning of an individual or collective identity—the preservation of "sameness" across time and space—is secured by memory. What we remember is determined by the identity we accept.[30]

The two theoretical oppositions presented above—memory that forms identity versus identity that forms memory, and space as a model of memory versus space as a model for memory—may be used to order our empirical experience of particular localities and the groups that inhabit them. In this sense, each opposition can be seen as a continuum. The first continuum, linked to the opposition between memory and identity, ranges from communities whose identities are firmly rooted in the past to communities that need to invent their past. The second continuum, linked to the opposition between memory and space, ranges from spaces that passively accumulate past events to spaces that are actively manipulated in order to orient social memory toward desired visions of the past. By combining these two dimensions, we can create a model that will help us to order the relationship among memory, space, and identity. This model is presented in table 6.1.

Table 6.1. Relationships among memory, space, and identity

| | Memory and identity | | |
		The past → contemporary "We"	Contemporary "We" → the past
Memory and space	Space as a "model of" memory	A	B
	Space as a "model for" memory	D	C

Type A represents "traditional communities." These communities have existed in the same space for a long time. They are relatively homogeneous and have fixed relations of power. Their members have a sense of continuity in their collective life. They define themselves by referencing the past and live in more or less stable spatial layouts that they do not manipulate. The center of Kraków as well as villages or some towns in the Carpathian are illustrations of type A communities.

Type B represents "new" communities, such as those consisting largely of immigrants. Because they are characterized by the coexistence of various, sometimes irreconcilable, forms of social memory, they can be considered heterogeneous. They must, due to this heterogeneity, first "imagine" themselves in the present and then "invent" a more or less commonly shared past. They have a settled spatial layout, which contains the accumulated signs of other groups that once lived there. As a rule, however, they do not manipulate space. Instead, they try to adjust to it, largely ignoring the traces of the past that surround them. Sometimes, however, they gradually come to identify with the past as it is remembered in space. History provides us with numerous examples of heterogeneous "barbarian hordes" that conquered civilized lands. These groups illustrate a type B relationship among memory, space, and identity.

Type C represents new communities that define themselves in and by their present. These communities actively manipulate their new spaces of life in order to build them into their invented traditions and imagined identities. Type C is well illustrated by the so-called Recovered Lands granted to Poland after World War II as a consequence of the Allies' political bargaining. Pieces of this territory were never even in contact with any geographical-political unit that might have been considered "Poland." Instead, the regained territories were a politically constructed space that legitimized Communist rule. After the German past was erased from local memoryscapes, these territories became an empty container into which elements certifying the land's eternally Polish character were added.

Type D represents traditional communities, which define themselves by their relationship to the past, but they actively manipulate the space they inhabit, removing traces of other collective memories, for instance. They may also erase ideological visions of history that were imposed on their territory, or retrieve memories that had previously been silenced or erased. This behavior is well illustrated by postcolonial societies that have preserved a sense of their common past. Many examples of type D behavior can also be found in the so-called de-communization of space in Eastern Europe after 1989.

Types A (traditional communities) and C ("manipulating" groups) can be considered "natural" because in both of these cases, we find consistency between the way that the communities form their identities and the way that their memory is contained within the spaces they inhabit. Types B and D are more interesting because they are characterized by a contradiction between their processes of identity construction and the spatial layouts in which this process takes place.

The boundaries between the four types are not fixed. Moreover, there are a variety of ways that communities may change how they produce themselves in and through space. New and "constructed" communities grow old and become traditional, for example. Traditional communities may modernize and be forced to reinvent themselves. Groups that manipulate space in order to invest it with their visions of the past may become successful—and thus come to treat their land as an untouchable model of their memory. People interested in digging into the past may discover other memories and thus subvert the official memoryscape. Communities that did not previously manipulate their space may change their attitude and begin to manipulate it. All of these possibilities for change make the model presented here a collection of "ideal types." Its application to particular cases requires a dynamic approach that assumes fluidity and acknowledges the unstable character of its categories.

In order to see how the model works in practice, let us now turn to the localities presented in the text and describe what has happened in each of them since World War II. In Polish historiography, the histories of these communities are usually interpreted as continuations of prewar times. The only change acknowledged in this historiography is the political transformation that took place due to Communist rule. The radical exchanges of population that took place in all of these localities is hardly seen as a central fact of their histories. Yet, at least half of each town's inhabitants were murdered or displaced on account of the war. These missing inhabitants were replaced by newcomers, a category that includes both people from neighboring villages looking for a better life and people resettled from Poland's former eastern territories.

It has, therefore, been difficult to unambiguously classify these communities. On the one hand, they were "traditional" in the sense that the halves of their populations that survived the war continued to live in the same places as had generations of their ancestors. On the other hand, they were "new" because newcomers filled the empty places in their social spaces. Old and new inhabitants alike had to "invent" themselves as communities without the aid of commonly shared traditions because such traditions did not exist.

The history of Żołynia exemplifies this difficulty. According to the census of 1921, the town's 569 Jews comprised 60 percent of its population.[31] By 1939, the number of Jews in Żołynia had grown to 598, but Jews now comprised only 12 percent of the total population.[32] This rapid decline in the percentage of Jewish inhabitants can be explained rather simply. As early as 1919, an initiative was developed to group the town of Żołynia together in a single administrative unit with a neighboring village, which was also known as Żołynia. The town of Żołynia and the village of Żołynia were formally united in 1928. Because the village had almost no Jews, the percentage of Jews in the new administrative unit was significantly lower than it had been previously in the town alone. This change was reflected in the composition of the town council. Żołynia's last town council before World War I had twelve Jews among its eighteen members. In the first election after the two Żołynias' unification, not one Jewish representative was elected to the council.[33]

The social profile of Żołynia had, therefore, already changed before World War II. Thus, the town's postwar population exchange was not as radical as in the other localities described here. Due to these changes to its profile before World War II, Żołynia can be defined as a traditional community. Wartime experiences, including the heroic narrative of resistance, were shared by Żołynia's surviving Polish community. Because the process of making Jews "invisible" commenced before the war, and the whole of the town's Jewish community along with all the material representations of its existence were destroyed during the war, the postwar exclusion of Jewish memory occurred spontaneously and without too much effort. Thus, we can place Żołynia between types A and D, although it is perhaps a bit closer to the former. What is more, the contemporary "reemergence" of the Jewish cemetery and the growing interest in Żołynia's Jewish past may be modest indications of an evolution toward type C, whereby a new definition of community is premised on a reshaping of the spatial frames of memory.

Rzeszów and Tarnów, where Jews constituted at least 50 percent of the total population before the war, witnessed the most radical population exchanges in the aftermath of the war and Holocaust. The character of these towns contributed greatly to the social transformations that occurred in both of them. As centers of Communist industrialization in an otherwise rural area, Rzeszów and Tarnów both attracted rural people to be turned into workers.

Jewish memory, wounded as it was, did live on. Tiny groups of Holocaust survivors populated both localities until the beginning of the 1970s. Perhaps it was for this reason that the non-Jewish inhabitants of Tarnów and Rzeszów did not display any particular interest in the remaining Jewish spaces. They may have simply assumed that this was a matter that the Jews should take care of. Because the few

Jews still living in Tarnów and Rzeszów did not have the means to do anything about the state of the towns' Jewish spaces, or perhaps because they preferred to stay "invisible," the spatial elements of Jewish memory either became increasingly dilapidated or were turned into communal property.

Tarnów and Rzeszów can be thus described as representations of type B. Both towns had to integrate new inhabitants and develop common identities including old and new. Yet, there was no significant intervention into the memoryscape in either case. Even these towns have changed over their histories, however. During the 1960s, the process of integration had largely been accomplished, and both towns seemed to be getting closer to type A. In the 1980s, the growing interest in discovering the towns' Jewish pasts, together with the development of commemorative activities, led to the transformation of memoryscapes. At this time, remnants of the Jewish pasts were highlighted in the cityscapes. Contemporary Tarnów and Rzeszów come, therefore, closer to type D. Both are communities that identify themselves by referencing the common past, but both also manipulate memoryscapes—though they now do so in order to preserve their Jewish pasts.

Łańcut, the town that lost about 40 percent of its population during the Holocaust, passed through the postwar process of population exchange relatively "naturally." As a "transfer space" between town and village, it has always been connected with rural people. It was precisely Łańcut's precarious position between town and village that revealed the significance of its Jewish presence. Łańcut was a shtetl, the space of which, Artur Markowski writes, was "something between the social space of a village and a town; a form that bridged village and town not only regarding the economy but also culture, religion and certain traditions or mental habits."[34]

Łańcut is therefore an example of a locality whose postwar spatial/temporal identity is located somewhere between type A and type B. The town has recently evolved toward type D, however, a trend that is indicated by the "musealization" of the synagogue building. The spatialized reemergence of an important element of the town's Jewish past has made Łańcut a model for the idea that Jewish tradition is something worth including in a town's local heritage.

Przeworsk, another town that lost 40 percent of its inhabitants on account of the Holocaust and then proceeded to erase the local Jewish presence, could be described in the postwar period as a mixture of type A and type C. The alterations that the town made to the Communist monument in 2000 suggest that since 1989, it has become a mixture of type C and type D. Through its de-communization of space, Przeworsk attempted to write a new version of its history that both officially redefines the community and continues the silencing of the Jewish past in public space.

It is worth noting that in many cases, the presence of the Jewish past is largely imagined and constructed yet simultaneously real. This is because local people involve the Jewish past in their activities. The Jewish past becomes, therefore, part of a "virtual multiculturalism,"[35] oriented toward the past and based on the "idea that various disadvantaged groups in society have equally valid views of history as that of the established culture of the majority."[36] Our understanding of the past, shaped as it is through palimpsest-like spaces, is therefore an exercise in multiculturalism that assumes a multiplicity of interpretations and rejects their ordering by the authority of any narrative closure.[37]

But our interpretive approach to the past(s) given in and through space is also an exercise in identity formation. The way we approach the past *is,* by and large, our contemporary identity. In this sense, the localities discussed here are sites of practice congruent with James Clifford's diagnosis.[38] According to Clifford, postmodern identities no longer presuppose a continuity of culture or tradition, and are mostly improvised locally from various collected pasts. Through these improvisations, different groups' pasts are mixed up and transformed. They become part of the local memoryscape, which is sustained on the one hand by the physicality of the space and the artifacts preserved within it, and on the other, by the way in which these artifacts are used as the props of local performances of identity.

Notes

1. Michel Foucault, "Of Other Spaces," *Diacritics* 16 (1986): 22–27.

2. See, for example, Edward W. Soja, "Postmodern Geographies: Taking Los Angeles Apart," in *NowHere: Space, Time and Modernity,* ed. Roger Friedland and Deirdre Boden (Berkeley: University of California Press, 1994), 127–162.

3. Gerard Delanty, *Social Theory in a Changing World: Conceptions of Modernity* (Cambridge: Polity Press, 1999), 71.

4. Ibid.

5. Hamzah Muzaini and Brenda S. A. Yeoh, "War Landscapes as 'Battlefields' of Collective Memories: Reading the *Reflections at Bukit Chandu,* Singapore," *Cultural Geographies* 12 (2005): 345.

6. Arjun Appadurai, *Modernity at Large: Cultural Dimensions of Globalization* (Minneapolis: University of Minnesota Press, 1996), 33.

7. Muzaini and Yeoh, "War Landscapes," 345.

8. William H. Sewell, Jr., *Logics of History: Social Theory and Social Transformation* (Chicago: University of Chicago Press, 2005), 172.

9. Lisa Yoneyama, "Timing the Memoryscape: Hiroshima's Urban Renewal," in *Remapping Memory: The Politics of TimeSpace,* ed. Jonathan Boyarin (Minneapolis: University of Minnesota Press, 1994), 103.

10. Akhil Gupta and James Ferguson, "Beyond 'Culture': Space, Identity and the Politics of Difference," *Cultural Anthropology* 7, no. 1 (1992): 6–23.

11. Clifford Geertz, "Religion as a Cultural System," in *The Interpretations of Cultures* (New York: Basic Books, 1973), 90–91.

12. Iwona Irwin-Zarecka, *Frames of Remembrance: The Dynamics of Collective Memory* (New Brunswick, NJ: Transaction, 1994).

13. James E. Young, *The Texture of Memory: Holocaust Memorials and Meaning* (New Haven, CT: Yale University Press, 1993), 116.

14. Karol Urban, *Cmentarze żydowskie, synagogi i domy modlitwy w Polsce w latach 1944–1966 (wybór materiałów)* (Kraków: Nomos, 2006).

15. Ruth E. Gruber, *Virtually Jewish: Reinventing Jewish Culture in Europe* (Berkeley: University of California Press, 2002).

16. Laurence Weinbaum, "Penitence and Prejudice: The Roman Catholic Church and Jedwabne," *Jewish Political Studies Review* 14, nos. 3–4 (Fall 2002): 132.

17. This book has been published in Polish as *Złote żniwa*. See Jan Tomasz Gross with Irena Grudzińska-Gross, *Golden Harvest: Events at the Periphery of the Holocaust* (Oxford: Oxford University Press, 2012).

18. Ireneusz Krzemiński, "Polacy i Ukraińcy o swoich narodach, o cierpieniu w czasie wojny i o Zagładzie Żydów," in *Antysemityzm w Polsce i na Ukrainie: Raport z badań*, ed. Ireneusz Krzemiński (Warsaw: Wydawnictwo Naukowe Scholar, 2004), 120.

19. Sławomir Kapralski, "The Impact of Post-1989 Changes on Polish-Jewish Relations and Perceptions: Memories and Debates," in *The Religious Roots of Contemporary European Identity*, ed. Lucia Faltin and Melanie J. Wright (London: Continuum, 2007), 89–104.

20. This is the English text on the table; spelling and styling as in the original.

21. Tarnów's memoryscape is therefore composed of the elements that serve as "models for" and those that are "models of." Among the latter, one should list the already mentioned Jewish cemetery as well as the bimah, the only remnant of the city's Old Synagogue. But since the area near the bimah recently became a site of various commemorative and artistic events, staged by Adam Bartosz, the head of the local museum, it may represent an interesting shift from a "model of" to a "model for."

22. The word "liberation" is a contested term in Poland. Since 1989, it has been argued that the concept is an ideological legacy of the Communist period and should be used carefully. Those less sympathetic to Communism would say that what happened in 1944–1945 was just a replacement of the Nazi German occupation with an occupation by the Red Army and its puppet regime. It was not, in other words, a real liberation.

23. Urban, *Cmentarze żydowskie*, 445.

24. The phrase is said to have been the last words of the Roman emperor Julian the Apostate.

25. Benedict Anderson, *Imagined Communities* (London: Verso, 1991).

26. David McCrone, *The Sociology of Nationalism: Tomorrow's Ancestors* (New York: Routledge, 1998), 52.

27. Zygmunt Bauman, *Mortality, Immortality and Other Life Strategies* (Cambridge: Polity Press, 1992).

28. Anthony D. Smith, *The Ethnic Origins of Nations* (Oxford: Blackwell, 1986).

29. David Lowenthal, *The Past Is a Foreign Country* (Cambridge: Cambridge University Press, 1985), 41–46.

30. John R. Gillis, "Memory and Identity: The History of a Relationship," in *Commemorations: The Politics of National Identity*, ed. J. R. Gillis (Princeton, NJ: Princeton University Press, 1994), 3.

31. Andrzej Potocki, *Żydzi w Podkarpackiem* (Rzeszów: Libra, 2004), 206–207.

32. Magdalena Kątnik-Kowalska, *By zdarzeń nie zatarł czas* (Żołynia: Gminny Ośrodek Kultury w Żołyni, 2002), 76.

33. See Żołynia Memorial, "Between the Wars," http://www.zolynia.org/betweenwars.html.

34. Artur Markowski, "Przestrzeń społeczna *sztetł* na przełomie XIX i XX w.—studium przypadku Wasilkowa na Białostocczyźnie," in *Świat NIEpożegnany: Żydzi na dawnych zie-*

miach wschodnich Rzeczypospolitej w XVIII–XX wieku, ed. W. K. Jasiewicz (Warsaw: Instytut Studiów Politycznych PAN i Oficyna Wydawnicza Rytm, 2004), 344.

35. Mirosław Bieniecki, "Wielokulturowość bez wielokulturowości (z notatnika badacza społeczności lokalnej we Włodawie)," *Kultura Współczesna* 42 (2004), 306–316.

36. Andreas Kitzmann, Conny Mithander, and John Sundholm, "Introduction," in *Memory Work: The Theory and Practice of Memory,* ed. Andreas Kitzmann, Conny Mithander, and John Sundholm (Frankfurt am Main: Peter Lang, 2005), 16.

37. Marek Szopski, "Dylematy wielokulturowości w metropoliach Europy," in *Tolerancja i wielokulturowość–wyzwania XXI wieku,* ed. Agnieszka Borowiak and Piotr Szarota (Warsaw: Wydawnictwo Szkoły Wyższej Psychologii Społecznej Academica, 2004), 71.

38. James Clifford, *The Predicament of Culture: Twentieth-Century Ethnography, Literature, and Art* (Cambridge, MA: Harvard University Press, 1996).

7 Jewish Heritage, Pluralism, and *Milieux de Mémoire*
The Case of Kraków's Kazimierz

Erica Lehrer

> Public spaces . . . can be sites of reconciliation between strangers who are wary
> of, but curious, about each other.
>
> —Elaine Gurian[1]

"Why would a Pole open a Jewish bookstore?" Jewish visitors ask. A non-Jewish Jewish bookstore would be cause enough for suspicion. But a Polish one? This combination violates the basic order of a Jewish universe built from grandparents' stories of deceitful Poles turning over Jews to the Nazis for vodka.

Zdzisław Leś is the owner of the Jarden Jewish Bookshop in Kraków, Poland. He recalled to me his inspiration for opening the shop:

> I visited this normal bookshop, in this very building, in which sat two boring women selling crime stories and third-class literature. And there was one shelf, maybe two small shelves, on which was written "Judaica." Ten titles! And I asked them, *"Do you know where you are?"* I thought it was a scandal, and I told these women so. So I took it over, threw out the other 90 percent of the books, and began to increase the Judaica. And now I have about 150 titles—in practice, all of what is published in Poland. And it is the only Jewish bookshop in Poland.[2]

Zdzisław used to direct Kraków's House of Culture, the omnipresent Communist-era center for community arts and cultural ideology, where he introduced a series called "Meetings with Jewish Culture." There were gatherings with authors of books, concerts of Jewish songs, and other events. At university, Zdzisław trained as a Slavicist. He attributed much of his sensitivity about Jewish influences on Polish culture to his familiarity with Polish literature. He poked fun at Polish ethnonationalism, noting that many of Poland's cultural heroes were of Jewish origin:

I don't know if you know that the best Polish poet of the twentieth century was Jewish. Bolesław Leśmian. And the best master of Polish language. Many Polish poets in the twentieth century were Jews: Tuwim, Leśmian, Słonimski. And they created, I think, more variety in poetry than others. In *Polish* poetry. . . . Isn't that a paradox? And some others fields, history for example, science. Maybe our stupid nationalists will finally understand that Polish folklore, which makes them have an orgasm, owes Jews a lot, and that their favorite potato pancakes are also a Jewish recipe, that our so-called folk art was also inspired by Jews and [our] dumb nation was only copying what they invented. So consider this: if so many Jews have done so much for Polish culture, why shouldn't two poor Poles like us do something for Jews?

Converging Memory Projects

The Jarden Jewish Bookshop is located in Kazimierz, a rare medieval Jewish quarter that survived World War II intact. Until the early 1990s, however, it was a largely empty, dilapidated part of Kraków. The most obvious evidence of hundreds of years of Jewish habitation were the many crumbling synagogues and entrance ways with visible impressions of mezuzot (small receptacles containing a biblical text traditionally affixed to door frames) that had been wrenched away in the wake of the brutal removal of the Jews by the Nazis. While Kazimierz is no longer a Jewish neighborhood in normative terms, fashionable Jewish-themed cafés and shops, run by ethnic Poles, now line the main square, beckoning customers with signs in Hebrew and Yiddish (or faux versions of them), and offering "Jewish" food, decor, and music.

His waggish rhetoric aside, the question Zdzisław poses begs exploration: just what are these Poles doing for Jews—and why? Many critical observers—foreign Jews perhaps most of all—have a ready answer. These "poor Poles" are not doing anything for Jewish culture, quite the opposite. They are skimming what is fashionable and marketable from Jewishness while uninterested in and unconnected to actual Jews, who are conveniently absent. Simply put, the notion "that preservation of the Jewish heritage of Poland lies partly in Christian hands . . . strike[s] some people as preposterous at best, and, at worst, in extremely bad taste."[3]

I seek to counter the popular view that interest in Jewish heritage in Poland today is merely a superficial fad, a view that is reinforced by the widespread embrace of the notion of "virtual Jewishness" that has proliferated since the publication of journalist Ruth Gruber's book by that name in 2002.[4] I suggest instead that the emergence of engagements with Jewish heritage in Kazimierz (and other sites in Poland) can be seen in important ways as the result of two overlapping subaltern memory projects—a local Polish one and a foreign Jewish one imported by tourism, both of which seek to expand narrow notions of nationhood by adopting new grounds, vocabularies, and materials for national and cultural identity building. Jewish heritage functions as an important tool for national reimagining in post-Communist Poland, and Poland is growing in significance for Western Jews seeking to rethink their individual and group heritage.

I have approached the process of reclaiming Poland's Jewish heritage from an ethnographic perspective: a micro-level view that seeks primarily to understand how local actors comprehend and navigate their changing social worlds, in conversation with the various other-cultural individuals they meet and whose own perspectives they must negotiate. While significant Polish state and regional initiatives engage with Jewish heritage in the form of major museum, monument, and educational projects, I focus on the grassroots level because it began significantly prior to the top-down initiatives, as well as because of its prevalence and activist quality. Most importantly, a ground-level view offers a window onto the significance of interethnic encounters for changes in individual subjectivity. Given the difficult history that underlies Jewish heritage in Poland, the open wound it remains for many Poles and Jews, and the touristic framework in which key encounters are taking place, I have tried to capture the quality of experience where tourists and locals meet. Doing so helps to illuminate the changing character of Eastern Europe's former "bloodlands." Here, sites of both killing and former life are being repurposed as sites of heritage, and they have become focal points for the significant moral, emotional, and political transactions as victims, witnesses, perpetrators, and their descendants, have come into increasing contact. These encounters suggest how coming to terms with historical wounds includes the reconfiguring of collective identities in ways that allow new relationships of self and other to emerge.

In Poland, Jewish heritage has functioned in important ways as a tool for Poles to reimagine their country in pluralist terms, a counterweight to rightwing rhetoric that stresses the longstanding, dominant conception of Polishness as essentially Polish-Catholic. In a contemporary demographic reality in which 95 percent of Polish citizens are baptized Catholics, Jewish heritage is both a vehicle to reclaim aspects of a prewar history of multiethnic coexistence across Polish terrain, as well as to envision a future Poland that may stand among peers in an increasingly multiethnic European Union. The Polish "Jewish memory" project is meaningfully contiguous with activist projects rooted in Poland's struggle for democracy. In the 1970s and 1980s under late Communism in Poland, grassroots interest in and activities on behalf of Jews represented a form of resistance against the government, which periodically wielded anti- (or occasionally philo-) Semitism as a political tool but otherwise censored Jewish themes.[5] Since the early 1990s in post-Communist Poland, non-Jewish "heritage brokers" have played essential roles in cultivating "Jewish space," where both Jews and non-Jewish Poles could begin to reimagine themselves in plural, interconnected ways.[6]

While not all of the post-Communist brokers have been idealistically motivated (and they are almost all, in a literal sense, opportunistic), neither have most of their projects been singularly mercenary. Rather, as has been suggested of culture brokering projects elsewhere, they may be better understood as representing "an honour, a responsibility, and something that can sometimes be turned to personal advantage and profit."[7] In publicly affirming Jewish culture, key brokers took social risks that the few, mostly old remaining local Jews were unable or unwilling to take. As international Jewish tourism and local Jewish confidence have grown, some brokers have productively engaged with these more conventional institutional and individual bearers of Jewish culture, renegotiating their roles along the way. While at times Jews function symbolically in this heritage industry, in Kazimierz in particular, culture and memory work has been a highly dialogic project in which the symbolic and the practical have intertwined, and the work of rethinking Polishness has overlapped with and been mutually catalyzed by processes of Jewish cultural heritage preservation, individual Polish-Jewish deassimilation, and Jewish community revival, to which non-Jewish Poles have made crucial contributions.[8] As sociologist Iwona Irwin-Zarecka notes of the pre-1989 period, "It would often be from these Catholic friends that a Jew brought up in silence learned some basics of Judaism and Jewish history."[9]

In parallel fashion, while facing the Holocaust remains a central motivation for much foreign Jewish travel to Poland, a growing minority of Western Jews seeks in that country more than an experience of evil and an opportunity to bear witness to genocide. A "memory project" discernibly developing among foreign Jews has drawn some to confront and reconsider their own community's refusal of Poland as a relevant part of Jewish heritage beyond the heritage of destruction.[10] Visiting Jews have increasingly seen in Poland an opportunity to reclaim aspects of their collective, as well as individual, genealogical selfhood that were lost or suppressed due to the broad effects of Holocaust trauma and the collective reorientation of Jewish communal identity toward Israel. Particularly as difficult questions about Zionism grow, there is a new appeal to alternative sites and formations of Jewishness including aspects of "shtetl" culture, klezmer music, and radical politics. Thus, while the incorporation of Jewishness into the Polish national narrative has been a prime mover in Kazimierz's character and success, individual Jewish quests to come to terms with Poland's broader Jewish heritage (beyond the Holocaust) have played an integral complementary role. As Amos, a French Jew in his early twenties, told me in the late 1990s while sitting in Café Ariel, one of Kazimierz's key Jewish-themed venues: "People come here [to Poland] and say 'It is awful, it is awful.' I say, 'No.' I don't come here to say it is awful. I just come to make peace with people. To *not* say, 'Okay, [see], it *is* antisemitic.' To try [instead] to make peace, and to make a place for that in my head. . . . I didn't want to go back to Poland to see antisemitism. I want to *stop* this."

While these emerging memory projects have followed multiple pathways, Kazimierz has functioned uniquely as a social catchment with an inherent *genius loci* that brings these projects into constant, meaningful contact. Over a fifteen-year span, I saw the Polish and Jewish projects not only converge but intertwine, catalyze, and most importantly reckon with each other in Kazimierz. The neighborhood has emerged as an important place for encounter and both memory and identity work, and a space that works against narrower, mono-ethnic, and thus more conflicting notions of Poland and its Jewish heritage—still dominant in both Jewish and Polish society—that pit Jewishness and Polishness if not always against, then in essential ways as distinct from, one another.

Much has changed in Kazimierz, and in Poland, since the first post-Communist Jewish tourist encounters with Poland and the proliferation of expressions of Jewish heritage in Polish public space. Diplomatic, business, educational, and artistic collaborations between Poland and Israel have increased, and on the Polish side, there has been an explosion of work by nonprofit nongovernmental organizations addressing Jewish themes.[11] But despite a few important American Jewish interventions, for Jewish visitors to Poland, there remains a widespread sense of apprehension; travel to Poland still feels for many like the breaching of time-space, a ritual entry into a traumatic mythico-history. Similarly, due to the minuscule number of Jews in Poland, most Poles have never met a Jew, and the sense of Jewishness as a socially touchy—if not outright taboo—topic endures. Indeed, the shock waves emanating from the public revelations of Polish complicity in Holocaust crimes following the publication of sociologist Jan Gross's books beginning in the early 2000s (along with subsequent scholarship and artistic production) have in some ways made Jewish subjects more sensitive than before.[12]

Kazimierz, more than just an evocative site for the projection and reception of representations of Jewish heritage, is a unique opening in which Jews and Poles regularly cross paths, a rare opportunity for geographically dissociated groups to experience "the face-to-face encounter that has traditionally grounded the ethical."[13] In this way, it suggests how heritage sites, despite their often superficial and stereotypical portrayals of culture and history, can form arenas in which painfully conflicting collective memories and national identities can be incrementally confronted, questioned, and expanded.

Jewish heritage initiatives in Poland—even in Kazimierz—are not always productive, and there is abundant evidence that engagements with them can result in painful incommensurabilities, misrecognitions, and retrenchment of positions—not to mention the cooptation of such initiatives by diplomatic narratives as grossly oversimplified signs of rosy past and present Polish-Jewish relations. But it should be recognized that heritage sites and spaces have special properties that make them powerful as self-making practices, available as much for morally and politically progressive practices of identification as for the celebration of ethnonationalism and its essentialized identity categories. The frequent, easy dismissal of places like Kazimierz as a "Jewish Disneyland"—a label suggesting a totalizing environment that reproduces normative identifications and constrains social interactions—needs to be challenged.[14]

Jewish Poland as Conflicted Heritage

The activist quality of the notion of a hybrid "Polish-Jewish" heritage—as illustrated by Zdzisław's statement above—must be understood in the context of the troubled symbolic landscape that Polish-Jewish relations were reduced to after the horrors of the Holocaust. This includes the immediate postwar years in which the few surviving, returning Polish Jews were often seen and acted upon as unwanted foreigners, as well as the later Communist government-sponsored antisemitic campaigns that emptied Poland almost entirely of Jews and Jewish social and memorial infrastructure. Whether today there exists a Polish-Jewish heritage—and what that heritage consists of—is a matter of popular dispute. In the postwar period, a divorce of Polish and Jewish memory occurred. Polish national memory was rearticulated by (Catholic) Poles, and Jewish memory of Poland was elaborated by Jews now largely residing elsewhere. This split was perpetuated and reinforced by Communist and ethnonational heritage practices, the latter within both the Polish and foreign Jewish communities.[15] New scholarship, in publications titled *Contested Memories* and *Imaginary Neighbors,* suggests contending frames of reference and charged symbolic engagements in which incommensurable Jewish and Polish national narratives of martyrology come head to head, particularly around the very sites of the Nazi genocide machinery.[16]

On the Polish side, the priorities of the postwar Communist state and the demands of Polish nationalism made the heritage of Poland's longstanding Jewish community invisible, unwanted, or irrelevant to what had become a mono-ethnic (Catholic) Polish nation.[17] While the Jewish past has become increasingly relevant in present-day, post-Communist Poland—particularly in the international diplomatic arena—its grassroots significance is shifting, uneven, and multivalent.[18] In the Jewish communal world outside of Poland, the *hegemonic* answer to the corresponding question of whether the Jewish people have a Polish heritage that extends beyond their near-demise during the Holocaust remained through the mid-2000s a relatively resounding "No."[19] The majority of Jewish travelers to Poland still visited primarily Holocaust-related sites, often continuing on (or returning) to Israel. These visits are frequently embedded in forms of state- and community-sponsored memorial tourism that use these countries as a stage to enact a Zionist-inflected pageant of national death and redemption, with an attendant either/or understanding of Polishness and Jewishness.[20]

The polarization of Jewish and Polish national visions of Poland's Jewish heritage at the turn of the twenty-first century is revealed by comparing two maps—one from an Israeli tourist agency specializing in youth tours to Poland and one from the Polish National Tourist Board.[21] Both maps show the terrain of today's

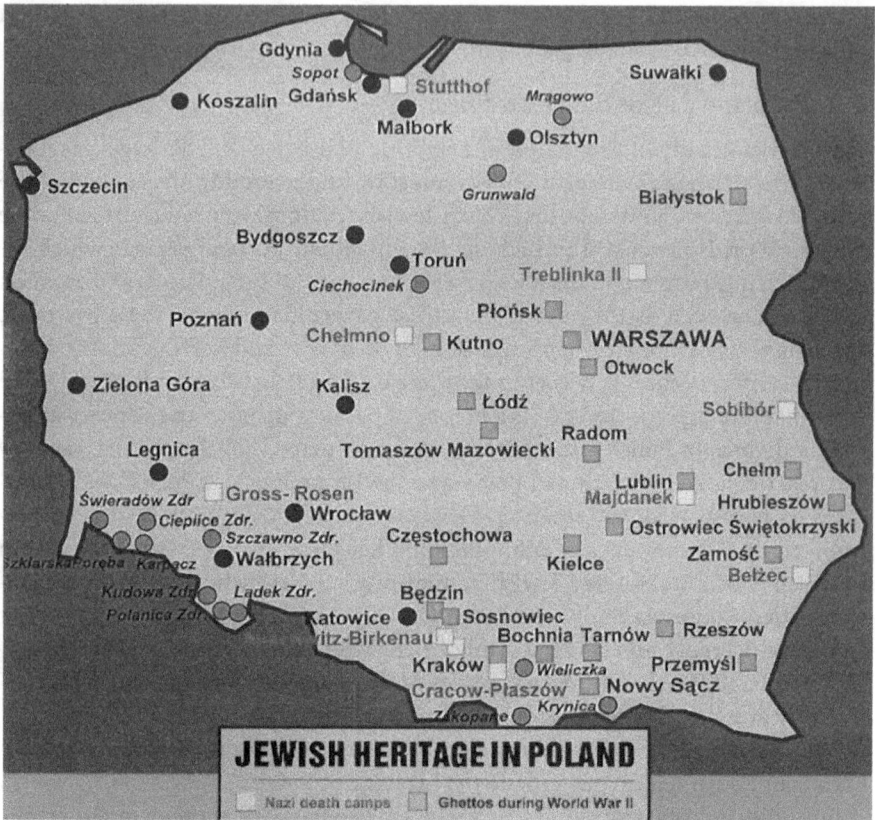

Map 7.1. Israeli map from the back cover of *Polin,* an Israeli tourist brochure advertising travel to Poland. Circa 2000.

Poland and are identically titled "Jewish Heritage in Poland." But the keys for each map—and the corresponding density of sites denoted—are strikingly different. The Polish map lists a range of historical Jewish locations, including key sites of Holocaust atrocities, but also features synagogues, Hassidic centers, and other sites of Jewish history and life. The Israeli map, by contrast, indicates *only* Nazi ghettos and extermination camps, a radical narrowing of what Poland's Jewish heritage might be seen to contain.[22]

These fixed, divergent representations serve as a backdrop on which to view the new grassroots activity around Poland's Jewish heritage, and the potential for new identity formation in relation to the dynamic social spaces these create.

Jews and Poles were "unequal victims" of Nazi crimes,[23] and recent historical scholarship suggests that Poles participated in Jewish persecution of and profiteer-

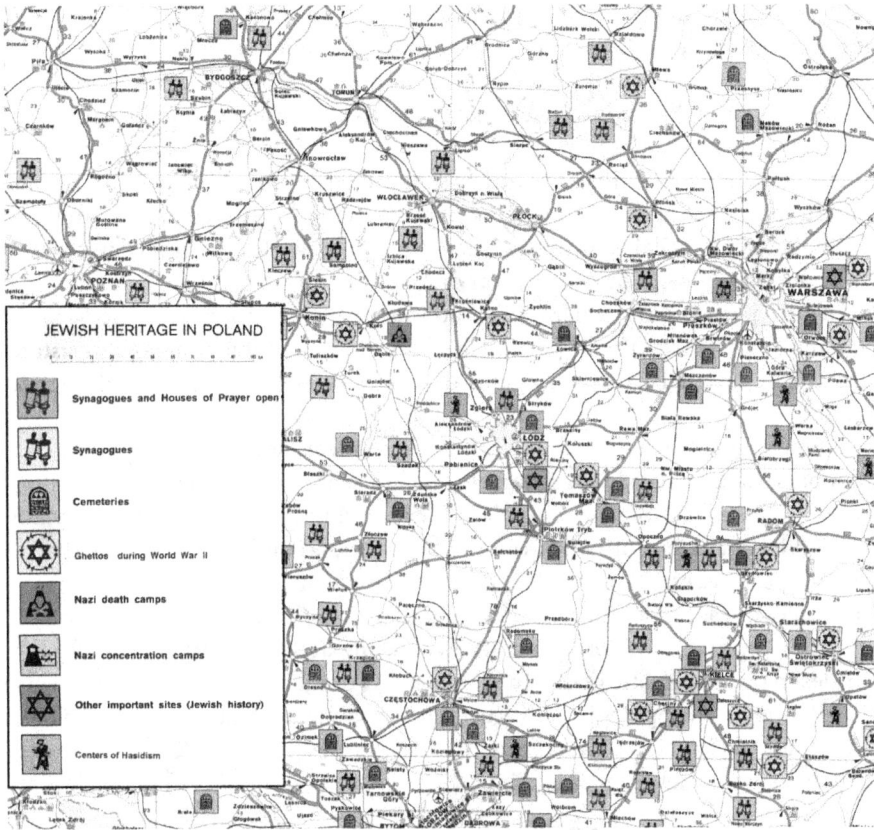

Map 7.2. Polish map excerpt from *Map of Jewish Heritage,* published by Centur/Polish Tourist Information Center during the late Communist era and since at least 2003 by the Polish Tourist Organization in Warsaw.

ing from Jewish expropriation to a greater extent than previously acknowledged, both during and after the war.[24] Compounding the injury, the Communist-era Polish state generally declined to acknowledge the Holocaust—the disproportional persecution and uniquely motivated attempt to exterminate the Jews—as distinct from the more general, brutal occupation of Poland and attendant persecution of ethnic Poles. While Holocaust consciousness has been publicly cultivated in the post-Communist era in new monument inscriptions, the popular media, and school history textbooks, so too has a Polish national narrative of martyrology, resistance, and aid, in which Jews play an ambivalent role (perceived at turns as competitors for victim status, Communism-embracing traitors, and ingrates unappreciative of Polish sacrifice).

On the Jewish side, Holocaust consciousness has grown in significance with the North American communal battle against assimilation and waning identification with the Zionist project in both Israel and the diaspora. Jewish Holocaust commemoration has tended to extract the Jewish experience from its larger wartime context, and from the larger fate and suffering of Poland in particular. While survey data in the past fifteen years has signaled both rising Holocaust consciousness among Poles and ambivalence about whether Jews suffered more than Poles, political scientist Claire Rosenson suggested that few "Jews can say anything at all about Polish losses during the war or even describe their situation under Nazi occupation," including "whether Poland was an ally or opponent of the Nazis."[25] The major Jewish youth travel-to-Poland programs have been at worst resistant, and at best slow, to modify their general disinterest in Polish history and perspectives.[26]

Since shortly after World War II, Poles and Jews have not in any significant numbers shared a physical territory, let alone a sense of shared culture or historical experience.[27] Unlike, for example, black and white Americans, South Africans, or conflicted citizens of Latin American countries, Polish-Jewish reconciliation has not been necessary, as the two groups no longer inhabit the same geographical space. In each side's narrative of victimhood, the other has served mostly to illustrate the first side's heroism or its own incomparable suffering. Despite major strides in the diplomatic realm, in many sectors of the Polish and Western Jewish populations, anthropologist Jack Kugelmass's 1995 statement that "Jews see Poles as witnesses, if not outright accomplices, to murder; Poles see Jews as ingrates," still describes widely shared sentiments.[28]

Hybrid Physical and Social Space

Two generations of Poles and Jews have had almost no contact with each other. Most Jews come to Kazimierz because it is on the way to Auschwitz. Through the mid-1990s, I knew many Jewish visitors who arrived in Kraków only to go directly by bus or taxi to the Holocaust's central symbol, returning the way they came. Those few particularly informed or with specific ancestral ties that brought them to Kazimierz would wander among crumbling facades bearing an occasional trace of flaking Hebrew lettering. Such visitors were struck primarily by the sense of Jewish absence, "particularly visible, since in spite of the destructive force of the war, the cultural landscape and urban fabric had survived."[29] Decades of economic stagnation made it appear as if time had stopped in the near aftermath of destruction, leaving a monument to the apocalypse. For local Poles, even the Jewish identity of the quarter had been lost; Krakovians knew it only as a slum.

But by the turn of the millennium, the gentrifying Kazimierz was strikingly different. Local heritage brokers had used the site to create "Jewish space" of a particular kind, beyond what Kraków's tiny "official" local Jewish community was able or willing to provide.[30] The venues that comprised this space—often advertised as "Jewish sites" in guidebooks—formed centers of gravity for Jewish travelers, and were transformative for provincial and Krakovian Jews seeking places to assemble. But per historian Diana Pinto, just as such Jewish space "cannot exist without Jews . . . neither can it exist only with them, for the space is not the equivalent of a community. It is an open cultural and even political agora where Jews intermingle with others qua Jews, and not just as citizens . . . present anywhere Jews and non-Jews interact on Jewish themes or where a Jewish voice can make itself felt." Pinto calls such space "the crown jewel" of a pluralist democracy.[31] Exceeding artifice or veneer—but also exceeding the bounds of Jewish community—Kazimierz venues have catalyzed a range of encounters and reckonings around Jewish heritage.

Kazimierz began to be perceived by local Jews as a *safe space*, free from widespread Polish suspicion and prejudice about Jews. Journalist Ruth Gruber noted in 2003 that "the district consciously forms a sort of 'Jewish zone' where different rules from the rest of the city—or country—may apply."[32] Further, Kazimierz possesses what Konstanty Gebert, a key figure in Poland's Jewish communal revival living in Warsaw, called in the late 1990s "ruach" (Hebrew for "spirit"), which made it a favored place for Jews from across Poland to come and "be Jewish." Not only have many Polish Jews felt it to be a rare place in Poland where one *can* wear a yarmulke (skullcap) openly, but as Stanisław Krajewski (a prominent figure in the Polish-Jewish community) told me in 2007, it is a place "where it feels *more* proper to wear one than not."

Similarly, Kazimierz venues were perceived by many as a *living space* in what visiting foreign Jews otherwise encounter largely as a landscape of death. Wojciech Ornat, owner of the quarter's first and most locally beloved Jewish restaurant, told me he opened his Jewish café in Kazimierz to counteract what he saw as the quarter's emptiness and sadness.[33] "One year ago," he said in 1995, "tourists saw only death. Now, with Café Ariel, they see life." An American Jewish professor who asked me for help in arranging an educational trip echoed those sentiments, telling me her group's meal and concert at Ariel "was a highlight of our trip—the first time after visiting concentration camps and cemeteries that the participants experienced Jewish life, not Jewish death."

Indeed, Kazimierz's liveliness and popularity led it to become a *space of social networking*. Foreign Jews (particularly Westerners) were sources of information, resources, meaning, and even legitimization of Jewish identity for many—especially young—Polish Jews. Michał, a Polish Jew in his early twenties in 2000, noted the importance of visiting Kazimierz for "meet[ing] people with whom I have an emotional connection. Even if I've never talked to them. I see them each week [on Shabbat] and I know they're like me [*tacy jak ja*]. They have the same problems. I know that I'm not alone."

Even older members of the tiny local community, who tended to mistrust much of the new Jewishness Kazimierz suddenly sprouted, nevertheless extended their social space to include some of these venues. Such old-timers developed the habit of visiting Café Ariel every Shabbat to enjoy the specially made challah and coffee that Ornat provided for them at no cost. Folklorist Eve Jochnowitz noted, "As soon as it opened, Ariel became the centre of all non-ceremonial Jewish activity in Cracow."[34]

Jonah Bookstein, a young American Jew from Detroit whom I met in Kraków in 1992 and who years later became the director of the Polish offices of the Ronald Lauder Foundation in Warsaw, was deeply involved in the early revival of Jewishness in Kraków. Together with late local Jew and "public character" Henryk Halkowski, Jonah organized many Jewish cultural and religious events at Café Ariel, like parties for Chanukah and Israeli independence day. "There were lots of guests; it was really fun. Jewish and non-Jewish both. Probably half and half." He maintains that

> what Wójtek [familiar form for Wojciech Ornat, Ariel's owner] and Gosia [his wife] did contributed *so much* to the Jewish atmosphere in Kazimierz, and in a very positive way. Jewish people felt comfortable—whatever Jewish community is there—and it's *small*—felt comfortable going to Ariel. That was the first time in who knows how long that you got guys from shul—these old [guys] coming from the shul and going to sit at a café! I think that was a very significant thing.

Mateusz, a Polish-Catholic student also present at the dawn of Café Ariel shared the sense of excitement about the experience and the people he met: "I was selling books there. And I was very happy, I was just sitting there and reading the books, having some free cookies and Coca-Cola, and listening to the bands, every night, with Jewish music and there were a lot of American Jews, Israeli Jews, [Jews from England, Holland, France], it was like, a lot of Jews! It was like, a *great place to be*." The opportunity to experience cultural difference without leaving home was a clear attraction of these new Jewish spaces. Indeed, Jewish spaces quickly began to draw in the "other others"—like gays, Protestants, and ethnic minorities—that were emerging or gaining visibility in Polish society, linking superficially single-issue Jewish memory activism and the heritage tourism industry to broader issues of social pluralism.

Heritage Brokers as an Interface

Heritage brokers form a "frontline" of local contact for visiting Jews; indeed, they may be the only locals that Jewish visitors meet. Thus they act as hosts, forming a key interface through which the symbolic meaning of heritage sites is produced, encountered, and understood[35]—and one that has evolved in response to visitor input.

Jewish visitors often wander into the Jarden Jewish Bookshop with a vague air of confusion, blinking as they leave the brightness of the square for the cool dimness that lies beyond the meter-thick medieval walls of the Landau Palace that houses it. Once inside, they gaze up at the shelves of Jewish books, wooden Jewish figurines, and political posters (*All different, All equal; 1 = 1. Intolerance = 0*) and then down at bearded Zdzisław, or his wife and co-owner, Lucyna, with her menorah earrings. They often seem unsure of what to make of this unanticipated array. Zdzisław calls the bookshop "a kind of club." He told me in the early 2000s,

> This isn't just a place where we sell books. Because tourists come and they ask us questions. Also inhabitants of Kraków come here and we talk with them. It was even shocking for us; people who write doctoral dissertations come here. They come here for scholarly consultations. Even if we don't have [a book] they ask us where in the world it exists. The tourists . . . don't just ask about the war, the Holocaust. They think we're some sort of information center for Jews in Poland. They expect that of us.

Small daily gestures suggested a desire on the part of non-Jewish heritage brokers for Jewish input, belying accusations that Kazimierz promulgates a static portrait of an idealized, ahistorical culture. While nostalgia has certainly been among the forces at play, its character and results are diverse, and its sources multi-directional, coming as much from visiting Jews as local Poles. The result has been an active dialogue about the past. For example, while Café Ariel had been using recipes provided by Róża Jakubowicz, the late matriarch of Jewish Kraków (and mother of Tadeusz Jakubowicz, the president of Kraków's official Jewish community), "Jewish grandmothers" from abroad critiqued them, telling Ornat in no uncertain terms how a kugel, cholent, or dish of chopped liver should be made.[36] He welcomed their input, even seeking out visiting Jews for impromptu cooking sessions in the café's kitchen, and tinkered with his dishes accordingly.

An example with broader impact is Kraków's annual Jewish Cultural Festival. The festival was started in 1988 by a couple of Poles with a few Jewish films and an intense curiosity about the culture they depicted. Today, it is an international event that draws 25,000 people over nine days to experience everything from Hassidic dancing and Jewish cooking to Yiddish and Hebrew language lessons, from lectures on religious and current political topics to world-class live music, culminating in a final outdoor concert in Kazimierz's main square that draws thousands of revelers and is broadcast nationwide on Polish television. It was through early encounters with Jewish musicians from abroad that Janusz Makuch, the festival's founding director, became "aware that [Jewish] culture was alive, and important for many people . . . that despite the Holocaust, there was a flow, a continuity of that culture," and that an entirely gentile Jewish cultural festival seemed inappropriate.[37] Over the twenty years of the festival's development, Makuch has also moved away from "nostalgic" themes of shtetl and klezmer to include avant-garde Jewish culture and current debates on Polish-Jewish history coming out of Europe, Israel, and the United States.

Organic Sites of Truth-Telling and Listening

Many scholars have noted that audience is crucial in acts of storytelling or testimony, especially in the context of Holocaust survivor narratives.[38] "Bearing witness to a trauma is, in fact, a process that includes the listener," and for the teller, the listener may be "somebody they have been waiting for a long time."[39] While much of this work focuses on formal interview situations, I observed the same dynamics when survivors or their descendants told their stories impromptu in the informal setting of Kazimierz's "Jewish" venues. This suggests the need to broaden our understanding of testimony and where it can take place. Especially with the institutionalization of survivor testimony collection projects, telling typically occurs in prearranged situations or official settings. But testimony may find more spontaneous outlets in less abstracted sites that evoke memory in vital, organic ways, in environments or landscapes whose sociality and physicality allows stories to "stick," creating the conditions for new communities of memory.[40]

One important category of listener for Jewish stories is other Jews with similar experiences. Beginning in the early 1990s and continuing to the present day, Kazimierz has been host to a kind of collective ingathering and re-embrace of lost or suppressed memory and experience, catalyzing various kinds of intra-Jewish reconciliation with the Jewish-Polish past. Barry Spielman of Tel Aviv wrote of "the very special attraction" that Kazimierz's main square held for him. He noted that people from all over the world "gravitated to this spot because they needed something," to "find some solace." He called Café Ariel "a sort of meeting place . . . a magnet, attracting all sorts of people," and mentioned by name certain locals and perennial visitors: "My uncle David, an Auschwitz survivor, immediately struck up a conversation with [another survivor who visits Kazimierz frequently]. Meanwhile my father was engaged in conversation with a white-haired gentleman from Israel who was also originally from Cracow. It turned out that they actually knew each other, and they went on reminiscing for quite a while. Could this be the reason people come back here?"[41]

Kazimierz also attracted non-Jewish Poles eager for—although often anxious about—an encounter with Jewishness. Visiting Jews often seemed drawn to tell stories of their wartime experiences, or their inherited pain, to ethnic Poles—particularly stories of pain caused *by* Poles. Visiting Jews' desire to tell difficult stories may be read on some level as a test of Polish empathy, engagement, and willingness to listen. An American Jewish woman complained to Zdzisław after taking the Jarden Bookshop's *Schindler's List* tour in the late 1990s that the guide, when they stopped at the nearby Płaszów concentration camp site, had said that "*only* 20,000 Jews" had been imprisoned there.[42] The woman was very upset and argued with the guide. Later, Zdzisław chastised the guide. "You stupid man!" he said, "Every half intelligent Pole knows that the situation of Jews and Poles was incomparable. For Jews, Płaszów was only a stopping place on the way to Auschwitz. It is not our job to argue this [numbers] question with our customers. This is a question for historians. We must provide a service for these very sensitive people."

Despite the fact that the guide may actually have erroneously inflated rather than downplayed the number of Jews interned at the Płaszów camp (and that the Jewish visitor may have inflated it even more), Zdzisław here highlighted the distinct difference of character in the overall fates of Poles and Jews during the war—that Jews were singled out for extermination as a group. More significantly, whereas in Poland a narrative of ethnic Polish wartime martyrology is hegemonic, Zdzisław saw his role as being sensitive to the primacy of the Holocaust framework for visiting Jews.

Intersubjectivity—Uncomfortable Encounters with Difference

Encounters between visitors and locals may prompt reconsideration of received understandings of Jewishness, Polishness, and antisemitism, as well as epistemological reflection about the sources of one's own knowledge.[43] The mere confrontation with Poles positively engaged with Jewish heritage can be a "reality-rearranging" experience for Jewish visitors.[44] Visiting Jews are often taken aback—whether pleased, angry, or ambivalent—by non-Jewish tour guides or shop employees deeply involved with and educated in Jewish ritual, history, and even languages (not infrequently to an extent greater than the visiting Jews to whom they cater). As an American Jewish lawyer involved with Jewish initiatives in Kazimierz told me, "There, some gentiles know so much about Jewish traditions that they're almost part of the community."

An exchange between a visiting American Jewish mother and daughter I interviewed in Kazimierz illustrates how the encounter with heritage brokers can provoke deep questions:

Mother: We definitely keep asking, and we keep saying to ourselves, "Do you think she's Jewish? Do you think the proprietor of that place is Jewish?" Every time we go in anywhere—we've *sort of* learned now that the answer is no. But particularly our first few days here [we kept wondering], "Is our guide Jewish? Can you tell if he's Jewish? Does he have a Jewish name? Would he have said something already?"

Daughter: But then again, what does it mean to be Jewish? That he doesn't self-identify as a Jew? I still think he could have had a Jewish grandparent but just wasn't telling us. So it's clearly . . . identity isn't very clear . . . We have a much more complex view as a result of this trip, wouldn't you say that? Of

Polish history, of Polish-Jewish relations. Much more complex. And I think we found it stunning that a young woman like Janina [their non-Jewish tour guide] would be so interested.

Confronting Jewishness configured in unfamiliar ways prompted self-questioning about identity and identification, genealogy, and participation.

Yet Jewish tourists are not passive recipients of narratives and information—however conciliatory—provided by Polish guides. In a "personal seizure and appropriation of the narrative resources made available by tourism," visiting Jews often resisted their Polish guides, challenging them openly, whispering disapprovingly to fellow travelers, or quietly doubting the guides' information.[45] Sometimes Jewish visitors simply commandeered the tours. Małgorzata, a twenty-one-year-old Polish guide from the Jarden Jewish Bookshop, was compelled to yield her prepared narrative to her client's recitation of her grandfather's memoir—and voiced enthusiasm about this development. "I never thought I'd meet someone with such a story!" said Małgorzata, adding that she is always learning more about Kazimierz from Jewish tourists. Another guide, Marta, echoed appreciation of such "teaching" by Jewish visitors, "because sometimes they know more than I do, so sometimes they correct me. It's really good." (Marta eventually converted to Judaism, and moved to Israel to marry).

Of course, the interactions were not always pleasant. Jewish tourists at times made use of a "captive" Polish audience to curse Polish ground. One man stood in the bookshop, loudly explaining the brevity of his visit. "One day is more than enough among these *stinkende vilde chayes*" (Yiddish for "stinking wild animals"). Many heritage brokers in Kazimierz learned to allow space for this kind of reaction, rather than becoming defensive, which might have only exacerbated the conflict. But there are other approaches. Jarden co-owner Lucyna, whose Hebrew-studying shop assistant overheard an Israeli customer in 2008 smearing Poland, reacted by quietly telling him as she rang up his purchases that she would be pleased to give him a 10 percent discount if he stopped saying such horrible things about Poles.

Two uncomfortable experiences of my own as a college student in the early 1990s shocked me into recognition of the limits of my own inherited view. First was my response to a Polish acquaintance, when he casually remarked that his father had been interned in Auschwitz, that I hadn't realized his family was Jewish. He replied—charitably revealing only a bit of the frustration he likely felt—that his family is *not* Jewish, and didn't I realize that ethnic Poles, too, were put in camps?

The second experience occurred when I began chatting with a young man selling small souvenir paintings of Kraków's historic sites. After a few minutes of pleasant banter, I asked him where he was from. He replied, "Oświęcim," which I had recently learned was the Polish name for Auschwitz. That Oświęcim is an

ordinary Polish town, and one that had been more than half Jewish before World
War II, was still relatively new to me. In any case, these realities didn't make a dent
in the much more significant fact that to my (American Jewish) mind, this man
had grown up in *Auschwitz*. I could not hide my consternation and said something along the lines of, "Oh my gosh that must be a *horrible* place to live." To
condense an exchange whose details have blurred over the years, what I remember clearly is that I was informed that the town is not the camp, that his parents
had been resettled there after the war not by their own choosing, that he enjoyed
a normal youth *thank-you-very-much,* and—most enduringly discomfiting for
me, because of the grain of truth it contained—was I trying to *shame* him?

It is clear that cultural critique is not solely the domain of visiting Jews, nor
is the direction of such critique aimed only at Poles. While Zdzisław of the Jarden
Bookshop sees his mandate as criticizing Polish distortions and ignorance regarding Jewishness, he and Lucyna also work to dispel misconceptions about Poland that Jews bring with them. As Lucyna told me:

> I fight sometimes with Jews [too,] because [they need to] understand [that just]
> as on the Polish side, [on] the Jewish side there's a kind of mythology, you know,
> from the years of the Second World War time, and it's not exactly the truth,
> what they're telling about Poles. Of course it's possible, you know, to break
> this. But it's a very long process; it's for generations. But somebody has to start
> something, anyway. In this way you can get what you want.

Zdzisław often lamented the lack of basic historical knowledge of many visiting
Jews, telling me stories like one about a Jewish group that called the bookshop
wanting a guide for Auschwitz—a *Jewish* guide, they specified. Zdzisław told them
that there is only one "half-Jewish" guide at Auschwitz, but that he could promise
them a competent guide for Auschwitz and Birkenau. "No, no," they responded,
"we only want to see Auschwitz." Zdzisław was furious, telling me, "They demand
a Jewish guide, but they don't even know that Birkenau is so much more important, where the vast majority of Jews died!" He said he had informed and chastised them, and that they had been surprised by the information.

Kazimierz's particular quality as a meeting ground also stimulated intersub-
jective reckonings of heritage among visiting Jews, at times within family groups
or between generations. As I was walking out of Szeroka Street with two American Jewish friends, an elderly man shouted excitedly across the square, "Oh! Jews!"
He hurried over, his two middle-aged daughters following. He was a Jewish Holocaust survivor, originally from Lvov, and now American. As is the norm among
Jewish tourists in Kazimierz, he told us his wartime story right then and there in
the middle of the road. I told them about the research that brought me to Poland.
The response came from one of his daughters: "How can you bear to live here?"
As I tried to formulate an answer, a local friend walked by and we exchanged a

few words. The survivor's face lit up. "You speak *Polish!*" he declared. "My kids never learned Polish," he added, shaking his lowered head with apparent regret. The same daughter, looking away, said to the air, "He never *taught* us Polish." A moment later she turned back to me and snapped, "Why do you speak *Polish?*"

Such encounters suggest the pain and ambivalence on both dangling ends of a broken cultural link between Jewishness and Polishness. Parent and child were divided by a deeply felt locus of identity, at once intimate and volatile: Polish language. Something that could have bound them together in intimacy (as well as to other Poles) binds them instead to opposite sides of a cultural-historical chasm.[46]

Identification: Expanding the Collective Self

Postconflict reconciliation consists, in part, in pursuing "more inclusive principles of present-day affiliation," or the expansion of group identity.[47] The dominant ethnonational understanding of Polishness (i.e., Pole = Catholic) has been a central problem for Polish-Jewish relations and notions of shared heritage. It can be argued that the naturalization of this conception of Polishness constricted the "universe of obligation" Christian Poles inhabited and in terms of which they acted toward their Jewish fellow citizens during the Nazi occupation.[48]

But identity categories are malleable, and Kazimierz is a place where broader conceptions of Polishness have been promulgated. Rather than only providing a space *for* Jews as a significant "other" in Poland (which they also do), Kazimierz heritage brokers actively call into question rigidly defined notions of Polishness and Jewishness altogether. As I have argued elsewhere, this made the site conducive for Poles to explore of a range of identifications with Jewishness, many of which are motivated by a progressive cultural politics.[49] It has been a place where otherwise contradictory identities could be reconciled.

Kazimierz has also accommodated visiting Jews who want to transcend the us/them binary promulgated by the hegemonic Jewish establishment by (re)claiming an embodied, emplaced identification with Polish-Jewish heritage. "My grandmother is from Poland," Adam, a twenty-year-old Jewish Australian told me, sitting on a low stone wall along a Kazimierz alley, adding quickly that his grandmother hates it when he expresses feelings of connection to Poland and had protested his visit. "She doesn't want me to think this way, but besides the atrocities, I know this is where [she] grew up. I see people on the street, going into fruit shops just like my grandmother did. I see their faces and think it's *amazing,* all these people who look just like my grandmother would've looked here." Such a cultural politics of geographic affiliation functions in interestingly asymmetrical ways. While an embrace of Israel may be a progressive gesture among Poles, for foreign Jews, a turn toward Poland, toward the diaspora as a site of ancestral rootedness, suggests resistance to hegemonic identity categories and postures. Marisa Davidson, a doctoral student in Jewish history, told me that she went to

Poland "hoping to connect." "Israel wasn't doing it for me," she said. "I wanted to find another way of thinking of myself as a historical Jew."

Conclusion

Much has changed in Kazimierz since the bulk of the research described here was done. Jewishness there has been both normalized (as a category of heritage experience and a living communal presence) and diluted by other interests. Today, if one feels Jewish, one may be encouraged to go to the new, Western-funded Jewish Community Centre—which stakes a powerful, normative claim for Jewish authenticity—rather than hang out at Klezmer Hois Café. Yet non-Jewish heritage brokers should be recognized for the Jewish space they helped to forge in the first post-Communist decades, as well as the supporting roles they continue to play as a more confident Jewish community struggles to emerge.

Sociologist Sławomir Kapralski has characterized the landscape of memory work in post-Communist Poland as a "complicated, multi-centred space in which critical attempts to reclaim memory from national myths and . . . silences, coexist with the mythologization of the past and . . . conspiracy to expunge inconvenient memory."[50] The heritage brokers I met in Kazimierz have been workers for the former cause, most particularly by calling into question one "crucial feature" of Polish national identity, namely "the belief that (ethnic) Poles have been the main victims of history in general and of WWII in particular."[51]

It may be that "the desire to work through one's own traumatic memory does not necessarily emerge from the self."[52] Encounters with the reality of the other can seed recognition, empathy, and new senses of "we." In this way, heritage spaces are not just *lieux,* but *milieux de mémoire,* where our abstracted, homogenizing national stories are called into question through the daily telling and living of our unique and overlapping individual stories. Thus, the possibility of pluralism may depend upon nurturing public spaces that draw estranged groups together to envision expanded versions of national and cultural heritage. If one listens closely, Kazimierz reveals two rare qualities. First, it is a space where people come because they can enact deeply felt truths about who they are and what they care about that may not find expression elsewhere because of their hybrid nature. Second, it is a place where Poles and Jews can be heard listening to each other's often difficult truths.

*   *   *

One summer evening, a Jewish family—grandfather, son-in-law, grandson—stood in the Jarden Bookshop, leafing through books. The father, after ascertaining my Jewishness, pointed to the grandfather and said, "He's from here. He didn't want to come back, but my wife wanted to see his town." Zdzisław asked if the grandfather could speak Polish. "Sure he can. Pop, speak Polish to the man," said the son-in-law. The grandfather leaned over the counter and began to tell his story to Zdzisław in a mix of Polish, Yiddish, and English. Zdzisław listened intently. The grandfather described being tied up—"like this," he said, pressing his wrists together as if bound—and turned over to the Nazis. "By Poles," he said, leaning closer to Zdzisław to make his point, "*Di Polyakn,*" he repeated in Yiddish. Zdzisław said nothing, only nodding, as if to encourage the grandfather to say more.[53]

Notes

An earlier version of this chapter was published as "Can There Be a Conciliatory Heritage?" *International Journal of Heritage Studies* 16, nos. 4–5 (July–September 2010): 269–288. The ideas in it are also more fully elaborated in Erica Lehrer, *Jewish Poland Revisited: Heritage Tourism in Unquiet Places* (Bloomington: Indiana University Press, 2013).

1. Elaine H. Gurian, "Singing and Dancing at Night," in *Stewards of the Sacred,* ed. Lawrence E. Sullivan and Alison Edwards (Washington, DC: American Association of Museums and Harvard University, 2004), 89.

2. Jarden has since expanded, and other Jewish bookshops have opened, two in Kazimierz and at least one in Warsaw.

3. Charles Hoffman, *Gray Dawn: The Jews of Eastern Europe in the Post-Communist Era* (New York: HarperCollins, 1995), 276.

4. See Ruth Gruber, *Virtually Jewish: Reinventing Jewish Culture in Europe* (Berkeley: University of California Press, 2002). For an extended consideration of the limitations of the notion of "Virtual Jewishness," see Erica Lehrer, "Virtual, Virtuous, Vicarious, Vacuous? Toward a Vigilant use of Labels," *Jewish Cultural Studies* 4 (2014): 383–395.

5. The antisemitic campaign of 1968 came as a wakeup call not only to "Poles of Jewish origin" but also to young members of the opposition, who attacked antisemitism as a discredited tool of the state. Michael C. Steinlauf, *Bondage to the Dead: Poland and the Memory of the Holocaust* (New York: Syracuse University Press, 1997), 109. Censorship also stimulated interest in Jewish history, and "re-inviting the Jew into Poland's collective memory stood . . . in opposition to the official efforts to make him disappear forever." Iwona Irwin-Zarecka, *Neutralizing Memory: The Jew in Contemporary Poland* (New Brunswick, NJ: Transaction, 1989), 127.

6. I use "heritage brokers" following Richard Kurin's "culture brokers," which he uses to describe individuals who bring audiences together and represent, translate, negotiate, or exchange representations or definitions of culture or cultural goods among them.

7. Richard Kurin, *Reflections of a Culture Broker: A View from the Smithsonian* (Washington, DC: Smithsonian Institution Press, 1987), 39.

8. Konstanty Gebert, "Jewish Identities in Poland: New, Old, Imaginary," in *Jewish Identities in the New Europe,* ed. Jonathan Webber (London: Littman Library of Jewish Civilization, 1994), 161–167.

9. Irwin-Zarecka, *Neutralizing Memory,* 90–91.

10. I take heritage to be the meanings and representations ascribed in the present day to artifacts, landscapes, beliefs, memories, and traditions understood as bearing traces of the (cultural or national) past.

11. On recent artistic projects, see Erica Lehrer and Magdalena Waligórska, "Cur(at)ing History: New Genre Art Interventions and the Polish-Jewish Past," *East European Politics and Societies* 27, no. 3 (2013): 507–540.

12. Gross's books that contributed to this debate include *Neighbors: The Destruction of the Jewish Community in Jedwabne, Poland* (Princeton, NJ: Princeton University Press, 2001); *Fear: Antisemitism in Poland after Auschwitz* (New York: Random House, 2006); and (with Irena Grudzińska-Gross) *Golden Harvest* (New York: Oxford University Press, 2012).

13. Michael Rothberg, *Traumatic Realism: The Demands of Holocaust Representation* (Minneapolis: University of Minnesota Press, 2000), 271.

14. For a critical reappraisal of the potential of even Disneyland itself, see Jane Kuenz, "It's a Small World after All: Disney and the Pleasures of Identification," *The South Atlantic Quarterly* 92, no. 1 (1993): 63–88.

15. Piotr Wróbel, "Double Memory: Poles and Jews after the Holocaust," *East European Politics and Societies* 11, no. 3 (1997): 560–574; Antony Polonsky and Joanna B. Michlic, "Introduction," in *The Neighbors Respond: The Controversy over the Jedwabne Massacre in Poland,* ed. Antony Polonsky and Joanna B. Michlic (Princeton, NJ: Princeton University Press, 2004), 1–49.

16. Joshua Zimmerman, *Contested Memories: Poles and Jews during the Holocaust and Its Aftermath* (New Brunswick, NJ: Rutgers University Press, 2003); Dorota Glowacka and Joanna Zylinska, *Imaginary Neighbors: Mediating Polish-Jewish Relations after the Holocaust* (Lincoln: University of Nebraska Press, 2007). See also Geneviève Zubrzycki, *The Crosses of Auschwitz: Nationalism and Religion in Post-Communist Poland* (Chicago: University of Chicago Press, 2006), and Slawomir Kapralski, "Auschwitz: Site of Memories," *Polin* 15 (2002): 383–400.

17. Gross, *Fear.* According to Gross, "the Holocaust became a nonsubject in Polish historiography" in this period (30).

18. Katrin Steffen surveys how Jewish themes polarize Polish society in her essay "Disputed Memory: Jewish Past, Polish Remembrance," *Osteuropa* 8–10 (2008): 199–218. Ruth Gruber questions the authenticity of contemporary engagements with Jewish heritage in her book, *Virtually Jewish: Reinventing Jewish Culture in Europe* (Berkeley: University of California Press, 2002). Magdalena Waligórska cautions that their most popular form—klezmer music—can be seen in instrumental terms, as a "rhetorical device" and "political correctness for all occasions." Magdalena Waligórska, "Fiddler as Fig Leaf: The Politicisation of Klezmer in Poland," *Osteuropa* 8–10 (2008): 227–238. Significant state-level steps have been taken on the Polish side. These include major interpretive changes at Nazi camp memorials, a formal apology in 2001 by then-president Aleksander Kwaśniewski for the pogrom at Jedwabne, and former Warsaw mayor and current Polish president Lech Kaczyński's donation of land and over 30% of the cost to create a world-class Museum of the History of Polish Jews in Warsaw.

19. The world class, multinational Museum of the History of Polish Jews, which opened in Warsaw in 2014, and new educational travel programs being developed by the San Francisco–based Taube Foundation, are interventions likely to have significant impact.

20. Scholarship by Jack Kugelmass (especially the ideas of "stage" and "pageant"), Jackie Feldman, Rona Sheramy, and Oren Baruch Stier characterizes such travel broadly in these terms. See Jack Kugelmass, "Bloody Memories: Encountering the Past in Contemporary Poland," *Cultural Anthropology* 10, no. 3 (1995): 279–301; Jackie Feldman, *Above the Death Pits, Beneath the Flag: Youth Voyages to Poland and the Performance of Israeli National Identity* (New York: Berghahn Books, 2008); Rona Sheramy, "From Auschwitz to Jerusalem: Re-Enacting Jewish History on the March of the Living," *Polin* 19 (2007): 307–326; and Oren Baruch Stier, *Committed to Memory: Cultural Mediations of the Holocaust* (Amherst: University of Massachusetts Press, 2003). Jewish individuals or family groups also seek personal heritage in specific towns, and other, comparatively marginal exceptions include Hassidic pilgrims to the tombs of dynastic Galician rabbis, genealogy enthusiasts who comb Polish archives, and fans of Yiddishkayt and klezmer who follow the festival circuit. But these groups are primarily interested in and hold in esteem prewar *Jewish* heritage, understood as a discreet entity situated

on a Polish backdrop, rather than a hybrid entity linked to Poles. An enduring example of the nostalgic view of East European Jewish culture as embodied in an idealized, hermetic shtetl is Mark Zborowski and Elizabeth Herzog's *Life Is with People: The Culture of the Shtetl* (New York: Shocken Books, 1995), especially as discussed in its 1995 introduction by Barbara Kirshenblatt-Gimblett. The fundamentally negative attitude toward Poland as a meaningful locus for Jewish memory is illustrated by the early difficulties in raising funds among American Jews for the Warsaw museum (see Robin Ostow, "Remusealizing Jewish History in Warsaw: The Privatization and Externalization of Nation Building," in *(Re)visualizing National History: Museums and National Identities in Europe in the New Millennium,* ed. Robin Ostow (Toronto: University of Toronto Press, 2008), 170–171). But change is afoot; the museum, as well as the Taube Foundation, are crafting new tourist itineraries, and Israeli State diplomatic efforts are also evident, e.g., Israeli ambassador to Poland David Peleg's categorical statement in a speech during Kraków's Jewish Cultural Festival in June 2008 that "Poland is not an antisemitic country."

21. While the Israeli Jewish and diasporic Jewish perspectives on Poland should not be conflated, they have common roots and are structurally intertwined in a shared pedagogy of youth pilgrimage, and thus can be meaningfully discussed together in this context. Their differences are also not particularly evident from the Polish point of view.

22. The full key of the Polish map lists, in this order, "Synagogues and houses of prayer open, Synagogues, Cemeteries, Ghettoes during World War II, Nazi death camps, Nazi concentration camps, Other important sites (Jewish history), Centres of Hasidism." For legibility, I have provided only a fragment of the Polish map, onto which I collaged the key. While the Israeli map is in English, the rest of the brochure to which it was attached is in Hebrew.

23. Yisrael Gutman and Shmuel Krakowski, *Unequal Victims: Poles and Jews during World War Two* (New York: Holocaust Library, 1986).

24. See Gross, *Neighbors;* Jan Grabowski, *Ja tego Zyda znam! Szanatazowanie Zydów w Warszawie, 1939–1943* (Warsaw: Instytut Filozofii i Socjologii Polskiej Akademii Nauk, 2004); Barbara Engelking, *"Dear Sir Gistapo": Denunciation to the German Authorities in Warsaw and Its Surroundings in the Years 1940–1942* (Warsaw: Instytut Filozofii i Socjologii Polskiej Akademii Nauk, 2003); and Dariusz Stola, "Fighting against the Shadows: The Anti-Zionist Campaign of 1968," in *Antisemitism and Its Opponents in Modern Poland,* ed. Robert Blobaum (Ithaca, NY: Cornell University Press, 2005), 284–300.

25. Claire Rosenson, "The Ball Is in the Jewish Court," *East European Jewish Affairs* 27, no. 1 (1997): 67.

26. For a discussion of Jewish travel, including such youth travel, to Poland, see Lehrer, *Jewish Poland Revisited,* 54–90.

27. Of course, the prewar situation was itself complex, with Jews having begun to assimilate into the Polish national mainstream only in the late nineteenth century.

28. Kugelmass, "Bloody Memories," 295.

29. Monika Murzyn, *Kazimierz: The Central European Experience of Urban Regeneration* (Kraków: International Cultural Centre, 2006), 120.

30. Per local scholar Edyta Gawron, "With respect to the material sphere, the Jewish Community [of Kraków] gained much. It was, however, unsuccessful in coordination of the activities aimed at rejuvenation and restoration of Jewish religious and cultural life. Thus, the present revival of Jewish culture has taken place in Cracow thanks to non-Jews with the help of the Jews from Israel and the Diaspora." Gawron, "Społeczność żydowskwa w Krakowie w latach 1945–1995" (Ph.D. diss., Jagiellonian University, 2005), 209, cited in Murzyn, *Kazimierz,* 394. The Ronald Lauder Foundation Youth Club, long situated in the Izaak Synagogue, was another significant site, but it publicized its Jewishness in Orthodox religious terms, implicitly discouraging non-Jewish participation and alienating many young Jews due to personality con-

flicts among its leadership. In spring 2008, a modern Jewish Community Centre (initiated by Charles, Prince of Wales) opened in the center of Kazimierz. While explicitly a space *for* Jews (rather than a "Jewish space" in Pinto's sense), given its savvy, young, Polish-speaking American-Israeli director, it may nonetheless also contribute to the latter.

31. Diana Pinto, "The Jewish Challenges in the New Europe," in *Challenging Ethnic Citizenship: German and Israeli Perspectives on Immigration* (New York: Berghahn Books, 2002), 251.

32. Ruth Gruber, "The Krakow Jewish Culture Festival," in *Focus on Jewish Popular Culture in Poland and Its Afterlife,* ed. Antony Polonsky and Michael Steinlauf, special issue, *Polin* 16 (2003): 364.

33. The restaurant, now called Klezmer Hois, has grown to include a hotel and klezmer cabaret, and an affiliated bookshop and publishing house, Austeria, a cutting-edge, bilingual (Polish/English) imprint for Jewish-themed works.

34. Eve Jochnowitz, "Flavors of Memory: Jewish Food as Culinary Tourism in Poland," *Southern Folklore* 55, no. 3 (1998): 226.

35. Barbara Kirshenblatt-Gimblett, "Theorizing Heritage," *Ethnomusicology* 39, no. 3 (1995): 367–380.

36. Jochnowitz, "Flavors of Memory," 227.

37. Gruber, "The Krakow Jewish Culture Festival," 365–366.

38. See, for example, Henry Greenspan, *On Listening to Holocaust Survivors: Recounting and Life History* (Westport, CT: Praeger, 1998); Lawrence L. Langer, *Holocaust Testimonies: The Ruins of Memory* (New Haven, CT: Yale University Press, 1993); Karl A. Plank, "The Survivor's Return: Reflections on Memory and Place," *Judaism: A Quarterly Journal of Jewish Life and Thought* 38, no. 3 (1989): 263–277; and James Young, "Holocaust Video and Cinematographic Testimony: Documenting the Witness," in *Writing and Rewriting the Holocaust* (Bloomington: Indiana University Press, 1988), 157–171.

39. Dori Laub, "Bearing Witness, or the Vicissitudes of Listening," in *Testimony: Crises of Witnessing in Literature, Psychoanalysis, and History,* ed. Shoshanna Felman and Dori Laub (New York: Routledge, 1992), 70.

40. Edward S. Casey, *Remembering a Phenomological Study* (Bloomington: Indiana University Press, 1987).

41. Barry Spielman, "The Streets of Kazimierz: A Personal Journey back to Poland and Jewish Kraków—A Second Generation Perspective," unpublished manuscript, 2000, 11–12.

42. Until mid-1943, all the prisoners at the Płaszów forced labor camp were Jews. In July 1943, a separate section was created for Polish prisoners. Except for "political prisoners," Poles served their sentences and were released. Jews remained in the camp indefinitely, or were sent on to nearby Auschwitz. For inmate population estimates, see Bernard Offen and Norman Jacobs, *My Hometown Concentration Camp: A Survivor's Account of Life in the Krakow Ghetto and Płaszów Concentration Camp* (London: Vallentine, Mitchell, 2008).

43. Anthropologist John Borneman stresses that preconditions for reconciliation must include "an appreciation of the intersubjectivity of the present" with the uncomfortable encounters with difference this entails. Borneman, "Reconciliation after Ethnic Cleansing: Listening, Retribution, Affiliation," *Public Culture* 14, no. 2 (2002): 286, 302.

44. I thank Stephanie Rowden for this turn of phrase, which she used to describe her own experience visiting Poland.

45. Saidiya Hartman, "The Time of Slavery," *The South Atlantic Quarterly* 101, no. 4 (Fall 2002): 769.

46. Such unanticipated encounters with cultural similarity or sharedness can be as provocative as confronting difference. Visiting Jews are often shocked by how familiar they find Polish food, habits, gestures, or phenotypes.

47. Borneman, "Reconciliation after Ethnic Cleansing," 286.

48. Helen Fein, *Accounting for Genocide: National Responses and Jewish Victimization during the Holocaust* (New York: Free Press, 1979).

49. Erica Lehrer, "Bearing False Witness? Vicarious Jewish Identity and the Politics of Affinity," in Glowacka and Zylinska, eds., *Imaginary Neighbors*, 84–109.

50. Sławomir Kapralski, "The Impact of Post-1989 on Polish-Jewish Relations and Perceptions: Memories and Debates," in *The Religious Roots of Contemporary European Identity*, ed. Lucia Faltin and Melanie J. Wright (London: Continuum, 2007), 98.

51. Ibid.

52. Joseph Rosen, "Beyond Memory: From Historical Violence to Political Alterity in Contemporary Space" (Ph.D. diss., York University, Toronto, 2008), 230.

53. Not infrequently when I have ended talks using this vignette, the first "question" from the audience will be from an elderly Jew (or occasionally a Pole) who begins, "I was born in Poland . . ." and proceeds to tell their own story, which inevitably exceeds (and usually challenges) my own analytical framework. As Zdzisław seems to, I also welcome such intrusions of the ongoing lived experience of these issues into the meager spaces I have attempted to create for them. I thank Birgit Meyer for bringing this dynamic to my attention.

8 "Lodzermensch" and Litzmannstadt: Making "Virtually German" Sites in Łódź after 1989

Winson Chu

Eᴜʀᴏᴘᴇᴀɴ ɪɴᴛᴇɢʀᴀᴛɪᴏɴ ʜᴀs led to a steady focus on reconciliation between countries that were once enemies. This process includes not just French-German reconciliation in the postwar period but also the improvement of relations between Germany and its Eastern European neighbors since 1989. Following the increasing partnership of Germany and Poland, there has been a concomitant boom in studies that examine not just historical events but also how today's Germans and Poles remember each other.[1] Yet the rush to better relations between Germany and Poland has likewise led some observers of German-Polish relations to warn of an uncritical and inadequate assessment of the past.[2] The showy displays of friendship between Germany and Poland have even been described as "reconciliation kitsch."[3] Moreover, the exchange of high words between state governments in Berlin and Warsaw can conceal what is happening at the regional and grassroots level. Polish-German politics of remembrance need to be understood in both their local dimensions and within the broader framework of memory politics in the European Union. How does historical memory "from below" reveal differences in German-Polish relations, and what are the effects of the interaction? Likewise, recent trends in Polish-Jewish relations have emphasized improving relations, but these are usually treated separately from the German-Polish context. What does looking at Polish-German and Polish-Jewish relations together tell us about new trends of nationalization in the new Europe, especially in the appropriation of multicultural pasts for national narratives?

This chapter argues that attempts in Łódź to recover a local German legacy fits into a European paradigm of reconciliation, but Polish-Jewish commemorations of the Holocaust often complicate these efforts to create a good German past. Conceived as a synthetic piece that weaves together historiographical issues with close readings, this work looks first at some recent trends in post-1989 Polish-German relations, especially in regards to European memory politics. It then gives a brief history of Łódź and considers attempts to conceal and recover

Jewish and German legacies there after the war and after 1989. The chapter ends with a brief example of how attempts to remember "blank spots" in Polish-Jewish history can run against a multicultural reconstruction of the past.

Historiographical Contexts: Landscapes of Memory

The collapse of Communist governments in Eastern Europe in 1989 and the speedy process of German reunification opened new avenues for communication and political and economic cooperation between Germany and its Eastern neighbors.[4] Germany was seen as Poland's biggest advocate in an expanding European Union, and the governments of the two countries were glad to offer their collaboration as a model of partnership in the new Europe. Scholarly cooperation between Germany and Poland led to concrete manifestations: a German Historical Institute began in Warsaw in 1993, and the Polish Academy of Sciences established its Center for Historical Research in Berlin in 2006.[5] Despite a noticeable cooling in the 2000s, economic and cultural ties between Germany and Poland have remained strong. Studies have shown that the Polish view of Germans has become more positive over time.[6]

The historian Norman Naimark has noted that the political integration in the European Union has also meant the attempt to create an "all-European version of past and future."[7] Likewise, Etienne François describes recent historical research as increasingly "European, transnational, and international."[8] This Europeanization of history has promoted the idea of being "united in diversity" as the future of the past for Europe.[9] As many scholars have noted, throughout Eastern Europe, the turn to a mythic multiculturalism in local spaces has become a common phenomenon. Especially the concept of "little fatherlands" or "little homelands" meshes well with European Union policies that have tried to develop cooperation across nation-state lines by supporting historical regions.[10] In this rediscovery of local spaces, supposedly backward borderlands can act as screens for idealized projections of interethnic coexistence.[11]

Is this transnational, multicultural "Europe" an "invention of tradition," in a way similar to how the "nation" has been described as a modern construct, an "imagined community"?[12] Certainly this multicultural picture of the past often seems contrived.[13] And while the new vogue for memory work is found throughout Europe and has a pan-European agenda, it can also be a distinctly nationalizing phenomenon: the search for "sites of memory" often simply redefines national insiders and outsiders.[14] Indeed, much of the ongoing memory work is undertaken in the name of erasing blank spots in various national histories, which includes uncovering what "we" have done to "others."[15]

Above all, these blank spots include issues of occupation and collaboration during the Second World War.[16] Here, it seems German society's reckoning with German crimes during the Nazi period has provided an important impulse for other countries to account for their own homegrown nationalisms and antisemitism. As Charles S. Maier has written, the (West) German model of "mastering the past" (*Vergangenheitsbewältigung*) has in many ways become a top German export item.[17] Yet in many Eastern European countries, historical research has also concentrated on uncovering the silences that occurred during the Communist period.[18] Since 2000, the Institute of National Remembrance, which investigates and documents "crimes against the Polish nation," subsumes the trauma of German rule in a broader framework of totalitarianism that spans 1939 to 1989.[19] Likewise, the European Union Commission has created programs to reconcile the different ways that particular European countries have remembered Nazi and Soviet legacies.[20] The city of Łódź exemplifies these changes in sensitivities and approaches, as well as in the need to find a usable past. Such attempts reveal the tensions not just in German-Polish but also in Polish-Jewish and German-Jewish relations.

Historiographical Contexts: Łódź

Like many of the twentieth century's great cities, Łódź grew dramatically in a short span of time. Located in the Russian share of the partitioned Polish Commonwealth, the budding textile industry of this "Polish Manchester" initially drew migrants from German-speaking Central Europe, but soon attracted workers from the Central Polish countryside and other parts of the Russian empire. With a population of about six hundred in 1820, Łódź reached half a million by 1914, making it the second largest city in the former Polish lands. The growth was accompanied by dramatic changes in the city's demographic composition: although more than 60 percent of the population was still German-speaking in 1862, the growing city became increasingly Polish-speaking.[21] At the same time, its sizable Jewish minority made it a center of Jewish life in Central Europe.

The term "lodzermensch" was coined during this time among nationalist writers, German and Polish, to describe the putative lack of national loyalty among Łódź's inhabitants, who were depicted as ruthlessly driven types who put money above all else, including ethnic and national loyalty. Władysław Reymont, who won the Nobel Prize for literature in 1924, popularized the term and its accompanying stereotype in his novel *The Promised Land*. Reymont demonized the "lodzermensch" for its foreign, urban qualities, which stood in contrast to the Polish agrarian lifestyle that he idealized.[22] Łódź's multiethnic composition survived both the First World War and the interwar period, when the city suffered severe economic hardship from the loss of Russian textile markets. Yet tensions were also apparent among Germans, Poles, and Jews in the city. When Hitler came to power in Germany, some demonstrators in Łódź ransacked German-owned stores and the German high school. German minority leaders also took this as an opportunity to break off relations with the Jewish population.[23]

On September 8, 1939, Nazi German troops occupied Łódź, which, for the next several months was referred to as "Lodsch" in official documents.[24] After several weeks of wrangling, Łódź became part of Reichsgau Posen (later renamed Wartheland) on November 9—a holy day of National Socialism. On April 11, 1940, Gauleiter Arthur Greiser announced that the name of the city would henceforth be "Litzmannstadt" in honor of General Karl Litzmann, who had managed to break out when his division was surrounded by Russian forces near Łódź early in the First World War. Not surprisingly, this battle was interpreted as a German victory over the Slavic menace, and the renaming of the city into the more German-sounding Litzmannstadt underscored the Reich's right to possess and remake the city. The city, like the "model Gau" it was in, was to play an exemplary role in Nazi plans to Germanize its newly won eastern territories.[25] The occupiers fortified their demographic position by bringing in ethnic German resettlers from the Baltic region and Soviet-occupied eastern Poland. Later, the Deutsche Volksliste was used to "re-Germanize" those Polish and other "elements" considered to be racially fit. As Soviet troops advanced in early 1945, German locals, resettlers, and administrators began to flee. Those who remained were mostly expelled in the following years.

The lingering perceptions of hybridity among Łódź's inhabitants led to intensified efforts by the occupiers to cleanse the city of undesirable elements. Łódź had the largest concentration of Jews in the territories directly annexed by Germany: 233,000 Jews lived there, making up roughly one-third of the city's population.[26] The German occupiers' creation of a ghetto for the Jews was completed in May 1940, when the ghetto was sealed. The Łódź Ghetto became the second largest ghetto after Warsaw. Thousands died from mistreatment, hunger, and disease. In early 1942, Germans began transporting the inhabitants to the death camps, including nearby Kulmhof/Chełmno. Łódź also became a major transit station in the "Final Solution" for Jews from Germany and occupied Czechoslovakia. One of the first ghettos to be established, it was the last to be liquidated.[27] The era of genocide, ethnic cleansings, and forced hardship left a permanent mark on the city.[28] At the same time, the Nazi German destruction of Łódź's Jewish population during the Holocaust meant that the city had become proportionately more "Polish" in 1944 than it had been in 1939.[29]

German and Jewish Legacies in Postwar Poland and Germany

The tense political situation after the war did not lend itself well to Germans getting to know Poland—nor for Poles to search for German legacies.[30] The people of Poland had suffered enormously during the war, and it is not surprising that postwar authorities were eager to demonize Germany and the Germans.[31] The Polish government's emphasis on Germany's crimes during the occupation also provided a convenient rationale for annexing much of East Prussia, Pomerania, and Silesia, all the more necessary because their "patron," the Soviet Union, had moved its own boundaries westward, at its Polish neighbor's expense.[32] The wartime Germanization and genocidal policies were thus followed by a "clean sweep" of the German population in the "Recovered Lands" of what became Western Poland.[33] German buildings and monuments throughout Poland were likewise reappropriated for Polish narratives.[34]

While Wrocław and Szczecin were cities in Germany before the Second World War (and Gdańsk had been made a Free City after the First World War), Łódź had been part of independent Poland and was largely Polish-speaking in the interwar period. Hence the caesura of 1945 between a German past and a Polish one played less of a role in Łódź. Yet the need during the Communist period to delegitimize the city's German legacy was nonetheless great. The increasing Nazification of German minority politics in the prewar period was taken as justification for the postwar expulsion of the Łódź Germans. Mirosław Cygański, a postwar historian of Łódź, argued that the city's Germans had acted as a "fifth column" in 1939; that the return of Polish lands was an act of "historical justice" for the German plans to exterminate the Polish people.[35] Similarly, the pre–World War II portrayal of factory owners in Łódź as ruthless and foreign capitalists reemerged all but unchanged in the socialist paradigm of class struggle.[36]

In West Germany, Łódź remained largely forgotten despite the role it had played during the war.[37] The city entered German popular culture briefly in the 1970s, when a German singer named Vicky Leandros sang "Theo, wir fahr'n nach Lodz," an interpretation of a First World War song that had originally been a Yiddish tune.[38] As the East European specialist Karl Schlögel wryly notes, the state of knowledge about Poland at the time was generally so low that many young Germans probably thought Leandros had simply made up the name "Lodz" for the song.[39] German histories of the city that did exist largely focused on the German communities in Łódź. The main carriers of "German Lodz" remained those expellee organizations of the Germans from interwar Poland, especially Landsmannschaft Weichsel-Warthe, and institutes devoted to the history of Germans in Eastern Europe.[40] Łódź expellees were not as vocal, however, as the groups that focused on the Sudetenland and Germany's lost eastern provinces.[41]

East Germany also had a complicated relationship with Poland that often prevented a deeper understanding between the two countries.[42] As elsewhere in Eastern Europe, the fate of the European Jews still took a backseat to the persecution of socialist protagonists; commemorations of Nazi crimes universalized the war, the perpetrators, and its victims. One East German book on Łódź had a chapter nominally devoted to the deaths of six thousand Jewish children, yet the bulk of the section focused on class struggle. Describing the different fates of the

factory owners and workers, the author wrote, "Killed in masses were only workers, socialists, communists, antifascists or people who did nothing more than be
Jews or Poles."[43]

The wider German public often knew Łódź best, if at all, for its ghetto, but
the specificity of the Łódź Ghetto itself was often lost in the wider landscape of
Holocaust sites. For those who were familiar with the Holocaust, Łódź was home
to a very polarizing figure in Chaim Mordechai Rumkowski, who led the ghetto's Jewish Council and who is often criticized for having cooperated with German authorities.[44] It was more edifying to concentrate on Warsaw, whose Warsaw
Ghetto offered a more inspiring history of Jewish resistance during its 1943 uprising.[45] Thus, Łódź remained on the peripheries of West and East German memory,
as well as in broader postwar discourses about the Holocaust.

"Virtually Jewish" and "Virtually German" Legacies in Poland after 1989

In the shadow of nearby Warsaw, Łódź had many problems finding its place in Poland's new post-Communist landscape. A severe economic downturn hit the city
as its former markets in the Soviet Union disappeared. Many people also began
leaving the city, which has recently resulted in Kraków's replacing it as Poland's
second largest city. Not surprisingly, some have looked to the past to find Łódź's
future. Many local histories, written accessibly, have appealed to residents to identify with their city.[46] In particular, boosters have actively promoted a more inclusive remembrance culture tied to the Europeanness of the city.[47] While previous
multicultural narratives only included Jews, Poles, and Germans, Łódź boosters have recently promoted the "city of *four* cultures": the Russian legacy is now
to add value to the Łódź "brand."[48] Today, the "Promised Land" sobriquet is no
longer used ironically as Reymont meant it. Several recent studies have focused
on Łódź's negative image and the attempts to improve it, especially in reimagining the German and multicultural past after 1989.[49] Yet the attempts to construct
these continuities in themselves have presented special problems. The complicated German-Polish-Jewish coexistence in the past and its demise must be re-
counted before the largely homogenous Polish present could be explained. It is
not an easy task. As the historian Ingo Eser notes, German and Jewish narratives
of Łódź still exist in separate strands.[50]

Jewish festivals and celebratory histories have gained prominence in towns
and cities across Poland, and the resurgence of multiethnic legacies may appear
impressive at first. Post-Communist Polish society has also done much to uncover
the "dark past" of the Holocaust.[51] At the same time, the market motivations of
"Holocaust tourism" and other attempts to reach out to Jewish tourists have become an integral part of this memory work. Some observers, such as the writer
Ruth Ellen Gruber, have critiqued the authenticity and agendas of such "virtually

Jewish" cultural products, which exist without a Jewish community.[52] Especially the commercialization of Jewish heritage in Poland, notably in Kraków, can appear to relegate Jewishness to a past that is purportedly "frozen in time."[53] As Joanna Michlic argues, there is still a remarkable silence in Poland about the Jewish past despite the prevalence of Jewish festivals and the growing awareness of Holocaust history.[54] Thus such commemorative politics and practices about multicultural-ism and Europeanism ultimately reveal how Poles—and Germans—view them-selves and their place in the world. Michael Meng, for example, has shown how the commemoration of Jews in postwar Germany and Poland has allowed both countries to return to an idealized past. This embrace—what Meng has termed a "redemptive cosmopolitanism"—has also kept Jews at a distance.[55]

These broader developments in European and Polish memory culture can be seen on the local level. Indeed, the history of the Łódź Ghetto exemplifies this complicated relationship of Jewish legacies both to the city and wider Pol-ish and German memories of the war.[56] As late as 2000, the geographer David M. Smith remarked on how the history of the Jews in Łódź, and especially the ghetto in World War II, represented a "moral geography of absence."[57] Yet this space has recently received more attention, especially in memorialization efforts led by Jerzy Kropiwnicki. A member of the national conservative Law and Justice party, Kropiwnicki was elected mayor of Łódź in 2002 and served until 2010. The com-memoration of the sixtieth anniversary of the liquidation of the Łódź Ghetto in 2004 included religious and civic leaders and international guests, and was to be a stark contrast to the rather muted fiftieth anniversary celebration.[58] Kropiwnicki also commissioned a large monument at the train station where Jews were de-ported to death camps.[59] Such public displays of remembrance are meant to en-courage today's city inhabitants to engage with the local past. Joanna Podolska, a reporter from the influential center-left newspaper *Gazeta Wyborcza*, has likewise contributed significantly to the growing body of work on Jewish life in Łódź.[60] In 2011, she became director of the Marek Edelman Center for Dialogue in Łódź.

Similar processes can be seen in the recovery of German legacies in Łódź, whereby the once culturally ambiguous "lodzermensch" has undergone a posi-tive "Re-Germanization" by Łódź city boosters. Poland's entry into the European Union in May 2004 was followed by the German-Polish year of 2005–2006. Under the rubric of the "Year of German-Speaking Lands," Łódź promoted events that showed the city's historical ties to Germans and Germany.[61] The URL for this site, now defunct, was www.lodzermensch.pl. One of the printed materials made for this occasion was a German-language trifold flyer to help visitors find out more about "important Germans in Lodz." The pamphlet quotes Mayor Kropiwnicki, who praised the Germans' "mentalities and modes of thought," including their ability to "plan far into the future" and their determination "to realize their vi-

sions."[62] Kropiwnicki, it seems, drew upon stereotypes of German industrious-
ness and relied heavily on the essentialization of national categories. Often considered a sign of "national indifference" in Central Europe, the "lodzermensch"
can be celebrated today as quintessentially German when the need arises.[63]

As with "virtual Jews," the dynamics of recovering and staging "virtual Germans" in Poland reveals more about contemporary Polish actors on the local and
national levels than about the German past itself. This positive "Re-Germanization"
of Łódź's past functions in the context of improving Polish-German relations, but
it largely excludes German-Jewish and especially Polish-Jewish narratives. Here,
a second and more negative form of "Re-Germanization" serves to distance Poles
from more controversial and complicated aspects in Łódź's history.

From "Lodzermensch" to Litzmannstadt

Scholars often portray the rediscovery of the multiethnic past as a new era of light
in contrast to the darkness of the totalitarian past. Yet this contrast also depends
upon terminological delineations, which can be found in the rediscovery of the
term "Litzmannstadt." The usage of the name Litzmannstadt has an important
function in this paradigm of multicultural remembrance by serving as a convenient break for ordering dramatic ruptures in the city's history. It clearly delin-
eates German wartime occupation from the period before and after. As a model
anti-Europe, Litzmannstadt destroyed not just hundreds of thousands of people
but also the functioning cosmopolitan world of the lodzermensch. This relationship can be found in several local histories.[64] One book by the local Germanist
Krystyna Radziszewska describes these two phases as "light" and "shadow," while
another book plays on the word "Łódź," which means boat in Polish, to describe
the sinking of the city in the war years.[65]

Nazi Germany's Litzmannstadt spelled not just the end of a "German Lodz"
but also of the "good German" of prewar Łódź. The German name serves as a
marker and is essential for maintaining the narrative of the prewar multicultural
past. While postwar historians like Mirosław Cygański focus on the threat of the
Germans within the city, the "lodzermensch" to Litzmannstadt narrative after
1989 emphasizes how the city's downfall came from outside forces. This externalization of the "bad German" aspects of the city's history fosters multicultural
memory politics by creating space to reclaim the positive aspects of German history in the city. "Lodzermensch" and Litzmannstadt thus exist in a zero-sum
game that maintains the purity of each, with the trauma of the latter essentially
constructing the former.

Several works in Germany have also relied on this Manichean narrative of
light to dark to tell the story of the end of the "good Germans" in multicultural
Central Europe. Thomas Urban, who writes often in the German press and has

published several books on German history in Poland, sees the end of the good Łódź already in 1933. At the same time, he emphasizes Polish provocations as an important factor in gradual Nazification of the German minority. In his overview of the war in Łódź, he focuses on the ghetto and the extermination of the Jews. Quite tellingly, however, Urban's chapter on the history of the city ends with the deportation of the last Germans after the war.[66] Georg Strobel, a West German historian who was born in Łódź, likewise wrote a "homage," which reads more like an obituary, to the multiethnic city of Łódź.[67] Finally, the Eastern European specialist Karl Schlögel also describes Litzmannstadt as the "anti-city" that resulted in the "liquidation of Łódź as a civilizational accomplishment from the nineteenth century." Yet Schlögel reveals the difficulties of separating "good" and "bad" Germans in the city's history when he writes that "the end of the Lodzermenschen came when the Germans arrived, and the last bits disappeared when even they were expelled from the city."[68]

Furthermore, Litzmannstadt can also be used in campaigns to clear up misconceptions that the Polish people had initiated or supported the Holocaust. Most notably, the Polish conservative newspaper *Rzeczpospolita* took part in a campaign to stop the usage of the expression "Polish concentration camps" in the media.[69] In this context of correcting misleading geographic labels, the city administration of Łódź under Mayor Kropiwnicki began promoting the usage of "Litzmannstadt Ghetto" instead of "Łódź Ghetto" in official commemorations.[70] Publications related to the 2004 commemoration of the ghetto's liquidation noticeably began rebranding the ghetto as the Litzmannstadt Ghetto.[71] This "Re-Germanization" campaign has also become much more explicit. In 2009, the sixty-fifth anniversary of the liquidation of the Łódź Ghetto commemorated the victims of the ghetto at the Radgoszcz-Radegast station. The ensuing publication was titled *The Restored Memory: The Anniversaries of the Liquidation of the Litzmannstadt Ghetto by the Germans, Lodz 2004–2009.*[72] The apparent need to add the qualifier "by the Germans" in the commemorative book was a recent development and had not been used in previous publications; the retroactive use for earlier ceremonies in the booklet reveals this prioritization.

Thus, the German-Polish past in Łódź is complicated by another group, the Jews, and their role in German and Polish memory politics. It is only in this triadic relationship of competing victimhoods that the payoffs and pitfalls in the attempts to uncover the German past in Łódź—and Litzmannstadt—can be understood. Significantly, the 2009 commemoration of the liquidation of the ghetto also included another ceremony in the nearby Survivors Park.[73] The city revealed a new monument topped by a large white eagle dedicated to Poles who had rescued Jews during the war. Taken together, these two commemorations thus stressed the role of Germans as perpetrators, Jews as victims, and Poles in saving the Jews.

Hence, "restoring memory" is as much about restoring the Good Pole as about remembering Jewish legacies by putting Germans—and the Polish people—back in their rightful places.

Conclusion

This renewed emphasis on the Germanness of the perpetrators has conflicted with local attempts to reclaim German-Polish-Jewish coexistence. At first glance, this may seem to conflict with Europeanist notions of national reconciliation and multiculturalism. Yet this renationalization is not a special Polish problem; rather, it is indicative of other countries, such as Germany, as in the case of the controversy on how to commemorate the victims of expulsions. Looking at localized memory politics such as those in Łódź, however, we can find many counternarratives that complicate such generalizations about the Europeanization of memory politics. Above all, we can see how transnational, national, and local institutions in Łódź have appropriated multicultural pasts into national narratives, a process that represents a "discursive ethnic cleansing" of the "lodzermensch."

Notes

1. See, for example, Andreas Lawaty and Hubert Orłowski, eds., *Deutsche und Polen: Geschichte, Kultur, Politik* (Munich: Beck, 2003). There is also a four-volume project underway called *Deutsch-Polnische Erinnerungsorte* (edited by Hans Henning Hahn and Robert Traba, published by Ferdinand Schöningh).

2. Klaus Bachmann, "Von der Euphorie zum Mißtrauen: Deutsch-polnische Beziehungen nach der Wende," *Osteuropa: Zeitschrift für Gegenwartsfragen des Osten* 50, no. 8 (2000): 853–871. Another early warning came in Albrecht Lempp, "Gemeinsam in einem Boot, nicht in einem Bett: Plädoyer für eine neue Sachlichkeit in den deutsch-polnischen Beziehungen," in *Erlebte Nachbarschaft: Aspekte der deutsch-polnischen Beziehungen im 20. Jahrhundert*, ed. Jan-Pieter Barbian und Marek Zybura (Wiesbaden: Harrassowitz, 1999), 118–128.

3. See, for example, Klaus Bachmann, "Die Versöhnung muß von Polen ausgehen: Wenn jeder Kredit, jeder Schüleraustausch, jede politische Handlung zwischen Polen und Deutschland von den Deutschen dem Schlagwort von der 'Versöhnung' untergeordnet wird, wird diese zum Versöhnungskitsch," in *Erinnerungskultur und Versöhnungskitsch*, ed. Hans Henning Hahn, Heidi Hein-Kircher, and Anna Kochanowska-Nieborak (Marburg: Herder-Institut, 2008), 18. The piece is a reprint of the original article that appeared in the left-leaning German newspaper *Die Tageszeitung* on August 5, 1994.

4. This transformation of cities in Eastern Europe has been studied in two recent volumes: John Czaplicka, Nida Gelazis, and Blair A. Ruble, eds., *Cities after the Fall of Communism: Reshaping Cultural Landscapes and European Identity* (Baltimore: John Hopkins University Press, 2009), and Thomas Bohn, *Von der "europäischen Stadt" zur "sozialistischen Stadt" und zurück? Urbane Transformationen im östlichen Europa des 20. Jahrhunderts* (Munich: Oldenbourg, 2009).

5. For problems and perspectives of Polish studies in Germany, see Dieter Bingen, Peter Oliver Loew, and Agnieszka Wenninger, eds., *Polenforschung in Deutschland: Eine Zwischenbilanz* (Bonn: Gesis, 2008), especially Hans-Jürgen Bömelburg, "Geschichte Polens in Deutschland," 15–20, and Claudia Kraft, "Kulturwissenschaftliche Polenforschung," 21–31.

6. Piotr Madajczyk, "Kriegserfahrungen und Kriegserinnerungen: Der Zweite Weltkrieg in Polen," in *Der Zweite Weltkrieg in Europa: Erfahrung und Erinnerung*, ed. Jörg Echternkamp and Stefan Martens (Paderborn: Schöningh, 2007), 108.

7. Norman M. Naimark, "The Persistence of the Postwar: Germany and Poland," in *Histories of the Aftermath: The Legacies of the Second World War in Europe*, ed. Frank Biess and Robert G. Moeller (New York: Berghahn Books, 2010), 27; Stefan Troebst, "Postkommunistische Erinnerungskulturen im östlichen Europa: Bestandsaufnahme, Kategorisierung, Periodisierung," in *Europa, Polen und Deutschland: Willy-Brandt-Vorlesungen 2003–2005*, ed. Hans-Joachim Gießmann (Baden-Baden: Nomos, 2005), 153–154, 187–191.

8. Etienne François, "Erinnerungsorte zwischen Geschichtsschreibung und Gedächtnis: Eine Forschungsinnovation und ihre Folgen," in *Geschichtspolitik und kollektives Gedächtnis: Erinnerungskulturen in Theorie und Praxis*, ed. Harald Schmid (Göttingen: V&R Unipress, 2009), 34–36.

9. On Germany's role in promoting this view, see Hermann Schäfer, "Erinnern für die Zukunft: Die deutsch-polnischen Kulturbeziehungen im Europa des 21. Jahrhunderts," in *Deutsche und Polen: Erinnerung im Dialog*, ed. Anna Hofmann and Basil Kerski (Osnabrück: Fibre, 2007), 90. Schäfer was the former president of the Stiftung Haus der Geschichte.

10. Schäfer, "Erinnern für die Zukunft," 89–90; Katarzyna Śliwińska, "'Heimat' als imaginärer Ort der Versöhnung: Zur polnischen 'Literatur der kleinen Vaterländer' und ihrem Ort in der Erinnerungskultur," in Hahn et al., eds., *Erinnerungskultur und Versöhnungskitsch*, 107–121; Robert Traba, "'Offener Regionalismus'—Bürgerinitiativen für die Entwicklung der polnischen Kultur," in *Inter Finitimos: Jahrbuch zur deutsch-polnischen Beziehungsgeschichte* 8 (2010): 64–65.

11. Hubert Orłowski, "Et in Arcadia ego? Heimatverlust in der deutschen und polnischen Literatur," in Barbian and Zybura, eds., *Erlebte Nachbarschaft*, 218, 223–224; Janusz A. Majcherek, "Der Mythos der Multikulturalität," in *Inter Finitimos: Jahrbuch zur deutsch-polnischen Beziehungsgeschichte* 8 (2010): 56–57.

12. See Eric Hobsbawm and Terence Ranger, eds., *The Invention of Tradition* (Cambridge: Cambridge University Press, 1983), and Benedict Anderson, *Imagined Communities: Reflections on the Origin and Spread of Nationalism* (London: Verso, 1983).

13. Heidemarie Uhl, "Kultur, Politik, Palimpsest: Thesen zu Gedächtnis und Gesellschaft am Beginn des 21. Jahrhunderts," in Schmid, ed., *Geschichtspolitik und kollektives Gedächtnis*, 48–49.

14. François, "Erinnerungsorte zwischen Geschichtsschreibung und Gedächtnis," 34; Uhl, "Kultur, Politik, Palimpsest," 43, 48–49.

15. Uhl, "Kultur, Politik, Palimpsest," 42. Uhl cites Volkhard Knigge, the head of the memorial foundation of the Buchenwald concentration camp.

16. Troebst, "Postkommunistische Erinnerungskulturen," 163.

17. See Charles S. Maier, *The Unmasterable Past: History, Holocaust, and German National Identity* (Cambridge, MA: Harvard University Press, 1988); Troebst, "Postkommunistische Erinnerungskulturen," 160–161. Troebst attributes the idea of a German industry standard in Vergangenheitsbewältigung to Timothy Garton Ash.

18. Krzysztof Ruchniewicz, "Polen: Abschied von der Martyrologie?" in *Politische Erinnerung: Geschichte und kollektive Identität*, ed. Harald Schmid and Justyna Krzymianowska

204 | Winson Chu

(Würzburg: Königshausen and Neumann, 2007), 199; Troebst, "Postkommunistische Erinnerungskulturen," 163.

19. *The Institute of National Remembrance Guide* (Warsaw: Instytut Pamięci Narodowej, 2009), 2.

20. "Action 4: Active European Remembrance," Education, Audiovisual, and Culture Executive Agency, European Union website, http://eacea.ec.europa.eu/citizenship/programme/action4_en.php.

21. Wiesław Puś, "Die Berufs- und Sozialstruktur der wichtigsten ethnischen Gruppen in Lodz und ihre Entwicklung in den Jahren 1820–1914," in *Polen, Deutsche und Juden in Lodz 1820–1939: Eine schwierige Nachbarschaft*, ed. Jürgen Hensel (Osnabrück: Fibre, 1999), 35–37.

22. Władysław Stanisław Reymont, *Ziemia Obiecana: Powieść*, 2 vols. (Warsaw: Gebethner i Wolff, 1899).

23. Janusz Wróbel, "Between Co-Existence and Hostility: A Contribution to the Problem of National Antagonisms in Łódź," *Polin* 6 (1991): 204–205; Beate Kosmala, *Juden und Deutsche im polnischen Haus: Tomaszów Mazowiecki 1914–1939* (Berlin: Metropol, 2001), 290–292.

24. This spelling better reflected the German pronunciation of "Lodz," which is how most German-language publications had spelled the city's name until that time, as well as after the war.

25. On the radicalizing role of the Reichsgau Wartheland and its Gauleiter, see Catherine Epstein, *Model Nazi: Arthur Greiser and the Occupation of Western Poland* (New York: Oxford University Press, 2010).

26. Florian Freund, Bertrand Perz, and Karl Stuhlpfarrer, "Das Getto in Litzmannstadt (Łódź)," in *"Unser einziger Weg ist Arbeit": Das Getto in Łódź 1940–1944; Eine Ausstellung des Jüdischen Museums, Frankfurt am Main, 30. März bis 10. Juni 1990*, ed. Hanno Loewy and Gerhard Schoenberner. (Frankfurt am Main: Amt für Wissenschaft und Kunst, Jüdisches Museum in Frankfurt/Main, 1990), 17.

27. Michael Unger, "Łódź," in *The Yad Vashem Encyclopedia of the Ghettos during the Holocaust*, vol. 1, ed. Guy Miron and Schlomit Shulhani (Jerusalem: Yad Vashem, 2009), 403–412; Laura Crago, "Łódź," in *The United States Holocaust Memorial Museum Encyclopedia of Camps and Ghettos*, vol. 1, part B, 1933–1945, ed. Geoffrey P. Megargee, Martin Dean, and Melvin Hecker (Bloomington: Indiana University Press, 2012), 75–82.

28. Recent works on the Holocaust in occupied Łódź include Andrea Löw, *Juden im Getto Litzmannstadt: Lebensbedingungen, Selbstwahrnehmung, Verhalten* (Göttingen: Wallstein, 2006); Gordon Horwitz, *Ghettostadt: Łódź and the Making of a Nazi City* (Cambridge, MA: Belknap Press of Harvard University Press, 2008); Peter Klein, *Die "Gettoverwaltung Litzmannstadt" 1940 bis 1944: Eine Dienststelle im Spannungsfeld von Kommunalbürokratie und staatlicher Verfolgungspolitik* (Hamburg: Hamburger Ed., 2009); Catherine Epstein, *Model Nazi: Arthur Greiser and the Occupation of Western Poland* (New York: Oxford University Press, 2010); and Adam Sitarek and Michał Trębacz, "Drei Städte: Besatzungsalltag in Lodz," in *Gewalt und Alltag im besetzten Polen 1939–1945*, ed. Jochen Böhler and Stephan Lehnstaedt (Osnabrück: Fibre, 2012), 299–321. On the postwar period, see Andrzej Lech, Krystyna Radziszewska, and Andrzej Rykała, eds., *Społeczność żydowska i niemiecka w Łodzi po 1945 roku* (Łódź: Wydawnictwo. Uniwersytetu Łódzkiego, 2010).

29. Sitarek and Trębacz, "Drei Städte: Besatzungsalltag in Lodz," 309.

30. Two publications dealing with recent German-Polish memory politics are based on papers delivered at the conference "Polish-German Post/Memory: Aesthetics, Ethics, Politics" in Bloomington, Indiana, in April 2007. See Justyna Beinek and Piotr H. Kosicki, eds., *Re-mapping Polish-German Historical Memory: Physical, Political, and Literary Spaces since World War II* (Bloomington, IN: Slavica Publishers, 2011), and Kristin Kopp and Joanna Niżyńska, eds., *Ger-*

many, Poland, and Postmemorial Relations: In Search of a Livable Past (New York: Palgrave Macmillan, 2012).

31. Elżbieta Opiłowska, "Erinnerungspolitik im deutsch-polnischen Grenzgebiet nach dem Zweiten Weltkrieg," *Inter Finitimos: Jahrbuch zur deutsch-polnischen Beziehungsgeschichte* 8 (2010): 111–113.

32. On the justifications given for expulsions, see Gregor Thum, *Die fremde Stadt: Breslau nach 1945* (Berlin: Siedler, 2003), 506.

33. T. David Curp, *A Clean Sweep? The Politics of Ethnic Cleansing in Western Poland, 1945–1960* (Rochester, NY: University of Rochester Press, 2006).

34. On this process in Breslau/Wrocław, see Thum, *Die fremde Stadt.*

35. Mirosław Cygański, *Mniejszość niemiecka w Polsce centralnej w latach 1919–1939* (Łódź: Wydawnictwo Łódzkie, 1962), 149–150.

36. Bianka Pietrow-Ennker, "Ein Klischee lernt das Zwinkern: Der 'Lodzermensch' verkörpert eine Lebensweise, die in Lodz wieder modern wird," *Frankfurter Allgemeine Zeitung,* January 3, 2002, 48.

37. Beate Kosmala, "Schwierigkeiten des Gedenkens: Das Ghetto Litzmannstadt als Erinnerungsort in Polen und Deutschland," *Zeitschrift für Geschichtswissenschaft* 55, no. 9 (2007): 743–761; Hans-Jürgen Bömelburg, "Lodz: Gegen den Strich," in *Deutsch-polnische Erinnerungsorte,* vol. 1, *Geteilt/Gemeinsam,* ed. Hans Henning Hahn and Robert Traba (Paderborn: Ferdinand Schöningh, 2014), 103. My thanks to Hans-Jürgen Bömelburg for providing his chapter to me in advance of publication.

38. See Valentin Polcuch, "Wie ein Schmonzeslied zum Schlager wurde," in *Lodz: Die Stadt der Völkerbegegnung im Wandel der Geschichte,* ed. Peter E. Nasarski (Cologne-Rodenkirchen: Liebig, 1978), 78, and Valentin Polcuch, "'Theo, wir fahr'n nach Lodz': Ein Schlager im Wandel der Geschichte," in *Lodz—"Gelobtes Land": Von deutscher Tuchmachersiedlung zur Textilmetropole im Osten. Dokumente und Erinnerungen,* ed. Peter E. Nasarski (Berlin and Bonn. Westkreuz, 1988), 11–12.

39. Karl Schlögel, "Lodz—Suche nach dem 'Gelobten Land,'" in *Promenade in Jalta und andere Städtebilder,* ed. Karl Schlögel, 2nd edition (Frankfurt: Fischer Taschenbuch, 2006), 126.

40. Wolfgang Kessler, "Lodz nach Lodz: Beobachtungen zu Erinnerung und Gedächtnis der Deutschen aus Lodz nach 1945," in *Lodz jenseits von "Fabriken, Wildwest und Provinz": Kulturwissenschaftliche Studien über die Deutschen in und aus den polnischen Gebieten,* ed. Stefan Dyroff, Krystyna Radziszewska, and Isabel Röskau-Rydel (Munich: Martin Meidenbauer, 2009), 163.

41. Jutta Faehndrich, "Erinnerungskultur und Umgang mit Vertreibung in Heimatbüchern deutschsprachiger Vertriebener," *Zeitschrift für Ostmitteleuropa-Forschung* 52, no. 2 (2003): 191–229.

42. See Ludwig Mehlhorn, "Zwangsverordnete Freundschaft? Zur Entwicklung der Beziehungen zwischen der DDR und Polen," in *Zwangsverordnete Freundschaft? Die Beziehungen zwischen der DDR und Polen 1949–1990,* ed. Basil Kerski, Andrzej Kotula, and Kazimierz Wóycicki (Osnabrück: Fibre, 2003), 35–40. In the same volume, see also Burkhard Olschowsky, "Die staatlichen Beziehungen zwischen der DDR und Polen," 41–58.

43. Margot Pfannstiel, *Łódź, mehr denn je "gelobtes Land": Auf literarischen Spuren in einer ungewöhnlichen Stadt* (Leipzig: VEB F. A. Brockhaus Verlag, 1979), 32.

44. Kosmala, "Schwierigkeiten des Gedenkens," 746; Sascha Feuchert, "Einleitung," in *Letzte Tage: Die Łódzer Getto-Chronik Juni/Juli 1944,* ed. Sascha Feuchert, Erwin Leibfried, and Jörg Riecke with Julian Baranowski and Krystyna Radziszewska (Göttingen: Wallstein, 2004), 7–8.

45. Kosmala, "Schwierigkeiten des Gedenkens," 743–744, 746.

46. On this process, see Ingo Eser, "Lodz—Blick(e) auf eine Stadtgeschichte," in Dyroff et al., eds., *Lodz jenseits von "Fabriken, Wildwest und Provinz,"* 54–55.

47. Craig Young and Sylwia Kaczmarek, "Changing the Perception of the Post-Socialist City: Place Promotion and Imagery in Łódź," *The Geographical Journal* 165, no. 2 (1999): 183–191; Andreas Kossert, "'Promised Land?' Urban Myth and the Shaping of Modernity in Manchester and Lodz," in *Imagining the City, Volume 2: The Politics of Urban Space,* ed. Christian Emden, Catherine Keen, and David Midgley (Bern: Peter Lang, 2006), 175–176; Joanna Michlic, "Łódź in the Postcommunist Era: In Search of a New Identity," in *Cities after the Fall of Communism: Reshaping Cultural Landscapes and European Identity,* ed. John Czaplicka, Nida Gelazis, and Blair A. Ruble (Baltimore: John Hopkins University Press, 2009), 281–303; Michael Fleming, "Legitimating Urban 'Revitalisation' Strategies in Post-Socialist Łódź," *East European Politics and Societies* 26, no. 2 (May 2012): 254–273.

48. The issue of the Russian and Soviet past has been analyzed in Craig Young and Sylvia Kaczmarek, "The Socialist Past and Postsocialist Urban Identity in Central and Eastern Europe: The Case of Łódź, Poland," *European Urban and Regional Studies* 15, no. 1 (2008): 53–70.

49. On Breslau being more alien than Danzig to Polish postwar settlers, see Thum, *Die fremde Stadt,* 45; Elizabeth Morrow Clark, "Reshaping the Free City: Cleansed Memory in Danzig/Gdansk, 1939–1952," in *Ethnic Cleansing in Twentieth-Century Europe,* ed. Steven Várdy and T. Hunt Tooley (Boulder, CO: Social Science Monographs, 2003), 313.

50. Eser, "Lodz—Blick(e) auf eine Stadtgeschichte," 55.

51. Joanna B. Michlic, "'Remembering to Remember,' 'Remembering to Benefit,' 'Remembering to Forget': The Variety of Memories of Jews and the Holocaust in Postcommunist Poland," Jerusalem Center for Public Affairs, January 3, 2012, http://jcpa.org/article/remembering-to -remember-remembering-to-benefit-remembering-to-forget-the-variety-of-memories-of-jews -and-the-holocaust-in-postcommunist-poland.

52. Ruth Ellen Gruber, *Virtually Jewish: Reinventing Jewish Culture in Europe* (Berkeley: University of California Press, 2002).

53. Monika Murzyn-Kupisz, "Reclaiming Memory or Mass Consumption? Dilemmas in Rediscovering Jewish Heritage of Krakow's Kazimierz," in *Reclaiming Memory: Urban Regeneration in the Historic Jewish Quarters of Central European Cities,* ed. Monika Murzyn-Kupisz and Jacek Purchla (Kraków: International Cultural Centre, 2009), 378. For a recent view on the pluralism of Polish-Jewish memory, see Erica T. Lehrer, *Jewish Poland Revisited: Heritage Tourism in Unquiet Places* (Bloomington: Indiana University Press, 2013).

54. Joanna B. Michlic, "Przerwane milczenie: O pamięci Zagłady w postkomunistycznej Europie," *Znak Miesięcznik,* no. 685 (June 2012): 30.

55. Michael Meng, "From Destruction to Preservation: Jewish Sites in Germany and Poland after the Holocaust," *Bulletin of the German Historical Institute* 46 (Spring 2010): 58–59. See also Michael Meng, *Shattered Spaces: Encountering Jewish Ruins in Postwar Germany and Poland* (Cambridge, MA: Harvard University Press, 2011).

56. Kosmala, "Schwierigkeiten des Gedenkens," 745, 754.

57. David M. Smith, *Moral Geographies: Ethics in a World of Difference* (Edinburgh: Edinburgh University Press, 2000), 68–72.

58. Michlic, "Łódź in the Postcommunist Era," 294–296.

59. Kosmala, "Schwierigkeiten des Gedenkens," 760–762.

60. Joanna Podolska, *Traces of the Litzmannstadt-Getto: A Guide to the Past,* trans. Dorota Dekiert (Łódź: Piątek Trzynastego, 2004). Despite the title, Podolska uses "Łódź Ghetto" in the text itself.

61. On the German-Polish year, see Schäfer, "Erinnern für die Zukunft," 87, 89.

62. Barbara Ratecka, "Auf den Spuren bedeutender Deutscher in Lodz. Ausstellung," pamphlet published by Urząd Miasta Łodzi, c. 2005.

63. On national indifference, see Tara Zahra, "Imagined Non-Communities: National Indifference as a Category of Analysis," *Slavic Review* 69 (Spring 2010): 93–119.

64. Krystyna Radziszewska, "Die Metropole Lodz: Eine Stadt zwischen Licht und Schatten. Lodzermensch und Litzmannstadt," in *Kulturraumformung: Sprachpolitische, kulturpolitische, ästhetische Dimensionen*, ed. Maria Katarzyna Lasatowicz (Berlin: Trafo, 2004), 123–132; Krystyna Radziszewska, *Tonąca Łódź (lata 1939–1945) (Das sinkende Boot [der Zeitraum 1939–1945])* (Łódź: Literatura, 2002). See also Marek Budziarek, *Łódź, Lodsch, Litzmannstadt: Wycinki z życia mieszkańców okupowanego miasta* (Łódź: Literatura, 2003), 5.

65. Radziszewska, *Tonąca Łódź*.

66. Thomas Urban, *Von Krakau bis Danzig: Eine Reise durch die deutsch-polnische Geschichte* (Munich: C. H. Beck, 2000), 173–177, 193.

67. See Georg W. Strobel, "Industriemetropole zwischen Orient und Okzident: Eine Hommage an die Vielvölkerstadt Lodz," in *Deutsch-polnische Ansichten zur Literatur und Kultur: Jahrbuch 1992* (Darmstadt/Wiesbaden: Deutsches Polen-Institut/Harrassowitz, 1993), 31–59; and Georg W. Strobel, "Das multinationale Lodz, die Textilmetropole Polens, als Produkt von Migration und Kapitalwanderung," in *Wanderungen und Kulturaustausch im östlichen Mitteleuropa: Forschungen zum ausgehenden Mittelalter und zur jüngeren Neuzeit*, ed. Hans-Werner Rautenberg (Munich: Oldenbourg, 2006), 163–223.

68. Karl Schlögel, "Suche nach dem 'Gelobten Land,'" *Bauwelt* 88, no. 48 (*StadtBauwelt* 136, December 26, 1997), 2699–2700.

69. Oliver Hinz, "Gedankenlose Wortwahl," *Dialog. Deutsch-Polnisches Magazin* 74–75 (2006): 64.

70. Bömelburg, "Lodz: Auf Identitätssuche," 106; Anna Gronczewska, "To, co Łódź zrobiła, żeby pamiętać, jest wyjątkowe," *Moja Łódź*, August 28, 2009, http://lodz.naszemiasto.pl/artykul /10183,to-co-lodz-zrobila-zeby-pamietac-jest-wyjatkowe-rozmowa-z,id,t.html.

71. *Żeby ten krzyk nie przeminął: Materiały z obchodów 60. Rocznicy Zagłady Litzmannstadt Ghetto 1944–2004* (Łódź: Urząd Miasta Łodzi, 2005). The publication for the fiftieth anniversary commemoration in 1994 was Jan Fijałek, Sławomir Abramowicz, Marek Budziarek, and Antoni Galiński, eds., *Zagłada Żydów z getta łódzkiego: W 50. rocznicę likwidacji getta łódzkiego* (Łódź: Okręgowa Komisja Badania Zbrodni przeciwko Narodowi Polskiemu w Łodzi—Instytutu Pamięci Narodowej and Muzeum Historii Miasta Łodzi, 1994).

72. *Przywrócona Pamięć: Obchody rocznicowe likwidacji przez Niemców Litzmannstadt Ghetto, Łódź 2004–2009 / The Restored Memory: The Anniversaries of the Liquidation of the Litzmannstadt Ghetto by the Germans, Lodz 2004–2009* (Łódź: Urząd Miasta Łodzi, 2009), 2, 62, 68.

73. The park was dedicated in 2004 during the city's commemoration of the sixtieth anniversary of the liquidation of the ghetto. It is interesting to note here that the Polish name, Park Ocalałych, can also be translated as "Park of the Rescued." More information can be found on the Marek Edelman Dialogue Center (also located in the park): http://www.centrumdialogu .com/en/about-us/survivors-park.

9 Stony Survivors
Images of Jewish Space on the Polish Landscape

Robert L. Cohn

LYING BENEATH ROME'S surface, the Forum, once the nerve center of the ancient city, confronts the visitor as a jumble of columns, arches, foundations, and reconstructed buildings. Ravaged by fire, sacked by the Ostrogoths, and pillaged by Christians observing the ban on pagan cults, the site was largely abandoned in the succeeding centuries, becoming pasture land for shepherds. Eventually its ancient stones, their provenance long since forgotten, were quarried for new construction elsewhere in the city. As Rome's sacred center of gravity shifted from the pagan Forum to Christian sites, a civilization fell largely into oblivion. One structure that escaped early destruction, however, was the Temple of Antonius and Faustina, preserved since the seventh century as the Church of San Lorenzo in Miranda, its Corinthian columns and inscriptions to Faustina and Antonius witnessing to its former and forgotten life. Not until the Renaissance, the Protestant Reformation, and the Enlightenment seriously challenged the hold of tradition was the stage set for the appreciation of the classical past as a distinctive era with its own integrity. Not until modern excavations revealed that the lower third of the Corinthian columns were hidden by the accumulated debris of centuries was the Forum revealed as the heart of ancient Rome.

When I visited the Forum, I was struck by the parallel between its sacked, forgotten, and then rediscovered ruins and the similarly destroyed, abandoned or recycled, and recently reembraced Jewish cemeteries and synagogues in Poland. There, however, a process that took hundreds of years in Rome was telescoped into a biblical generation. As the pagan voices that would have lamented the end of Roman culture were eventually silenced, those few Jews who survived the Holocaust and chose to stay in Poland were in the main unable to lay claim to and preserve Jewish property. And the Communist governments succeeded in repressing and nearly expelling the public memory of the Jewish past.[1]

In the case of ancient Rome, it was the French Revolution that catalyzed a different vision of the past. Peter Fritzsche explains how the deep rupture of the revolution gave birth to a new sense of history for which the past became the site of alternative identities that rendered the present insecure. Ruins were seen for the first time not as part of the natural cycle of degeneration but as windows on particular historical events. Ruins carried a kind of half-life power to inspire and frighten by providing evidence of counterlives, potential futures that never came to be.[2] Françoise Choay shows how the French Revolution and the Industrial Revolution that followed stimulated the preservation and restoration of the newly recognized architectural patrimony.[3]

A similar radical shift in perspective arose toward the Jewish past in Poland in the wake of the political and cultural ferment beginning in the 1970s that culminated in the end of Communist rule. At the same time that some Catholic and secular intellectuals had begun to expose and criticize Polish wartime and postwar behavior toward Jews, a small group of young Poles of Jewish and mixed backgrounds was reclaiming a Polish-Jewish identity and attempting to renew a living Jewish presence in Poland. Poles and Polish Jews began to recognize what remained of synagogues and cemeteries as traces of a Jewish cultural record that had been marginalized and delegitimized, but that could be seen now as witnesses to a newly valorized past. As in postrevolution France, the past took on an independent identity. Jewish material remains, which had been blended into ongoing Polish towns and cityscapes, assumed a new significance. Indeed, in recent years, many Jewish sites have been transformed from what Barbara Kirshenblatt-Gimblett would call "zones of repudiation" into Pierre Nora's *lieux de mémoire*, places where memory crystallizes and expresses itself.[4] Nora suggests that without *milieux de mémoire*, environments in which tradition reigns and the present flows continuously from the past, we nominate and dedicate *lieux de mémoire* to stop time in its tracks and nudge us to recall a past age.[5] The stones that the postwar builders of Poland rejected have thus become the cornerstone of memory. By means of these "cultural outtakes" (Kirshenblatt-Gimblett again), a Jewish map of a Poland once thick with Jews and Jewish history now bleeds through a Poland whose present Jewish population is very thin. It is a map "with its own points of reference, layers of association, and sometimes different names for rivers and towns. A separate Jewish map that is yet inextricably of Poland, and interwoven with Polish fate."[6]

That map emerges like a palimpsest, a reused ancient manuscript whose original ink eventually becomes visible behind its newer text. Just as Andreas Huyssen reads some contemporary cities as spatial palimpsests, "as lived spaces that shape collective imaginaries," so we can read the Polish landscape at large.[7] Here partially restored synagogues and fenced, though largely empty, Jewish cemeteries dot the landscape in the midst of Polish towns where no Jews live. These structures, unlike "intentional monuments," memorials purposefully constructed to remember a hero or event, are accidental witnesses to the past. Choay, referring to the medieval patrimony in postrevolution France, calls them "historic" monuments, "constituted *a posteriori* by the converging gazes of the historian and the *amateur,* who choose it from the mass of existing edifices."[8]

If heritage is "the transvaluation of the obsolete, the mistaken, the outmoded, the dead, and the defunct, . . . created through a process of exhibition," how is the formerly rejected Jewish heritage being transvalued?[9] Here I examine three forms of exhibition in order to understand how each "as a new mode of cultural production in the present that has recourse to the past" represents that past.[10] First, I look at two examples of synagogues *in situ,* a ruin and a restoration, before turning to several volumes of photographs of Jewish cemeteries and synagogues. Composed in succeeding decades, these books trace changing attitudes toward Jewish sites. Third, I explore the proliferation of images of and perspectives on Jewish spaces on the internet. Multiple portals and websites make visible not only contemporary representations of commemoration and restoration but also virtual communities of concern, which transcend national and religious boundaries.

Synagogues *In Situ* Ruined and Restored

Because sacred places—synagogues and cemeteries—are the most visible evidence of prewar Jewish life and death, they have become the most visible spatial markers of public memory. With the exception of those structures belonging to newly active communities in major Polish cities, most are restorations with primarily educational and commemorative aims. In the town of Działoszyce, for example, about seven thousand Jews comprised 80 percent of the town's population in 1939. Few came back after the war, and none stayed.[11] On a hot July day in 1998, the remains of the synagogue, a hulking roofless form, sits solitary at the end of a road near the town square. Vegetation surrounds and penetrates the structure: weeds and wild shrubs cascade from niches in the upper courses of the walls, and brush sprouts out of the ground that was once its floor. Broken beer bottles and syringes are scattered around, suggesting the profane use to which this once sacred site has been put.

In the 2005 documentary *Hiding and Seeking,* filmmaker Menachem Daum captures the reactions of his sons and wife, whose parents lived in Działoszyce and survived the war in hiding, upon seeing the synagogue for the first time. Overcome with emotion, Mrs. Daum asks her sons to say the Kaddish with her. The sons, to this point in the film dismissive of the gentile world and of the entire "roots" journey on which their father has brought them, break down and weep. Do they lament the Nazi terror inflicted upon their family, the postwar abandonment and profanation of a holy place, the destruction of a Jewish civilization?

Ruins, Svetlana Boym opines, foster thoughts about human frailty, the passage of time, and the unpredictability of change, nostalgia fraught with mourning and melancholy. This kind of nostalgia she terms "reflective," focusing on *algia*, longing and loss.[12] At ruins of synagogues and cemeteries, I—like perhaps other Jewish visitors—dwell on the absent, mourn for a world that is no more, know that it is gone forever.[13] Coming in contact with the ruins of a sacred place is an end in itself, an opportunity to "remember" a lost Jewish world, a world constructed from each visitor's own prior exposure to European Jewish life and filtered through the knowledge of the Holocaust. The encounter with such *lieux de mémoire* deepens, Fritzsche suggests, "the sense of irreversibility, which denies to the present the imagined wholeness of the past."[14] It is the sense of being cut off from that past by the rupture of the Holocaust that produces the melancholy of nostalgia.

If the ruins of the Działoszyce synagogue inspire moments of reflective nostalgia, the reconstructed synagogue in nearby Pińczów evokes what Boym calls "restorative" nostalgia, which aims at *nostos,* the return home, the desire to revive and rebuild. Yet while Boym undercuts this desire by seeing it as leading to the erasure of trauma in favor of idealized, "invented" origins, the Pińczów project aims to include the now absent Jewish community in the history of the town. The restoration of this early seventeenth-century synagogue was the object of a long-term commitment by the Pińczów Regional Museum beginning in the 1970s, long before Jewish foundations began to support such projects. By 1998, the building was secured, the roof rebuilt, the floor relaid, the grounds landscaped, and the fallen massive stone aron ha-kodesh (Torah ark) returned to its place. When I visited again in 2009, designs and inscriptions on the walls and ceilings had been revealed. Located on the corner of a quiet street surrounded by new houses, the synagogue's grassed and fenced lot sits well below the street level.[15] The cavernous sanctuary serves as an exhibition space featuring a display of photographs and drawings illustrating highlights of prewar Jewish life in Pińczów. One photo shows a collage of portraits of the fifteen Poles and fifteen Jews who comprised the city council in the late 1920s. The synagogue aims to revive a memory of Poles and Jews living together in harmony.

Around the perimeter of the synagogue grounds is a retaining wall built of fragments of Jewish gravestones recovered from sheds, yards, and stone paths after the cemeteries in Pińczów had been built over. A number of intact matzevot stand upright against the wall. Although survivors soon after the war sometimes mortared together such gravestone walls around cemeteries, the location at a synagogue is unusual: as sites that convey ritual pollution, a Jewish cemetery is typically located at some distance from a synagogue, and at the least separated from it by a proper wall. Here, in contrast, the evidence of both Jewish life and Jewish death is concentrated in one location.[16]

As an historic monument, in Choay's sense, the synagogue restores the memory of a Jewish religious world and of the integration of Jews in the life of the town.

Moreover, as a division of the museum, the synagogue is officially guarded as part of local heritage. Yet the tombstone wall transforms the site into an intentional monument as well, a sacred memorial to the Holocaust. In its brokenness, the wall remembers less the individuals whose graves its stones, now largely undecipherable, once graced than their murdered descendants. Furthermore, the conjoining of synagogue and cemetery creates a single venue to represent Judaism. Whereas the synagogue, when it supported a living community, fit into Jewish architectural, social, religious, and economic networks as a Jewish sacred space, now it stands out from its Polish environment. Physically, it is cut off from its surroundings by its lower elevation, its tombstone wall and metal fence, and its Renaissance architecture, so different from the postwar buildings adjacent to it.[17] Unlike the ruin of the Działoszyce synagogue, which denotes abandonment and loss, however, the restored Pińczów synagogue represents a moral effort to remember. With the synagogue, the town revives some knowledge of its Jewish past and so protests against the second death of forgetting.[18]

Cemeteries and Synagogues Photographed

In 1976, as reconstruction proceeded in Pińczów, Monika Krajewska had just begun to photograph Jewish gravestones in towns all over Poland. She explains that while other socially conscious friends were searching for a multicultural Polish past buried under decades of Communist-enforced uniformity and finding abandoned Russian Orthodox churches, she and her husband set out to discover the formerly Jewish world that surrounded them. Hitchhiking around the country, they found graveyards everywhere—on hilltops, next to gas stations, running into cornfields. They cleared shrubs and thorns, photographed matzevot, made rubbings, and deciphered inscriptions and iconography.[19] Krajewska's pioneering photographic work was issued in two collections of images, *A Time of Stones* (1983) and *A Tribe of Stones* (1993). *Time,* along with a public exhibit in 1981 in Warsaw, first exposed this world of Jewish ruins to public attention.[20]

Through this medium, Krajewska brought together scattered, isolated, and largely forgotten Jewish spaces and promoted awareness of and reflection on the Jewish past.[21] "The camera," Paul Williams notes, produces "an instantaneous abduction of the object out of the world into another world, into another kind of time."[22] Or, as W. James Booth says, "The photograph both stops time and allows that frozen past to be evoked again. It is thus ultimately related to those sentiments of memory, nostalgia, and regret, to the presence of an absence, and in that way to the doing of justice as well."[23] Seen today through the inevitable lens of the Holocaust, such photos redouble that out-of-time sensation, the nostalgia, and the regret. In its representation of a palimpsest of Jewish spaces, photography exposes a topography of loss.

Each volume makes distinctive contributions to a memory of Jewish death. The stunning black-and-white photographs in *Time* are identified by location but otherwise not annotated. They appear to be arranged in no particular order, but rather as markers of a single Jewish necropolis spanning the Polish landscape. Occasionally, meditative verses from Polish and Polish-Jewish poets, white text on black background, interrupt the flow of images, enveloping them in a chorus of sad voices. Some pictures train in on individual matzevot whose inscriptions can be clearly read but remain untranslated. The shared space of camera and epitaph engenders an intimate connection with the dead for the viewer; the undeciphered gravestone becomes relic.[24] In other photos, a long view captures graveyards in their rural or urban backgrounds nestled within a variety of Polish landscapes. The few stones poking out of a woodsy hillside in Chęciny overlook miles of planted fields against a hilly horizon. Sheep graze among the broken stones in Tykocin.[25] In Karczew near Warsaw, the few remaining stones push out of a field of sand that, through the camera's filter, appears as a moonscape. In some photos, vines and underbrush embrace and obscure tombstones; in others, trees frame them as backdrops. Image upon image of forgotten, abandoned, unknown, and yet strangely beautiful graveyards evoke a melancholic mood in the face of a world lost and gone forever.

The second book, *A Tribe of Stones,* however, frames a similar collection of photos with different text to produce a more informed evocation of prewar Jewish death. Besides providing background notes on each photo, Krajewska explains in an introduction the history of Jewish cemeteries in Poland, customs of Jewish death and burial customs, and the iconographic symbols and epitaphs on the tombstones. English translations of many of the Hebrew epitaphs give non-Hebrew readers a window into the individual dead. The words and images tell stories of human charity and devotion, reveal Jewish occupations and community service, tell of priests and rabbis and virtuous women, and celebrate learning and industry. This new text makes the photos come alive in the context of a meaningful Jewish civilization in Poland. Rather than viewing anonymous dead whose traces are spread over the countryside, we see the traces of particular persons whose lives were deeply rooted in Jewish tradition and anchored in the towns in which they lived and died. While melancholy remains, this volume heralds an attitude of belonging to Poland claimed by the renewed Jewish community of which Krajewska is a member. The memory of the Jewish past here also serves as a summons to a Jewish future.

Separated by little more than a decade from Krajewska's work, a more recently published anthology is a measure of the ongoing progress in the dissemination of knowledge and memory of prewar Judaism. This book, with photos by Chris Schwarz and text by Jonathan Webber, focuses on Jewish Galicia and includes images not only of cemeteries and synagogues but also of Holocaust sites and contemporary acts of remembering.[26] The structure of the book promotes a positive view of Polish memory work: ruins in chapter 1 are followed by restorations in chapter 2; sites of Holocaust death in chapter 3 precede Holocaust memorials in chapter 4; and the last chapter pictures both Jews and Poles in acts of remembering. While the photos and accompanying text may trigger multiple reactions—sadness, sanctity, horror, mourning, inspiration—the volume aims not only to commemorate a Jewish world but also to celebrate those who seek to remember it.

This collection differs from those of Krajewska in several ways. First, here the photographs are in full color, a deliberate choice, Webber notes, to convey the presentness of the sites.[27] Monochrome, at least in an age when most visual media are polychrome, suggests age and timelessness. The boldness of the colors in Schwarz's photographs, even in those of faded ruins, makes this old world come alive and impinge upon the viewer in a dramatic way. Second, the images of restored Jewish architecture and of people engaging in Jewish remembrance and celebration lend a hopeful forward-looking dimension to "traces of memory" that might otherwise point only to the past. Like the Galicia Jewish Museum itself, the book is dedicated to the future of Jewish memory in Poland. Third, the full descriptions of each photograph and extensive historical and religious background given in the endnotes ground the images in Jewish civilization. The traces cut off from their culture by the Holocaust are thereby called back to the culture from which they sprang. Their pasts are restored, their identities renewed. Finally, Webber's notes repeatedly suggest the moods and attitudes that the images can engender. While perhaps overly prescriptive, these observations frame the photos in the welter of emotions that accompany any sympathetic encounter with the Jewish past.

The three volumes considered here chart a path of increasingly rich contextualization of their photographs in the Jewish past and Polish present. Each also offers its own aesthetic of ruins and restorations. Krajewska's gravestones show "human construction at the mercy of nature's deconstruction," while Schwarz's color images give the traces new life.[28] Displaying and juxtaposing the multiform Jewish remains that crisscross Polish space and history, these books yet picture prewar Judaism as a whole and holy civilization.

Jewish Spaces on the Internet

Cyberspace offers new possibilities for remembering and representing Jewish spaces. Individual synagogues, cemeteries, and towns boast their own websites, while portals facilitate wide-ranging coverage of hundreds of Jewish sites at once. Moreover, blogs enable searchers to form online, virtual communities for discussion and discovery. If before the fall of Communism and the rise of the internet the Polish memory of Jews inside Poland developed largely independently of the Jewish memory of Poland outside, the internet facilitates joint communities of memory that transcend national and religious boundaries. To some degree, though, the proliferation of images of cemeteries and synagogues on the web reduces their aesthetic impact. Copies of copies, digital images made from other images, they lack the artifactual, precious quality of the original photographs of Krajewska and Schwarz; most lack attribution altogether. But in their multitude and variety, these images in cyberspace and their contextualizations enable multiple perspectives on the representation and commemoration of prewar Jewish spaces.

The vast number of websites authored by Jewish and Polish organizations, municipalities, museums, and individuals makes it difficult to generalize about them; each offers a different collection and configuration of resources that frame a Jewish narrative. Some have more images, others more text; some have a nostalgic tone, others are more academic. Some focus on the past, others the present. Still, some trends emerge, some common patterns of remembering, forgetting, and imagining a lost "Jewish world." Here I examine websites that represent a single synagogue or cemetery, index multiple synagogues and cemeteries, and place Jewish traces within the wider context of renewed and ongoing Jewish life in Poland.

To begin, consider the online version of the synagogue at Pińczów discussed earlier. On the Pińczów Regional Museum homepage in 2010, it was named as one of five permanent exhibits, alongside displays of prehistoric remains, parks with regional flora and fauna, and famous people in the Pińczów area. On a second museum page, a partial Torah scroll was displayed as one of six sample artifacts from the museum just below a portable wooden shrine from a Catholic church and a bronze-age hatchet. In these contexts, the synagogue and the Torah assumed a place within the town's historic family. The synagogue's own page sets its restoration within a brief history of the Jews of Pińczów, called so populous a Jewish town that it gave rise to the expression "crowded as Jews in Pińczów."[29] Between the wars, we are told, "they constituted a completely different world, with separate language, religion, and customs," living in the area around the synagogue and dressed in skullcaps and gabardine caftans. Here the Jewish world remembered is a religious one: the Jew is of the generic Orthodox variety. This essentializing description gives no hint of the diverse political and religious factions within the Jewish community, nor of the tensions between them and their fellow Poles. Indeed, Polish farmers, the text notes, hid several hundred Jews from the Germans, only to be shot along with them when discovered. This portrayal of an irenic relationship, as in the photo of the town council in the synagogue gallery itself noted above, forms the backdrop for reclaiming the synagogue as integral to the town's heritage. As the only material remnant of prewar Jewish Pińczów, the synagogue in this online museum gives rise to a memory of a valued but exotic religious community.

Turning from synagogue to cemetery, one can find still active cemeteries, such as those in Łódź and Warsaw, which maintain their own websites. Łódź's site provides in four languages a map of the enormous graveyard, the largest Jewish cemetery in Europe, searchable by quarter and revealing the names of those buried in each.[30] The result of painstaking research on records and gravestones, the site thus witnesses to the individual dead, both those who have descendants to remember them and the vast majority who do not. By contrast, the site of the Warsaw Jewish cemetery on Okopowa Street maintained by the (Orthodox) Religious Community of Warsaw offers no such necrology.[31] Instead, it supplies descriptions, photos, or drawings of the cemetery and its history, Jewish burial practices, matzevah iconography, and tombstones of famous rabbis and Talmudists. In Polish only, the site provides to a Polish audience an education in the sanctity and beauty of the cemetery, thus valorizing the sacred history of the community that buried its dead there.[32]

Second, a number of portal websites are devoted to making the scattered and forgotten architecture of Jewish life and death visible to Polish and international audiences. Perhaps most intriguing is www.kirkuty.xip.pl (Kirkuty), a portal that links to about five hundred Jewish cemeteries and was "created by a person of non-Jewish ancestry." Each link delivers a page that narrates a short history of Jewish settlement in a Polish town, the names of its important Jewish leaders, and a description of its cemetery along with photos of the cemetery and of individual matzevot. Links to other sites, such as online Jewish memorial books, mutual aid societies, and even video tours provide further resources. The homepage also connects to a blog in Polish with a steady, up-to-date stream of remarks by visitors offering brief memories, information, and questions about particular graveyards and individuals buried there.

On its homepage, Kirkuty (Polish for a Jewish cemetery) casts its representations of Jewish cemeteries as an encounter with the sacred, what Rudolph Otto called the *mysterium tremendum et fascinans,* an overwhelming experience of fear and fascination at once.[33] The website notes,

> The fate of Jewish cemeteries has been tragic. Today we often don't know—or pretend that we don't know—what lies behind an old wall or in a forest nearby. *Jewish cemeteries are very special places.* Hidden somewhere out of the way, covered with high grass, they intrigue us with their atmosphere and we find delight in the Hebrew scriptures [inscriptions] laboriously and artistically forged by unknown craftsmen.

With a hint of social self-criticism ("pretend"), the site aims to reveal the hidden, to bring into view what has heretofore been off-limits. It promises to provide an alternate map of Poland, a look behind those walls and into those forests that lie just beyond quotidian existence into a sacred world. The "atmosphere" of abandonment bespeaks the numinous; the sacred Hebrew language, unknown to most visitors to the site, and the anonymity of the craftsmen enhance the mystery.

Videos of cemeteries linked to the Kirkuty site expand the sense of the sacred by inviting users on a virtual pilgrimage. The eight-minute video at the cemetery at Oświęcim (Auschwitz), for instance, begins with a disembodied hand opening the cemetery gate. The camera scans a snow-covered graveyard, occasionally focusing in on particular matzevot but mainly offering long views of rows of them from a distance. No people are shown, and no voices are heard; you are alone. The cemetery is fenced, and the gravestones appear upright and, under the snow, well-tended.[34] Frequently the camera pans skyward to show barren trees and an occasional bird. Mournful choral and orchestral music, including the theme from the soundtrack of the film *Schindler's List*, imposes a lugubrious mood on an otherwise silent scene. As a virtual pilgrim, do you try to imagine those buried here? Remember instead the fate of those without graves but turned to ashes in the death camp only a short distance away?

The portal of the Foundation for the Preservation of Jewish Culture (FPJH), in contrast, focuses on restoration projects.[35] Its "Chassidic Route" site, for instance, encourages not virtual but actual pilgrimage through towns in southeast Poland and Ukraine where Hassidic dynasties once flourished. Recalling the pilgrimages that prewar Hassidim would make to these towns to visit their rebbes or their tombs, the project joins the sites on a single map. Explaining that Hassidism was "one of the most important currents ever to come into being within Judaism," the sponsors promote its memory through further restoration efforts in the towns. The project constructs a pilgrimage route that never existed as such, because disciples for the most part visited the court or tomb of their own rebbe but did not travel on a circuit to the towns of others. By representing these towns as stations on a pilgrimage route, the project constructs a nostalgic memory of Hassidic Jewish piety as a hook on which to hang "the development of profiled tourism, based on Jewish cultural heritage." Yet another site on the FPJH portal, "To Bring Memory Back," promotes Jewish heritage in a different way. It encourages Polish school students to discover the "multicultural history of their towns" through activities such as interviewing the elderly, taking photos of remaining landmarks, and creating artworks. These two projects emanating from the same portal illustrate the active role of the internet in the construction of the multicultural heritage that it claims to represent.

Another site, more a blog than a portal, celebrates the selfless acts of ordinary Poles who have dedicated themselves to renewing cemeteries and synagogues in their towns. The opening banner of the Jewish Heritage Conference site states its theme: *Hayyim*, Hebrew for "life." The blog centers on reports of two conferences, in 2008 and 2010, organized in memory of Ireneusz Ślipak, who labored for over twenty years to restore the Jewish cemetery of the town of Warta. In the opening article of the blog, Jewish filmmaker Menachem Daum calls Ślipak a *tsaddik* ("saint"), and Rabbi Michael Schudrich calls the conference participants "heroes."[36]

Included on the site are several short documentary videos by Daum made at the conference. Like the narrator on the Kirkuty site, restorers interviewed here speak of their work in explicitly religious language. Ślipak, in archival footage taped at Warta, testifies, "This is a holy place. Its devastation forced me to act. I feel these are the older brothers of Christians." With the "elder brother" metaphor, a frequent trope of Pope John Paul II, Ślipak casts his labor as Christian duty: the need to resacralize what has been profaned. Indeed, his work fulfills the pope's challenge to non-Jewish Poles, in a speech in Poland in June 1997, to care for Jewish cemeteries that had been neglected, "places that are of particularly deep spiritual, eschatological, and historical significance."[37]

In a second video, Szymon Modrzejewski, a thin man in his forties (with a cool Mohawk haircut), who has been caring for abandoned Jewish and Ukrainian cemeteries in southeast Poland for a quarter of a century, says, "These are our cemeteries. I can't see the history of Poland without the history of Jews and Ukrainians. . . . Communists tried to make our culture uniform. Respect for differences was not respected. I felt that something had to be done." As he fits together the shards of a gravestone like the pieces of a jigsaw puzzle, he speaks about the need to renew the Polish heritage torn apart. The work, he remarks, "is becoming something that I cannot even give a name to. . . . With every tombstone my heart grows. I've made many friends among the dead, I hope, and also many among the living." Although he might not think of his work as explicitly religious, Modrzejewski's unnamed passion bears the echoes of religious experience.

Finally, a quick survey of general portals reveals a concerted effort to mainstream the material heritage of the Jewish past as Polish heritage and further to claim that past as an integral element of present Jewish life in Poland. These sites aim to be informational and inclusive. The site Polin: Polish Jewish Heritage (http://polin.org.pl/start/), sponsored by the FPJH and maintained by the Jewish Studies department at Łódź University, wants to make available history and photos of all the places where Jews lived before the war. Click any green arrow on its map of Poland and a more detailed local map will appear, studded with red arrows, each a link to a particular town with a prewar Jewish community. At each link is a history of the Jewish community and contemporary and archival photos of Jewish buildings, cemeteries, and monuments, as well as information on any restoration projects underway. Similar in some respects is the Diapositive Information Service mounted by the Adam Mickewicz Institute in Warsaw.[38] A link to a page called "Traces of the Past" provides an interactive map of towns in Poland with Jewish connections. Mouse over a red square on the map and the name of the town with its Jewish connection pops up; click on the name of the town on the list to the right and you find a discussion of its Jewish history and of the traces of its cemeteries and synagogues. These discussions constitute one chapter of an education in Jewish heritage and contemporary life; other pages reference the Shoah, current Jewish organizations, Jewish books, events, and festivals. Both websites imprint Jewish maps on Poland to show how integral Jews were in the country.

The most recent major portal is Virtual Shtetl, the online arm of the Museum of the History of Polish Jews recently opened in Warsaw.[39] Describing itself as "a bridge between the history of Polish-Jewish cities and the modern multicultural world," it functions as a cyber-museum without barriers and is available in seven languages. The website is devoted to Jewish history in Poland and focuses on the history of towns and biographies of famous people. At last check it featured 47,136 photos, 732 videos, 78 audios, and 1,745 towns. But it is more than a reference tool to the past, though it includes an extensive glossary and bibliography. Virtual Shtetl also supports an online community inviting visitors to join and post text, photos, videos, and audios. Members thus contribute to the construction of a new-age shtetl spanning Jewish time and space, and connecting Jews, Poles, and others in a common effort to remember.

*　*　*

In his discussion of identity and memory, W. James Booth distinguishes between two different forms of memory that mediate the distance between past and present.[40] For the first, the past remains present as a living deposit of tradition, barely noticed or clearly distinguishable from the past. Memory here is embodied in habit, manners, way of life, and landscape. On the other hand, the second sense of memory obtains where a community has been cut off from its past, where the past is regarded as completed and visible only in its traces. Here memory must struggle with the absence and the traces, must stoke the flickering embers to keep the past present.

The exhibits—material, photographic, virtual—of synagogues and cemeteries examined above are all weapons in that struggle. While ruins like those at Działoszyce denote for visitors a dead Jewish community, a restoration like Pińczów's is an effort to recall a long Jewish history in the town and so honor its memory, however idealized. The photo anthologies portray a palimpsest of Jewish traces rising on the Polish landscape. While Krajewska's first volume represents gravestones as symbols of loss, the second appreciates and deciphers them as witnesses to past Jewish life and as a legacy for a potential Jewish present. Webber sets Schwarz's stunning photographs in a broad and deep historical context, and shows how alive Jewish memory is in Poland today. Cyberspace facilitates not only the ongoing construction of an enormous online library of remnants of the Jewish past but also spotlights the ways in which this past is being taken up as part of Poland's multicultural heritage. Constant and universal access enables the creation of virtual communities of interest transcending ethnic boundaries. If the proliferation of internet sites is any indication, cyberspace will continue to provide a firm foundation for the ongoing representation of the stony survivors and the Jewish past that they mediate.

Notes

1. See Michael Steinlauf, *Bondage to the Dead: Poland and the Memory of the Holocaust* (Syracuse, NY: Syracuse University Press, 1997), 62–88; Iwona Irwin-Zarecka, *Neutralizing Memory: The Jew in Contemporary Poland* (New Brunswick, NJ: Transaction, 1989), 35–74.

2. Peter Fritzsche, *Stranded in the Present: Modern Time and the Melancholy of History* (Cambridge, MA: Harvard University Press, 2004), 5–25, 98–107.

3. Françoise Choay, *The Invention of the Historic Monument*, trans. Lauren M. O'Connell (Cambridge: Cambridge University Press, 2001).

4. Barbara Kirshenblatt-Gimblett, *Destination Culture: Tourisms, Museums, and Heritage* (Berkeley: University of California Press, 1998), 160; Pierre Nora, "Between Memory and History: *Les Lieux de Mémoire*," *Representations* 26 (1989): 7–24.

5. Although my concern here is with actual physical places, *lieux* for Nora refers to sites in its broader meaning including archives, commemorations, eulogies, resolutions, and other means of calling up the past.

6. Eva Hoffman, *After Such Knowledge: Memory, History, and the Legacy of the Holocaust* (New York: Public Affairs, 2004), 232.

7. Andreas Huyssen, *Present Pasts: Urban Palimpsests and the Politics of Memory* (Stanford, CA: Stanford University Press, 2003), 7.

8. Choay, *The Invention of the Historic Monument*, 13.

9. Kirshenblatt-Gimblett, *Destination Culture*, 149.

10. Ibid.

11. Abraham Langer, "During and after the War," *Yizkor Book of the Jewish Community of Działoszyce and Surroundings*, transl. of *Sefer yizkor shel kehilat Działoszyce ve-ha-seviva* (Tel Aviv: Hamenora, 1973), http://www.jewishgen.org/Yizkor/Dzialoszyce/Dzialoszyce.html#TOC.

12. Svetlana Boym, *The Future of Nostalgia* (New York: Basic Books, 2001), 55, 41.

13. See also, e.g., Jonathan Webber and Chris Schwarz, *Rediscovering Traces of Memory: The Jewish Heritage of Polish Galicia* (Bloomington: Indiana University Press, 2009), 29–43.

14. Fritzsche, *Stranded in the Present*, 65.

15. In a prewar photo, the synagogue lot appears to be at and not below street level. Perhaps the postwar buildings surrounding the synagogue were built atop wartime ruins.

16. At the Old Jewish Cemetery in Kraków, adjacent to the Remuh Synagogue, gravestone fragments were also collected to form what came to be known as the Wailing Wall, though here the wall does not surround the synagogue.

17. Monika Murzyn notes importantly that heritage is always being reselected and reshaped, and that it serves various "users" in different ways. While it may serve to integrate communities, it may also serve tourist purposes. "Cultural Heritage in Time of Change: Opportunities and Challenges," in *Cultural Heritage in the 21st Century: Opportunities and Chal-*

lenges, ed. Monika A. Murzyn and Jacek Purchla (Kraków: International Cultural Centre, 2007), 139–154.

18. See the philosophical meditations on the role of memory in political identity and the practices of justice in W. James Booth, *Communities of Memory: On Witness, Identity, and Justice* (Ithaca, NY: Cornell University Press, 2006), 72–121.

19. Monika Krajewska, *A Tribe of Stones: Jewish Cemeteries in Poland* (Warsaw: Polish Scientific Publishers, 1993), 11–14.

20. One earlier book of photos of cemeteries and synagogues by Zalman Gostyński, *Des Pierres Racontent* (Paris: Abexpress, 1973), a bilingual French-Yiddish edition, likely did not have wide circulation in Poland. Similarly, photographer Chuck Fishman's volume, *Polish Jews: The Final Chapter* (New York: New York University Press, 1977), was published not in Polish but in English. A small selection of its stunning photos, both of people and gravestones, are now available on the internet: http://www.chuckfishman.com/gallery.html?folio=Portfolio &gallery=Polish%20Jews%3a%20The%20Final%20Chapter%201975. *Time of Stones* was published in Polish and some other languages by Interpress, the official Polish Communist news agency, as one of the first books on a Jewish theme after the Solidarity movement made possible greater freedom. It was thus aimed at both a foreign and Polish audience, while *Tribe of Stones,* published ten years later only in English, was aimed at a foreign market alone. In Poland and other Eastern bloc countries during Communist times, some conscientious individuals made it their mission to document and photograph largely abandoned Jewish cemeteries. One example is Jan Herman in Czechoslovakia: *Jewish Cemeteries in Bohemia and Moravia* (Prague: Council of Jewish Communities in the Czech Socialist Republic, 1982).

21. Of course, photography has long conveyed the world of Eastern European Jews. Such prewar collections as Roman Vishniac's of Jewish life or Arthur Levy's of Jewish gravestones depicted the poignancy of that world even before it ceased to exist. Roman Vishniac, *Polish Jews: A Pictorial Record* (New York: Schocken, 1965); Arthur Levy, *Jüdische Grabmalkunst in Osteuropa* (Berlin: Verlag Pionier, 1923).

22. Paul Williams, *Memorial Museums: The Global Rush to Commemorate Atrocities* (Oxford: Berg, 2007), 62.

23. Booth, *Communities of Memory,* 24.

24. Elizabeth Hallam and Jenny Hockey, *Death, Memory and Material Culture* (Oxford: Berg, 2001). The authors here are speaking of photographs of the dead themselves, but their point about relics applies as well to photos of gravestones.

25. Monika Krajewska, *A Time of Stones* (Warsaw: Interpress, 1983), 57, 77.

26. Webber and Schwarz, *Rediscovering Traces of Memory.* This collection is a selection of the images exhibited at the Galicia Jewish Museum, itself founded by Schwarz.

27. Webber and Schwarz, *Rediscovering Traces of Memory,* 13.

28. Robert Ginsberg, *The Aesthetics of Ruins* (Amsterdam: Rodopi, 2004), 319.

29. Muzeum Regionalne Informacja Turystyczna w Pińczowie, http://www.muzeumitpinczow .eu/viewpage.php?page_id=17.

30. http://www.jewishlodzcemetery.org.

31. Jewish Community of Warsaw Jewish Cemetery, http://beisolam.jewish.org.pl/pl-d /index-pl.php.

32. A necrology is found, however, on a second website, the Internet Database of the Warsaw Jewish Cemetery at Okopowa Street (http://cemetery.jewish.org.pl/), which provides an interactive platform for finding the graves of individuals. Enter a surname and retrieve an image of the person's gravestone and a table including all the information on the stone.

33. Rudolph Otto, *The Idea of the Holy* (1923; reprint London: Oxford University Press, 1950), 12–40.

34. Brandon Blache-Cohen, director of an Amizade service learning program in Oświęcim, however, reports that the cemetery is not well tended most of the year (pers. comm. with the author, December 17, 2010).

35. The foundation was established by the Union of Jewish Communities in Poland and the World Jewish Restitution Organization. On its website, it defines its mission as "to protect and commemorate the surviving monuments of Jewish cultural heritage in Poland. The Foundation is active in regions whose location far from major cities makes it difficult for Jewish communities to provide adequate care. Our area of operation covers nearly two-thirds of Poland." http://fodz.pl/?d=3&l=en.

36. The article is reprinted from *The Jewish Post and News*, September 8, 2010, and describes the 2010 conference in Szczekociny.

37. Quoted in Ruth Ellen Gruber, *Virtually Jewish: Reinventing Jewish Culture in Europe* (Berkeley: University of California Press, 2002), 76.

38. http://www.diapositve.pl.

39. Virtual Shtetl, http://www.sztetl.org.pl.

40. Booth, *Communities of Memory*, 33.

10 Reading the Palimpsest

Konstanty Gebert

ONE WAY OF understanding the ongoing impossibility for Jews and Poles to understand each other is to look at the cognitive trap into which the two nations have fallen. They both believe that, because they share a common geography, they also share a common history. In fact, they do not: different dates and events mean different things to both, and there is simply no consensus between them about history, especially that of the last one hundred years.[1] The only thing that reconciles the two warring memories is the shared geography they grow out of.

But does it really? As Diane and David Roskies have noted, "Ask the average Pole where Khelm is and he may or may not know. But as any Jew can tell you, whether he has been to Poland or not, that Khelm is the most famous fools' town in the world. It may seem strange that two nations living on the same soil would have an entirely different relation to the same place, but that's the way it happened. Jewish geography is simply not the same thing as *goyish* geography."[2]

Fair enough—it is not. For one thing, the names differ. While Khelm is just a transcription of the Polish name of Chełm according to the principles of English phonetics, some other place-names can be more daunting. It takes insider knowledge to understand that Ger is Góra Kalwaria, Amshinov stands for Mszczonów, and that Lemberg is really Lwów. Or is it? For while Lwów today is Lviv, for half of the past century it was Lvov, and for all of the previous one and then some it was, well, Lemberg.[3] Throw in two different Jewish alphabets, and two different goyish ones, and maps on which borders come alive and crawl from end to end like venomous snakes, and it is surprising that there can be any shared geography at all.

Yet while the two histories are at war, the two geographies, starting with the very place-names, simply differ. Sometimes it is just a question of small shifts across the map: in the sixteenth and seventeenth centuries, the Jewish Kraków, whose inhabitants called it Kuzmir, and which was known to the residents of the Polish Kraków (who never knew they were living in Kroke) as Kazimierz, was not inside the Polish Kraków as it had been before, and would be after, but alongside it, the result of a temporarily successful expulsion of the Jews. Sometimes it was a question of demography. When Jews made up two-thirds of the population, as in Apt, it did not matter all that much that they were "really" living in Opatów.

In Varshe, the proportions were reversed, and the city's Jewish inhabitants knew full well that they were living in Warszawa. The problem was different: the city's non-Jewish majority did not want them there. Possibly neither did the gentile minority in Opatów, but the town did not see pogroms; Warsaw did.

Differences in place-names did not only express linguistic idiosyncrasies; they were shorthand for different perceptions. "The Jewish quarter in Warsaw occupied [in the early twentieth century] one fifth of the city. There were no drawbridges or guards on its borders: the ghetto had been abolished long before, but nevertheless there still existed an invisible wall that separated the quarter from the rest of the city."[4] Poles and Jews lived in different geographies: what was familiar for the one was foreign for the other. To be sure, the barrier was permeable and routinely crossed, and yet the juxtaposition of two geographies remained valid. It lasted up to the moment (for the three years of the culmination of the Shoah in Poland, 1941–1944, historically were but a moment) when the Jews were exterminated and disappeared, and their gentile neighbors took over—and took in—their geography, or what remained of it after the German destruction.

Seventy years on, what remains of this Jewish geography? Of the Jewish buildings and places, symbols, sights, and signs? History rarely has seen a disappearance that sudden, a rupture, as it were, of a culture so clearly diverse from the one that followed it in the same physical settings. In fact, the few examples that do come to mind are still almost from the same time and place: the expulsion of the Germans from German territories incorporated into Poland immediately after World War II, and the concomitant flight of the Poles from Polish territories incorporated simultaneously into the Soviet Union. Quite often, the same people would have seen the extermination of the Jews, and then would have fled their hometowns in the East, where it had happened, to take over in the West the homes of Germans who were being expelled. The pervasive character of this experience of extermination, expulsion, and flight is one of the factors that explain why the appalling violence of the destruction of the Jews, still visually evident two generations later in the spaces where it happened, did not make on the gentile witnesses an impact sufficiently strong for them to relate to the gaping absence that remains.

The Polish social anthropologist Sławomir Kapralski has for years been studying the ways that Jewish memory is present—or absent—in contemporary Polish spaces.[5] In a powerful essay on "virtual multiculturality," he analyzes the modes of representation of that memory, and concludes it can become musealized, excluded, segregated, destroyed, or preserved.[6] All these, with different variations and more, can be seen not only in southeastern Poland, where a surprising number of Jewish monuments have been preserved, but even in Warsaw, which was razed to the ground by Germans and then selectively and limitedly reconstructed after the war. Yet there is another way altogether to conceptualize the way Jewish memory functions in public spaces of Warsaw today: the palimpsest, layer upon layer of text, written on and erased from the same piece of parchment.

Until recently, Jewish memory had not been musealized in Warsaw. Kapralski exemplifies this form of representation describing the town of Łańcut, in which the synagogue, almost the sole remaining trace of a Jewish community that made up 40 percent of the town's prewar population, long used as a warehouse, was eventually restored to its baroque glory and now houses a museum of the extinct Jewish civilization. In Warsaw, the presence of a living Jewish community prevented the conversion of the Nożyk shul, one of the two surviving of the 240 synagogues, shuls, and shtiblach (tiny Hassidic prayer houses) that existed before the war, into a museum: Jews simply continued to daven there.[7] This, however, meant that Poland's capital, in which 30 percent of the prewar population had been Jewish, has to date no Jewish museum, apart from a tiny exhibition in the Jewish Historical Institute. This is about to change, however, with the new Museum of the History of Polish Jews, scheduled to open in 2014. Contrary to what obtains in Łańcut, and consistent with the specificity of postwar Warsaw, it will musealize not an existing "post-Jewish" structure, but a post-Jewish absence. Housed in a new, striking building located in the center of a vast plaza in the heart of what had been the Jewish district, where remnants of prewar buildings had survived into the early 1960s, it will not exhibit Jewish objects but virtually recreate Jewish spaces, such as an eighteenth-century shtetl or interwar Jewish Warsaw. This, of course, is virtualization squared, indeed cubed. What remains authentic is the physical location, which by now has nothing Jewish in it.[8] What will be Jewish will be new, virtual, and imagined: the museal reenactment of a memory that had been thoroughly eradicated.

But though the Nożyk shul represents a form of Jewish presence—life, not just memory—absent, for tragically natural reasons of location from Kapralski's typology, for precious few Jews survived in Poland and kept on simply living there, it is hardly a simple continuation of what was.[9] The architect who designed this synagogue never could see it the way we do now. When completed in 1901, it stood inside a courtyard, surrounded by residential buildings of which only the truncated fragment immediately south of the shul, known as the "white building," is still remaining. The district was then a warren of narrow alleyways and tenements in which each family often had only one or two rooms for itself. Only now, after the destruction of World War II, can we actually see the building in its simple, elegant neoclassical shape. Zalman Nożyk, a successful and pious businessman, had built the building and donated it to the Warsaw Jewish community; his only request was that when *Yizkor* (the mourning prayer) was said, it be said also for him and his wife. The shul was Orthodox, but modern with a now-unused place for a choir above the aron ha-kodesh (Torah ark), something unthinkable even in Modern Orthodox shuls today. It survived the war because the Germans used it as a stable for their horses. Badly damaged, it reverted to Jewish use after 1945, and to Jewish ownership after 1989.

Provisional repairs could not prevent the deterioration of the shul, and in the early 1980s, the government allowed its renovation with the goal of rededicating it for the fortieth anniversary of the Warsaw Ghetto Uprising. When workers broke into the compartment behind the aron ha-kodesh, which is nowadays the children's room, they discovered stacks of Hebrew books. Not knowing what to do with them, they started dumping them outside; a group of young Jews rushed to the rescue and carried them to an unused room in the white building. Stamps on their pages indicated that the books were the property of small communities around Warsaw, probably brought into the shul just before the war for safekeeping: no one imagined that the shul itself might be in danger. The books had remained safe there; taken out of the cache and exposed to the ambient air, they started molding. The only way to save them was to kill the mold with gas—and so an urgent search for a gas chamber for surviving Jewish books was started. Most were eventually saved. As part of the renovation, an ugly but much-needed office annex was added to the building—and the shul was rededicated in April 1983.

The white building itself is a living memorial to a rare presence in contemporary Poland: Jewish continuity. Before the war, it used to house a Jewish outpatient clinic, as attested to by fading Yiddish inscriptions on the staircase. Residents included the Melchior family. Ghetto-period documents belonging to them, including school copybooks and unused ration cards, were discovered when the building was being renovated twenty years ago. For a time after the war, when the Nożyk shul was in disrepair, davening moved to a temporary shtibl (small room) improvised on its ground floor. It now houses different Jewish institutions and organizations—and was just barely spared execution at the hands of the Jewish community, which intended to allow its demolition so that the plot it stands on could be used for the construction of a skyscraper next door. The move would have assured the community its financial solvency—and would have amputated its historical memory. Mercifully, the plans eventually came to naught.

Much of what remains of contemporary living Jewish Warsaw can be found between the shul and Grzybowski Square next door. A picture taken here would be a cliché hard to beat. At one end of the square, we have red brick semi-ruined buildings, their doors and windows barred, apparently waiting to finally crumble. At the other end, a postwar building houses the Yiddish theater, Jewish organizations, and rented offices (including at one time some for Deutsche Bank), between them a huge Catholic church—and in the middle a polished modern plaza with water jets and benches. If one knows that the ruins stand on Próżna Street, which had been part of the ghetto—and that the street's name in Polish means "empty"—the irony reigns supreme. Here, one would like to exclaim, Jewish memory has been obliterated and denied.

Yet the houses on Próżna Street stand ruined because a series of investors, one of them Jewish, had bought one side of the street with the intention of turning it into a Jewish center, but never delivered until now. An Austrian company is converting the buildings for office and commercial use, meticulously reconstructing the facades and gutting everything else. The end result will be virtually authentic, that is, a make-believe. The houses on the other side of the street remain authentic but stand empty and continue to decay, because the city is still trying to ascertain rights of ownership, if any. The Nazis and then the Communists did a thorough job of destroying records and denying rights. Yet all agree that the street must be preserved and revived. It is the only fragment of the former ghetto in which houses on both sides of the street are still standing, and, in fact, before the ghetto, it was a part of Warsaw's elegant downtown. Before the German occupation in 1939, there had been no ghetto in Warsaw, and the northern district, heavily populated by Jews, merged imperceptibly with the rest of the city, becoming gentrified as one walked south and west toward the city's center. Yet one cannot see it now: it was razed by the Germans, and the Soviets built a huge skyscraper in its place. As one walks toward it, one sees a marker indicating the location of the ghetto wall: an upright plaque, a trail on the pavement—a line, now invisible, that for a few years separated life and death.

These markers have been put up by the city in some two dozen locations to indicate the places where the ghetto wall used to be. They come as a surprise to many who run into them in the historic—and reconstructed—New Town district, where otherwise there is no mention of the thriving Jewish population that had lived there, or in the Krasiński Gardens, which now include the erstwhile location of Nalewki Street, the Jewish quarter's commercial thoroughfare. Again, a form of memory absent from Kapralski's typology: it might be called memory restituted.

On Próżna Street, partial reconstruction proceeds apace, and maybe the sort of the northern side will be finally sorted out. Zalman Nożyk, who lived in the house on the corner on the first floor, would no doubt be satisfied. He would have certainly found all those goings-on unsettling, but the huge church next door would not have surprised him a bit. It stood there in his time, the Catholic part of Warsaw blending with its Jewish part. In the 1930s, its parish priest was Maurycy Godlewski, a well-known antisemite. The same Godlewski risked his life during the ghetto to smuggle Jewish Christians—yes, there were several thousand of them, Warsaw's Jews blending with Warsaw's Christians—out to the "Aryan side." Yes, he was motivated more by religious solidarity than general humanity, but the Germans would not have cared—to them a Jew was a Jew, no matter how many times dipped in the baptismal font. In fact, the Germans did burst into the parish office in July 1942, and took away all who had sheltered there. One of those saved, the great hematologist Ludwik Hirszfeld, described his escape from the ghetto through the church in his memoirs.[10] The same church in the 1990s used to house an antisemitic bookstore—and was the site of extremely moving penitential prayers in which on the sixtieth anniversary of the Jedwabne pogrom in 2001, Poland's Catholic bishops asked God for forgiveness for the crimes their coreligionists had committed. In that massacre, committed a few days after the Germans had invaded the part of Poland previously under Soviet occupation since 1939, several hundred Jews were murdered by their Polish neighbors. A plaque on the bell-tower declares that the church "honors the memory of Poles who died trying to save Jews in World War II."

On the modern plaza, recently designed and completed, you might notice two large stones. One, its top partially removed to reveal what looks like a bullet, is a monument to the arms-makers of the Polish underground in World War II. Another smaller and less exposed one marks the site of a great socialist demonstration against the tsar in 1905, when Poland was part of the Russian empire. It is difficult to go anywhere in Warsaw without seeing markers of the city's violent past. But that second stone also points to another story. In the same year, Jewish socialists, members of the Bund, fought a major battle here. Plac Grzybowski was then a red-light district, and many of the brothels, as well as many of the women who worked there, were Jewish. The Bundists, whose socialism was based on a fundamental belief in human dignity, considered this outrageous and attacked the brothels to free the women and disrupt the trade. The thugs, Jewish and gentile, fought back, and soon a gun battle was raging in the center of Warsaw. The tsarist police had a hard problem to solve: should they be on the side of the criminals or of the subversives? The cops joined forces with the mob. The Bundists were ultimately defeated, but the brothel trade never picked up again on plac Grzybowski. No commemoration of that particular incident can be found, however.

And how did Deutsche Bank get into the picture? That is simple: they were renting offices from the Jewish Socio-Cultural Association, which owns the building. Built under Communism in the late 1960s to house the Yiddish theater and other Jewish institutions, it was completed just as the antisemitic campaign of 1968 got underway. As some fifteen thousand Jews were forced to leave the country, the building on plac Grzybowski became the refuge of obstinate diehards who were willing to try everything, even rotten compromises with the regime, to maintain a Jewish life and presence. The Jewish paper and publishing house were closed down, fewer and fewer people dared to come. But those who did could for a moment feel inside as if they were on the Jewish street again, even if no conversation was safe, there as elsewhere, from snooping ears. But the theater played on, even when most of the actors had fled and had to be replaced by young Poles who knew no Yiddish and learned their roles by rote. Even when most of the audience had fled, and theatergoers were handed headphones and listened to the Polish translation of that memorized Yiddish. A grotesque travesty? Possibly. Yet the theater endured and still plays on—and there are again more Jews among the actors and even in the audience. Still, there is a price to be paid for everything, and the theater, which under Communism relied on subventions doled out by the same government that had expelled its audience, after the democratic transformation recovered its freedom but had to generate income. Thus vacated offices were rented out and Deutsche Bank found for a time its new Warsaw address. They have since moved, and the premises are now occupied by the offices of the Cosmopolitan Building—a huge residential skyscraper rising next door to the theater and shul. In the original plans for the skyscraper, the building was to expand onto the plot on which the white building now stands.

What remains of Jewish Warsaw is scattered across the huge expanse of the former Jewish district, but Jewish continuity is limited roughly to the tiny enclave by plac Grzybowski. But to understand how the city got to being what it is now, one has to move elsewhere, through the entire district of Muranów, built after the war on the ruins of the ghetto.[11]

As one stands at the intersection of John Paul II and Solidarity Avenues, one could be well excused for thinking that there is nothing of Jewish interest in the city—actually, for thinking there is very little of interest, period. Billboards advertising cars and junk food compete with electronic signs promoting a local "gentlemen's club" and do little to alleviate the overpowering drabness of the area's Stalinist architecture. Even more modern buildings, clearly of post-1989 vintage, do not make the area merrier or more interesting. Sure, Poland has every reason to commemorate its twin heroes of the late twentieth century, the trade union that brought down Communism in a peaceful revolution and the pope who provided the inspiration for the movement. But what is there of Jewish interest?

Although one might not know this, in prewar Warsaw, this was the heart of the Jewish district. No John Paul II or Solidarity Avenues then, but a maze of small streets and alleys, bursting with humanity, chockfull with signs in Yiddish; Polish, written or spoken, was barely a distant second. Solna, or Salt Street, took up the eastern half of the pope's avenue of today, while Leszno Street, grander, actually was as large as the trade union's avenue. But Solna did not continue north beyond Leszno: that area was too densely built over.

If standing at the northeast corner of the intersection and looking south, one sees the entrance to the Femina cinema, at the ground floor of an apartment block built just a few years before the war and very modern for its day. The Femina opened in 1941 as one of the best theaters in the Jewish district, which since had become the German-enforced ghetto. When looking left toward the east, one sees a church, one of the three that served the needs of Jewish Christians in the ghetto. Looking right, one notices, a few houses beyond the intersection, the impressive building of the courthouse, a major monument of interwar Poland's state architecture. While the main entrance from Leszno Street was during wartime within the ghetto, gentiles having business with the courts, which did not cease to operate in wartime, could access it through a back entrance on Biała, or White, Street. The street still exists, but none of the houses now standing on it was built before the war. Open to both sides, the court building was a major escape route for the inmates of the ghetto.

And if one were to turn back and look beyond the northwest corner on John Paul II Avenue, one would notice a small gap between the 1950s-vintage building on the corner and the modern, small commercial pavilions now lining that part of the street. Through the gap, one can see what seems to be the ground floor of the corner building continuing—but instead of a window, one sees only a wall. This is because that is no ground floor but rather the external boundary of the pile of rubble from the ghetto on which the district of Muranów was built after the war. Part of the ghetto's rubble was transported to the other side of the Vistula River, which bisects the city, and served to build a major sports stadium. The remainder was bulldozed and fixed—and the new district was built on top. Today's ground floors are at prewar second-floor level. Ruins of houses lie underneath.

This is why in Warsaw, each time earthworks are done, for street construction or the laying of pipes or foundations, one expects to find human remains. The entire city is a vast cemetery, with thousands of bodies from the Ghetto Uprising of 1943 and the Warsaw Uprising of 1944 still buried beneath its buildings and streets. When unearthed, they are taken out to be reburied. But then a problem arises: which cemetery? A practical rule of thumb has evolved. If found around the postwar John Paul II Avenue, which bisects the former ghetto, they are most probably Jewish and buried at the Jewish cemetery.[12] When found around Jerusalem Avenue, however, which was and remains one of the city's principal streets, and the scene of heavy fighting in 1944, they are assumed to be Catholic and are reburied at a Catholic cemetery.

None of this palimpsest nature of Warsaw is apparent at first sight, yet all of this is of crucial importance for any understanding of the city's rich and impressive Jewish past. Were one to look around beyond the symbolic intersection described above, one would find vestiges of prewar Jewish life: a building that used to be a school, a ruin that used to be a prison, the site of a famous yeshiva. And if one looks down on Warsaw from one of the many high-rises, one sees clearly that the city has two street grids, superimposed on top of one another and coexisting uneasily. Prewar streets, their traces visible through the facades of a few surviving houses, lead nowhere. Modern thoroughfares cut a building in half. The palimpsest is difficult to read. And in the rare places where the ancient text is clearly visible, not obscured by contemporary writing, the difficulty is replaced with moral discomfort. Such as in this particular place.

It looks familiar, with the nagging, unpleasant familiarity of something once seen and forever etched on one's memory—even if one had not wanted to remember it. And one did not—even though consciously we all profess that this should be preserved in memory for ever. Yes, agreed, but why my memory? Why take in this burden?

Or maybe it does not look familiar, but banal, another uninspiring, drab cityscape with buildings that seem not to belong, as if assembled together from different, unmatching Lego sets.

It all depends on whether one has seen Yael Hersonsky's film.[13] Or the one still photo reproduced in so many history books.

There is a bridge, a high bridge, chockfull with people. Behind the bridge, slightly to the left, there is a four-story apartment building standing at the intersection of two streets, its corner rounded off in a nice architectonical touch. And under the bridge there is a street. Not a river, not a ravine, not a railroad line, not a highway—but a street. An ordinary street. Something's wrong.

Yes. The people on the bridge are wrong. They are the wrong kind of people for the street underneath. That street is for the people who don't wear armbands. Or kippot. Or payess. For the people who do not have to get papers proving they actually have the right to live. For Aryans. And the wrong people—actually, it is wrong even to call them people: they're Untermenschen—cannot cross that street. Cannot mingle with the right kind of people. This is why they have to use the bridge. And you are standing where the bridge used to stand.

If you turn west, the building with the rounded corner is still there. That is how you recognized it, the detail having become engraved in your memory. You looked at it when you looked at the photo and did not want to avert your gaze, yet at the same time not wanting to look at the people on the bridge. They are all dead, you thought. They just think they're alive. They will all soon be smoke. So you looked at the building in the background instead. And yes, they all became smoke, and the building is still there.

There is nothing special about it. But it is there and they are not.

Turn around and face east. In front of you there is a church, St. Charles Borromeo. During the ghetto, it stood almost at the thin end of the wedge that, starting from Saxon Garden, bisected the ghetto into its large northern and small southern parts. The wedge ended where you stand, and originally traffic between the two parts was regulated by a system of gates, which would block Chłodna Street on both sides of Żelazna to enable ghetto traffic between the two parts, and then Żelazna on both sides of Chłodna, to allow "Aryan" traffic to flow. The bridge was built later, because the hinged gate system was cumbersome.

On your left you spot a survivor: the elegant building at Chłodna 20. Another picture of the bridge, taken from your current vantage point, also has it in the background. But in that picture, the people on the bridge are few, and the building does not have to relieve your gaze. Yet it is worth remembering: this was where Adam Czerniaków lived, on the second floor on the right. There exists a picture of the bridge taken from his window. You can see on it the *putto* that still sits on the apartment's external windowsill. Czerniaków, chairman of the German-appointed Judenrat, committed suicide in July 1942 when he realized the scale and end of the German "resettlement" scheme. The entrance to the building is locked, but try to slip in after someone who has the code to the door. You will see three courtyards, one following another, the connecting passageways gently flowing to ease the eye. Big Warsaw tenements were built like that, the rent getting less the deeper in one went.

To reach St. Charles Borromeo Church, which stands next to where the bridge used to be, from downtown Warsaw in wartime, one had to follow the wedge. The ghetto walls were quite wide apart at first, but then they moved closer, as the sides of the wedge raced to their meeting point at the bridge. Those walking down the street could not, one is tempted to think, avoid the feeling that it is they who were walled in; that the ghetto was closing its arms around them in a trap from which there was no escape. On Easter Monday 1943, as they walked to the church for mass, they could hear the shooting: the ghetto uprising had started. Soon after, walls of flame and smoke arose behind the ghetto walls.

It is not that those labeled "Aryans" had chosen or wanted that label, or were safe or indifferent. Often they were neither. In retaliation for attacks by the underground, Germans would execute dozens of Polish hostages. The plaques with the Maltese cross you see on the walls of Warsaw buildings mark such sites. And many felt human compassion for their neighbors on the other sides of the walls; a daring few risked their lives to save them. But walking to the church, they knew that there were then just two kinds of people: the wrong kind and the other kind.

If one continues walking down Żelazna, one should keep one's eyes peeled for buildings that do not belong—or rather, buildings that belonged then, which is why they do not belong today. Some try to pass, not at all looking the wrong way. Other ones are unmistakably marked. One will notice how one's eyes grow keener, one's thoughts sharper, one's analytical skills honed with even a bit of practice. Yes, one can now tell each from the other with much more assurance. They will not escape.

Of course they don't fit. The buildings on both eastern corners of Krochmalna at Żelazna are jarring. Although badly in need of restoration, they are still inhabited; they are also much taller than the apartment houses on Próżna. These were rent-producing tenements, the bane of penniless renters, and the source of landlords' fortunes. Isaac Bashevis Singer lived in such a tenement further down Krochmalna, at number 10; the building no longer exists. If Próżna was the elegant, assimilated downtown of the northern district, Krochmalna was its beating Jewish heart.

One courtyard, similar to the triple one visited at Chłodna 20, could house, for instance, two separate shtiblach of two different Hassidic orientations; a synagogue for mitnagdim, the opponents of Hassidism; numerous workshops, shops, and stores. Singer's Krochmalna, described in his memoirs, *In My Father's Court* and *Love and Exile,* and in the novel *Shosha,* was populated by Hassidim and Communists, mystics and prostitutes, assimilated students and pious shoemakers. An entire universe:

> Nr. 13 [on Krochmalna] bordered on the ill-famed Krochmalna Square, where pickpockets and hoodlums loitered, and dealers in stolen goods carried on their trade. The houses facing the Square also harbored a number of brothels. Even regular commerce was carried on in an underhand manner: if one wanted to buy a *tchaste*—a kind of chocolate-covered cracker—one pulled numbers from a hat or spun a wooden wheel. Yet in the same houses dwelt decent men, pious women, chaste girls. There were even a few Hassidic study houses.[14]

Past the intersection with Grzybowska Street, which leads back to Grzybowski Square, one can see on the right one of the two surviving fragments of the wall of the Warsaw Ghetto; on the left, yet another set of three semiruined survivor buildings. Waliców 14 was the address of Władysław Szlengel, the poet of the ghetto.[15] All but unknown outside Poland, and not very widely read even there, he was the author of powerful poems about the isolation and despair of the ghetto dwellers, made prisoners of what had been their homes, their district. Szlengel wrote his poetry in Polish. He was emblematic of those Jewish writers born at the turn of the century for whom Polish was the mother tongue. He was certainly aware of the unavoidable irony of writing in Polish while separated from the rest of Warsaw, the rest of Poland, by the ghetto wall built by the Germans.

Szlengel's poems survived mainly in the underground Ringelblum archive, a vast collection of documents concerning the life of the ghetto, assembled by a group of underground activists led by historian Emmanuel Ringelblum. It was preserved in metal containers in the cellars and mostly recovered after the war. But years after the war, a resident of suburban Warsaw discovered copies of these poems, concealed in a cunning cache under the surface of an old table he had started chopping up for firewood. That table might have stood in one of the semiruined buildings on Waliców, or indeed in an elegant salon on Próżna. And there is no way of knowing what was lost forever in tables long destroyed—or is still waiting to be discovered in tables that yet survive.

The gate of the building at Waliców 10 has small metal half-domes gracefully filling in its two corners, rising one foot or so above street level. Such adornments served a practical purpose: they ensured that carriages entering the gate were sufficiently clear of its walls to avoid damaging them or the carriages themselves. The half-dome at Waliców 10 can also be seen on a photograph from the ghetto period. It shows two men loading a corpse on a handcart. Another human body, so emaciated that it hardly rises above the pavement, lies nearby, across the gate.

Szlengel could have easily seen this scene from his window. Had he not survived, to die eventually in the ghetto uprising, he could have been that body. And the anonymous body in the photo could well have been that of another Szlengel, another Hirszfeld, whose work, not concealed in a cunning tabletop, would not have reached us. Or it could have been the body of a nobody, whose life had made no impact on the world but who had the extraordinary privilege of having his death witnessed. Immortalized when already dead.

Others were not so lucky. They went to Stawki.

Stawki was the northern, poor end of the Jewish district. Buildings were usually rundown and low. This was an area of small artisans, cheap boarding-rooms, and slums. Just north of it were railroad sidings used for unloading rail freight. Yet two modern buildings, one on each side of the street, indicated that Stawki had a future. Those buildings housed schools, attended mainly by Jewish students. The buildings were, in the ghetto, to become the Jewish hospital (northern side) and the SS headquarters (southern side). Stawki Street between them was blocked with a wall, which created an enclosure. Beginning on July 22, 1942, thousands of people would be forced into it, and then on to the trains to Treblinka.

Only a few photos of the Umschlagplatz remain, and that is not surprising. What is surprising is that they were taken at all. Why would anyone want to document the place where humanity ended? But looking at them, we see clearly the two modern buildings—modern also in the sense of being contemporary. They survived, while the shtiblach and the schools, the residences and the shops, all went up in flames. As if to defiantly assert that death has a better purchase on existence than life.

The school buildings at the Umschlagplatz are now used for educational purposes again. The former hospital is a complex of high schools; the former SS headquarters, the department of psychology of Warsaw University. Until 1983, the site of the former Umschlagplatz was all but unmarked. A gas station was built there, and only a small plaque in Yiddish (with spelling mistakes) and Polish reminded passersby of what had been. In 1983, when Poland was ruled by a Communist military government, which had crushed the Solidarity movement and was boycotted by the West, the authorities, under general Wojciech Jaruzelski, decided to play up the fortieth anniversary of the ghetto uprising by organizing a host of events and inviting Jews worldwide to attend (including from Israel—the first such invitation since Poland broke off relations in 1967). This was done in the hope of attracting reciprocal Western goodwill.

At the same time, independent commemorations of the ghetto uprising were banned for the first time. The uprising's deputy commander, Marek Edelman, had since the antisemitic campaign of 1968 refused to attend official ceremonies; in the late 1970s, young Jews active in the opposition Jewish Flying University joined him. These ceremonies took place undisturbed, but in 1983, the authorities forbade them, and jackbooted police physically prevented participants from laying their flowers at the Umschlagplatz monument. This generated outrage among non-Jewish onlookers, and a spontaneous protest demonstration began. A young Solidarity activist read out a letter of support from Solidarity leader Lech Wałęsa, who had been detained by police to prevent him from joining in the ceremonies. He was jailed for six months for this offence—and after 1989, became independent Poland's first minister of defense.

The gas station was finally torn down in 1987, and in 1988, for the forty-fifth anniversary, the existing Umschlagplatz monument was built. In the 1990s, protests notwithstanding, developers seized plots of land around the Umschlagplatz, including buildings that had been part of the deportation complex, and leveled them to build the high-rise apartment blocks that now dominate the area.

These, too, belong to the palimpsest. When reading its texts, we should concentrate not only on what has been overwritten but on the overwriting as well. It testifies that there is no new text: no matter how desperately writing might try to break from the past, it remains but a comment on it: illuminating or obscuring, noble or vile, but unable to exist on its own. The present can be read only through the prism of the past. The past was somebody's present, and had already then to be thusly read. The texts speak to each other, even if they have never met other than on this same piece of mortally tired, blood-soaked old parchment.

So, finally—relax. In the heart of the city, this green island, created by a Saxon prince elected the eighteenth-century king of Poland, is a joy for the eyes, sweetness for the lungs. This is where the Polish and Jewish worlds of Warsaw would meet, walking down the same paths but never mingling. Until 1939, the imposing Saxon Palace used to separate the garden from the square opposite it. All that remains of it now is the Tomb of the Unknown Soldier, originally located in the middle of a majestic, two-story colonnade that connected the two parts of the palace. The truncated columns on top of the tomb, and the colonnade amputated at both its ends, today give a much more dramatic setting to the simple slab under which he lies than the splendor that was before German bomb met Saxon stone.

The Saxon Garden was a contested area. Antisemites would complain that Jews spoil the beauty of the spot by their vile looks and jarring voices; young thugs would sometimes attack Jewish passersby, and themselves be attacked by Jewish posses, which stalked the garden; police then, often unsuccessfully, would engage both. This made strolling in Saxon Garden and the Krasiński Garden by the Old Town a question of principle. Saturday afternoons, after services, were dedicated to the shabbes shpatzieren, Yiddish for a Saturday walk. But Jews would eventually return to their own districts, having again staked the ground but despairing of ever owning it. Sundays in the gardens belonged almost exclusively, by force of custom, to the gentiles.

One of the first German regulations after they conquered Poland was to ban Jews from entering public gardens. When the ghetto was created, it included almost no green spaces, and whatever greenery there was soon became firewood or was eaten by cold and starving ghetto dwellers. Children grew up, for the pitiably few years left them, without knowing the meaning of tree and flower, let alone forest or field. In Yael Hersonsky's film, a survivor of the ghetto comments on German propaganda footage showing a ghetto woman arranging flowers in a vase: "What nonsense. Flowers? We would have eaten them."

Notes

1. For a discussion of this argument, see Konstanty Gebert, "Separate Narratives: Polish and Jewish Perceptions of the Shoah," in *Conflict and Memory: Bridging Past and Future in (South East) Europe,* ed. Wolfgang Petrisch and Vedran Džihić (Baden-Baden: Nomos Verlagsgesellschaft, 2010).

2. Diane K. Roskies and David G. Roskies, *The Shtetl Book: An Introduction to East European Jewish Life and Lore* (Jersey City, NJ: Ktav, 1979), 45.

3. If you think that was difficult, think Yehupetz instead of Kiev, and Zvihil instead of Nowogród Wołyński.

4. Bernard Singer, *Moje Nalewki* (Warsaw: Czytelnik, 1993).

5. Actually, it would be more precise to speak of "post-Jewish" memory in the sense of that extraordinary Polish word, *pożydowski.* Literally meaning "post-Jewish," it was originally coined in the immediate postwar period to designate Jewish property left behind and seized by new owners. Simultaneously, another neologism, *poniemieckie,* or "post-German," appeared to refer to formerly German property in the territories annexed from Germany whose owners were being expelled. Both terms seemed to imply that the former owners have incomprehensibly disappeared, leaving their property behind.

6. Sławomir Kapralski and Mirosław Bieniecki, *Wirtualna wielokulturowość: Pamięć żydowska w przestrzeni wybranych miejscowości Polski południowej i wschodniej,* unpublished manuscript. The reference is, of course, to Ruth Gruber's trailblazing *Virtually Jewish: Reinventing Jewish Culture in Europe* (Berkeley: University of California Press, 2002), a magisterial study of how a new culture "about Jews" has filled in the void left by the Shoah. See also Sławomir Kapralski, "(Mis)representation of the Jewish Past in Poland's Memoryscapes: Nationalism, Religion and Political Economies of Commemoration," in *Curating Difficult Knowledge: Violent Pasts in Public Places,* ed. E. Lehrer, C. E. Milton, and M. E. Patterson (New York: Palgrave Macmillan, 2011), 179–193.

7. The other, a neoclassical early nineteenth-century synagogue in the district of Praga, was blown up by the Communist authorities, who had no use for it, in the mid-1960s.

8. The Jewish city survives underneath, however, in the cellars of buildings that had stood there, and their decaying contents. Archaeological digs, which preceded the laying of the foundations of the museum, unearthed a set of ghetto-period documents.

9. Much of the material that follows has been used, edited, and amended in the "Field Guide to Jewish Warsaw and Krakow," produced by the Taube Center for Jewish Life and Culture, Warsaw, 2012. This innovative publication allows users to gain an in-depth appreciation of the history and present of Jewish communities in these two major Polish cities. Future editions will be expanded to include other localities.

10. Ludwik Hirszfeld, *Historia jednego życia* (Warsaw: Czytelnik, 1946); English translation, *The Story of One Life,* ed. Maria A. Balińska and William H. Schneider, trans. Maria A. Balińska (Rochester, NY: University of Rochester Press, 2010).

11. The district has in recent years generated huge interest among a younger generation of Poles who are coming to terms with the un-naturality of the Stalinist housing development built on the rubble of a district whose inhabitants, one-third of the prewar population, have been erased from the city's memory. In *Festung Warschau* (Warsaw: Wydawnictwo Krytyki Politycznej, 2011), photographer Elżbieta Janicka documents and dissects the way postwar—and especially post-1989—Polish memory has taken over and occupied the area, infusing it with its own symbolic meanings. Jerzy Majewski, the leading historian of the city, reconstructs the streets and buildings of prewar Jewish Warsaw in *Żydowski Muranów i okolice* (Warszawa: Agora, 2012). In her *Stacja Muranów* (Wołowiec: Muranów Station, Czarne, 2012), Elżbieta Chomątowska documents both the remaining traces of memory and the history of postwar construction, blending the two into a powerful narrative of identity formation. And in a stunning novel, *Noc żywych Żydów* (Warsaw: WAB, 2012), Igor Ostachowicz describes "Jewish zombies" emerging from Muranów's cellars to bother the Polish inhabitants.

12. The avenue was projected already in the interwar period and built in the 1950s. It originally carried the name of Communist revolutionary Julian Marchlewski, and was renamed John Paul II only after 1989. For some reason, the name did not stick, and people often refer to it, tongue-in-cheek, as John Paul Marchlewski Avenue.

13. Israeli documentalist Yael Hersonsky produced "A Film Unfinished" (2010) using German documentary footage of staged scenes shot in the Warsaw Ghetto. The footbridge figures quite prominently in it.

14. Isaac Bashevis Singer, *In My Father's Court* (New York: Farrar, Strauss and Giroux, 1975), 17–18.

15. The HyperTexts: Władysław Szlengel, http://www.thehypertexts.com/wladyslaw_Szlengel _Jewish_Warsaw_Ghetto_Poet_Poetry_Bio_Picture.htm.

11   A Jew, a Cemetery, and a Polish Village
A Tale of the Restoration of Memory

Jonathan Webber

THE LONG AND distinguished history of the Jews of Poland, spanning more than eight centuries, reached its climax in the twentieth century when Poland was home to the largest Jewish community in the world, comprising approximately 3.5 million people. It was destroyed almost in its entirety during the Holocaust. Today, the Jewish population of Poland, concentrated in only about a dozen cities, is in the mere thousands, less than half of 1 percent of what it was before the Second World War. Despite the massive destruction, there are many physical traces of the Jewish cultural heritage still to be found, but they are randomly scattered, often quite banal, and usually in poor condition. So it is hard nowadays to sense the immensity of the Polish-Jewish past, in terms of its spiritual, political, artistic, literary, intellectual, architectural, and other cultural achievements.

Perhaps the clearest present-day evidence of the exceptional size and geographic spread of the pre-Holocaust Jewish community of Poland are the well over one thousand abandoned Jewish cemeteries in the country, standing not only in large cities but also in small market towns and in innumerable rural settings across the countryside. Among the elements of the Jewish built environment, cemeteries are far more likely to have physically survived than synagogues and prayer houses, because the latter were set upon by the Germans for the purpose of conscious destruction (very often, and very effectively, by setting them on fire). Perhaps only 250 of such buildings have survived in the whole country, although with relatively few exceptions, they have usually been converted to other uses and are hardly recognizable for what they once were.[1] Cemeteries, which are much more laborious to destroy, thus frequently constitute the only clear physical proof that Jews ever lived in such places at all, when other obvious traces of their past have long since vanished.[2] If there are surviving tombstones, complete with long literary inscriptions and decorative symbolic imagery, such cemeteries offer further evidence of the rich Jewish culture and elaborate civilization that once existed in Poland. Yet abandoned Jewish cemeteries—and given the exceedingly thin geographical spread of Poland's present-day Jewish community, the vast majority of them are, by definition, abandoned[3]—are often hard to find: overgrown with decades of accumulated vegetation, surrounded by bushes or high walls, they are usually not signposted or marked on local maps, and may be some distance from the center of the town or village. Unless outsiders have a specialist interest in the subject, they would be completely unaware of their existence.

Yet a cemetery's physicality (its visibility or accessibility) is not the decisive factor in its cultural presence for *local* people.[4] My experience as a foreign anthropologist researching Jewish cemeteries in southern Poland throughout the 1990s brought me, quite early on, to this realization. Memory, quite simply, is not located first and foremost in what is physically verifiable, but rather in what remains in people's minds as recollections of the past. On numerous occasions, I stood in the main market square of a small town and asked local people about the Jewish past. They were perfectly articulate: "You see that house? That's where the rabbi—his name was Steiner—used to live. It was a wooden house, but it's not there anymore." I could, of course, see no wooden house, but it was clearly present in the mind's eye of the villager showing it to me. I would be told that in fact all the houses in the market square used to be inhabited by Jews. There were rich Jews here, there were poor Jews there, a distillery here, a leather shop there. Fifty years after the beginning of the German occupation, elderly informants could still rattle off the names of those Jews: they had been to school with them and could remember their names as if it was yesterday. There was something surreal about standing in the market square and being described a detailed reality for which I had no physical verification.

I would ask about the Jewish cemetery. "No problem," the villager would say. "Straight down the hill for half a mile, and it's there on the left-hand side of the road." Often I would indeed find an abandoned Jewish cemetery. But many was the time that I would pace the half mile back and forth, back and forth, until I gave up and had to return to the market square and ask someone to take me there. The local people knew precisely where the Jewish cemetery was, even if it was invisible to an outsider. Such cemeteries were not just abandoned, they were obliterated: the fence was gone, the tombstones had vanished. All that remained were empty plots of land. Yet for local people, the cemetery was still there. The categories of nothingness and emptiness, I realized, could be rich with content—even if nothing could actually be seen.

Interestingly, classical Jewish law similarly recognizes such empty places as cemeteries. Cemeteries are not regarded as such only when they are fenced off and contain within them serried ranks of tombstones. On the contrary, a cemetery is considered a consecrated, eternal resting place for those who are buried there, a place that must be maintained out of respect for the dead. A Jewish cemetery, in other words, always remains a Jewish cemetery. Even if it is completely abandoned and devastated, even if human beings can see nothing there, God remembers, and God can see who is buried there, just as God can recall all the human beings who have ever lived.

The Jewish cemetery of the village of Brzostek in southern Poland was one such place—a small, rectangular piece of land with no boundary fence enclosing it, lacking any sign of tombstones. When I first visited Brzostek, I was directed to the cemetery by local people in the market square without hesitation. They said it was about 300 yards away, beside a country lane. When I arrived at the place they had described but unable to identify if I had found the right spot, a neighbor came out of her house and confirmed that, yes, I was standing right in front of the Jewish cemetery, and she even pointed out its precise boundaries, which extended to the edge of a car repair workshop beside the road. It was midsummer, and she proudly drew my attention to the fact that, although the adjacent farmland was in use for agricultural purposes, the site of the cemetery had been left fallow, as the farmer had no right to that piece of land. Indeed, once this had been pointed out to me, the two shades of green became clear—the fallow grass of the cemetery (albeit cut down for hay or manure) versus the green of the farmed land. The boundary between those two shades of green formed an easily discernable line— the farmer knew precisely where the Jewish cemetery was, as did the neighbor. So in some sense it still *was* the Jewish cemetery, even for these local people, despite the absence of a Jewish community in Brzostek or a functioning synagogue, and the fact that no burials had taken place for more than sixty years. I began to wonder about the status of this memory: Would future generations of farmers and neighbors preserve it? Or would it slowly die out? Could this memory ever be remobilized in quite new ways? Anthropologists are used to the idea that surface realities are not always reliable guides to unfolding, lived experience: subliminal knowledge (for example, regarding an ostensibly "lost" ethnic identity) can surface at unexpected moments, often long after its associated cultural practices have disappeared. Might this abandoned cemetery, then, have a future?

I had a personal interest in these speculations: Brzostek was the birthplace of my paternal grandfather. His family had emigrated to England in 1880 when my grandfather was then a young child. It was a poor village with about 1,300 inhabitants, of whom about 400 were Jews—in other words, about a third of the population.[5] Brzostek is situated about 20 miles southeast of Tarnów, a big city 50 miles east of Kraków; it is not at all well known, certainly not in Jewish history. It did not have a long Jewish history (Jews began to live there only during the early part of the nineteenth century, and established a community in Brzostek only in about 1850). There were no famous people who came from there, no renowned rabbis buried there whose graves pilgrims would visit. The antisemitic disturbances that punctuated life there from time to time were fairly typical of other such modest villages in the region. Likewise, what happened in Brzostek during the Holo-

Figure 11.1. The Jewish cemetery of Brzostek in the 1990s: empty and unfenced. Photograph by Chris Schwarz, Galicia Jewish Museum, Kraków

caust followed the classic pattern—the Jews were ordered by the Germans to assemble in the summer of 1942 in the market square, from where some were taken away to be murdered in a nearby forest; others were deported to the death camp at Bełżec. In that sense, the history of Jewish Brzostek is unremarkable.[6] Because of the small size of its Jewish community, there was never a Brzostek *landsmanshaft* (association of émigré Jews from the locality) as was created by Jews from many larger Jewish communities in Poland whose members had emigrated to New York, Tel Aviv, and elsewhere.

There was a fair-sized synagogue in the village, 150 yards down the hill from the market square; after the war it was converted into a student dormitory/hostel. The building thus still stands, but no symbolic detail is left, whether outside or inside, that would indicate its former identity, nor is there a commemorative plaque. Nowhere in Brzostek was there any overt acknowledgment that Jews ever lived there at all, let alone that one-third of its population was taken away and brutally murdered. There is one exception, however: the lane down to the former synagogue is named "ul. Żydowska" (Jewish Street), and there is an official sign bearing that name at the top of the hill. That name, and that street sign, was introduced only after the war—prewar Brzostek was too small to need official street names.

Perhaps it was that lone street sign, immediately across the road from Brzostek's municipality building, that triggered my inkling that somehow, somewhere in Brzostek the memory of its Jewish past still lived on, and was perhaps capable of being reawakened, in a manner more demonstrative than what the unacknowledged synagogue building or the "invisible" cemetery would otherwise have led an outsider to imagine possible. These three elements—the street sign, the synagogue building, and the cemetery—were in no way symmetrical, but together they formed the cornerstone of a plan I fashioned to restore and reconsecrate the Jewish cemetery.

The Plan and Its Dramatis Personae

The cemetery restoration project in Brzostek may have begun as my own idea, but the process, from start to finish, was essentially a dialogue, an exercise in what I have come to think of as Jewish cultural diplomacy. If the cemetery was to be restored, my first question was: in whose name will this act of reclaiming the local Jewish heritage be undertaken? Given that there are no Jews living in Brzostek, if the cemetery were indeed restored, who would look after it? Formulated in this way, the problem's answer was obvious: since the local Polish villagers still regarded the empty space as "their" Jewish cemetery, it was with them that I needed to begin.

But first, I needed the advice of a "culture broker," an individual who could not only bring a foreign Jew (myself) together with the local ethnic Poles, but also provide both sides with the necessary reassurances of good intent. A foreign Jew (even one with local origins and a record of public work in Poland on heritage-related issues, as I had) could not merely impose his proposal onto reluctant, unwilling Polish villagers. The matter is not at all straightforward. Dealing with the physical debris of Poland's multicultural past (including traces of the former presence of a number of other minorities, not only those of the Jews) poses large questions, at both national and local levels, intersecting with many difficult, if not intractable, issues. These include the consequences of major changes to Poland's international boundaries after the Second World War, the repatriation to Poland of ethnic Polish refugees from territories that then came to be outside Poland's sovereignty, the abandonment of private property formerly belonging to local people (especially but not only Jews) who had fled or been taken away to be murdered, and the failure (up to the time of writing) of successive governments in Poland to provide for its restitution. All such issues are surrounded by controversy (sometimes in the context of political debates) and, in some cases, by a latent sense of national shame, even if the ostensible historical causes were attributable to the actions of a foreign German occupier and subsequently by foreign-imposed Communist rule.

Claims by foreigners or outsiders who assert a moral authority on the basis of having once been insiders—Jews with Polish origins, to give the obvious relevant example here—can in such a context be deeply destabilizing and indeed inhibit a slower, more organic response by local people to the issues they know they eventually need to deal with. A refusal or even a reluctance to deal with their claims is often still interpreted by Jews simply as ongoing evidence of Poland's troubled antisemitic past, although the issues are in fact considerably broader than Jewish or Holocaust-related matters alone. There is thus an additional dimension here. Jewish popular stereotypes about Poland, including the mythologized historical image of the shtetl as an autonomous Jewish space, have encouraged Jews nowadays to treat Polish-Jewish issues as if they functioned in some sort of sociopolitical vacuum. But the shtetl never was, and indeed never could have been, an entity where Jews had full independence or cultural autonomy in isolation from its non-Jewish environment. The shtetl was neither a legal nor a political entity, and was in any case run by municipal councils, following the law of the land. Popular Jewish memories of Poland largely tend to exclude details of regular contact by Jews with their Polish neighbors—much as Polish local histories, similarly, have tended to make only passing mention of Jews, even if they were the majority population. But Polish-Jewish life was of course deeply influenced by these daily interactions and cultural influences, whether in the field of architecture, food, music, clothing, or folk medicine, and much else besides.[7]

Awareness of all this meant that I felt it both ethical and expeditious to demonstrate common courtesy, cultural sensitivity, and the desire for Polish-Jewish dialogue—it was not that I was coming back to Brzostek "on behalf of the Jewish people" to reclaim a Jewish cemetery, or to reclaim my personal family history. Those thoughts were certainly part of it, but only one part of the larger picture. I was concerned also with local feelings and the desire to contribute to good Polish-Jewish relations. I knew this in theory, but at the outset of this practical project, I could have no idea of how it would unfold in practice. I did know perfectly well, however, that from the early 1990s, immediately after the fall of Communist rule and with the manifest encouragement of both national and local governments, the memorialization of the Jewish past in Poland had steadily become an established genre, not only in the large cities such as Kraków but also in quite a few smaller places as well, even though the actual number of restorations, as measured in absolute terms, was still relatively low compared to the overall size of the challenge.[8] What I didn't know was how a village such as Brzostek would respond to such an initiative. But I was convinced that the project would not be best presented as belonging exclusively to foreign Jews—after all (if for no other reason), a restored Jewish cemetery would still need input from local people for its ongoing maintenance.

There had already been a successful Jewish cemetery restoration project in the small market town of Pilzno, Brzostek's neighbor 10 miles to the north. This had come about in the late 1990s through the intervention of a family of Hassidic Jews now living in the Boro Park neighborhood of Brooklyn, New York. The Jewish cemetery of Pilzno still had a few surviving tombstones, but it was unfenced and neglected. The initiative to restore it came from Joseph Singer, an elderly New York rabbi born in the town who had immigrated to the United States as a young man before the war. Rabbi Singer now wanted to honor his father, who had been the chief rabbi (*av beit din*) of this small Jewish community, and he instructed his eldest son, Duvid, to arrange that the cemetery be refenced and that a memorial tombstone, listing the key rabbinical personalities of the town, be erected at the site. Duvid Singer realized that he could not do this on his own, and he turned for help to Adam Bartosz, the director of the regional museum in nearby Tarnów. Bartosz had long been seriously interested in the local Jewish heritage, having authored a significant book on the subject, and during my fieldwork in southern Poland beginning in the late 1980s, I had gotten to know him well.[9] Bartosz came to me for advice, and I encouraged him to get involved in the project. Since then he has become the key local culture broker in this field, spearheading a number of other Jewish heritage initiatives in the region, including the preservation of an important local Holocaust memorial site, and arranging open-air Jewish concerts in Tarnów and an annual Jewish culture festival.[10]

Thus it was that Bartosz agreed to accompany me in early 2007 on a visit to Leszek Bieniek, the mayor (*wójt*) of Brzostek, to propose the idea of a restoration project of the Jewish cemetery there. During the meeting, I emphasized that the purpose of the restoration was to help to give back to Brzostek an important part of *its own history,* its Jewish history. I wanted Bieniek's assent not only to the restoration of its Jewish cemetery but also to the erection of a public plaque on the main square in memory of the Jews of Brzostek. Restorations of a Jewish cemetery in Poland are primarily regarded by Jews as a private Jewish matter (a religious or cultural duty, for example because of ancestors buried there) and so do not include that latter feature, probably because foreign Jews, especially those from shtetl backgrounds and lacking a strong secular education, do not always see the relevance of a Polish context in understanding their local Polish-Jewish past. But to me, reaching out to the local community was vital; that is, after all, what Jewish cultural diplomacy requires. I stressed that the project was not an exclusively Jewish affair; indeed, I was hoping for as full a participation of Brzostek people as possible, in particular the local school and the local priest. I don't know if he could imagine just what I had in mind, but when the priest came to a subsequent meeting, I told him that once the restoration of the cemetery was complete, there would be a ceremony of reconsecration. I invited him to take part in that ceremony. He was astonished. "How can I take part in a Jewish ceremony?" he asked. I told him this was perfectly possible, and that it would be a considerable honor, for both the Jews and the village as a whole, and would add gravitas and prestige to the occasion. I described it as an interfaith event, with his own participation publicly announced. He could read a psalm or two in Polish as well as some other suitable prayer of his choice.

The director of the local school was also present at this meeting. I explained to her that in raising funds for this project, I envisaged establishing an annual cash prize for the best students each year in any academic field—on the one condition that for clear educational reasons the prize be known as "The Jews of Brzostek Memorial Prize." Much more than a cemetery restoration project narrowly defined, the idea to restore Brzostek's Jewish memory in the broader terms I had suggested charmed the mayor, the priest, and the schoolteacher. By getting them involved from the start, they understood themselves as key stakeholders in a village-wide project. Needless to say, the contract to build the new fence was given to a small, local Brzostek company. The involvement of local people thus began to gather momentum. Armed with the support of these fundamental local figures, I could then develop the rest of the project. It took well over two years from that first meeting with the mayor until the reconsecration could take place.

The first, and without a doubt the most laborious, aspect of the project was determining the precise boundaries of the cemetery. The neighbor and the farmer knew those boundaries in agricultural terms (the neighbor had the common-law rights to the hay), but if a fence was to be constructed, formal legal and cartographic specifications in the land registry were needed. It emerged that the Brzostek municipality had no official records specifying the precise boundaries; any such records, including the Jewish community records, had presumably been lost during the war, and a search had to be made in the archives of surrounding towns to see if anything reliable could be found. Furthermore, although all prewar Jewish cemeteries (along with Jewish communal property more generally, and as opposed to private property) were eligible under a national Polish law of 1997 for formal restitution to the Jewish religious community of Poland, the boundaries of the piece of land in question needed verification by the office of Michael Schudrich, the chief rabbi of Poland. What concerned Rabbi Schudrich was something even more precise than what might have concerned the municipal cartographers: given that the duty in Jewish law to preserve a burial-ground means that graves should on no account be disturbed, the digging of foundations for the new boundary fence must not disturb the bones of those who might have been buried immediately adjacent to the perimeter. Further, should a fence be wrongly positioned, some graves could be excluded, which, quite apart from other considerations, might also give rise at a future date to such graves being disturbed.

These matters were complicating my romantic idea of "memorializing the Polish-Jewish heritage." The Jewish community of Poland, as represented by its chief rabbi, was clearly a stakeholder—it was the owner of that piece of land and had to be listened to. After much searching over many months, Lucyna Pruchnik, secretary of the mayor's office, eventually found a prewar map with the boundaries of the Jewish cemetery marked on it. But far from solving the problem, it revealed a most unexpected difficulty, because it showed that the Jews of Brzostek had enlarged their cemetery in the 1920s by acquiring an additional piece of land alongside the original plot. In other words, the cemetery extended further down the road than the neighbor had informed me. It turned out that the car repair workshop had been built on top of part of the cemetery extension. Rabbi Schudrich explained to me that the 1997 law did not allow for the destruction of buildings that had been erected on Jewish cemeteries after the war if such buildings had been there for at least twenty years, and that we would therefore have to live with the workshop—even if it could be proved that there had been burials prior to the war in that part of the cemetery.

So how could a new boundary fence be erected along that side of the cemetery adjoining the workshop? Would it not by definition be excluding graves originally within the cemetery precincts? The solution we eventually came up with was simple and elegant. The fencing on that fourth side would be visually different from the other three sides, so as to demonstrate this boundary was not included in the restoration project. We did this by offering the owner of the workshop a fence that matched *his* other fences, rather than that of the cemetery. And as for the risk of disturbing graves at the perimeter, that was solved by asking Adam Bartosz to ask the local Brzostek contractor to agree to the presence of a special representative of the chief rabbi when the contractor was digging the foundations. If any bones were discovered during the process, he would cease work immediately. That part went very smoothly: no bones were discovered. Still, the problem of defining the boundaries delayed the construction of the fence by well over a year, during which time the cost of steel (the major component of the fence) actually doubled from the original estimate. Rabbi Schudrich had to make two visits to Brzostek from his base in Warsaw (five hours away by car), and the cost of having his representative supervise the digging was expensive (travel, accommodation, and other expenses). The costs of the project were growing apace.

At this point, I asked Adam Bartosz to draft a budget, including the reconsecration ceremony and (at my request) a souvenir booklet for the people of Brzostek. With this, I was finally in a position to go to the last set of stakeholders—the financial sponsors—and explain that all the necessary preconditions had been met. Part of this was straightforward. My grandfather Joseph had become a wealthy businessman in England, and on his death, his children established charitable memorial trusts in his memory. So it was not especially difficult to persuade the trustees (which included some of my cousins) to fund the Brzostek cemetery project in his memory—after all, Brzostek was his birthplace. Also, a Jew from my synagogue in London, the late Shiya Tager, had recently put up a plaque on a nearby Jewish institution in memory of his parents; to my astonishment, I noticed that it indicated that his father was born in Brzostek. I knew his son, Romie Tager (who happens to be a cousin of my brother-in-law); if Romie's paternal grandfather had been born in Brzostek, he had precisely the same kin relationship with Brzostek that I did. The family trustees agreed that I should approach him to see if he would be interested in splitting the costs, a proposal to which he readily agreed, rapidly resolving the financing. Romie Tager's only condition was that we arrange a suitable memorial tombstone for his Brzostek family, to be erected inside the cemetery and consecrated at the same time as the cemetery reconsecration.

My cousins, however, quite correctly pointed out that perhaps there were other Jews, elsewhere in the world, who had Brzostek origins and who would also like to be involved. One of my cousins, Rosemary Eshel, had in fact done quite a lot of research on the Jews of Brzostek, a project that had led her to discover prewar photographs, memoirs, and a handful of "Brzostekkers" (as we began to call them) in Australia, Israel, the United Kingdom, and the United States. These people included just one person, Adam Szus, then aged ninety-one and living in Sydney, Australia, who had adult memories of prewar Brzostek. My cousin suggested we announce the project in the Jewish newspapers in these countries to see if other Brzostekkers would come forward to share the costs or at least support the event through their presence. This part of the story was a mixed blessing. On the one hand, I was glad at the thought that the reconsecration ceremony might be attended by a range of Brzostekkers and their extended families. On the other hand, I was conscious of the possible consequences if they were equal stakeholders. What if they had quite different ideas about Polish-Jewish relations, the objective of a cemetery restoration, or the wording of suitable inscriptions, including the plaque on the main square? How would I reconcile such differences of opinion? My own family were also not fully agreed on these points, some of them being at first unconvinced about the need for the plaque on the main square and indeed about the whole strategy of cultural diplomacy that I had committed myself to from the outset. They knew little about Polish history and what they thought they knew about it was in fact based on conventional Jewish stereotypes that demonize Poland for its so-called endemic antisemitism. Some of the family discussions thus came to be dominated by impromptu seminars I found myself conducting on the complexities of Polish-Jewish relations over a history of more than eight centuries, and in the end, the family withdrew their objections. But how would I deal with a diffuse, transnational stakeholder group of people I didn't know but who might want to push their own views as regards the nature of the project? What if they would not accept the presence of the parish priest of Brzostek at the reconsecration ceremony? I entered this phase with some trepidation, but finally, perhaps because none of the Brzostekkers (except for Tager) contributed financially, they kept quiet, whatever their private views might have been.

There was one significant disappointment: my failure to engage in the project the family of the last rabbi of Brzostek, Rabbi Chaim Wolkenfeld. Through my cousin I succeeded in tracking down his grandson, who lives in Boro Park, and I went to meet him. The Wolkenfeld family had provided prewar Brzostek with three generations of community rabbis from 1873 onward.[11] Rabbi Chaim

Wolkenfeld was murdered by the Germans in July 1942 in Strzegocice, a hamlet just outside Pilzno; the precise location of the gravesite there is known, although the family has not yet decided to provide it with a marker.[12] What I had hoped for was a family representative to come to the reconsecration ceremony and to provide a memorial stone listing these rabbis, similar to what the Singer family had done for the cemetery in Pilzno. Maybe the absence of the Brzostek rabbinate in the project at that time (due to other commitments, as it turned out) eased my burden—it was one less potential stakeholder for me to be concerned about. And with that one important exception, everything was now in position; the plan was complete.

As far as Brzostek itself was concerned, I had not realized at the start that my overture to the mayor in fact would fall on such fertile ground. Not only was the mayor perfectly enthusiastic, but it turned out that Lucyna Pruchnik, the Brzostek municipality secretary, had in any case been in touch with the Australian Brzostekker Adam Szus for some time, and had been slowly collecting whatever data he could provide about prewar Jewish Brzostek. It was Lucyna who eventually found the map I needed, and came to know more than I could have imagined about Brzostek's Jewish heritage. It was as if a Jewish heritage restoration project was an event just waiting to happen, and my plan was simply the catalyst.

Restoration and Reconsecration

As the date for the reconsecration approached (fixed a year beforehand for a Sunday afternoon in mid-June 2009), I began work to find ways of widening the circle of local Brzostek villagers who could become interested in the public restoration of their locality's Jewish past, since the preservation of memory would ultimately depend on local involvement. The important thing was to see if local people could be energized by the project.

I had agreed with Adam Bartosz that we would produce a souvenir booklet in Polish to be distributed free of charge to every household in the village. What, though, should it contain? I had a visiting Ph.D. student from Kraków who was researching the history of the shtetls of southern Poland, and I asked her to see if she could find anything of interest published in Poland on the Jews of Brzostek. Within days she discovered three fascinating articles published by two local Brzostek historians, Wiesław Tyburowski and Renata Tyburowska.[13] Tyburowski's texts were socioeconomic studies of the history of the Jews of Brzostek. Tyburowska's article was particularly interesting, as it concerned Jewish burials in Brzostek—in fact, it listed the names of all 450 Jews who had been buried in the Jewish cemetery there from 1894 to 1938. Among these were four people named Tager, a fact about which our sponsor, Romie Tager, was especially pleased to hear. His family had not really preserved the date- or name-specific memory of those individuals, and he immediately decided that the memorial tombstone he wanted in the cemetery should bear the details provided in Tyburowska's list.

These three articles had been published during the years 1993–1998 in a local Brzostek historical yearbook. If I had needed any further proof that the time was ripe, if not overdue, for a restoration project, here it was. These local historians had been energized years earlier as regards their local Jewish heritage. It turned out that the Brzostek municipal archive had duplicate copies of virtually all documents recording Jewish births, marriages, and deaths covering that forty-four-year period, and it was these documents that provided the basis for the research undertaken.[14] We decided that our commemorative booklet would include two of these research papers (including the one listing the names of the Jews buried in the cemetery), as well as a fine nostalgic essay by Lucyna Pruchnik's daughter Kornelia titled "Shtetl Brzostek"; numerous prewar photographs of Brzostek Jews collected by Lucyna Pruchnik and captioned with the names of those depicted; and an essay by Adam Bartosz, with accompanying photos, on the story (as he saw it) of how the Jewish cemetery came to be restored. I wrote an introduction.[15]

The contractor completed work on the cemetery fence a good nine months before the ceremony. As word spread in the village, Adam was informed by the Brzostek Friendship Society (a group of local history enthusiasts) that about a dozen Jewish tombstones had been discovered in local farms and barns; they had been scavenged as building materials or for paving, during the war or after. While recognizable by their Hebrew inscriptions, most of them were in poor condition, fragments rather than complete tombstones. Nevertheless, the contractor agreed to talk to the current owners, and if they were amenable, he would fetch the stones and install them upright in the cemetery, as if they had always been there, spread out randomly across the empty space. They could not be installed directly above the graves they related to, as even if the stones themselves could be identified, information about who had been buried where was lacking from the records. In the large rectangular area of the cemetery, measuring about 75 by 20 yards, a handful of tombstones were thus returned. While somewhat forlorn, they began to physically substantiate what locals already knew—that this was the Jewish cemetery and was about to be formally reconsecrated as such.

Meanwhile, the director of the local school, who had evidently grasped and indeed welcomed the educational importance of the whole project, began in earnest to energize her students about the upcoming event. I had imagined that the annual school prize in memory of the Jews of Brzostek would be given to the best student in a field such as physics or chemistry, but the school director came up with quite a different idea. Realizing that her students knew nothing about the history or culture of the Jews of Poland, let alone about the Jews of Brzostek, she engaged a scholar to come from Warsaw to give a series of lectures on the subject. A bus was hired to take the top class to Kraków, to let them see the synagogue buildings and Jewish museums of the former Jewish district of Kazimierz. The art teacher encouraged the students to take photographs of what they were seeing and arranged a photography competition on the subject. The Polish literature teacher encouraged the students to write essays describing what they saw, and organized an essay competition. The music teacher asked me to send a song book so that the students could learn Jewish songs, in Hebrew or Yiddish. And the parents were asked to dig out—whether from their memories or books—whatever recipes of Polish-Jewish foods they could find, so that they could prepare a suitable banquet at the school on the day of the reconsecration, to entertain the assembled guests in an authentically Jewish manner.

This energizing of the local people, young and old, was far beyond anything I could have imagined, let alone instigated. It pointed to a latent desire that the cemetery project merely brought to the surface. I knew a Polish artist in Kraków named Marta Gołąb, who specialized in the old Polish-Jewish art of paper-cutting (now virtually forgotten as a folk art among Jews). I asked her if she would design an original, commemorative paper-cut to be used both on the cover of the souvenir brochure and the reconsecration invitation, which I intended to have delivered to every household in Brzostek. I wanted to let everyone know that the whole village was invited. Imagine my surprise when Marta informed me that she had been raised in Brzostek, and that an aunt of hers was still living in the main square there! Before I knew it, the school director had arranged for Marta to have an exhibition of her work in the school to accompany the celebration.

About six weeks before the reconsecration, Adam Bartosz sent me an e-mail saying that the contractor, who had been busy installing the archway over the new entry gate to the cemetery, wanted to apologize that he had inadvertently left the gate unlocked one night. Someone had evidently arrived with a tractor and dumped another dozen or so tombstones inside the cemetery. What should he do? By this point, nothing was really surprising me anymore. We instructed the contractor to simply re-erect these tombstones as well. I asked Adam to send me photos of the inscriptions, just in case I could sufficiently decipher any of the names and dates to link up with those on Renata Tyburowska's lists. I shall never forget the moment when I saw the name Fishel Schönwetter on one of the stones. The family name Schönwetter ("fine weather") is unusual and memorable, and it was easy enough to find Fishel Schönwetter as entry no. 243 in Renata's list: he died in 1913, aged fifty-two. I had been in e-mail contact with an American Jew from New Jersey named Mark Schönwetter, born in Brzostek and a child survivor of the Holocaust. He had said he would like to come to the ceremony, and had given me the names and dates of his father and grandfather. His father had been the distinguished lay head of the Jewish community in Brzostek until he was shot in a mass grave in August 1942. Fishel was in fact Mark's grandfather. Now I could inform him that we had found his grandfather's tombstone, and I invited him to add a memorial plaque to it in memory of his father also. At a village level, with very small numbers, these were particularly moving developments, quite different from what would be the case in a big-city cemetery restoration, supported by well-documented information disseminated by a large transnational *landsman-shaft*.

At last, the big day arrived. The proceedings began at the main square with the unveiling before a group of invited guests of the public plaque in memory of the Jews of Brzostek. The events were the antithesis of a private Jewish matter to which some local notables had been invited. Rather, the proceedings took place under the official auspices of the municipality of Brzostek, and the invitation, while bearing the names of the two principal sponsors (the Webber and Tager families), bore prominently Brzostek's official coat of arms and the logo of Adam Bartosz's museum in Tarnów.[16] The commemorative plaque was affixed to the side wall of the town hall (a few months earlier, Brzostek had been upgraded once again to a "town"), immediately facing the sign "ul. Żydowska." Assembled at the top of the narrow lane beside the main square, flanked on either side by the Jewish Street sign and the new plaque, were the notables: the mayor, the chief rabbi of Poland, the parish priest, the president of Kraków's Jewish community, along with mayors of neighboring towns and villages and a number of local newspaper and television journalists. About one hundred in all, the group included a busload of people we had transported from Kraków, including about thirty Brzostekkers. The colored bunting was removed as the plaque was formally unveiled, and some of the notables gave short speeches. The text of the plaque, which had been formally approved by the district authorities (who accepted it without changes) read as follows:

קטסוֹיזב ק״ק רכזל

IN MEMORY OF THE JEWISH COMMUNITY
OF BRZOSTEK—ITS RABBIS AND TEACHERS,
SHOPKEEPERS AND ARTISANS,
AND ALL ITS FAMILIES—
AND IN MEMORY OF THE 500 JEWISH
MEN, WOMEN, AND CHILDREN OF BRZOSTEK
MURDERED BY THE GERMANS IN 1942
IN THE PODZAMCZE FOREST, IN THE BEŁŻEC DEATH CAMP,
AND IN OTHER UNKNOWN PLACES[17]

The group then proceeded to the cemetery, a ten-minute walk down the hill; the police had closed off the roads to prevent motor traffic disturbing the event. As we turned the corner before the cemetery, the sight that greeted our eyes astonished us. Lucyna Pruchnik had asked me beforehand how many people we expected, and how many chairs should be put out. I thought perhaps fifty, or maybe a hundred. But the entire area in front of the cemetery was packed with people, young and old—about six hundred of them, most in their Sunday best, undeterred by the intense summer sun. Most of the men were wearing suits, as were the students from the high school; some of the latter were acting as ushers, handing out skullcaps and cold drinks. The priest was dressed in gorgeous multicolored robes, complete with crucifix. Earlier that day, he had mentioned the event in his sermon and encouraged people to come. As Lucyna later explained, the number of people attending represented almost half the population—at least one person for every household in Brzostek.

The crowd was clearly captivated by what they saw. What had been a desolate, empty field now boasted an elegant fence with ceremonial gates, adorned with a Hebrew inscription in large lettering: *Hashem natan, vehashem lakach, yehi shem hashem mevorach* (The Lord gave, and the Lord has taken away. Blessed be the name of the Lord).[18] There was no need to state "this is a Jewish cemetery"—the inscription in Hebrew said it all. At my request, Adam Bartosz opened the ceremony by intoning those Hebrew words, and then translating them into Polish. But what was truly breathtaking was the sight of the cemetery now filled with tombstones. Once the people of Brzostek had seen for themselves that the Jews were taking their cemetery seriously by refencing it, they too took the cemetery seriously: stone after stone was brought back, from farm after farm, courtyard after courtyard, one by one, by local people, and reinstalled by the contractor. There were now more than fifty of them. Spaced apart across the full span of the cemetery, some of them grouped around the central commemorative monument we had prepared, these tombstones, of different shapes and sizes, different types of stone, and with different styles of inscription, together made a tremendous impression. And they were fully visible from the lane, as from the start I had envisaged a fence of metal railings rather than a high solid wall, so that what was inside the cemetery would not be private, unseen, "other" Jewish space (as is unfortunately the case with many other Jewish cemetery restorations), but rather become an integral part of the town's visual space.

I had not prepared a formal speech (having been too busy with overseeing the administrative details), but other than expressing formulaic thanks to the mayor and his colleagues, what I found myself saying was an outpouring of gratitude to the people of Brzostek for returning the tombstones:

> We humans forget the past. We forget even our own ancestors after a couple of generations. But the Jewish tradition says that God remembers everyone who ever lived, even those whom we have forgotten. I never knew the people who were buried here in this cemetery, but what you have done by bringing back their tombstones is nothing less than God's work—to restore their memory with respect and with dignity. Thank you for what you have done, for this act of friendship and human solidarity before God.

Figure 11.2. The Jewish cemetery of Brzostek in 2009. Photograph by Jonathan Webber

Figure 11.3. The speakers at the ceremony in 2009 to reconsecrate the Jewish cemetery of Brzostek (from right to left): the chief rabbi of Poland, the president of the Jewish community of Kraków, the mayor of Brzostek, the parish priest of Brzostek, the director of the regional museum in Tarnów (acting as master of ceremonies), and the anthropologist (at the microphone). Photograph by Connie Webber

The local people could see from the lineup of dignitaries who had taken the time to come (and make speeches) that this was a significant event. A letter sent by the Israeli ambassador was read aloud, as was a letter from the grandson of Rabbi Chaim Wolkenfeld. Although present-day ceremonies in Poland to rededicate cemeteries or install monuments, while not particularly numerous, are well publicized in the local media, and in that sense give the impression of constituting an established genre, in my experience, there is no fixed formula. Cemetery reconsecrations are simultaneously religious and civic events, and as such are necessarily cultural inventions, stimulating multiple emotions and multiple memories. Much may, however, be left unsaid in the official speeches on such occasions, especially as regards local details of Holocaust-related events, although from time to time there are some notable exceptions. What I chose to do—and for which I produced a printed liturgy in Hebrew, Polish, and English—was to divide the ceremony into two parts. First, while the crowd was seated, there were speeches and prayers delivered from a podium erected immediately outside the cemetery, as a ceremony of rededication. Then came the second part, when all those present were invited to leave their seats and actually enter the cemetery, where a different set of Hebrew prayers (the El Male Rachamim and the Kaddish) was recited, as a ceremony of reconsecrating the terrain of the cemetery itself, together with its new main monument. For example, during the first part, Mark Schönwetter spoke poignantly from the podium about being a child Holocaust survivor from Brzostek, about what had happened to his family (despite having had the opportunity to escape deportation in 1942, his father chose to accompany the rest of the Jews to their fate), and about his emotions on this day of his return. During the second part, a memorial prayer was recited for his grandfather, immediately beside his reerected tombstone, and another memorial prayer for his father.

Between the two parts of the ceremony, the crowd was invited to pace the full length of the cemetery along the road; psalms were recited (in each of the three languages), and—following a local Hassidic custom used at the rededication of the cemetery in Pilzno some years earlier—cloves of garlic were handed out to people by the ushers with the request to throw them over the fence into the cemetery, an act symbolizing the cleansing of ritual and spiritual impurities. After each psalm, Chief Rabbi Schudrich blew the shofar, an astonishingly powerful sound in the open air, reverberating in the hills beyond. As the crowd began to enter the cemetery, the ushers handed out skullcaps and small stones for people to place on the individual tombstones, following Jewish custom. Then the Eshet Chayil (Proverbs 31:1–31), a prayer in praise of women, was sung—once again, a mystical tradition used at Pilzno, symbolizing the return to the cemetery of the Divine Presence, understood as embodying female virtues. Twenty candles in protective glass holders had been prepared, and a variety of women were called up by name, one by one, to place these at the foot of the new central monument. The first of these was the daughter of Bronisława and Wojciech Dziedzic, righteous Poles who risked their lives to save Jews during the German occupation (among them Mark Schönwetter and his sister, both of them present there that day). Krystyna Oleksy, deputy director of the Auschwitz State Museum (who had come more than 100 miles to be at the ceremony), was invited to light the second candle. The monument was a simple slab of stone, with an inscription solely in Hebrew, which read, "This monument is in memory of the Jews of Brzostek buried in this cemetery, and in memory of the five hundred Jews of Brzostek without a resting place who were brutally murdered by the Germans in the Holocaust, most of them in 1942 in the Bełżec death camp and the Podzamcze forest near Kołaczyce. May their souls find eternal repose and their memory be forever blessed." Affixed to the entry gate of the cemetery were translations, one in English and one in Polish. The final element of the ceremony was to offer all participants a glass of vodka, which was served immediately outside the cemetery—as a *lechayim*, a toast to life, symbolizing for the ceremony participants the return to the normal world from the world of the dead.

I had no doubt that some of the elements of this ceremony were naturally unfamiliar to locals. But that was how I had conceptualized this—as a ceremony that combined recognizable (if not well-known) features to offer cultural anchorage alongside the strange and the unknown, articulating the otherness of Jewish culture and tradition (or Catholic tradition, for the foreign Jewish Brzostekkers) while drawing it a bit closer to home.

A reception at the school followed. In the main hall of the school, banquet tables had been set up, laden with the Jewish food prepared according to the recipes sourced by the parents. In adjoining rooms, the results of the photography competition were on display, as well as an exhibition of Marta Gołąb's papercuts. There were more speeches, extremely warm on both sides. The school had even produced a souvenir brochure of its own on the Jews of Brzostek. The concert of Jewish songs provided by the students was superb, their pride and enthusiasm palpable. My sister and I presented the prizes to the students, along with gifts to Mayor Bieniek and Secretary Pruchnik. The gift we found for the school made a unique surprise: in 1926, on the 150th anniversary of American independence, arrangements were made through the American embassy in Warsaw for every school in Poland to sign a birthday card. The originals are preserved in the Library of Congress, but thanks to JewishGen (a genealogy association), we were able to locate the signatures of the pupils from Brzostek and to offer the school director a framed copy of the two relevant pages. It is a particularly moving document, not only for its evidence (the signatures) that Jewish and Polish children sat together at the same school benches in Brzostek in 1926, but also because of the knowledge that most of those Jewish children would have lived no more than another sixteen years before being taken away to be murdered. The school had not been aware of the document and was evidently pleased to receive it.

The Holocaust is clearly an omnipresent subtext for any effort to memorialize the Jewish past in Poland. So the day ended with a visit to a mass grave located in a forest a few miles away, within the municipal boundaries of Brzostek. The 160 Jews who were murdered there on August 12, 1942, actually came from the next village, called Jodłowa (more or less the entire Jewish community of that village was brought to an end on that one day). It was fitting that we concluded the day's events with prayers recited for the souls of those people, though the mayor of Jodłowa, who had been with us throughout the day, said in his short speech at the mass grave that he hoped that sometime in the future, he would merit the chance to do for his village a restoration of Jewish heritage like that which had been done at Brzostek. An overwhelmingly welcome initiative, this expanding project of heritage restoration seemed poised to spark others. The empty Jewish cemetery of Brzostek, it seemed, had contained far more than could have been imagined.

Afterword

The Holocaust is, of course, much more than a subtext. The sheer magnitude of the displacement—the terror and the suffering, the stupendous loss of life, the destruction of entire communities, the uprooting of previously multiethnic settlements, and the devastation of the local heritage—echoes down the generations. Even now, much of this is still too raw for Jews to be reconciled to, alongside the controversies over Polish-Jewish relations during those terrible times, which continue to rumble not far below the surface. There is not, and cannot be, a quick fix. Dealing with the reduction of a particularly long and distinguished Jewish record in Poland to a desolate, silent, melancholy landscape of ruins and rubble requires patient, sensitive attention and may take generations.

The evident goodwill of a small village community in attempting to recover and revalue its Jewish past is thus in one sense little more than a footnote to the wider picture. I am not even sure that I could use the word "typical" to characterize the story that I have set out above. But on the other hand, the story speaks for itself. The cultural dialogue that marked the events in Brzostek clearly generated much enthusiasm, particularly as regards the return of the tombstones—even if the reconsecration ceremony included strange, exotic, and unfamiliar elements, or the Jewish food served by the local people at the banquet was not, in fact, kosher, and even if some of the important details of what actually happened locally during the war years were not publicly referenced (let alone discussed or analyzed). The texture of the memory was plain for all to see: the attendance of the six hundred villagers and the suited ushers calmly handing out skullcaps can perhaps be taken as symbolizing how preexisting subliminal knowledge can be transformed into social reality, given the right conditions. In that sense, I offer the story as a modest contribution to the ethnography of nostalgia.

When I set out to restore and reconsecrate the Jewish cemetery in Brzostek, I had wondered about its future. I am writing this twenty months after the ceremony, and during that time, I have had no opportunity to return to the village (or town, as it is now correctly called). I have not done follow-up fieldwork to find out how local residents today think about the Jewish heritage of their town. But I am aware of the central fact that the restored cemetery is not a functioning cemetery. Even if it does now appropriately honor those who are buried there, the place has become a museum of sorts, the reinstalled tombstones forming a lapidarium. In that sense, the cemetery has not returned to its prior state; rather, it is a new cultural creation, an effect of the complex cultural displacement caused by the Holocaust, overlaid by the organic processes of present-day memorialization. The acknowledgment in post-Holocaust Poland of a "Jewish heritage" is, perhaps by definition, a new concept. It is thus authentic and inauthentic at the same time, a new layer of memory that both illuminates and obscures what was there before. The neighbor and the farmer, along with many other local people, had always known that empty piece of land as the Jewish cemetery. It was privileged, insider knowledge, inaccessible to the uninformed outsider. Today it has become public Polish knowledge, and indeed at the reception in the school, the mayor proudly handed me a newly printed map of his town, clearly showing the Jewish cemetery marked on it. I do not suppose Brzostek will ever host a Jewish culture festival, as Adam Bartosz does in Tarnów, doubtless inspired by the highly elaborate annual festival in Kraków.[19] Brzostek has really nothing much to show of its Jewish past. The plaque, however, with its Hebrew lettering on the wall of the town hall in the main square is surely important (despite residual Polish skepticism, since Communist times, about plaques and other monuments on main squares), and I suspect that local people, and especially the schoolchildren, will gradually, and in an unsensational manner, absorb more of the historical facts about their town's having had a substantial Jewish population and thus become epistemologically acclimatized to constitutive events and to the local presence of a (re)constructed Jewish heritage they share with literally hundreds of other small towns the length and breadth of Poland.

That is more than enough of a reward as far as I am concerned.[20] Let me conclude, then, on a personal note. It was a privilege for me to have had the opportunity to engage in a project like this, which (I confess) did offer me the chance to sneak in some of my own ideas about the multidimensionality of Jewish space in Poland (especially as regards a cultural history of Jewish interaction with its Polish neighbors) and thus the importance of Jewish cultural diplomacy in the context of such a revival project. The cemetery restoration was not just a private

Jewish initiative for private Jewish purposes; it was also, as I saw it, a reflection of the broader desire to give back to Brzostek part of its own history. But, as I discovered, the events were simply waiting to happen—the process had begun quite some time before I found myself involved, and is likely to continue long into the future. Jewish space always was multidimensional; nowadays, in a setting where Jews no longer live, it still is multidimensional, but much more explicitly in dialogue with its cultural environment. The realities cannot be measured only by the presence or absence of private Jewish initiatives or other specific, tangible projects. Recognizing that is the key modality underpinning any local efforts at reconciliation with the past—that, at least for me, was the main moral of the story.[21]

* * *

But the story continues. Since this chapter was written, there have been further developments, which are worth a brief summary here. First of all, the existence of a reconsecrated Jewish cemetery in Brzostek has over the past three years attracted three more Jewish families with roots in the town to come forward with the wish to erect memorials to their family members buried there. The newly constructed layer of memory of this cemetery-lapidarium has in that sense enabled the place to come to be seen by such Brzostekkers as a bona fide place of memory, even with a future that includes organic growth. A ceremony to dedicate these new tombstones was held in June 2012, once again in the presence of a large crowd that included the local mayor, the chief rabbi of Poland, and the local priest (now deacon) of the parish of Brzostek. These dignitaries took part in that ceremony as the first element of a memorial day during which two further ceremonies were also held.

One of those ceremonies was the dedication of a monument deep in the Podzamcze forest, some 10 miles away, where a sizeable percentage of the Jews of Brzostek (the exact number is not known) were murdered by the Germans in August 1942, shot into a mass grave. Establishing a memorial there had been intended from the beginning of the cemetery project, but the precise location was unknown to me at that time. After much research, the mass grave was found to have been in a clearing of the forest (now completely overgrown with vegetation), up a steep hill, 500 yards from the nearest road and lacking any present-day access path through the woods. The support and encouragement of the local mayor and other municipal officials to memorialize this tragic spot, and their participation along with many local people (as well as Brzostekkers from eight foreign countries) in a formal consecration ceremony marking the seventieth anniversary of the massacre, are details worthy of another article. Suffice it to say here, it was clearly part of the ongoing, organic texture of memory that the cemetery project in Brzostek had brought to the surface three years earlier.

The third formal ceremony that day came about through the initiative of an Australian Jew with roots in Brzostek. Having been in contact with me and thus aware of the memory work being undertaken, he had decided to erect a new thanksgiving tombstone at the grave of a Polish woman who died in 1979 who had risked her life during the war by hiding two Jewish girls. One of those girls was his mother. So on that day in June 2012, the new tombstone was dedicated at an interfaith ceremony at the Roman Catholic cemetery in Brzostek, attended by the dignitaries and a large local crowd, including the Australian ambassador to Poland. The chief rabbi spoke of the enormous importance of honoring the memory of a person who had risked her life to save others.

The Polish-Jewish cultural dialogue was by now an established genre in Brzostek, plain for all to see. Hence the celebration at the local school, which also took place that day, together with the awarding of the annual prize in memory of the Jews of Brzostek and a sumptuous buffet lunch for a hundred invited guests, was truly joyful and relaxed. The school put on a richly illustrated exhibition on the Jewish social history of Brzostek, and the students offered a cultural performance (song and dance, together with poetry readings) and a screening of their own excellent, homemade film depicting a Polish-Jewish past in a contemporary Polish setting.

The detailed structure and content of the "Brzostek Memorial Day 2012" obviously constituted a new script. But as I have been suggesting all along, in the perception of local people, the script existed in advance of the memorialization events themselves, and in that sense, was instantly intelligible and meaningful. Even in this remote rural environment, distant from the relatively well-honed commemoration events of the large cities in Poland, it was clear to all those present that memory is far from being something coterminous with those very elderly who can still recall prewar times. On the contrary, the strongly educational element of the entire Brzostek project has confirmed that energetic intercultural dialogue can genuinely help a recovery of history and a reconciliation with the past, which can amplify personal and communal identities in fruitful ways. More, I would imagine, is yet to come.[22]

Notes

1. A figure of 1,200 Jewish cemeteries in Poland is suggested by Weronika Litwin on behalf of the Warsaw-based Foundation for the Preservation of Jewish Heritage in Poland (www.fodz.pl); see her "Synagogues and Cemeteries: What Is Being Done and What Needs to Be Done?" in *Poland: A Jewish Matter,* ed. Kate Craddy, Mike Levy, and Jakub Nowakowski (Warsaw: Adam Mickiewicz Institute, 2010), 156. See also Samuel Gruber and Phyllis Myers, with Eleonora Bergman and Jan Jagielski, *Survey of Historic Jewish Monuments in Poland: A Report*

to the United States Commission for the Preservation of America's Heritage Abroad (New York: Jewish Heritage Council, World Monuments Fund, 1995). They suggest that there are a further four hundred Jewish cemeteries in Poland that may have been deliberately bulldozed or built over during the Second World War or in the aftermath of the war (ibid., 31–32). On the number of synagogue buildings and prayer houses that have survived in Poland, as well as a survey of the varying uses they have been put to, see the landmark article of Eleonora Bergman and Jan Jagielski, "The Function of Synagogues in the PPR, 1988," *Polin* 5 (1990): 40–49, although, since that publication was prepared, many of those uses have changed, and continue to change.

2. Indeed, in those cases where an entire village was destroyed during wartime, a surviving Jewish cemetery may also constitute the only proof of the age of the village itself. This is the case, for example, with the town of Lutowiska in the Bieszczady mountains in southeastern Poland, near the Ukrainian border.

3. Litwin says that of the 1,200 Jewish cemeteries in Poland, 30% (about 360) are in a state of complete ruin, and a further 30% have neither any tombstones nor a boundary fence (Litwin, "Synagogues and Cemeteries," 156).

4. The point should not be overgeneralized: even if the ordinary outsider finds the abandoned Jewish cemetery hard to find, or so overgrown with vegetation that it is physically impenetrable, certain sectors of the local population may nevertheless know the site perfectly well (children may play there, or alcoholics may find the place convenient, due to its privacy). But it should be noted that, because of population movements following the end of the Second World War, many local populations may consist heavily of postwar ethnic Polish incomers (e.g., from former Polish lands in what is now Ukraine) who have no personal knowledge of prewar Jewish life in the town or village where they now live. One point particularly worth mentioning here, however, is the ritual associated with All Souls' Day (in early November), when the common custom in Poland is for people to visit the local cemetery (and/or such other cemeteries where friends and relatives are buried) and light candles in remembrance of the dead. It has become increasingly common for groups of local schoolchildren, accompanied by their teachers, also to visit their local *Jewish* cemetery on All Souls' Day and light candles there—and in that way keep the memory of their vanished Jewish population as a living educational reality. The annual visit may be undertaken even if the Jewish cemetery is some distance away from the town or village centre, and even if it requires some skill or ingenuity to get inside (because of the vegetation or the need to find the key to the entry gate). I suppose, however, that this would be done only at Jewish cemeteries that still retain classic, visible features of a cemetery, i.e. including (some) tombstones and/or a boundary fence, and so would not be normally undertaken at cemeteries that retain neither of these two features.

5. On the Jewish demographic and socioeconomic history of Brzostek, the best source is Wiesław Tyburowski, "Żydzi w gminie wyznaniowej Brzostek: Przemiany społeczno-gospodarcze w latach 1894–1938," *Rocznik brzostecki* 4 (1998): 74–98, reprinted in *Cmentarz Żydowski w Brzostku*, ed. Adam Bartosz, Natalia Gancarz, and Janusz Kozioł (Tarnów: Muzeum Okręgowe w Tarnowie, 2009), 15–35. For details of the history of Jewish communal life in Brzostek, see Avraham Wein and Aharon Weiss, eds., *Pinkas hakehilot: Entsiklopediyah shel hayishuvim hayehudiyim lemin hivasedam ve'ad le'achar sho'at milchemet ha'olam hasheniyah. Polin,* vol. 3, *Galitsiyah hama'aravit veshleziyah* (Jerusalem: Yad Vashem, 1984), 73–74. An extremely brief English-language note on the Jews of Brzostek can be found in Shmuel Spector, ed., *The Encyclopaedia of Jewish Life before and during the Holocaust,* 3 vols., (New York: New York University Press, 2001), 1:207.

6. Neither Brzostek itself nor its Jews significantly prospered before the war: the place did not develop as it was situated relatively far (12 miles) from the nearest railway, and although it once enjoyed formal status as a "town," it lost it in 1934 when it officially became a village once

again. The population remained static over several generations, although the Jews, who numbered about five hundred by 1939, grew to slightly more than one-third.

7. Historians certainly recognize that there is a need for new social and economic histories of shtetls (whether these be towns or villages) that focus on both Jews and Christians and their contacts with each other. The subject raises many theoretical and methodological questions regarding the embeddedness or otherwise of Jewish culture in its non-Jewish environment. For important reviews of the topic, see *Polin* 17 (*The Shtetl: Myth and Reality*, 2004), and M. J. Rosman, *How Jewish Is Jewish History?* (Oxford: Littman Library of Jewish Civilization, 2007), esp. 82–110.

8. After the fall of Communist rule in Poland in 1989, numerous restoration projects have taken place across Poland, especially in the larger cities but also in smaller market towns. In that sense, the country is now unrecognizable compared to what it was twenty years ago. For a review of some of these efforts in southern Poland, see Jonathan Webber, *Rediscovering Traces of Memory: The Jewish Heritage of Polish Galicia* (Oxford and Bloomington, IN: Littman Library of Jewish Civilization and Indiana University Press, 2009), 162–163. There are quite a few agencies involved in this work, including private Jewish initiatives as well as *landsmanshaftn;* perhaps the most active single agency is the Warsaw-based Foundation for the Preservation of Jewish Heritage in Poland, which claims that in 2009 alone, it was responsible for cleaning up and refencing no less than twenty-seven Jewish cemeteries in the country (Litwin, "Synagogues and Cemeteries," 156). There is, however, still no centrally coordinated master plan for this work, which appears to vary rather substantially from place to place, for example as regards to the aesthetics of the fencing, entry gates, and new monuments, or the style and content of relevant inscriptions—let alone the cultural diplomacy or other strategy vis-à-vis the local Polish community setting. Such projects are slowly becoming seen as "mainstream" within Polish society (especially when taken in context with the growth of Jewish museums in Poland and of Jewish Studies departments at Polish universities), although, at the same time, it should be noted that completed projects are really very few compared to the vast number of abandoned cemeteries that still require attention.

9. Adam Bartosz, *Tarnowskie Judaica* (Warsaw: PTTK Kraj, 1992).

10. Since then he has published (inter alia) *Żydowskim szlakiem po Tarnowie / In the Footsteps of the Jews of Tarnów,* Polish-English-Hebrew edn., trans. Annamaria Orla-Bukowska and Hanoch Fenichel (Tarnów: Muzeum Okręgowe w Tarnowie, 2007), and "From the House of Chaim," in Karol Majcher, *Bobowa: Historia, ludzie, zabytki* (Warsaw: Przedsiębiorstwo Wydawnicze Rzeczpospolita, 2008), 178–185.

11. For details of these Brzostek rabbis, see Meir Wunder, *Me'orei galitsiyah: Entsiklopediyah lechakhmei galitsiyah,* 6 vols. (Jerusalem: Makhon Lehanstahat Yahadut Galitsiyah, 1978–2005), 2:764–765.

12. For the gravesite location, see Kornelia Pruchnik, "Sztetl Brzostek," in Bartosz et al., eds., *Cmentarz Żydowski w Brzostku,* 52n2. While this chapter was in press, I learned that the municipal authorities in Pilzno had unexpectedly decided, despite protracted negotiation with the office of Rabbi Schudrich, to proceed unilaterally with marking the site. Rabbi Schudrich's office had not been informed at the time about the erection of a small monument, which took place in November 2013, nor had any consecration ceremony been held with prayers recited in memory of the dead. This news surfaced some months later, while Adam Bartosz and I were in the process of making further inquiries about the future of the site. The inscription on the monument refers to fourteen Jews being murdered there by the Germans in the summer of 1942 (no precise date is given); Rabbi Wolkenfeld is not mentioned specifically. In correspondence with Rabbi Schudrich's office, the Pilzno municipality, which owns the site where this mass grave is located, explained that according to their rules, Rabbi Wolkenfeld could not be

named on the monument because there was no eyewitness who could be found today to testify that the rabbi was in fact among that group of fourteen Jews. It is a sad ending to a sad story; perhaps in the future Rabbi Wolkenfeld's family will agree to a commemorative monument in the Jewish cemetery in Brzostek.

13. Wiesław Tyburowski, "Społeczność żydowska okręgu metrykalnego: Brzostek w latach 1894–1938," *Rocznik brzostecki* 1 (1993): 61–77; Tyburowski, "Żydzi w gminie wyznaniowej Brzostek"; and Renata Tyburowska-Rams, "Cmentarz Żydowski w Brzostku," *Rocznik brzostecki* 3 (1997): 61–78.

14. As explained by Tyburowski, "Społeczność żydowska."

15. Bartosz et al., eds., *Cmentarz Żydowski w Brzostku.*

16. The souvenir booklet itself was officially published by the museum.

17. The one line in Hebrew at the top reads, "In memory of the Jewish community of Brzostek"; underneath that (but not reproduced here) was the Polish translation of the English text that appears below.

18. This is a quotation from the Hebrew Bible (Job 1:21), which also occurs in the funeral liturgy.

19. There are numerous ways in which Jewish Kraków acts as a role model for developments in Poland elsewhere, as evidenced, for example, in the decision of the Brzostek school director to take her students on a trip there in order to see the place for themselves. On the Jewish Culture Festival in Kraków, see, for example, Ruth Ellen Gruber, *Virtually Jewish: Reinventing Jewish Culture in Europe* (Berkeley: University of California Press, 2002), 45–50, or, for a particularly poetic description of the significance of the Kraków festival by its director Janusz Makuch, see his "The Jewish Culture Festival, Kraków," in Craddy et al., eds., *Poland,* 131–135.

20. The (quite unexpected) reaction of the Polish Ministry of Culture to formally present me at the ceremony with a medal marking my contribution to Polish culture was greatly appreciated, even if somewhat excessive—though in the eyes both of the local Poles and the visiting Brzostekkers, it probably underscored the significance of the occasion. The more modest gift I received from the mayor, a set of keys to the Jewish cemetery of Brzostek, felt very appropriate and is certainly greatly cherished.

21. The two Jewish journalists who reported the story in the foreign press predictably emphasized a one-dimensional Jewish view, although (to be fair) the warmth and enthusiasm of the local population was certainly given proper coverage, especially the return of the tombstones; see Dina Rosell, "Brzostek's Moving Moment of History," *Jewish Tribune* (London), July 20, 2009, 16, and Johanna Ginsberg, "Family Helps Polish Town Reclaim Its Painful Past: Survivor and His Kin Return for Restoration of Gutted Cemetery," *New Jersey Jewish News,* July 30, 2009, an article based on a long interview with Mark Schönwetter. The local Brzostek magazine *Wiadomości Brzosteckie* carried a particularly long article on the reconsecration in its July 2009 issue, which included not only a dozen photos of the event (including a picture of the participants on the front cover) but also reproduced as its centerfold the full two pages of the signatures of the Brzostek schoolchildren who signed the American birthday card in 1926.

22. Perhaps one indication of the organic growth of memory is the substantial coverage of the 2012 events in the Polish media. In addition to the official website of the Brzostek municipality, which posted an article and over 250 photos under the rubric "70th anniversary of the extinction of the Jews of Brzostek," as well as a 25-minute film showing highlights of the ceremonies (see "Dzień Pamięci Żydów z Brzostku," http://www.itvpoludnie.pl/wiadomosci /Dzien-Pamieci-Zydow-z-Brzostka,898), the website of the neighboring small town of Kołaczyce, where the mass grave in the Podzamcze forest is located, also posted a 20-minute film showing highlights of the consecration ceremony of the new memorial there, which was available

A Jew, a Cemetery, and a Polish Village | 263

for several months afterward. The ceremonies were also featured in a front-page article in the weekend supplement of *Dziennik Polski* for July 6, 2012 ("Brzostek mój dom," http://www .dziennikpolski24.pl/pl/magazyny/magazyn-piatek/1230253-brzostek-moj-dom.html), which interestingly included some Holocaust narratives. The story included details about how Israel Schönwetter (Mark's father) renounced the opportunity to escape and instead ended up with the rest of the Brzostek Jews in the Podzamcze forest, as well as a tragic story from Ruth Wachner Pagirsky, an eighty-six-year-old woman born in Berlin who came to the Brzostek ceremonies in 2012. She had been visiting her grandparents in Brzostek in 1942 (then aged sixteen), only to see them being shot publicly in the market square for refusing to follow the order of a German soldier who wanted her grandmother to cut off the beard and side-curls of her grandfather. There were at least two international English-language reports about the Brzostek ceremonies: one article in the *Times of Israel* (Connie Webber, "Poles and Jews Restore the Jewish Memory of Brzostek," July 1, 2012) and one that appeared in a news report of the JTA (Jewish Telegraphic Agency) on June 19, 2012, from Sydney, Australia, focusing on the dedication of the new memorial in the Roman Catholic cemetery in Brzostek to the Polish woman who had rescued two Jewish girls during the German occupation ("Tomb of Courageous Polish Non-Jew Is Rededicated," http://www.jta.org/news/article/2012/06/19/3098381/tomb-of-courageous -polish-non-jew-is-rededicated).

12 The Museum of the History of Polish Jews

A Postwar, Post-Holocaust, Post-Communist Story

Barbara Kirshenblatt-Gimblett

THE DECISION TO call Warsaw's newest museum the Museum of the History of Polish Jews is strategic. By referring to Polish Jews, rather than Jews in Poland, the museum's name points to the integral and transnational nature of the story—integral, because Jews were (and are) not only "in" Poland but also "of" Poland, and transnational because their story is not confined to the territory of Poland. To speak of Polish Jews rather than Polish Jewry is to keep open the diversity of Polish Jews, rather than to treat them as one body. To not be the Jewish Museum Warsaw, the pattern of Jewish museums in Hohenems, Vienna, Berlin, Munich, Prague, Brussels, Copenhagen, Budapest, Dublin, Moscow, and London, among others, is to question assumptions about what constitutes a "Jewish museum" in postwar Europe. Last but not least, the Warsaw museum does not differentiate and join Jewish museum and Holocaust (or tolerance) center, in contrast with the new Jewish Museum and Tolerance Center in Moscow.

Once home to the largest Jewish community in the world, Poland today is home to one of the smallest, the result of genocide, emigration, and assimilation. Most Jews of "Polish origin" broadly conceived do not live in Poland. They have created Jewish museums in their new homes and dedicate them largely to their successful immigrant histories in places where they now form a critical mass. While the Holocaust looms large for them as for Jews everywhere, the history of Polish Jews before and after the Holocaust does not. Those whose families once lived in the historic territory of Poland make up an estimated 70 percent of the more than 13 million Jews in the world today. They should be prime stakeholders in a Museum of the History of Polish Jews in Poland, in the very place where their deep ancestral story took place, rather than in New York or Tel Aviv or Melbourne or Cape Town. The relationship of Polish Jews to their own history, to Poland, and to those who live in Poland today is fraught. No less sensitive is the relationship of Poles who are not Jewish—in Poland and abroad—to the Jewish past of their hometowns and cities, and no less important is the history of Polish Jews to how they understand themselves and their own history.

The Museum of the History of Polish Jews is an agent in the history that it presents and not simply a mirrored reflection of it. To better understand the transformative potential of this museum in postwar, post-Holocaust, and not least post-Communist Poland, this chapter provides an account of its evolution and compares it with the Jewish Museum and Tolerance Center, which opened in November 2013 in Moscow.

Rising from the Rubble

The Association of the Jewish Historical Institute of Poland, a small Jewish nongovernmental organization established in Poland right after the war, initiated the project to create a Museum of the History of Polish Jews shortly after the United States Holocaust Memorial Museum opened in 1993 in Washington, DC. It was an idea of Grażyna Pawlak, executive director of the association at the time, and her colleagues. They were impressed by the Washington museum. In 1998, Jerzy Halbersztadt, a historian and at the time project director for Poland of the Washington Holocaust Museum, became the director of the Polish museum project and led its development until 2011. The museum, its architecture, and its core exhibition are a result of his vision and leadership. A key figure in the early concept for the Warsaw project was Jeshajahu Weinberg, the Washington museum's first director and the visionary who conceptualized its permanent exhibition. He had earlier created Beit Hatfutsot: Museum of the Diaspora, a pioneering narrative museum that opened in Tel Aviv in 1978.

For the first ten years, the Museum of the History of Polish Jews was a project, not an institution. The association had no money, and there was no museum as yet, so the project team did the one thing they could do—they created a plan for the exhibition. This museum is unusual because it was created from the inside out. The creators did not start with the building and then think about the exhibition. They started with the story the museum would tell. That story would define the kind of institution the museum should be: a cultural and educational center dedicated to the history of Polish Jews. The building would need to be an appropriate expression of that mission and place of open dialogue inspired by it.

My connection to the project began in 2002, when Jerzy Halbersztadt invited me to spend a week in Warsaw to review the Outline of the Historical Program and the Masterplan for the exhibition, which Event Communications, a design company in London, had developed. They began working on the project in 2000 and completed the Masterplan in 2003. Event Communications specializes in multimedia narrative exhibitions. Such exhibitions start with a story, rather than with a collection. At that point, the project had a very modest collection be-cause it was starting from scratch. It had only just begun to gather material for the exhibition. To tell a story of one thousand years, we could not limit ourselves to what could be shown through objects from a collection, even if we had free access to every public and private collection of material related to the history of Polish Jews. There are simply not enough of the right objects to support this epic story.

In 2005, what had been a project became a museum, at least on paper. The association succeeded in forming a unique private-public partnership with the Ministry of Culture and National Heritage and the Warsaw city council to estab-lish the museum as an institution. The city gave the land, covered the cost of the building—approximately $65 million—and oversaw the construction. The min-istry was responsible for the basic operating costs. The association was to create, produce, and install the exhibition, and raise the funds, about $40 million.

In the same year, an international architectural competition for the building was held. This was the first successful international architectural competition for a public building in Poland, and probably still the only one. Architects who par-ticipated in the competition were given the exhibition Masterplan and asked to design a building that would communicate the mission of the museum and pro-vide a proper home for the exhibition.

As a result of the competition, there was now an architect, Rainer Mahlamäki of Finland, and concept for the building. His winning design was noteworthy for its deference to the Monument to the Warsaw Ghetto Heroes thanks to its mini-malist exterior, clad in glass fins, and geometry, which echoes the shape of the monument. The drama of the building is inside. Indeed, the interior of the build-ing required an engineering tour de force to create the monumental organic forms and largest (and suspended) glass window in Poland. The result is a house of light, reflection, transparency, and openness, with vistas right through the building to the monument on one side and the memorial park on the other. The interior, with its soaring volumes and warm sandy surface, creates a chasm across which there is a bridge, a fitting metaphor for the history of Polish Jews, whose history was fractured by the Holocaust, and for the museum, whose mission is to create bridges across time, continents, and people.

The groundbreaking followed shortly after. We were ready for the next stage of exhibition development, scheme design (there were three stages—Masterplan, Scheme Design, and Detail Design). At this point, in April 2006, I was invited to join the team as the program director of the core exhibition. In 2011, with detail design complete and the production of the exhibition about to begin, we began working with Nizio Design International, a Polish design firm. The Museum of the History of Polish Jews opened the building and began its educational and cultural programs in April 2013 on the occasion of the seventieth anniversary of the Warsaw Ghetto Uprising. The grand opening and unveiling of the core exhibition is scheduled for October 2014.

The museum tells the story of what was once the largest Jewish community in the world, and also a center of the Jewish world on the very site where that history took place. The museum faces the Monument to the Warsaw Ghetto Heroes. It stands on the site of the Warsaw Ghetto and prewar Jewish neighborhood. It completes the memorial complex. Until now, to honor those who died, one remembered how they died—at the monument. Today, we can honor them, and those who came before and after, by remembering how they lived—at the museum.

The museum is one of the largest museums dedicated to Jewish history in Europe, with about 175,000 square feet, 130,000 square feet of usable space, and more than 45,000 square feet dedicated to the core exhibition. It is now in Warsaw's tourist guidebooks as one of the top ten attractions in the city, along with the Royal Castle. Some 180,000 visitors came to the museum in the first four months, 6,000 of them in six hours in May 2013 on Warsaw's annual Night of Museums—and this before the core exhibition opened. Projected figures are over 500,000 visitors a year.

Narrative Space in the Absence and Presence of Objects

The exhibition uses the principle of narrative space to present the one-thousand-year history of Polish Jews. An exhibition is not only a visual experience. Above all, it is a spatial experience. Only if the visitor moves does the story unfold—in a particular place, in a specific moment, and not simply in the abstract space of a gallery. Scenography plays a vital role in defining the space of the story. Our approach is more black box than white cube, more theater than gallery. Each of the seven historical galleries has its unique architecture and scenography. Only when visitors step into the core exhibition will they understand why we describe this exhibition as a "theater of history."

Visitors enter the story from a grand staircase that leads from the parterre to a "forest," a space of historical imagination where they will hear the legends Jews told themselves about how they came to Poland, why they stayed, and how Poland got its name: "Polin" in Hebrew, which according to legend means "rest here" (*po-lin*). When entering the hand-painted medieval gallery, visitors cross the threshold between legend and history. They experience a shift from night to day, from forest to clearing, from the first signs of Jewish presence in the eleventh century to the creation of complete Jewish communities, at least fifty of them, by 1500.

As they enter the next gallery, *Paradisus Iudaeorum*, visitors have a spectacular view of a 430-square-foot topographical model of Kraków and nearby

Kazimierz, where there was a Jewish neighborhood. The model of the city is animated by a panoramic multimedia projection directly onto its three-dimensional surface, inviting the interaction of visitors, who become walkers in the city.

Exiting this open-plan gallery, which presents the rise of Jewish civilization in the Polish-Lithuanian Commonwealth, visitors then enter the intimate space of the private noble town. This story is set in the period following the 1648–1649 Khmelnytsky Uprising and other cataclysmic events that decimated Jewish communities and left the Commonwealth in ruins. It was in these towns, where Jews made up a large percentage of the population, that a distinctive form of Jewish settlement emerged. Never a literal recreation, these settings are composed from projections of period images on the facades of thematic spaces: marketplace, tavern, home, church, and synagogue.

In contrast with the intangible media of light, sound, and projection is the tangible wooden synagogue ceiling and roof, the centerpiece of this gallery, which was created with traditional tools, techniques, and materials. Every mark on every timber tells the story of a specific building tradition, a particular tool, and the unique hand that held it. The timbers are "signed" thanks to these marks. The names of donors have also been inscribed on the pegs that hold the whole structure together.

With the partitioning of the Commonwealth by the Russian, Prussian, and Austrian empires, modernity challenged the integral Jewish way of life that had flourished in the Jewish towns of the Commonwealth. A multimedia railway station symbolizes the rapid pace of change. The story of Jewish life in the partitions during the long nineteenth century comes to an end with World War I and the collapse of the empires.

The centerpiece of the interwar years gallery that follows is a street created by means of projections on relief street facades. Some historians view this short period as a "second golden age," despite economic hardship and rising antisemitism during the late 1930s. This was a period of dynamic Jewish political parties and social movements, and vibrant modern Jewish culture in its many forms.

Perhaps the clearest example of "story space" expressed architecturally is the Warsaw Ghetto section of the Holocaust gallery. "Life in the shadow of death" is set in claustrophobic spaces—the walls are slanted, the atmosphere disorienting and anxious. Visitors climb stairs and stand on a bridge like the one that joined two parts of the Warsaw Ghetto. Like those in the ghetto, they look down on the "Aryan street" and see what seems like normal life. Visitors will encounter the reality of that world—occupied Poland under German terror—only when they exit the second part of the ghetto exhibit, "life in the face of death," and enter the "Aryan street" from below. They then see what they saw from the bridge, but from a new perspective. What seemed normal from afar is revealed as a terrifying reality up close.

In 1939, there were about 3.3 million Jews in Poland. By war's end, 90 percent of them had been murdered. But the story does not end with the Holocaust. For those few who survived, the dilemma was whether to stay or leave. The two options confront each other on opposing walls that line the postwar years gallery. By 1989, although there were very few Jews in Poland, there were also signs of the renewal of Jewish life on a small scale and growing Jewish presence in Polish consciousness. Again, visitors experience the historical moment spatially. They are no longer in a gallery. They now find themselves enfolded in the building's very architecture—a space that soars from below ground to the roof of the building, a space filled with natural light and hope.

Challenges

Money, time, and the scope and scale of the project itself were a challenge, as was starting from scratch with everything—original research, collection development, and above all conceptualization of both the museum and exhibition. We did not want to present a master narrative or to reduce the main messages of the exhibition to sound bites. Rather, we had to create a dynamic environment that orients the visitor and encourages him or her to explore, which required a balance between clarity and richness.

It was not easy to convince people of the value of creating the painted ceiling and timber-framed roof of the wooden synagogue that once stood in Gwoździec, today in Ukraine—and especially in the way that we did. Today, this 85 percent scale structure stands in the eighteenth-century gallery. Installed beneath this celestial canopy is the 100 percent scale Gwoździec painted bimah, the platform from which public readings from the Torah scroll take place. This ensemble is the centerpiece of the gallery and signature feature of the museum as a whole. From the exhibition level, visitors look up to the ceiling. From the public level above, they can see the timber-framed roof, which extends up through an opening into the modern architecture of the museum itself. Through a cutaway in the roof, visitors can see its timber-framed structure.

We worked with Handshouse Studio, a nonprofit educational organization in Massachusetts whose mission is to recover lost objects. While the original object, in the sense of the original material, can never be recovered, the knowledge of how to build it can—but only by building it, which is what we did, using traditional tools, materials, and techniques. It was expensive and it was complicated to organize—about three hundred international volunteers, craftspeople, scholars, and artists collaborated in creating the structure in nine workshops in the open-air folk architecture museum in Sanok, as well as in masonry synagogues in towns and cities across Poland. This project represents the gold standard in museum education and community outreach. Local residents were invited into the workshops and encouraged to take an interest in the Jewish past of their town and its synagogue. It was a challenge to convince the project's management that this approach was worth the cost and effort—it would have been considerably cheaper to have a theater prop maker simply make a copy of the painted ceiling.[1] In the end, this is a new kind of object, an actuality, and not a copy, facsimile, recreation, reproduction, or reconstruction—it is a recovered object. Its value lies in the knowledge recovered by building it.

Expectations

Perhaps the biggest challenge as the opening of the core exhibition neared is the expectations of our multiple stakeholders and audiences. Understandings of this history differ, as do expectations as to how it should be told and with what emphasis. Some worry that we are creating a museum of antisemitism—that the museum will be anti-Polish, or not pro-Polish enough. Others worry that we will avoid the subject of antisemitism or treat antisemitism as relatively insignificant. Some are concerned that we will not give enough emphasis to prominent Communists who were of Jewish origin—and to the related problem of Żydokomuna, the stereotype that all Jews were Communists and all Communists, or the worst of them, were Jews. Or that too little attention will be given to the Righteous among the Nations, those who saved Jews during the Holocaust, or alternatively to those who betrayed Jews.

Some believe that the story of Polish Jews should be told more or less strictly within the territory of Poland in any given period. Others believe that the history of Polish Jews is an international and transnational story, that Polish Jews are a part of a wider Jewish diaspora, and the story of Polish Jews as a diaspora should be prominent. Some believe that the exhibition should begin and end with the Holocaust. There are debates about perspective: Do we tell the story from a "Polish" or "Jewish" perspective? Or from some other "objective" perspective or from multiple perspectives? Is this a Polish museum, a Jewish museum, or something else? Who is the museum for? Is it primarily for the Polish public or for an international Jewish public—in addition to anyone else who might visit it?

One of the biggest challenges is the expectation that the history of Polish Jews is at bottom a history of Polish-Jewish relations, and that assimilation should be a prominent, if not the most prominent, thread throughout this history—assimilation as a mark of success, indeed, the ultimate success, of Polish Jews. The emotionally charged need to feature exemplary "Poles of Jewish origin" comes not only from Polish stakeholders but also from Polish Jews themselves. The desire to showcase achievement arises at least in part from what Zygmunt Bauman has called "unrequited love." Their love of Poland was not reciprocated. "Unrequited love" is all the more bitter when experienced with stigma. The celebration of exceptional individuals, especially those who are highly assimilated, is a way that some individuals manage what sociologist Erving Goffman has called "spoiled identity," an identity "spoiled" by antisemitic stereotypes and traumatic experiences, by feelings of shame and fear, and by the ultimate insult of outright rejection. Bauman's personal story is a painful case in point.[2]

Who Is Telling Whose Story to Whom and Why?

How perfectly do mission, story, stakeholder, and audience align? In Warsaw—and in European Jewish museums more generally—the fit is imperfect, and it is in this imperfection that their great potential lies. "Perfect fit" museums—Jewish museums that are largely by, about, and for Jews—generally celebrate the success of immigrant Jewish communities or the success of the State of Israel against the dark backdrop of Europe. They aim to instill pride and confidence, strengthen the Jewish identity of a new generation, and put forward a positive self-image in opposition to negative stereotypes. To put the issue provocatively: Outside of Europe, Jewish museums are often immigration museums by another name. In Israel, almost all are national museums. And in Europe, virtually all are, de facto, Holocaust museums.

At first glance, Jewish museums outside Europe display a neat alignment that binds mission, story, stakeholder, and audience. The perfect fit of American Jewish museums (like their counterparts in the United Kingdom, Australia, and South Africa) align mission—strengthening Jewish identity and continuity—with support from their local Jewish communities.

The idea that a Jewish museum outside of Israel would be initiated, created, and supported primarily by the state is, from an American perspective, surprising. I do not know of even a single similar case in the United States, but for much of postwar Europe this is rather the rule. Indeed, it is inconceivable outside Europe that the national government, state, or city would create a Jewish museum in the relative absence, indifference, or even opposition of local Jews, rather than at their urging. "We're here. We don't need a museum," some Jews in Vienna and Berlin have said, and their history as postwar immigrants, often from the Soviet Union, is not the history that local Jewish museums in Europe generally tell. That the local Jewish community living there today could be indifferent to—or even against—the creation of a Jewish museum is simply counterintuitive from a North American perspective. It would be less surprising if *non-Jews* were the skeptics. This is decidedly not the case in Poland.

Recent European Jewish museums are essentially attempts to recover stories of success that have been overshadowed by the Holocaust and persisting stigma of antisemitic stereotypes. While European Jewish museums generally bring the story forward to the present, Jewish museums located outside of Europe more often turn their backs on postwar Europe. For such museums, the story of Jews in

Europe is a closed story. For this and other reasons, Jewish museums in Europe are poised to play a unique role—to reopen a story largely forgotten, untold, and unknown.

To open the story is to speak to the particular conditions of postwar, post-Holocaust, and post-Communist Europe—and to unsettle easy assumptions about who is Jewish, what Jewish looks like, what it means, and why it matters. This is not quite what one might expect in the "perfect fit" Jewish museums—they may be too perfectly aligned for these to be such pressing questions. More pressing for them is the work of consolidation, confirmation, affirmation, and celebration of the Jewish experience in all of its diversity, often expressed as Jewish "identity," continuity, and contributions. The misalignment of Jewish museums in Europe makes them more interesting because it has the potential to shake up the assumptions of those—myself included—who have been privileged to live in "intact" or "whole" Jewish families and communities, the very communities that create and support the Jewish museums that reflect their experience, in North America, Australia, South Africa, and Israel.

To say that European Jewish museums are "Holocaust museums by another name" is to think in terms of two modes of Holocaust memory. The first is to remember the genocide. This is the mission of bona fide Holocaust museums. They generally embed this catastrophic event along an axis of genocide rather than along an axis of Jewish history. Even when Holocaust museums locate the genocide along an axis of history, it is along the lines of various national histories—French, German, Macedonian, Lithuanian—but not Jewish history. Indeed, Salo Baron, the great Jewish historian, did not consider the Holocaust to be part of Jewish history. He believed that it was part of European history, part of the history of World War II.[3]

The first mode of Holocaust memory honors those who died by documenting how they died—the genocide. This is perpetrator history, even when largely reported by the victims, an approach pioneered by Yad Vashem. The second mode, a defining feature of European Jewish museums, honors those who died by remembering how they lived and does so in the very places where their stories took place and continue. It is in this respect that Jewish museums in Europe today are "Holocaust museums by another name." It is no accident that the Jewish Museum Berlin sets the two-thousand-year history of German Jews within an architectural program that is Holocaust through and through: its jagged form, a fractured Star of David, brutal materials—concrete and zinc—constant reminders of violence and void.

In contrast, the architectural program for the Museum of the History of Polish Jews sets one thousand years of the history of the Polish Jews within a house of glass. Located on the site of the Warsaw Ghetto and Warsaw's prewar Jewish neighborhood, the building faces the Monument to the Ghetto Heroes. This building, with its understated geometry and shimmering glass fins, its transparent and reflective architecture, houses a multimedia narrative exhibition and educational and cultural program that completes the story and the memorial complex.

A challenge for this museum, as for virtually all Jewish museums in Europe, is to resist an overwhelming teleological narrative driving inexorably to the Holocaust as its inevitable endpoint for the preceding millennium of Jewish history. Holocaust narratives start with hate. The logical endpoint—the teleology of hate— is genocide. The core exhibition of this museum does not begin with hate and does not end with genocide—the Holocaust was a cataclysmic event, to be sure, but the story does not end there. Nor can antisemitism account for what made possible a thousand years of continuous Jewish presence in Polish lands, the place that became home to the largest Jewish community in the world and a center of the Jewish world. Jews living here created a civilization whose legacy lives on in Jewish communities across the world today, including Poland.

A Museum in Place and Time

What does *postwar* mean? A period after death and destruction, after a radical reconfiguration of European space and massive relocation of populations. Where does the wider society find itself, in a story that is defined for them by war, rather than by genocide? Some feel that their traumas have been overshadowed by the success of Holocaust commemoration. At the Museum of the History of Polish Jews, the wider public should be able to find themselves virtually *everywhere* in a story that offers an integral history, a history "in common," if not a "common history." Some experiences were "shared" and others not, even during the same events in the same time and place.

What does *post-Holocaust* mean for countries that once had large and vibrant Jewish communities? Today, they may have small—even minute—Jewish communities and ones that are differently constituted than before the war. Is the museum in any sense for or about them?

What does *post-Communist* mean for the Eastern bloc? In the case of Poland, it means the very possibility of creating the museum. This would have been inconceivable under Communism—and there are now Jewish museums and Holocaust museums being planned in other post-Communist societies.

A Tale of Two Post-Communist Museums: Moscow and Warsaw

In Moscow, "Jewish museum" means something else altogether. Two new Jewish museums recently opened there. The Museum of the Jewish History in Russia, a small private museum, opened in May 2011 and has formed an interesting collection of objects. The Jewish Museum and Tolerance Center opened in November 2012 in the vast Bakhmetyevsky Bus Garage, a treasure of constructivist industrial architecture designed by Konstantin Melnikov and Vladimir Shukhov and completed in 1926.[4] The state gave the building to the Federation of Russian Jewish Communities in 1999. Today, the Jewish Museum and Tolerance Center is part of the largest complex of Jewish services in Moscow—an estimated 150,000 Jews, although the last census puts the number at 70,000, are dispersed across this megalopolis. Those services include a synagogue and community center, mikvah (ritual bath), Jewish day school and yeshiva, Shaarei Tsedek (health services) for seniors, kosher soup kitchen and grocery, medical center, publishing house—and now a museum. The Moscow museum is a project of the Federation of Russian Jewish Communities, which is led by Habad Lubavitch Hassidim. This is not the first museum created by Habad—the first is the Jewish Children's Museum, which opened in 2007 across the street from the Lubavitch headquarters on 770 Eastern Parkway in Brooklyn, New York.[5] But the Moscow museum is by far the largest and most ambitious—and a sign of others to come.

There is a "perfect fit" of sorts here, and its expression sets this museum apart from all others in Europe, if not the world. Like the Museum of the History of Polish Jews, this museum offers a multimedia narrative exhibition dedicated to the history, in this case, of Russian Jews. There was a plan to have Hollywood's Universal Studios create the exhibition, but finally Ralph Appelbaum Associates in New York City, one of the largest and most prestigious exhibition design firms in the world, was chosen. Appelbaum took responsibility for most of the project, including much of the research—in consultation with a team of historians in the United States, Russia, and elsewhere. The final result is a professionally prepared history exhibition, wrapped around a Jewish core that gives expression to the essential values, vision, and mission of the organizers—in a word, a unique Jewish museum.

Habad's mission is to strengthen Jewish religious observance and to reach out to Jews who are not observant. The rationale here is that Jews who do not go to the synagogue may go to a museum, and Habad will meet them there. To be sure, the museum is not for Jews only, and Russian and international visitors will find much of interest too, but the message to them is of a different order. Running down the center of the building is the Jewish core of the entire exhibition and expression of the Moscow museum's essential and essentially Jewish message:

- The history of the Jewish people according to the Bible is presented in the Beginnings Theater, a "4-D Animated Experience," which ends with the destruction of the Second Temple in 70 CE. The fourth dimension is tactile and propioceptic—shaking seats and mist.
- The story of the Diaspora includes an introduction to Judaism and ends with the partitioning of the Polish-Lithuanian Commonwealth, thanks to which Jews suddenly appear en masse in the Russian empire.

- The shtetl, a transhistorical—though essentially premodern—icon of an integral Jewish way of life, consists of a synagogue and interactive Torah scroll, heder (Jewish religious primary school) and animated book, shtibl (Hasidic prayer and study room), and multimedia Sabbath table, as well as a market stall and presentation of Jewish occupations, but no church.
- A memorial to victims of the Holocaust. It faces the far end of the gallery, where there are dramatic panoramic films of World War II and the Holocaust.

Lining the outer walls of this Jewish core is "Judaism: A Living Religion," a transhistorical presentation of Jewish religious life and counternarrative to the Paradise Lost of the shtetl. The message of this core is that the integral Jewish way of life represented by the shtetl might have been lost to assimilation and Communism, but Judaism remains a living religion despite everything, transcending time and enduring against all odds. The Jewish core is spectacular—modeled figures, recreated environments, large multimedia elements, engaging interactive presentations. Judaism: A Living Religion is largely graphic, with some objects, and gives greater emphasis to Jewish religious observance in Russia today.

Confronting the Jewish core are the historical exhibits along the outermost walls of the exhibition space. Experienced independently of the Jewish core, they appear to be a straightforward presentation of the history of Russian Jews from the nineteenth century to the present, period by period—through vivid panoramic films, recreated settings, interactive components, video interviews, and occasionally objects and documents. But seen as the envelope that encloses the Jewish core, they represent the forces that all but destroyed Jewish religious life in Russia: assimilation, secularization, genocide, and Communism. In this way, the exhibition's counternarrative harnesses the agency of display to reverse the course of history—a history that suppressed Jewish life and Jewish religious life in Russia. This is the way the exhibition speaks to its Jewish visitors. The expectation is that the museum's Russian and international visitors will be most interested in the Beginnings Theater and its Bible stories, the World War II films, and the Tolerance Center.

How does the Museum of the History of Polish Jews, also a multimedia narrative museum, differ from the Jewish Museum and Tolerance Center in Moscow? Whereas the Moscow museum projects a definitive future, the Warsaw museum offers an open-ended past. The present is a work in progress leading to a future as yet unknown. Polish visitors are expected to be in the majority, though time will tell, and the majority of Jewish visitors will come from abroad—the Jewish community of Poland, once the largest in Europe, is today one of the smallest.

While both museums offer a multimedia narrative exhibition—and both employed the best international design firms—the key messages and approach to historical narration are very different. The history of Polish Jews, as told at the Warsaw museum, begins in the tenth century. The history of Jews in Russia proper—when they come to understand themselves as Russian Jews is another question—begins with the incorporation of a large partition of the Polish-Lithuanian Common-wealth into the Russian empire at the end of the eighteenth century.

The decision to start the story with Genesis, as a story of the Jewish people, is coherent with the Jewish religious core—and Jewish essence—at the very center of the Moscow museum's exhibition. So too is the decision to place the transhistori-cal shtetl—the Paradise Lost of an integral Jewish way of life—within the Jewish core (as already noted, there is no church in this shtetl), and to divide this core from the wider history that encloses—and threatened—it. It is for this reason that this shtetl is the true starting point for this telling of the history of Russian Jews. Shtetl represents what was lost to the forces of modernization. What replaced it is represented by a nineteenth-century café in Odessa, where visitors can join Sholem Aleichem, Simon Dubnow, and Pauline Wengeroff, beautifully rendered white figures, at interactive café tables and explore modern Jewish culture and politics. Surrounding the café tables is a panoramic multimedia presentation of the processes of modernization and Jewish responses.

The Warsaw museum's approach is based on different metahistorical prin-ciples.[6] First, Jewish religious life is integrated into the overall narrative. It is not treated transhistorically or normatively, but rather historically and situationally, as an evolving and adaptable part of Jewish life. Visitors are introduced to fun-damental aspects of Judaism incrementally as they arise in particular situations and periods, and not within a display dedicated to Judaism as such. We draw on rabbinical responsa, codifications of Jewish law, commentaries, autobiographies, and mystical and homiletic works to illuminate the specificity of Jewish spiritual life in various periods, whether the emergence of new spiritual trends, efforts to reform Jewish religious education, crises of religious authority, new forms of re-ligious leadership, or new ways of defending tradition in the face of new chal-lenges—what Hans Ulrich Wehler calls "defensive modernization."[7]

It is in the interwar gallery that we "deconstruct" the icon, first by presenting the historical reality of Jewish life in towns and cities across the length and breadth of the Second Polish Republic—without a trace of nostalgia. About 50 percent of the Jewish population before 1939 lived in large cities (Warsaw, Vilna, Kraków, Łódź, Lwów, Białystok) and the rest in towns large and small. The towns and smaller cities were fully twentieth-century places, albeit on a more limited scale. It is in Kazimierz Dolny, the setting for so many films and plays, novels and poems, memoirs and travel reportage, paintings and drawings, that we present the mak-ing and unmaking of the icon most fully.

Third, we treat the millennium of continuous Jewish presence in the historic territory of Poland as an integral history, and not as a separate Jewish history in a

Polish context. The history of Polish Jews is an integral part of the history of Poland, and the history of Poland is not complete without a history of Polish Jews. This is a *relational history*, which is not the same as a history of Polish-Jewish relations. A history "in common"—a story of coexistence, competition, conflict, and cooperation—is not the same as a "common history." Indeed, multiple perspectives on "events" (are they the same events if experienced so differently?) are central to the historical narration. It is in this sense that we take a relational rather than contextual approach. This is not about a Polish context into which Jews are placed. The history of Polish Jews is not a footnote to Polish history.

Last but not least, we strive to avoid a *defensive history*—a history whose starting point is the correction of misperceptions, antisemitic stereotypes, and the like. A proper historical account should achieve that goal, but not defensively, which is generally the starting point for tolerance education. Rather, our approach might be termed "constructive engagement," and our goal is to create a "trusted zone" for engaging difficult subjects. Like the Moscow museum, the Warsaw museum is itself part of the history it presents and an agent in that history.

Resisting Teleology

The teleological pull of the Holocaust is felt perhaps most strongly in Poland, the epicenter of the Shoah. The Germans built all the death camps on Polish soil. Material evidence of the genocide is pervasive in the Polish landscape, whether as death camps or mass graves. So too is the memorialization of the genocide in dedicated memorials, exhibitions, books, and public debates. When Poland and Jews are uttered in the same breath, the immediate association is Holocaust and "Polish antisemitism."

In a sense, the whole country is already a Holocaust museum—that is how organized groups who come to Poland to commemorate the Shoah experience Poland. If not for the story that the Museum of the History of Polish Jews tells, one thousand years of Jewish life in Poland would vanish into the axis of genocide, and the history of Polish Jews would be reduced to a lesson in (in)tolerance. The world would forever know more about how Jews died than about how they lived—and would know virtually nothing about how they continue to live, albeit on a small scale, in Poland today. Recovering a story of one thousand years matters here in a special way—as does a historical narrative that situates the Holocaust within that long period. This story must not be reduced to a history of antisemitism and a teleology of genocide.

Jewish museums in Europe have a special role to play. They are in the very places where the history they present took place. They are a product and agent of that history. Their prime opportunity is to take a closed story, a story closed by the Holocaust and then Communism, and to open it again. The story is not over. Many people say that "the story ends with the Holocaust, the Holocaust is the absolute end"—and that is indeed how the story is often told. But here, in Europe, Jewish museums take the story all the way up to the present and into the future. Indeed, the new core exhibition at the Jewish Museum Vienna, which opened in November 2013, begins with the postwar period and works back in time.

As already noted, the number of Jews in Poland today is small—those who can be counted number about four thousand, with estimates of the rest ranging from twenty to sixty thousand. But Jewish presence in Polish consciousness is enormous. We take this situation—small numbers, big presence—as the organizing concept for the last chapter in the historical narration. The Museum of the History of Polish Jews as an educational and cultural institution—with the exhibition of the history of Polish Jews at its core—is also a way to support the renewal of Jewish life in Poland, however small in scale. That renewal is taking many forms, only one of which is religious. An important task is to lift the fear and shame that led parents to hide their "Jewish origins" from their children. The "misalignments" of so-called Jewish museums of Europe, the Warsaw museum included, could challenge assumptions of Jews living elsewhere about what it means to be a Jew, to be a whole Jew, a true Jew, an authentic Jew—to see what "Jewish" looks like in postwar, post-Holocaust, postcolonial, post-Communist Europe.

Jews are a "sensitive subject" in Poland, as is the stigma of "Polish antisemitism." People of good will in Poland are acutely aware of its specter. The Warsaw museum has a role to play here too, a role complementary to, but different from, teaching tolerance. The history of Polish Jews must not be reduced to a history of antisemitism and Polish-Jewish relations to a history of Polish antisemitism.

Once very diverse—multidenominational, multilingual, and multinational—Poland today is relatively homogeneous: borders were redrawn, populations were relocated, 3 million Polish Jews were lost to the Holocaust, most of those who survived left, and most of those who stayed assimilated. Today, Poland is essentially Catholic and Polish, though a closer look reveals greater diversity both religious and regional. Nonetheless, immigration to Poland is not yet the significant factor that it is in other parts of Europe, while emigration, whether temporary or permanent, is strong thanks in part to the European Union. The history of Polish Jews, one of several minorities that formed part of the fabric of Poland throughout most of its history, is a way to recover Poland's historic diversity.

Finally, Jewish museums can offer the constructive model of engagement noted above. They can complement Holocaust museums, which start from the negative past. Jewish museums also address difficult issues, but within a longer and wider historical narrative. While the chasm created by the Holocaust can never be repaired, European Jewish museums can build bridges across the rupture. Those bridges could reconnect Jews abroad to their own histories in Europe. They could reconnect people living in Europe today to the Jewish past of their own towns and cities—and to those who descend from the Jews who once lived there.

Notes

This chapter is adapted from the keynote address delivered at the annual meeting of the Association of European Jewish Museums in 2011 in London. I would like to thank colleagues at that event for their comments and those who were kind enough to read an earlier version of this chapter and offer their suggestions: Shelley Horenstein, Erica Lehrer, Samuel Kassow, Ewa Klękot, Arkady Kovelman, Corinne Kratz, Jeffrey Shandler, and Marcin Wodziński.

1. The synagogue project was made possible by a generous gift from Irene Pletka.

2. Zygmunt Bauman and Keith Tester, *Conversations with Zygmunt Bauman* (Cambridge: Polity Press, 2001), 17; Erving Goffman, *Sitigma: Notes on the Management of Spoiled Identity* (New York: Simon and Schuster, 1963).

3. See David Engel, *Historians of the Jews and the Holocaust.* (Stanford, CA: Stanford University Press, 2010).

4. I visited these two museums in February 2013 together with my colleagues from the Museum of the History of Polish Jews. I spent two full days at the Jewish Museum and Tolerance Center and have agreed to serve on their Academic Advisory Board.

5. Barbara Kirshenblatt-Gimblett et al., "Jewish Children's Museum: A Virtual Roundtable on Material Religion," *Material Religion* 3, no. 3 (2007): 405–426.

6. Moshe Rosman, "Categorically Jewish, Distinctly Polish: The Museum of the History of Polish Jews and the New Polish-Jewish Metahistory," *JSIJ Jewish Studies: An Internet Journal* 10 (2012): 361–387.

7. Cited in Marcin Wodziński, "How Modern Is an Antimodernist Movement? The Emergence of Hasidic Politics in Congress Poland," *AJS Review* 31, no. 2 (2007): 24.

Epilogue
Jewish Spaces and Their Future

Diana Pinto

THE VERY TOPIC of this book of scholarly articles—Poland's Jewish spaces, their different natures, their growing numbers, their geographical diversity, and their importance in the context of Poland's own democratic development—would have been simply unimaginable even for the most optimistic observer of the early 1990s. Poland "back then," with its minuscule Jewish community resurfacing in a country whose own tormented national history produced a long tradition of martyrology as well as Communist and Catholic taboos, a country with a strong reputation, in the eyes of the wider world, for unremitting antisemitism, seemed hardly the context in which one would predict the commemoration of Jewish death, and even more importantly, an ever-growing celebration of Jewish life and culture.

I must confess that the Polish case lay at the furthest point of my horizon when I coined the term "Jewish spaces" in the mid-1990s.[1] I argued then that Clio being Europe's predominant muse, the Jewish past with its physical and symbolic traces, not just of death but even more importantly of life, would inevitably come back to the fore as a vital piece of the continent's culture as it moved toward a democratic pluralist future. Mine was a theoretical exercise. There still was not much to confirm it on the ground.

At the time, I was trying to address a uniquely European condition. Given the extermination of two-thirds of European Jewry in the Holocaust, I argued that remembering the past and celebrating Jewish life across the newly liberated continent could not be the work of Jews and Jewish communities alone. Rather than bemoaning this situation, I saw in the birth of such pluralist Jewish spaces a blessing that could indeed become Europe's Jewish trademark.

Israel was its own Jewish space, and in America, there were sufficient numbers of Jews around to fill all of the positions linked to Jewish community life, broader culture as well as academic studies, so that these habitats remained by and large "Jewish." I am now pleased to see that younger, non-Jewish American scholars specializing in German and Polish history have begun to examine Jewish issues linked to their fields, as some of the chapters in this book attest. But it is Europe that remains the laboratory of Jewish and non-Jewish cooperation in the strengthening of Jewish culture on the continent.

In the 1990s, Poland's Jewish spaces were still by and large inchoate. The country's pluralist democracy—the key element in any viable and flourishing Jewish space—was a work in progress, but the "progress" to many in the Jewish world seemed rather slow, and when it picked up speed, it was seldom given the benefit of the doubt by those Jewish activists bent on taking the memory of Poland's vanished Jews out of the grip of "the Poles."

As the chapters in this book testify, Jewish spaces have not only grown apace with Poland's own youthful pluralist democracy. They have often been at the center of its growing pains, the very symbols over which the wider Polish society has split as it struggles with contending visions of its own national past. Jewish spaces now exist in the smallest of local settings, in the big cities, inside universities, in bookshops, in music festivals, in concert halls, and in restaurants well beyond the initial settings of Kraków and Warsaw. The soon-to-be-opened Museum of the History of Polish Jews may well become their crown jewel, but a crown jewel, it is important to stress, whose right to exist was vehemently disputed for the longest time by many Jews around the world. Poland, in brief, has become a full-fledged European democracy precisely because it can commemorate and celebrate its manifold pasts.

The time has come to reflect now on the larger implications of these European Jewish spaces, of which the Polish case is perhaps the most eloquent. Has their function ended now that most towns, cities, regions, and countries throughout Europe have established or helped to establish—along with their Jewish communities or diasporas—Holocaust memorials, Jewish museums, Jewish cultural centers, renovated former synagogues, and protectively enclosed cemeteries, and helped to foster a rich Jewish book, music, film, video, and photographic culture? Can European societies return to "business as usual," happy that by having paid homage to the Jewish past and present, they have in effect celebrated their own present-day pluralist disposition and values?

I would argue just the opposite. The major pluralist and democratic significance of these Jewish spaces is just beginning to exert its influence. The impact of these spaces will be crucial as nations across Europe confront their multiple identities, including the development of their own brands of European Islam (mainly in Western Europe), but also the incorporation of the continent's numerous indigenous minorities—including Roma—into a wider public discourse. Jewish spaces in this context thus carry a more universal function. They can even serve as models for future Christian spaces, since Christianity is fast becoming another minority religion in an increasingly secular, multicultural Europe. Such spaces help to combat prejudice. They offer more complex national readings, confront head-on historical misunderstandings and taboos, and offer a vision of pluralist life. This is important in today's Europe, where many play with the notion of a golden age of monolithic nation-states, but also in Israel and in the wider Jewish world, where the present-day Jewish diasporic condition is still viewed as fragile and endangered in general, and all the more so in Europe.

To understand the significance and novelty of these Jewish spaces, which bring together Jews and non-Jews in the evocation of Jewish life, one has to situate them in the continuum of identity that goes from the most internal, community-linked settings all the way to the most open-ended universal context. Jewish spaces, it is important to stress, do not encompass internal Jewish community life. Jews, as all other religious or ethnic communities, are masters (within the respect of the national law of course) of their own religious and cultural spaces in which non-Jews can participate but only as guests who have to accept the rules and cultural givens of the house. I call these Jewish-Jewish spaces. Such spaces, such as community-owned museums, can be open to the outside world and even influenced by it, but they belong to Jews.

On the other end of the spectrum, there are the national and universal spaces. Jews participate in them as full-fledged citizens in the former and as human beings like everyone else in the latter. Jewish religious stands, cultural practices, and worldviews are legally protected, integral parts of a bigger democratic and human rights picture. They are listened to and integrated into a wider pluralist setting and inside the universal "cacophony" (think of the internet) as one voice among others. In these contexts, the Jewish narrative has no exclusivity, but it is accepted along with all other narratives in a political climate that is no longer tainted with the institutional and political antisemitism of the prewar past.

The Jewish spaces that concern the authors in this volume occupy a conceptually new middle slot on the identity spectrum. Their originality stems precisely from the fact that Jews and non-Jews stand as equal participants in these spaces, unlike in the Jewish-Jewish spaces, but the references of these Jewish spaces are *Jewish-inspired,* unlike the national and universal spaces. In other words, Jewish spaces are built around a Jewish narrative of the past and present they seek to commemorate and celebrate. This narrative is, of course, in turn transformed or enriched by the very presence of the non-Jews who help to foster it. Here, non-Jews are not guests but *co-actors.* The space however, remains a "Jewish-friendly" space, unlike the national pluralist space, which is neutral.

Indeed, the novelty of these spaces lies precisely in the fact that the national, regional, local, and civil society institutions that play a major role in creating them are favorably disposed to the Jewish story. This was not the case in the past, when Jewish themes were most often studied with an alternative, often antisemitic perspective in mind, be it Christian theological, racial, national, or cultural—like Semitic Studies in theological faculties (both Catholic and Protestant) or Hebraic Studies in nineteenth-century German universities where Jews were not allowed to teach unless they converted. Jews were expected to integrate into a national narrative by converting explicitly (Heinrich Heine's ticket into Western civilization) or by removing or hiding the Jewish meaning behind their German words (Franz Kafka). Today, these Jewish-friendly spaces are anchored firmly in the Jewish narrative. Non-Jews within them accept it as a starting point for their own pluralist reflections. These spaces are thus both the product and the fountainhead of such a paradigmatic shift.

Given this context, it is easier to understand why the creation of Jewish spaces in contemporary Poland has been fraught with such tension and complexity. Both sides had to readjust their positions in the pluralist spectrum of identities. Both sides had to lose their identity monopoly, and contemplate the other not as a foe in a zero-sum game but as a partner. This was of course easier said than done as most of the chapters in this volume attest, but I am convinced that it has indeed *been done*. Jewish life has returned to Poland. Jewish references are living pieces of an increasingly open national discourse. This is an enormous achievement.

It goes without saying that not all is utopian in these Jewish spaces, as some have pointed out. But the misunderstandings, negotiation, at times even conflict built into them are part of their vitality and ensure that they not become museums. This is what makes the Polish case so interesting and symbolic. The living Jewish component of Poland's Jewish spaces does not come only from the country's small Jewish community. It also encompasses Jews of Polish origin from around the world, Israelis who are not just going to Auschwitz, transnational Jews, and some Polish non-Jews who have not just assumed the role of "bridges" to Jewish culture but of cosmopolitan "honorary Jews" in their own essentially monocultural Polish setting. Such non-Jews are key actors in their own national pluralist stakes. This complex juxtaposition of identities around Jewish themes thus points the way to a new type of normality.

On this count, how is one to classify Auschwitz? The fraught process of its historical transformation from the camp of Polish martyrs into a present-day consensus that favors the preponderance of its Jewish victims played a key role in Poland's—and not only Poland's—pluralist democratic development, as Poles and Europeans wrestled with the complexities of their pasts. The contrast between the 1995 and 2005 commemorations of the liberation of Auschwitz illustrates this point. In 1995, the Polish President Lech Wałęsa chose to focus only on Polish suffering in his speech as a way of righting the old Soviet "anti-fascist" narrative. In 2005, historical truth was respected, this time at Birkenau, with the suffering of the Jews preceding the suffering of the Poles, followed by the suffering of the Romas. Nevertheless, Auschwitz and all Nazi death camps are, in my opinion, the ontological opposite of a Jewish space. They incarnate Jewish powerlessness at the hands of non-Jews bent on destroying the very traces of Jewish life, and should be referred to instead as a "Jewish void."

But what are the long-term prospects for Poland's Jewish spaces? It is one thing to argue, as I have done earlier, about their central importance in the strengthening of a pluralist setting, and quite another to wonder how long they can continue to exist as *ongoing* centers of Jewish and non-Jewish interaction. I have no doubts whatsoever about the centrality of Auschwitz or Warsaw's Museum of the History of Polish Jews (to take the two extremes) in the European or even the world's "memoryscape" in the long-term future, as well as the complex sociological collage of Kraków's Kazimierz. Similarly, throughout the country, artwork and the beautifully restored buildings will also survive.

What about the more marginal Jewish spaces? They cannot rest alone on the pious memory of what will become an ever more distant past. What will happen in the long run to all those former shtetls, where it is often relocated Poles whose origins lay in the lands taken over by the Soviet Union who are doing their best to revive a local Jewish past? What will happen once the survivor generation who was born there, and their children and grandchildren, pass away? Can one assume that the internet and its burgeoning communities of "descendants from" can maintain a living memory? Who, then, will be interacting with the local Poles? Will occasional Jewish tourists suffice? Can one imagine highly orthodox Jews making a comeback of sorts? They incarnate Jewish life and have an ongoing presence in Poland's Jewish-Jewish spaces, but how extensive are their contacts with non-Jews? In brief, there is a danger that Jewish spaces may be epiphenomena tied to a very specific political and cultural moment.

At present it seems far-fetched to think that Poland will be once again the home of new Jewish immigrants. An influx of new Jewish presences from abroad exists in the country's major cities as they open up to a globalized economy, but I am not sure these Jews think of themselves as "new Polish Jews." It could very well be that in our globalized world, Jews will continue to flock to Poland as sojourners, including those Israelis and others who have reclaimed Polish passports. But Jewish spaces will endure only if these transnational Jews care about such spaces and work to fill them with life. Inevitably, the life in question will be *present-day life*, not the memory of the life that was. And of course, non-Jewish Poles must also continue to be animated by a similar, forward-looking interest in Jewish life. If not, such spaces will become archeological sites and centers of historical research—both highly important but not quite what is at stake here. Therein lies the challenge.

We do not know what the future will hold, but one thing is certain: Poland's Jewish spaces have played (and continue to play) a highly positive and enriching role in the country's democratic culture. Equally important, theses spaces are transforming the mindsets of Jews around the world as they discover a more positive reading of the European past and present. We should celebrate this achievement, but it is up to all of us to ensure that the pluralist fruits of Jewish space continue to enrich the future.

Note

1. The first formulation appeared in "A New Jewish Identity for Post-1989 Europe," JPR Policy Paper no. 1, June 1996, Institute for Jewish Policy Research, London.

Contributors

Winson Chu is associate professor in the Department of History at the University of Wisconsin–Milwaukee.

Robert L. Cohn is the Philip and Muriel Berman Professor of Jewish Studies in the Department of Religious Studies at Lafayette College, Easton, Pennsylvania.

Konstanty Gebert is a noted Polish journalist and prominent spokesperson for Poland's post-Communist Jewish community.

Sławomir Kapralski is a researcher at the Institute of Philosophy and Sociology of the Polish Academy of Sciences and a lecturer at the Centre for Social Studies/ Graduate School for Social Research in Warsaw.

Barbara Kirshenblatt-Gimblett is University Professor and professor of Performance Studies at New York University, and program director of the core exhibition for the Museum of the History of Polish Jews in Warsaw.

Erica Lehrer is associate professor in the History and Sociology–Anthropology departments at Concordia University in Montreal, Canada, where she also holds the Canada Research Chair in Post-Conflict Memory, Ethnography, and Museology.

Michael Meng is assistant professor in the Department of History at Clemson University, South Carolina.

Monika Murzyn-Kupisz is assistant professor in the UNESCO Chair for Heritage and Urban Studies in the Department of Economic and Social History at the Kraków University of Economics.

Diana Pinto is an intellectual historian living in Paris. She has lectured and published widely on minority issues in Europe, and has been a senior fellow of the London-based Institute for Jewish Policy Research and consultant to the Political Directorate of the Council of Europe.

Stanisław Tyszka received his Ph.D. from the Department of History and Civilization at the European University Institute in Florence. He is an assistant professor on the Faculty of Applied Social Sciences and Resocialization at the University of Warsaw.

Magdalena Waligórska is assistant professor of East European History and Culture at the University of Bremen.

Jonathan Webber is a British social anthropologist now living in Kraków, Poland, where he is a professor at the Institute of European Studies at the Jagiellonian University, having taught for twenty-eight years at the universities of Oxford and Birmingham. His academic research interests and publications have focused on modern Jewish society, Holocaust studies, Polish-Jewish Studies, and Jewish heritage issues.

Geneviève Zubrzycki is associate professor of Sociology and director of Polish Studies at the University of Michigan, where she is also affiliated with the Frankel Center for Judaic Studies.

Index

Jewish writers and, 233; in multiethnic Łódź, 195; polonization of Szczecin and, 103, 107
Polishness, 174, 175; Catholicism and, 4, 26, 41n26, 161, 186; Jewish memory and, 7; received understandings of, 183; redefinitions of, 4, 8, 173
Polska Kronika Filmowa [PKF] (Polish Newsreel), 78
Pomerania, 92, 102, 105, 197
poniemieckie ("post-German"), 103, 236n5
post-space, 110
power relations, 150
Poznań, city of, 56, 59, 83
pożydowski ("post-Jewish"), 103, 236n5
prayer houses, 50, 55, 56, 60, 93, 122, 238; destruction of, 238; "Judaica Foundation" on site of former prayer house, 62; shtiblach (Hassidic prayer houses), 225, 232, 234
prisoners of war, Soviet, 20, 38n8
Promised Land, The (Reymont), 195
Property Commission for the Catholic Church, 52
property restitution, 4, 11, 46–47, 245; Jewish heritage preservation and, 55–65; legislation concerning, 47–53; social reception of claims, 53–55
Pruchnik, Kornelia, 249
Pruchnik, Lucyna, 245, 248, 249, 251–252
Prussian Law (1847) on status of Jews, 50
Przeworsk, town of, 157–158, 160, 161, 166
psychoanalysis, 84
public sphere, 12, 74, 89n

Radio Maryja, 27
Radziszewska, Krystyna, 200
Rajkowska, Joanna, 82–83, 95
Rajzman, Eliasz, 93
Rakoczy, Bishop Tadeusz, 27
Ralph Appelbaum Associates, 274
Rapaport, Natan, 76
Recovered Lands (German territories annexed to Poland), 31, 90, 94, 103, 110, 112n5; German population expelled from, 197, 224; as politically constructed space, 163
Red Army, Soviet, 17, 19, 38n7, 124, 168n22, 196
Regulatory Commission for Jewish Religious Communities, 47
Regulatory Commission for the Evangelical Church of the Augsburg Confession, 52
Regulatory Commission for the Polish Orthodox Church, 52
religion, 12n5, 161

Religious Union of the Mosaic Faith, 48
respatialization, 107, 111
Reymont, Władysław, 195, 198
Ringelblum, Emmanuel, 233
ritual slaughter (*shehitah*), 13n8
Romania, 48
Roma people, 3, 11, 104, 111, 281, 283
Roosevelt, Franklin D., 94
Rosenson, Claire, 178
Roskies, Diane and David, 223
Rothberg, Michael, 3
Rozen, Mikołaj, 109
Rubin, Hadasa, 93
Rumkowski, Chaim Mordechai, 198
Russia, post-Soviet, 273–277
Russian empire, tsarist, 195, 228, 268, 274, 276
Russians, 16, 111
Rzeczpospolita (newspaper), 41n35, 201
Rzeszów, town of, 155, 165–166

Sabor, Agnieszka, 148n74
Sachsenhausen concentration camp, 92
Sasak, Jan, 157–158, 160
Sasnal, Wilhelm, 95
Schaper, Edzard, 68n31
Schindler's List (film), 217
Schlögel, Karl, 197, 201
Schlör, Joachim, 99, 100
Schönwetter, Fishel, 250–251
Schönwetter, Israel, 263n
Schönwetter, Mark, 250–251, 254, 255, 263n
schools, Jewish, 93, 104, 122, 125
Schudrich, Chief Rabbi Michael, 56, 218, 245–247, 254, 261n12
Schwarz, Chris, 213, 214, 215, 219
Sejm (parliament of Poland), 47, 49, 51
Semitic Studies, 282–283
Shields, Rob, 95
Shoah. *See* Holocaust (Shoah)
Shoah (Lanzmann film, 1983), 1, 2
Shosha (Singer), 233
"Shtetl Brzostek" (K. Pruchnik), 249
"Shtetl Route" tourist trail, 92
shtetls, 115, 121, 135, 139, 140, 173; Jewish museums and, 275, 276; Jewish past revived by relocated Poles, 284; landscape of Jewish memory and, 116; nostalgia for idealized provincial past and, 140; as social spaces between town and village, 166; tourism and, 126
shtiblach (Hassidic prayer houses), 225, 232, 234

www.ingramcontent.com/pod-product-compliance
Lightning Source LLC
Chambersburg PA
CBHW071839270326
41929CB00013B/2049